6.6.18
$30.00

THE
DESIGN OF
CHILDHOOD

ALSO BY ALEXANDRA LANGE

Design Research: The Store That Brought Modern Living to American Homes
(with Jane Thompson)

Writing about Architecture: Mastering the Language of Buildings and Cities

The Dot-Com City: Silicon Valley Urbanism

THE
DESIGN OF
CHILDHOOD

How the Material World Shapes Independent Kids

ALEXANDRA LANGE

BLOOMSBURY PUBLISHING
NEW YORK · LONDON · OXFORD · NEW DELHI · SYDNEY

BLOOMSBURY PUBLISHING
Bloomsbury Publishing Inc.
1385 Broadway, New York, NY 10018, USA

BLOOMSBURY, BLOOMSBURY PUBLISHING, and the Diana logo are trademarks of
Bloomsbury Publishing Plc

First published in the United States 2018

ISBN: HB: 978-1-63286-635-6; eBook: 978-1-63286-637-0

LIBRARY OF CONGRESS CATALOGING-IN-PUBLICATION DATA IS AVAILABLE

2 4 6 8 10 9 7 5 3 1

Typeset by Westchester Publishing Services
Printed and bound in the U.S.A. by Berryville Graphics Inc., Berryville, Virginia

To find out more about our authors and books visit www.bloomsbury.com and
sign up for our newsletters.

Bloomsbury books may be purchased for business or promotional use. For information on bulk
purchases please contact Macmillan Corporate and Premium Sales Department at
specialmarkets@macmillan.com.

To Paul and Romy, who opened my eyes

CONTENTS

INTRODUCTION

In 1924, Lillian Moller Gilbreth found herself a widow with eleven children. She and her late husband, Frank Gilbreth, were the inventors of motion study, breaking tasks down into minute component parts to figure out how to speed up repetitive tasks and reduce worker fatigue. The couple was also the subject of *Cheaper by the Dozen*, a 1948 bestselling biographical novel written by two of those children. While Frank Gilbreth was alive, he and Lillian worked for industries ranging from construction to medicine to rehabilitation. Lillian had a PhD in psychology, and she eventually became the second woman member of the American Society of Mechanical Engineers and the first female engineering professor at Purdue University. She wrote or co-wrote many of Frank's books, often anonymously, as it was thought that a woman's byline might undermine their authority. After Frank's sudden death, even longtime clients were reluctant to renew their contracts with her alone, and she had to reestablish herself as a sole female practitioner. Unwilling to let Gilbreth, Inc. perish with its male founder—and still needing to provide for her children—she did just what many professional women of the present day do when presented with an obstacle: She pivoted.

First, she established a course in motion study, headquartered at her Montclair, New Jersey, home and office.[1] If companies did not want her services, they might still send their employees to her for training, as teaching was considered a woman's profession. This would allow her to travel less and spend more time with the family. Next she began to think about areas of industry in which being a woman and a mother might be an asset rather than a liability.[2] Even when Frank was alive, they tested many of their ideas on their children, establishing "the one best way" to take a bath, to train preteens to touch-type, and to chart age-appropriate chores for each child. The couple pioneered the use of short films to study how jobs were performed, and they once set up camera equipment in their laboratory to film five of their children getting their tonsils out. The ensuing hijinks provided enough material for *Cheaper by the Dozen* and a sequel, *Belles on Their Toes*. In the latter Frank B. Gilbreth Jr. and Ernestine Gilbreth Carey write of their mother: "If the only way to enter a man's field was through the kitchen door, that's the way she'd enter . . . Mother planned, on paper, an efficiency-type kitchenette of the kind used today in a good many apartments. Under her arrangement, a person could mix a cake, put it in the oven, and do the dishes, without taking more than a couple of dozen steps."[3]

Her kitchen plans got her a contract with General Electric, then coverage in the newspapers, and then an offer by a newsreel company to film this unicorn, a woman engineer with eleven children, baking an apple cake in her "efficiency kitchen." The cake was a must, as it was the only dish Gilbreth could prepare: Her family had employed a cook during her childhood, and the Gilbreth household had included a couple of servants so that both parents could work. Studying films of women in their kitchens, Gilbreth counted the number of steps required to walk from pantry to stove to sink and the number of operations required to measure, stir, bake, and wash up while making a cake. She then rearranged the elements of the kitchen to put stove and prep counter side by side, with ingredients stored above, pans below, and the refrigerator nearby. A cart within arm's reach provided a second work surface and could be wheeled over to the sink when the task was done. The arrangement was L shaped, one of three efficient setups used in most contemporary kitchens, where a fixed island typically replaces the cart. (My kitchen is a U, yours may be a C.) Though her biographer Jane Lancaster points out that Gilbreth seemed little interested in getting other women out of the kitchen, when her daughter Ernestine married Charles Everett Carey in 1930 and asked her mother for a kitchen design as a wedding present, Lillian created one she branded the Teamwork Kitchen, with a butcher's apron for Carey and cupboards engineered for his greater-than-six-foot height.[4]

Gilbreth saw an opportunity where others did not, turning sexism to her advantage. Even while Frank was alive the Gilbreths had seen the home as a site of labor, and they applied four critical eyes to repetitive everyday tasks. Dad "believed that most adults stopped thinking the day they left school—and some even before that. 'A child, on the other hand, stays impressionable and eager to learn. Catch one young enough,' Dad insisted, 'and there's no limit to what you can teach,'" wrote the younger Gilbreths in *Cheaper by the Dozen*.[5] Though Frank and Lillian used their children to demonstrate that motion study could be child's play, it wasn't until Lillian was faced with the possibility of a world without work outside the home that she turned her research within those walls—and designed her own escape hatch.

Cheaper by the Dozen has always been one of my favorite children's books, but it wasn't until I began to write my own book about children that I figured out why. Frank Gilbreth's attitude toward raising kids came across as entirely modern. He saw them as little sponges, to be spoken to as adults and provided with the tools to teach themselves. Their eagerness to learn was a better approximation of his own lust for learning than the spirit of most workaday adults. Lillian Gilbreth's career transformation, in widowhood, planted an early clue that critical thinking could be applied to toothbrushing as well as production lines. As a tidy little girl who wanted a place for everything, I loved the idea that there was a better way to do anything, and I became conscious of my own movements and arrangements. When I cook dinner using a minimum number of bowls, cutting boards, and pans, I think of Lillian. When in my early thirties I finally had the chance to design my own kitchen, multiple childhood readings of *Belles on Their Toes* made mapping a work triangle a snap. A children's book taught me most of what I needed to know.

More personally: When I had a child, I found myself more focused at home than on the distant architecture that had been my topic—partly by choice, partly because the 2008 recession eliminated much of my freelance work. But even as I happily played with my son, I couldn't turn my critical mind off. At first it was the construction site on the carpet: I am a design critic married to an architect, so naturally our baby gifts included three or four different sets of building blocks, in cardboard, foam, and wood. Was one set better than the other? Who chose the colors, the sizes, the illustrated fruits? As he became more mobile, it was the high chair and the stroller: Do we buy the one he needs now, or can we find one that will grow with him? As we explored the neighborhood, I wondered why the playground's bulbous plastic parts seemed so different from the metal-frame geodesic dome that I climbed in my own backyard. He went to school and the classroom was arranged not in rows of tiny desks but in sections: block corner here, child-size tables and chairs there, a rug beyond, even though the building itself seemed made for kids in grids. Navigating the city with a baby carrier and then a stroller (and then a stroller and a preschooler) I was suddenly aware of curb cuts and subway elevators, of small parks in which one could rest, and streets so wide we never made it across before the countdown clock ended.

To have a child is to be thrown suddenly, and I found rather miraculously, back into the world of *stuff*. Dirty stuff, clean stuff, sleepy stuff, heavy stuff. Today's world of apps promises you freedom from so many things: phone calls, food preparation, driving, but even the Gilbreths found there were limits to efficiency when it came to child-rearing. You can outsource the laundry, but you still have piles of clothes. You can speed up the toothbrushing, but you can't replace it with watching a video of toothbrushing. Babies love iPads, but they still need to play with actual blocks. In what initially felt like a limitation, I found my next topic, as Gilbreth found hers. I studied the landmarks of my son's territory as it grew from rug to house, school to playground to the whole city (under my supervision). This history is not unknown—though it has barely diffused beyond specialized audiences—but it seems particularly important to revisit it now. Middle-class parents today obsess over their children's food, their kindergarten curriculum, their sports prowess, their test skills, drilling down on daily rituals as if one worksheet, one piano lesson might make all the difference. But the kitchens, classrooms, playing fields, and bus stops in which kids eat, learn, run, and chat are as important as the activities they support. Loris Malaguzzi, who developed the Reggio Emilia preschool and primary-school curriculum with parents in and around that Italian city, called environment "the third teacher": The adult in the classroom has a role, but so does the classroom itself, stocked with materials for children to manipulate and create, accessible on low open shelves, provocative of imagination.[6]

I came to see each successive stage of childhood development as an opportunity for encounters with larger and more complex environments; as each challenge is met, the child needs to find another within her grasp and set herself the task of mastery. (Because so many of the texts I consulted were written before 1970 and refer to the child solely as a "he," I'm going to take the opposite tack in my text.) Malaguzzi is far from alone in this belief in child-led and object-oriented learning. Psychologist Jean Piaget, whose theory of the child mind came to dominate late twentieth-century education, theorized that knowledge has to be learned from experiences, like by putting a block under a blanket and then finding that it still exists, or, in a later stage, by dropping blocks from different heights and seeing what happens. Through active experiment children construct their understanding of the world—just one of tens of building metaphors embedded, almost subconsciously, in the language of childhood.

That's why each chapter in this book starts, like this one, with a children's story. The more research I did on design and childhood, the more I realized that the authors I'd loved since the age of four dramatize, at least in part, what the experts describe in far more abstract language. The freedom of the child in the city after a blizzard: That's architect Aldo van Eyck, but it is also *The Snowy Day*. The joy of scavenging materials to build a playhouse: That's Simon Nicholson's theory of loose parts, but it is also *The Borrowers*. Theory and practice united in delight. If Lillian Gilbreth is better known for her lightly fictionalized exploits than her pioneering work, so be it: Her children's accounts of growing up efficiently provide as good an introduction to motion study as most will need. Thoughtful tales, beautifully illustrated, are an illuminating source on childhood when based on careful observation. Picture books, along with the toys, equipment, and childhood spaces that are the primary "texts" for this book, are the products of as much engineering, experiment, and thought as the office buildings and museums I was wont to write about. They may be for children, but that doesn't mean they are childish. I had to get over my own unconscious bias toward writing about kids—revealing myself as both a critic and a mother—in order to take them seriously.

•

BLOCKS SEEM SO basic. And yet we find them teaching the architect and the scientist, the fabulist and the fact finder. Progressive education in the United States and Europe—education not based on the primer and the lash—begins when a teacher places a block before a child and watches what happens. In chapter one, we tour a shop's worth of building toys, showing the dazzling claims for their efficacy in action. This history leads from Friedrich Froebel's wooden cubes, intended to demonstrate the crystalline structure of nature, through the magic of the "automatic binding brick," better known as LEGO, to constructed online worlds, like *Minecraft*, that exploit parents' long-standing association of the plain, the geometric, and the wood with the idea of the "Good Toy." In chapter two, I describe the first territory children are able to explore: the house, describing how manufacturers began to ply parents with furniture promising better deportment, improved health, increased creativity, and, most of all, *storage*. (Where else would you put all those toys?) Storage becomes a leitmotif of the family home, which first bulges with attics, basements, and garages, and then streamlines with carports, built-ins, and kid-size cupboards. Pushed and pulled by the perceptions of children's space needs, the average size of the American house grows from 980 square feet in 1950 to 1,660 square feet in 1973 to 2,600 square feet today. Pioneer girl Laura Ingalls didn't have her own room. She owned a single doll, handmade by her mother. And she went to school in a one-room schoolhouse, a surprisingly durable architecture of education that served students well into the twentieth century.[7] Chapter three walks the child to kindergarten, comparing the view from the shared desk in the one-room schoolhouse to that of the "campfire" in today's project-based learning environments.

Children's lives, however, are not lived solely indoors. Before cities established dedicated play spaces, the streets were children's ball court, social center, and jungle gym. Chapter four further explores the neighborhood, where schoolkids, bored by their own backyards, should be able to access open space on their own. I discuss the history of playground design, and the contentious role designers play in it. The first playgrounds in Boston were piles of sand in empty lots, which allowed children of all sizes to build the cities of their dreams; junk playgrounds, introduced after World War II, added tools and real construction to the mix. While the aesthete in me thrills to the abstract playscapes of Isamu Noguchi, after a day of building with blocks in the classroom, why should the schoolyard's equipment be fixed and impervious to children's ideas of fun? From the late nineteenth century on, writers, thinkers, educators, and politicians wanted to get children out of the city. Off the streets, out of apartments, into private homes, and bused to suburban schools. Children were to be their parents' problem, and the building of playrooms and the purchasing of play equipment—a swing set for every yard!—created an ideal of childhood that was privatized and consumer-driven. In chapter five, we (like the child approaching adolescence) reach the outermost ring and look at the urban fabric that holds together home, school, playground, and streets, which, in an ideal world, would safely enclose childhood's domain. Over the past century, urban designers have offered alternatives to this age-segregated model, which fences children off from their own city. From Progressive Era suburbs that put a premium on community space to mixed-use modern developments that reject the narrative that high-rises are unsuitable for children to new towns built like old villages—a little bit dense, a little bit forested—planners have sought models of urban life that might make every member of the family happy.

Certain themes emerge and reemerge from chapter to chapter, irrespective of the increasing scale of the problems they discuss. This is a book about design, but many of its figures, like Lillian Gilbreth and Caroline Pratt, creator of the classic unit block, aren't called designers. Many of those figures also happen to be women, unusual for architecture and design history. Work with children was seen as a woman's job—Friedrich Froebel may have launched the kindergarten, but he chose women to staff it because of their supposedly nurturing nature—so when you look at design for children you find female educators, therapists, philanthropists, and clients seeking solutions to problems. If the inventors are men, this work is likely to be seen as minor. As curator Juliet Kinchin writes, "In the case of male designers in particular, the experience of engaged parenting and teaching is often treated as a sideline or aberration—not least by the designers themselves—and downplayed as a formative influence on their more publicly appraised work, or omitted altogether."[8] For women working in the field, it may have been their only option, leaving them without the opportunity or inclination to minimize their kid-size work.

Parallel to the topic of who designs for children lies a bigger question: Do children need design at all? Or, rather, how might they be enabled to design the toys they need and experiences they desire for themselves? The act of making that designers find so satisfying is built into early childhood education, but as they grow, many children lose opportunities to create their own environment, bounded by a text-centric view of education and concerns for safety. Despite adults' desire to create a safer, softer child-centric world, something got lost in translation. Jane Jacobs said, of the child in the designed-for-childhood environment: "Their homes and playgrounds, so orderly looking, so buffered from the muddled, messy intrusions of the great world, may accidentally be ideally planned for children to concentrate on television, but for too little else their hungry brains require."[9] Our built environment is making kids less healthy, less independent, and less imaginative. What those hungry brains require is freedom. Treating children as citizens, rather than as consumers, can break that pattern, creating a shared spatial economy centered on public education, recreation, and transportation safe and open for all. Tracing the design of childhood back to its nineteenth-century origins shows how we came to this place, but it also reveals the building blocks of resistance to fenced-in fun.

CHAPTER 1

BLOCKS

Antoinette Portis's 2006 children's book *Not a Box* comes wrapped in brown paper. It resembles a cardboard box in flattened form, its bold Impact font in the style of the classic post office rubber stamp: all red, all caps. On the back cover there's a more explicit nod to shipping: "This End Up." But the story it tells is more complex. "Why are you sitting in a box?" asks a voice offstage. "It's not a box," replies our hero, a rabbit drawn with three rough black lines.[1] In the pages that follow, we see the rectangle of the box, drawn in black, morph into a racecar, a mountain, a howdah, a rocket, via red lines, seemingly drawn in haste, that are literally outside the box. In answer to repeated questions from the same offstage voice, the rabbit doesn't bother to explain. She just repeats, "It's not a box." What the box is, is whatever she imagines it to be. The voice's humdrum questions are slowing her down, boxing in her creativity. She is ready to take off while adult specificity would keep her grounded.

Portis's book, in design and content, reminds us that many of our longest-serving toys have no baked-in narrative. Simple shapes and sturdy materials encourage free play and meet the child at her level. She may get in the box, color the box, cut the box, stack her box with a friend's. The box is merely a vehicle for building structures—real or imaginary—of increasing complexity. The box, like its cousin the block, has been central to early childhood education since the late seventeenth century, when John Locke, in his influential epistolary book *Some Thoughts Concerning Education* (1693), wrote of a father who replaced educating his children by repetition and force with educating them by using a game played with four wooden blocks pasted with all the letters of the alphabet, one block for vowels, the other three for consonants. The father, wrote Locke, "has made this a play for his children, that he shall win, who, at one cast, throws most words on these four dice; whereby his eldest son, yet in coats, has played himself into spelling with great eagerness, and without once having been chid for it, or forced to it."[2]

Today's toy aisles reflect the pedagogical ideas of Locke and the educators who followed him in the eighteenth and early nineteenth century, notably Johann Heinrich Pestalozzi and Friedrich Froebel, who believed that children had to touch and observe for themselves in order to learn. With the latter half of the twentieth century came child psychologist Jean Piaget's "constructivist" theory of cognitive development, which dominates present-day early childhood education: Young children learn through experiences, constructing information for themselves by manipulating physical objects, with teachers as guides rather than sources of information.[3] In *Raising America*, her history of "a century of advice about children," Ann Hulbert describes the Piagetian child as "an independent experimenter investigating a world of objects, solving the epistemological problems of space, time, causality, and categorizing."[4] The offstage voice questioning what the rabbit is doing needs to wait or, in what educators would call "scaffolding," ask questions that draw the rabbit out. Not *Why are you sitting on that box?* but *What is that box today? What happens to your stuffed rabbit if you put it inside that box? What do you think would happen if you piled up two boxes? Let's see if you are right.* The child learns through her senses as she puts the box through its paces and as she reencounters the box in different settings and with different groups of children. Bookseller materials prepared for the launch of *Not a Box* suggested bookstores hold their own "Bring Your Own Box" events, inviting children to bring a cardboard box and providing "scissors, markers, crayons (especially red), construction paper, glue sticks, and any other arts-and-crafts supplies you have." (Thematic snacks included juice boxes and animal cracker boxes.)

Play with boxes hasn't always been so regimented and supervised. When I was a child, the purchase of a new washing machine was a cause for celebration in my neighborhood, as it meant access to a new playhouse in somebody's yard. This was an experience we shared with decades upon decades of children before us. Corrugated cardboard boxes were first introduced in the late 1870s and slowly replaced wooden crates as the preferred wrapper for objects of all sizes, from crackers to kitchen appliances. As the objects contained grew larger—by 1940, 44 percent of American homes had a mechanical refrigerator, up from 8 percent in 1930[5]—the play potential of those boxes increased. A shoebox was fine for a diorama, but everyone wanted something you could get *inside*.

Dr. Benjamin Spock once touted the cardboard box as an inexpensive alternative for parents who couldn't afford store-bought playthings like toy cars or a ready-made jungle gym. Better to give your child "a packing box. By turns it's a bed, a house, a truck, a tank, a fort, a doll's house, a garage," he wrote.[6] But that didn't mean its commercial potential went unnoticed. In 1951, Charles and Ray Eames—married collaborators who practiced in Los Angeles and designed their own Pacific Palisades house like a grown-up Erector Set—assembled a neighborhood they called

Carton City out of the cardboard boxes used to ship their company's iconic parti-colored Eames Storage Units. They designed surface graphics for the boxes suggesting where doors, windows, and awnings might be cut through the corrugations. The same year, the Eameses created The Toy, manufactured by Tigrett Enterprises, which offered children the chance to make their own prefabricated structures, more colorful and lightweight than Carton City.[7] The Toy (even the name suggested that it might be the only toy a child needs) combined thin wooden dowels, pipe cleaners, and a set of square and triangular stiffened-paper panels in green, yellow, blue, red, magenta, and black. Children could run the dowels through sleeves on the edges of the panels to strengthen them and then attach these struts at the corners. The Toy took the cardboard box beyond the right angle, allowing for the creation of gem-like haunts or twisting towers. In September 1951, *Interiors* also wrote up The Toy, presenting its simple assembly and graphic design as "a happy change from the intricate, puzzling, super-mechanical constructor set which has been the standard building toy since little Gilbert wore knickers."[8] Creative Playthings, a New York City–based store that sold modern and educational toys, put a fiberboard playhouse in their catalog as early as 1967, with a pitched roof and scored windows and doors.[9] That catalog also included a list of Piaget's four stages of childhood development—helpfully illustrated with Creative Playthings products. But although the cardboard box has been marketed, it can scarcely be improved. So potent is the form that the cardboard box was inducted into the National Toy Hall of Fame in 2005.[10] Other constructive entries in the Hall of Fame include alphabet blocks, the Erector Set, Lincoln Logs, LEGO bricks, and the Tinkertoy.

That we need a book like Portis's to remind us that a box can spur the imagination is a commentary on how far toys have traveled since Locke's day. As a number of writers have argued, children's toys and children's play are a space dominated by intense commercial energy and an ever-increasing explicitness of purpose.[11] But the toys in the Hall of Fame represent another trend that runs as counterpoint through much of this hungry selling. From the beginning of the mass-produced toy industry, designers, manufacturers, artists, and educators have made toys intended to teach. In the postwar period, these were ennobled as "Good Toys," a catchall term for playthings that encouraged imagination, stimulated the mind, promoted active play, and eschewed violence.[12] Such toys were produced internationally and exhibited a similar simplicity of form, truth to materials, and absence of decoration. They were the cardboard box commodified, with copy on their packaging touting creativity, quiet, and hours of solo play. They were rarely advertised on TV but were often on display as symbols in model homes and dream houses—"Good Toy" equals good parenting.

If there is a Good Toy (educational, useful, unadorned), there must also be a Bad Toy (flimsy, decorated, a symbol of conspicuous consumption). The definition of *good*, though, is a moving target, keeping time with educational theory. Circa 1800, maps, puzzles, and games taught geography and etiquette; circa 1850, scientific instruments and construction sets often required the assistance of an adult; circa 1900, educators stressed simplicity: wooden beads, wooden blocks.[13] Toys reveal the attitudes of adult society. It is parents and educators who read the leaflets included in building sets claiming they will turn a child into an engineer, an architect, or, nowadays, a computer programmer.

Historians trace the opposition between Good Toy and Bad Toy back to the dawn of the marketing of toys in the late eighteenth century. As tastemakers pushed for increased "parental interference" in children's lives, encouraging everything from breast-feeding to setting aside space for a nursery in the home, the sales of children's goods—including blocks, didactic games, and picture books—followed suit.[14] In *Practical Education* (1798), educator Maria Edgeworth describes the need for a "rational toy-shop," selling "balls, pulleys, wheels, strings, and strong little carts" as well as "pieces of wood of various shapes and sizes, which they may build up and pull down."[15]

Industrial woodworking and printing businesses were the first makers of building toys for the middle class, both in Europe and America. Some early block sets, following Locke, used the six sides as an opportunity to display symbols: letters, numbers, or stories, often taken from the Bible. Designer and historian Karen Hewitt describes these early commercial products as "dipped in honey," sweetening learning by treating the toy like an advertisement for itself, with multicolor imagery made possible by chromolithography, a then new printing technology. To focus the child's mind on letters, it would be better if alphabet blocks weren't all colors of the rainbow, or if the colors corresponded to a next step in reading, like differentiating vowels from consonants. In recognition of this, twentieth-century Montessori alphabet sets use blue for vowels and red for consonants. Like other Montessori materials, the blocks are supposed to be "auto-educative" so that children can teach themselves with minimal adult interruption.[16] The lesson is baked into the design. Some nineteenth-century block sets were made up of abstract geometric shapes, for pure building. Still others were building-specific, often linking the child's play to the history of architecture in his or her country.[17] The most popular building sets, produced well into the twentieth century, shared the literalness of the alphabet and biblical toys. As Brenda and Robert Vale write in their history of construction toys, *Architecture on the Carpet*, "in America Lincoln Logs perpetuated the legend of the frontier and Wild West in its many versions of miniature log cabins, and in Britain black-and-white Tudor Minibrix were sold with a grainy photograph of seventeenth-century houses in the village of Weobley in Herefordshire, so redolent of 'olde England.' "[18]

In the twentieth century, as middle-class mothers became primary caregivers without household help, they absorbed the message that they should be playing with their children themselves, rather than parking them in front of solitary distractions. But what to do when you have housework? The Good Toy is the solution. Starting in the 1920s, *Parents* magazine ran a column titled "Toys That Teach." Playskool, which sold desks and blackboards for use at home, used the slogan "Learning while playing" in the 1920s, and "Toys that build kids" in the 1960s.[19] Media studies professor Ellen Seiter writes, "Supplying a toy just so a mother could win time to herself did not jibe with the increasing emphasis on a mother's constant monitoring and stimulation of her child. But the emphasis on toys and learning, the idea that toys—as well as mothers— could also teach, solved this problem nicely."[20] LEGO, having successfully associated itself with "creative play," used its advertisements to stress the bricks' use for quiet, nonviolent play: "Let somebody else's child get his kicks tracking a little kid through a gun sight" read an ad from 1966, describing the viewpoint of today's highly realistic first-person shooter games long before their creation. And the names for two of the game modes in *Minecraft*, Creative and Survival, echo the Good Toy/Bad Toy, thoughtful/violent split. While danger lurks in Survival mode, you don't have to fight or die in Creative, and you have unlimited resources, that is, an infinite number of blocks. The construction toy is simultaneously a blank slate and an object for the projecting of competing desires, whether it is made of cardboard, wood, plastic, or pixels. The imaginative play fostered by objects like The Toy happens side-by-side with the manipulation of block sets emblazoned with numerals, pictures, and Bible stories, and these two modes have been present since the origins of the toy industry in the late eighteenth century. This history undergirds the more specific case studies of building toys that follow, examples chosen to highlight both the influence and ubiquity of the form in classrooms and playrooms, as well as a few toys that, in a burst of adult creativity, twist away from geometry toward biology. The apparently unsatisfiable two-hundred-year quest for the ideal educating object, the elusive Good Toy, metaphorically links wooden cubes to the latest video games, and physically links 3-D-printed connectors to classic Tinkertoys.

•

You are four. You sit at a low table, a companion on either side on a long bench, your feet just touching the ground. The wooden table before you is marked with a grid of thin lines, four inches apart, stretching to the edges. A teacher appears behind you with a wooden box. She places it on the table in front of you, slides back the bottom—you didn't even see the lid!—and lifts the box. In front of you is a wooden cube. You touch it and it comes apart. Oh no! But your teacher just smiles and leaves you to examine the parts. It is not one cube but eight. You begin to stack them into a tower. This is kindergarten.

The cardboard box is a vehicle for the imagination, a building block light enough for a child to lift, an illustration of the translation of dimensions into volume. The wooden block is what it is: solid, natural, untransformable. To Friedrich Froebel, the block was where to begin an education. When he set up the first kindergartens in the early nineteenth century, he gave children wooden blocks and would-be teachers a system that he believed would unfold the mysteries of nature and mathematics through the fingers and the senses. Blocks weren't something to be dumped out on the floor but tiny sculptures presented with ceremony. I've seen one of the original Froebel block sets made by Milton Bradley, their first American manufacturer. Almost cubic itself, the box of blocks has a pleasant heft and mystery. Slide back the top and you see another cube of cubes nestled inside. In this crystalline arrangement, children might discover the world.

Froebel, born in 1782, was a polymath, gifted in drawing and other forms of visual communication. As a teenager, he trained as a woodsman in Germany's Thuringian Forest, learning about botany and forestry and drying, mounting, and classifying his own sets of local flowers and leaves. At university in Jena, he listened to lectures on mathematics and science, and he imagined working as a cartographer, translating information into graphics. He looked for work as a surveyor, considered becoming an architect, and then decided to teach. In 1805, he accepted a position at the Frankfurt Model School.

It turned out to be a place where, via drawing, handwork, and the experience of nature, children were taught an organized version of the stitched-together education that produced Froebel himself. The school was run by a follower of Johann Heinrich Pestalozzi, who trained educators from across Europe and the United States at a series of homelike model schools he founded between 1798 and 1825, inspired by the idea of childhood described in Jean-Jacques Rousseau's *Emile, or On Education* (1762).[21] Pestalozzi's groundbreaking decision was to eliminate the one-directional rote learning that had come to dominate organized schools. Positive reinforcement, capitalizing on children's innate curiosity, replaced a system of dictation and rigid codes for good behavior. Instead, children were given "object lessons," starting with observation of minerals, plants, and animals, learning to represent them on the page first as abstracted lines, angles, and curves and building up to more realistic representation. Educators supported students as they found their way to their own conclusions through manipulation and observation. In his novel *Leonard and Gertrude* (1781), Pestalozzi suggests that a mother might teach her children to count by numbering the steps from one side of the room to the other, and teach them the decimal system by observing the ten panes of glass in each window. The alphabet was taught via cutout letters that students could touch and manipulate, a tactile technique still present in Montessori education. Alongside these instructional objects and drawing exercises, Pestalozzi schools also encouraged singing (primarily of Protestant hymns), dancing, and experiencing the outdoors. Geography was taught on nature walks, botany and geology by collecting samples, mathematics with apples and stones.[22] Older children might make relief maps of local terrain. Touch was to lead to thought, thought to learning.

Pestalozzi believed women were uniquely suited to be teachers, theorizing that they would encourage children as ersatz mothers rather than discipline them like masters. The title of Pestalozzi's widely read book of 1801, *How Gertrude Teaches Her Children: An Attempt to Give Directions to Mothers How to Instruct Their Own Children*, also put education in women's hands. In that book, he lays out the four essential elements of his educational theory: that children learn best when they follow their own interests; that perception is the source of all learning; that children learn best through activity, so physical education must be part of coursework; and that ethical and moral education come from love and trust, which first develops between mother and child.[23] His attitude toward gender norms may trouble us today, but as kindergartens spread, teaching became one of the best paths to employment for women. Education historian Barbara Beatty calls the kindergarten movement, which built on Froebel's teaching and materials, one of the first women's movements.[24] Popularized by women in America and Europe, kindergarten came to be seen as a supplement to, rather than a replacement for, child-rearing at home, which eased its path to acceptance.

Froebel's key contribution was to add a set of standardized materials to Pestalozzi's theory of early education. The materials, and the detailed teaching method, made the Froebel kindergarten into a model that could travel—and it did. Froebel set up his first kindergarten, designed for very young children, in 1837; by 1850, Froebelian kindergartens had opened in England, India, Belgium, and France, and the preschool movement in the United States gained new momentum from women who had been taught by Froebel and emigrated to America. "This early acknowledgement of children as something other than small, stupid people engaged in useless activity set the stage for the acceptance of child psychology and the Child Study movement at the end of the nineteenth century," writes Norman Brosterman in his study of Froebel, *Inventing Kindergarten*.[25] Changing the form of school, from rows of desks and an emphasis on reading, writing, and arithmetic, to an open room and outdoor garden with child-size furniture, blocks, and songs, made it more palatable to parents.

Froebel's uniform playthings were inspired by an unlikely model. On a two-year break from teaching, from 1814 to 1816, Froebel hid himself from the world while organizing the mineralogical museum at the University of Berlin. This meditation on the physical qualities of crystals, the prelude to organizing them by a new scientific method, gave him deep insight into the patterns of nature. Crystals were too precious to place in the hands of children, however. To make his spheres, cylinders, and cubes, Froebel would return to the material of the forest: wood. He called his first ten teaching objects *gifts* to emphasize the ideal relationship between adult and child.

If the word *gift* suggested the spirit, *kindergarten*, a word of Froebel's invention, suggested the form: half garden, half schoolroom.[26] Froebel designed a model "garden for the children," with communal flower and vegetable plots running down one side of the yard and individual beds of herb, oil, cereal, and field plants down the other. Seats labeled with each child's given name sat in the center. Indoors, children sat at long slate-topped tables marked with a grid. The space in front of each child was her work space, into which the gifts were offered one at a time, to be used until the child had derived all the lessons from them that she could. In the influential *Kindergarten Guide* (1877), Froebel acolytes Maria Kraus-Boelte and John Kraus write, "As long as the child is happy, it is best not to interfere; when no longer contented alone, let the mother or kindergartner take her own box, and show one or more examples of formation, for the purpose of calling out new ideas."[27] Kraus-Boelte, who had studied the method with Froebel's widow, set up a kindergarten on East Twenty-Second Street in Manhattan in the 1870s. One of her students, Ruth Burritt, ran the Kindergarten Cottage at the Centennial Exposition in Philadelphia in 1876.[28] The woman tying all of these pieces together was Elizabeth Peabody, a transcendentalist and crusader for early childhood education, who organized the pavilion, convinced printer Milton Bradley (best known as the father of the board game industry) to manufacture the materials, and wrote a kindergarten guide of her own.[29] The kindergarten was to be "a commonwealth or republic of children," she wrote, "contrasted, in every particular, with the old-fashioned school, which is an absolute monarchy."[30] The ratio of one adult to one child might do in infancy, but as children got older and more active, "a sufficient society of children" was "the indispensable thing." Though Froebel is credited as "inventing kindergarten," it is women who both implemented and popularized the idea, adapting his sometimes rigid methods to the real children they encountered across the European continent and in the United States. As with design, women in education were often limited professionally to working with the smallest children. Without their translation, early childhood education might look very different.

The first gift was a set of colored balls, squishy and crocheted, with a loop of string to allow a child to swing them. The second gift consisted of a cube, a sphere, and a cylinder, made of maple, with thin wire loops embedded so that they could be hung from a rack on short strings. A drawing of the three forms, stacked on top of one another into a pillar, became a symbol of kindergarten, and a stone version of the stack stands on Froebel's grave.[31] The third gift, those eight wooden cubes, would prove the most influential in form and concept.

Froebel believed children have a natural tendency to take things apart. The cubes, once freed from their box, would be pushed across the table, "falling apart." Children would then have to "mend" the blocks back into their original cube, noting in the process that they were making a cube from cubes. "From a knowledge of the outside, instinct prompts the desire to know the inside, and, therefore, children, at this age—to the regret of their parents—usually destroy their toys," wrote the Krauses.[32] Froebel had clearly observed this tendency to destroy, and he harnessed it, creating a toy with destruction (and subsequent construction) as part of the play. While the child revealed the nature of the gift, she would also reveal something of her inner life, expressing her understanding through play. The simplicity of his blocks contrasted with those commonly available at this time: the didactic toys, with alphabets and numbers, or the building toys, molded and painted to look like real architectural materials. The third, fourth, fifth, and sixth gifts also consisted of different numbers of blocks. With each set of blocks, the children would be led through three types of activities. The first exercise involved building representations of things they might see in their environment —"forms of life" rendered in the chunky, abstracted way we might now called pixelated. Another

Gift 2: Sphere, Cylinder, and Cube. Kindergarten material based on the educational theories of Friedrich Froebel. Manufacturer: J. L. Hammett Co. c. 1890. Wood and string, closed: 2½ x 2⅞ x 10 x ¼ dz (6.4 x 7.3 x 26 cm). [Gift of Lawrence Benenson. Digital image © The Museum of Modern Art/Licensed by SCALA/Art Resource, NY]

exercise would involve "forms of beauty": pinwheels, stars, snowflakes, quilt blocks, and windmill blades, each one using all of the blocks in the box. The third activity was "forms of knowledge," that is, early mathematics, demonstrating the fractional and equivalent relationships of different arrangements.[33] These gifts were like the crystals Froebel studied: elements in the grammar of nature that had to be touched, stacked, dangled, and rearranged in order to learn about geometry, gravity, time, and symmetry. *Is that all?* the nineteenth century parent may well have said, but Froebel and his followers demonstrated that the unmarked block was, indeed, enough. As the choreographed lessons detailed in books like the Krauses' melted away in favor of freer-form exploration of stacking, sorting, and representing with blocks, what remained was

Gift 6: Blocks. Kindergarten material based on the educational theories of Friedrich Froebel. Manufacturer: Milton Bradley Co., Springfield, MA. c. 1880–1900. Maple, 3½ x 3⅝ x 3⁹⁄₁₆ dz (8.9 x 9.2 x 9 cm). [Gift of Lawrence Benenson. Digital image © The Museum of Modern Art/Licensed by SCALA/Art Resource, NY]

the idea that you could begin an education—begin a life of learning—with a wooden cube.

Frank Lloyd Wright's early exposure to Froebel's method became a well-worn anecdote in his autobiography. "For several years I sat at the little kindergarten table-top ruled by lines about four inches apart each way making four-inch squares; and, among other things, played upon these 'unit-lines' with the square (cube), the circle (sphere) and the triangle (tetrahedron or tripod)—these were smooth maple-wood blocks," Wright later wrote. "The virtue of all this lay in the awakening of the child-mind to rhythmic structures in Nature . . . I soon became susceptible to constructive pattern evolving in everything I saw."[34] Brosterman cites examples of work by Wright and Le Corbusier, who also attended a Froebel-influenced kindergarten, that closely resemble Froebel gifts. How much their adult work was influenced by their early childhood education is hard to determine—both also had influential adult mentors and lived in a moment when design began to embrace abstraction. Yet looking at one of Wright's stained-glass windows, where the organic repetition of, say, a hollyhock is transformed into straight lines, triangles, and squares, one can see an echo of the abstracting influence of the gifts, and hear Froebel describing his tools as the "building blocks" of nature.

After the gifts, which remained unchanged by children's manipulations, the second part of the Froebel system consisted of ten craft "occupations," where children would modify the materials through piercing, cutting, weaving, or folding with colored sheets of paper. At the 2012 Museum of Modern Art exhibition *Century of the Child*, the results of a number of these Froebel activities were displayed in the first gallery of the exhibit, where they established at a glance the connection between progressive education and modern art.[35] Influential designers and design teachers had close links to the method. Buckminster Fuller's geodesic domes owe a direct debt to the nineteenth gift, peas-work, where wooden sticks are connected hub-and-spoke-style with dried peas or cork. Fuller told an interviewer, "One of my first days of kindergarten the teacher brought us some toothpicks and semi-dried peas, and told us to make structures. With my bad sight, I was used to seeing only bulks . . . The other children, who had good eyes, were familiar with houses and barns . . . When the teacher told us to make structures, I tried to make something that would work. Pushing and then pulling, I found that the triangle held its shape when nothing else did."[36] Froebel's intent was to reveal the hidden structures of life, as well as the child's internal powers, and Fuller, with his bad eyesight, may illustrate that better than most. He was building by touch and experiment rather than appearance. The shock of recognition that present-day designers see in Froebel's kindergarten is not hard to trace: Their teachers, and their teachers' teachers, as well as their design heroes, learned from Froebel. But while designers and architects derived inspiration from the deceptive simplicity of his materials, educators were extending his "object lessons" in urban and radical directions.

•

CLASSROOMS AT CITY and Country School appear to be at least 50 percent blocks: ranged on shelves, categorized by size, labeled by name, and adjacent to big areas of floor free of tables and chairs. Caroline Pratt, who founded the school in Manhattan's Greenwich Village in 1914, let blocks be her curriculum, at least through third grade. When I visited a kindergarten class on a rainy winter morning 103 years later, I found children still learning the same way. A chart on the wall, created on Monday, established teams of children that would work together on a structure (teaching cooperation), and the name of the structure they had in mind (teaching planning). These kindergartners had begun by doing research and taking pictorial notes. By Tuesday, the day of my visit, I could see the teams' structures, including Yankee Stadium, a space shuttle, and the Plaza Hotel. At the Plaza, the makers had overcome gravity by making a hand-cranked elevator out of a block, paper, yarn, and a pulley (teaching science). They were inspired by Hilary Knight's foldout schematic of Eloise exploiting the Plaza's elevator bank, an illustration that remains one of the great visuospatial moments in children's literature. The space shuttle team populated their vessel with wooden figures whose white paper wrappings marked them as astronauts (teaching social studies, about people and their work). Pratt's method was for children to learn everything by observing, questioning, and making. "Everything," in Pratt's view, meant the structures of their world, not the structure of the universe. If in kindergarten you build one structure (real or fictional), by third grade, referred to at City and Country as the 8s, the class will tape out a city map on the floor and make custom buildings out of wood from their woodshop, as well as wallpaper, cardboard, mesh, and fabric.

Froebel started children off with blocks, but he made them follow his plan. Pratt was part of a new generation of trained teachers who rebelled against his narrow idea of object-oriented learning. Kindergarten materials had entered the American middle-class mainstream by the 1870s, sold by mail order and, by 1900, in the Montgomery Ward catalog.[37] Milton Bradley, one of two competing manufacturers of Froebel's gifts, tried to expand his market by adding letters to the cubes, radically changing their purpose. But more substantive developments came from people like Anna Bryan, who founded a series of free kindergartens in Louisville. She found children far more interested in creative play than in Froebel's instructions: "When it was time to play with the gifts," she observed, "the children made beds, chairs, tables, stoves, and cupboards with the blocks instead of the prescribed designs."[38] Bryan trained teachers who would work for John Dewey at the University of Chicago's Laboratory School, where children played with real objects and learned handwork, cooking, and housekeeping. "Nothing is more absurd," Dewey wrote in an essay titled "Froebel's Educational Principles," "than to suppose there is no middle ground between leaving a child to his own unguided fancies and likes, or controlling his activities by a formal succession of dictated directions."[39] Alice Temple, a teacher who worked with Dewey, spoke at the International Kindergarten Union convention in 1900 and criticized the Froebel craft occupations as too abstract: "Let him weave a little basket of vegetable fiber on a wire frame, or a rug of heavy candle wicking for his playhouse rather than a small, easily torn and comparatively useless paper mat."[40] Kindergarten—Froebel's word—had become an accepted part of American childhood, but what kindergarten entailed, by the early twentieth century, was up for grabs.

"I was seventeen when I taught my first class—a one-room school in the country—and I had none of the benefits of normal school, teacher training, nor even, possibly, had ever heard the word *pedagogy*," Pratt writes in her 1948 memoir, *I Learn from Children*.[41] Though Pratt would go on to get a teaching degree at Teachers College in New York City, she always believed that her education, and, indeed, the history of education, paled in comparison to what she learned observing her charges. Pratt believed in the importance of materials and hands-on learning. Her diploma was in manual training and kindergarten methods, and she taught woodworking at the Philadelphia Normal School for Girls from 1894 to 1901, where she was expected to be "able to correlate and co-ordinate the woodworking with the language, arithmetic, and other work of the school."[42] Girls at the school were taught to make working drawings, measuring and adding until they were accurate, and then to use carpentry to produce in three dimensions the designs on their drawings. The connection between making and thinking, and the usefulness of craft in teaching more abstract concepts, was central to this curriculum, but choice was limited.[43] When Pratt had an opportunity to lead her own woodworking classes at Hartley House, a settlement house in Manhattan's Hell's Kitchen, she began to experiment: She let children choose their own models, though they still had to start with a plan; she let them make (and remake) their objects by their own method; and she let the children take their completed work home. They were not completing an exercise to be put back in the box by nightfall but pursuing their own visions. She found that discipline and motivation took care of themselves when she ran the classroom this way.

In her memoir, Pratt is dismayed by the fear of waste that seems to permeate education:

> I once asked a cooking teacher why she did not let the
> children experiment with the flour and yeast, to see

whether they could make bread. She said in a shocked
voice, "But that would be so wasteful!" . . .

Once in our school I watched a little girl take sheets of
good drawing paper, one by one, from a pile—I counted
up to fifty. She made a little mark on each one with a
crayon, and threw it away. Fifty sheets of paper wasted,
and nobody said, "Don't!" . . . That little girl was in
school for the first time, and terrified . . . Those fifty
sheets of paper were a beginning for her; she drew, then
played with blocks, then answered the child who played
beside her on the floor, and in a few weeks she had begun
to find her way through the jungle of her own terrors
and was learning to be a happy, busy little schoolgirl.[44]

What other teachers see as waste, Pratt sees as a necessary richness. Pratt
set herself the task of designing blocks on a more generous pattern, offering
the freedom of the woodshop without tools, putting enough blocks in the
classroom for there to be material to waste, but maintaining a sense of
preparation. Modern, urban children could not easily gather "play material
from the life around them," and her toys were intended to fill that gap.[45]
Beginning in 1908, Pratt also produced a line of wooden toys, jointed
dolls, and farm animals, intended to be immediately recognizable as well
as plain enough to spur children's creativity (sewing clothes, building a
house). Pratt separated her "Do-Withs" that "seem to be inviting you to
come play with them," from "Do-Nothings," uninspiring toys that just
sit there, and "Look-Ons," wind-up toys that perform on their own.[46]
The Do-With Toys were made by Pratt in a Greenwich Village workshop and sold at Gimbels department store, but despite extensive press
coverage, her toy business failed. By 1913 she had another project, her
Play School, where the blocks were a central part of the curriculum for

the eleven four- and five-year-olds at what may have been the first nursery school in the United States.

Pratt's blocks are commonly referred to as unit blocks, and these were staples of my own childhood, at home and at school. The basic brick is 5½ by 2¾ by 1⅜ inches (140 by 70 by 35 millimeters), a 4:2:1 proportion. Unit blocks are large enough to use on the floor but small enough for three-year-olds to manipulate. On the wall of former principal Kate Turley's office at City and Country, there was a one-page sheet naming all of the blocks that make up a classroom set. First there is the "brickie" or the "unit," workhorse of the system. Next are a "squarie" or "half unit," a "middlie" or "double unit," and a "longie" or "quad"—four units long. Pratt's blocks, a version of which I played with throughout my own childhood, and which are now ubiquitous at most preschools, foreshadow some of the modular pleasure of LEGO, as smaller parts can be combined to make larger wholes out of squares, triangles, or arches with semicircular openings. The blocks with the one-by-two proportion always seem to be used most quickly, forcing children to assemble more idiosyncratic pieces—the squares, the right triangles—back into satisfying bricks, teaching basic principles of geometry, by the by, the same way Froebel's cubes-in-a-cube did. A half unit split along its long axis is a "butterie" due to its resemblance to a stick of butter; a half unit split diagonally along the short side is a "ramp," and along the long side a "triangle." Children get to discover for themselves that a squarie, a butterie, a ramp, and a triangle are all half units. The cute nicknames are used for the classes of three- and four-year-olds, while the mathematical terms are introduced in kindergarten, with the five-year-olds. "Strive for consistency," reads that instructional page, so that the whole school, children and adults, will speak the same block language.

The larger scale of the unit blocks, as well as the sets of wooden boxes and blocks Pratt later developed for outdoor play, were inspired by the

Block Structures in a MacDougal Alley Classroom, City and Country School. 1916–1921.
[Courtesy of the City and Country School Archives]

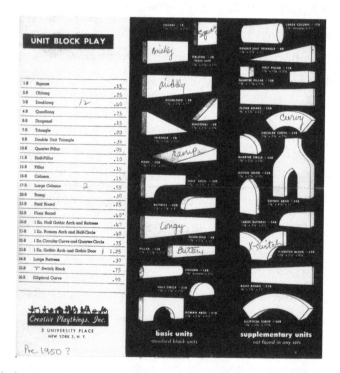

Unit Block Play, Creative Playthings, Inc., New York. c. 1950. [Courtesy of the City and Country
School Archives]

work of another female reformer, Patty Smith Hill. An educator at Columbia University Teachers College, Hill wrote dismissively of the size of Froebel's blocks: "The tiny cubes, circles, squares, and triangles inherited from Froebel's day are poor materials for construction at this stage of child life, as one slip of immature fingers, or even a deep breath, may annihilate the child's production in the twinkling of an eye."[47] Brought up playing with bricks, barrels, and boards, and making her own toys in the carpentry shop at the female seminary her father ran, Hill was well positioned to develop her own larger-block system. Eventually manufactured by Schoenhut Piano Company, a major turn-of-the-century toymaker, Hill's blocks used metal rods or pegs to attach the wooden structures together. Buildings could be more stable, more permanent. A set of her floor blocks included large pillars, blocks, wheels, and rods, with some pieces as long as three feet. Construction happened not on a table but on the floor, and because of the scale (sixteen times larger than Froebel's one-inch unit), children had to recruit compatriots to help, adding a social dimension to learning about shape, number, and construction.[48]

Up to this point, blocks had been thought of as a toy for one, maybe two children, a solitary pursuit that taught fine motor skills and structure, symmetry, and mathematics. But Hill, and then Pratt, saw that blocks could be a connector as well as a physical challenge. Hill's blocks standardized a different kind of play, that of making forts in the woods, or playhouses in the backyard, that was large scale, imaginative, and cooperative. When early childhood educators today talk about developing social and emotional skills, they often argue that shared play with larger-scaled cardboard blocks is just as important as learning to write or to stack. (Another part of this is playground interaction. We'll get to that later on.) As children increasingly work with digital tools, the social life of platforms is also an important design element, and in recent years, researchers have looked at how to teach manners for the virtual play space. In a 2013 *Economist* Explains piece written for unit blocks' one hundredth birthday, the anonymous author lists many of the long-standing claims for their educational benefits: "Co-operative building develops language and social skills. The 'unit'-based measurements of halves, doubles and quadruples, combined with columns, ramps, curves, buttresses and other specialised shapes, lay the foundations for basic maths and geometry. Balance and collapse teach the nature of gravity. Ramps and columns can be used to make simple levers and fulcrums. The need to place blocks carefully develops hand-eye co-ordination. Does all this ascribe too much educational potential to simple chunks of wood?"[49] The author's conclusion is *No.*

•

HILARY PAGE'S FATHER worked in the lumber trade. Early on, he noticed his son's interest in creating his own toys and games. One year, as a gift, he brought young Hilary two tons of scrap wood from the local sawmill, and Hilary worked with this private woodpile for several years, using it as a base for new inventions. As an adult he praised his father for setting him on his path, telling an interviewer he "had an intelligent father who in his childhood gave him the opportunity to develop his own ideas for making toys."[50] The woodpile lies behind many classic building toys. Froebel, Hill, and Pratt understood wood and woodworking intimately, were exposed to the material as children, and trained in the tools used to transform it into products for human use. Manufacturers of nineteenth-century toys had often started making them as a side line to use up scrap, repositioning their businesses when they found kid-size playthings more profitable than adult wares.[51] Page also began his toymaking career with a heap of timber and a plan.

At Shrewsbury Public School in Shropshire, England, Page showed an early entrepreneurial gift, turning his interest in photography into a business developing photos for other students. After school he followed his father into the timber business but, in 1932, at age twenty-eight, he decided to act on his lifetime interest in toys. He opened a store called Kiddicraft at 6 Godstone Road, Purley, Surrey. The small shop carried wooden toys imported from Russia, including *matryoshka* nesting dolls, stacking rings, and other playroom classics. Page was spurred to this enterprise, as Pratt had been before him, by a deep disappointment in what was on offer for children:

> It was not until I first became a father, twenty years ago, that the puzzling difficulty of selecting a suitable toy for a very young child struck me forcibly. I spent many an hour meandering around the toyshops and, in the process of my talks with the assistants, I discovered a general lack of understanding and consideration for the play-value of the toys they were selling all day. I tried to explain to them that toys need not necessarily be designed, manufactured and sold in shops as such, and that some of the most important playthings I had come across were improvised from everyday household equipment such as saucepans and saucepan lids, cotton reels, empty tins, etc., but they were quite disinterested in this particular aspect and undoubtedly felt I was a perfect nuisance.[52]

While running his store, Page scheduled visits to local nursery schools every Wednesday, playing with the children on the floor and figuring out which toys were most engaging to them. As he played, Page became disenchanted with wood as the primary material for children's toys. Everything for children, he observed, went in the mouth, and it was impossible to create a paint or enamel that didn't flake or get bitten off. Children's toys should be able to be washed every day, and wet wood quickly degrades. The solution was molded plastic: "Dust and germs cannot cling to the bright shiny surface, and the range of bright colors is most attractive and interesting to the child," he wrote in an essay for the 1946 *Daily Graphic Plastics Exhibition Catalog* titled "Plastics as a Medium for Toys."[53] Later, Page points out the importance of "perfect design" for the creation of quality toys. Work has to go into the making of a thoughtful mold before the first toy is struck as, unlike with wood or metal, you can't thicken a wall after the fact. "Baby's toys are subjected to extremely hard wear; almost inevitably they will be thrown out of the pram on to the ground, and an article which is quickly broken is in every way most unsatisfactory."

In 1936, Page formed a separate company, named British Plastic Toys Ltd. (Bri-Plax), to manufacture molded toys using thermoplastic urea-formaldehyde. His partners at Kiddicraft were dubious about plastic's potential, but he persisted, producing his first range of plastic toys, branded Sensible Toys, in 1937. Most of these were based on the classic wooden toys he had been importing from Russia, but they were lighter weight and more durable. Among the offerings were stackers called Building Beakers and Pyramid Rings, nesters called Billie and His Seven Barrels, and teethers and rattles made of linked triangles. Versions of all of these can still be found in the baby aisle of any major big-box store.

But Page also produced something new: the Interlocking Building Cube, patented in the United Kingdom in 1940, a cubic plastic block with four raised bumps, or studs, on the top and an open bottom into which those studs fit tightly. A black-and-white image from a box top, circa 1939, shows a tower of eight cubes, with two side by side forming a T on top of a base: a configuration possible, but improbable, with squaries. A few more cubes scattered on the tabletop show the interlocking mechanism from the top and bottom. The text reads, "Building Cubes have always been 'favourite' toys during the first five years. BRI-PLAX INTERLOCKING

BUILDING CUBES are miles ahead of the ordinary painted or polished ones, as they build up so much better. They are self-coloured and it is impossible for a child to remove the slightest trace of the material or colour, even with constant sucking, biting and gnawing. They are completely hygienic and can be washed indefinitely."[54]

A postwar box lid for the cubes, in full color, shows essentially the same arrangement of bulging tower and strewn-about cubes. This time, however, a boy and girl are playing with them together—notably, the girl is building the tower, the boy is helping—and the following has been added to the promotional text: "This toy teaches finger-control, balance and patience." By 1953, the educational claims for toys had grown more specific, and Kiddicraft wanted its bona fides to be known. There's no parent in the picture, either, because Page had strong feelings about children being left alone to explore materials: "It is a great mistake to present a child with a toy and then take immediate steps to make sure he knows exactly how the creator of that toy intended it to be used."[55]

During World War II, all nonessential plastic production ceased, and Page returned to his roots, touring the country with a lecture on "Children in Wartime." He wrote a second book, titled *Toys in Wartime* (1942), that showed families how to make their own playthings out of household objects, recycled boxes, and other kinds of "scrap." But as soon as materials became available, Page began production again. He had the lead in plastic toy production because of his prewar experiments, and Page had something new to add to what was now known as the Kiddicraft line for older children. Marketed for ages seven and up, "self-locking building bricks" were smaller, with a basic 2 x 4 studded piece with an open bottom. As with Pratt's unit blocks, the system built upon a basic 1 x 2 brick. Slits in the side allowed two-dimensional doors, windows, and cards printed with literal bricks to be inserted between the plastic pieces, and sets also included "finish" pieces with smooth peaked tops, intended for the gable of

Bri-Plax Interlocking Building Cubes, A Hilary Page Design. Made in England. 1939.
[Photograph by Chas Saunter, hilarypagetoys.com]

Kiddicraft Interlocking Building Cubes, A Hilary Page Design, box lid. Made in England.
1950. [Photograph by Chas Saunter, hilarypagetoys.com]

a roof or the top of a wall. Page patented the 2 x 4 brick in 1947 and took out later patents on side slits and the baseplate.

"Self-locking building bricks" made their debut at the 1947 Earls Court Toy Fair, where the Page family built a life-size display, including sturdy skyscrapers as tall as his five-foot-six daughter, Jill. In a print advertisement from 1948, a boy proudly shows off the cottage he built with the Kiddicraft bricks: ". . . and here's the House that *I* built." Copy aimed at purchasing parents reads, "Made to scale and locking together easily and perfectly they provide the basis of an endless variety of realistic models."[56] The abstraction of the cubes, which were aimed at the same preschool audience as Froebel's and Pratt's blocks, gives way to the older-child realism of bricks. At a time when the British construction-toy market was dominated by Meccano, an engineering toy with metal parts used to make working machines, the Kiddicraft copywriter may have felt older children needed a bigger, more ostensibly productive challenge than simply stacking.

You may have been thinking, as you read the story of Page's invention, *Don't self-locking plastic building bricks sound a lot like LEGO? Isn't LEGO from Denmark?* LEGO founder Ole Kirk Christiansen introduced plastic Automatic Binding Bricks in 1949, in Billund, Denmark, building on his company's success making wooden toys. So which came first? It wasn't until a 1980s patent case between U.S. toy manufacturer Tyco and LEGO that the connection between Page's Kiddicraft and LEGO was revealed. LEGO sued Tyco when the latter began manufacturing interlocking bricks in Hong Kong, where Page's 1947 British patent would have had jurisdiction. A story covering the lawsuit in the *Mail on Sunday* melodramatically referred to the Kiddicraft bricks as "The Ghost That Is Haunting Lego Land."[57] In testimony by Godtfred Kirk Christiansen, one of Ole Kirk Christiansen's sons and the longtime managing director of LEGO, Godtfred said that he and his father had seen

Page's bricks before they created their own, as they had received samples when they bought their British injection-molding machine in 1947. "With the cooperation of a tooling works in Copenhagen, we modified the design of the brick, and moulds were made. The modifications in relation to the Kiddicraft bricks included straightening round corners and converting inches to cm and mm, which altered the size of the brick by approx. 0.1 mm in relation to the Kiddicraft brick. The studs on the bricks were also flattened on top."[58] LEGO settled with the owners of Page's company, which had become Hestair-Kiddicraft in 1981. "Page had the idea and Lego took the idea that he himself could not commercialise," the patent agent for Hestair-Kiddicraft told the *Mail on Sunday*. Page's widow said Page himself had never seen LEGO.

By the early 1950s, Page had moved on to another toy idea, Kiddicraft Miniatures, which reproduced real life in even more exacting detail. He planned three hundred tiny models of food and household items, licensing brand names from manufacturers to make them as accurate as possible. Page produced two hundred of them, but he could not honor all of the agreements he made. The stress of the enterprise brought his company near collapse, and Page committed suicide on June 24, 1957. Kiddicraft continued, but it never figured out how to capitalize further on Page's insight. Though the popularity of LEGO bricks today seems a forgone conclusion, the Danish company, like Kiddicraft, struggled for years to convince parents that they needed a plastic, interlocking brick alongside their wooden blocks. For a time, LEGO was the interloper—the Bad Toy in the Good Toy aisle—trying to make the case for itself as educational, creative, *necessary* for childhood despite its unnatural material and array of colors.

•

LIKE OTHER BLOCK innovators, Ole Kirk Christiansen started out as a carpenter. He founded his business in 1916, making simple furniture and cabinetry for houses in Billund. During the Depression, he started to make toys and small household objects in order to make ends meet, and eventually he decided that playthings were the better business in a sluggish economy.[59] As LEGO legend has it, he created a competition for his employees to rename the company, a competition he ended up winning with LEGO, a contraction of the Danish *leg godt*, or "play well."[60] The toys the rechristened LEGO company made in the 1930s were wooden cars, boats, and pull toys shaped like animals. They did produce blocks, but with letters, numbers, and illustrated animals on the sides.

In 1947, a British salesman came to Billund and visited Christiansen, selling him on the company's plastic injection-molding equipment. When the new machine arrived, it came with samples of what it could produce, including the Kiddicraft bricks. It took LEGO several years to perfect their designs and find a reliable source of the raw plastic they needed, cellulose acetate. In 1949, the company first produced a fish-shaped rattle, a bear in an airplane, and the new, unmarked building bricks in a variety of bright colors.[61] The bricks came in two sizes, either 2×2 or 2×4 studs on top, with side slits, and panel windows and doors. The blocks were released as gift sets in four different sizes. Catalog pages from 1950 show houses, skyscrapers, and other edifices built out of combinations of the red, green, white, and tan bricks, demonstrating the capabilities of the different sizes of sets. These first LEGO bricks were only available in Denmark and didn't sell well. In the early 1950s, neither Kiddicraft nor LEGO had success with the binding bricks, although other plastic toys had become widely accepted and were selling well. Both companies were treating them as abstract elements, like wooden blocks, but consumers didn't see them as essential in the same way. LEGO had to make a city where everyone wanted to play.

What changed the game for LEGO was the System of Play, announced at the 1955 Nuremberg Toy Fair. LEGO needed its own universe and, thanks to a chance encounter between Godtfred Kirk Christiansen and the buyer for the top Copenhagen department store, Magasin du Nord, that universe came to be. On a trip to the 1954 London Toy Fair, the buyer told Godtfred that most toys seemed to be one-offs, and that there was no toy *system* on the market.[62] Godtfred looked at the company's product line and decided that LEGO Mursten, or bricks, had the most potential for such far-reaching organization. Until then, LEGO bricks had been between categories, too small to appeal to younger children in the manner of wooden blocks or the Kiddicraft bricks, but the wrong scale to be mixed with other cars or play figures. System of Play brought together all of the company's existing sets, plus new elements, into a unified town plan. The company's existing boxes already included a number of architectural models, to which LEGO added a large vinyl mat, marked with streets and blocks, new 1:87-scale vehicles, trees, bushes, and signs that matched the so-called HO standard size used for model railways. On the mat was the instruction "Build your own LEGO town." Finally LEGO was additive, expansive, and architectural, a worthy rival for a previous generation of engineering-based construction sets and train sets that had sprawled over the linoleum floors of basements and playrooms.

The desire for expansion matched the postwar building and baby boom, and the toy finally entered the zeitgeist. Magasin du Nord allowed LEGO to set up a large display on its ground floor for the System of Play and sales improved, allowing the company to add sets, year by year, to a single imaginary town that must always be in need of something new. Today, the LEGO Group is often criticized for stoking the cycle of consumer desire, sequestering LEGO bricks in individual branded universes, and launching new sets on a fashion cycle, but this has been part of the company's sales strategy for longer than people realize. The free play celebrated in their ads of the 1970s and early 1980s reflects a brief moment in American culture when the kindergarten values—embedded in wooden blocks—returned to the forefront, but that has by no means been the status quo for toys in the home. LEGO's rivals were the pop guns and action figures of the television universe, in whose company it looks positively sedate.

System of Play laid out a large, car-centric town on a grid plan, rationalizing and modernizing the village. Over the next few years, the company added a gas station, a fire station, a car showroom, and a church, as well as accessories made of metal, including motorcyclists, traffic police, street lamps, and even a Volkswagen Beetle. The architecture of the initial Esso gas station, garage, and VW showroom looks like Danish functionalism of the 1920s and 1930s, white buildings with rounded corners.[63] On the website Brick Fetish, LEGO historian Jim Hughes writes that Godtfred hoped the set, with its many traffic-related additions, would teach street safety as part of its educational value.[64] The System of Play was strictly an indoor toy, allowing children to play city-planner-as-God in the comfort of their own living rooms—a development that Maaike Lauwaert, author of *The Place of Play* (2009), associates with children's forced retreat from society as their activities became more regimented and parent-controlled. The playroom, well stocked with toys, was supposed to replace the pleasures of the urban, social street. According to Lauwaert, "In the 1950s, the playroom became an integral part of architectural practices. While the mid-19th- and early 20th-century guidebooks on housekeeping advocated a separation of the child from worldly affairs, a distancing of the child from the adult world, 1950s architects designed homes that centralized the child and play in the recreation area and the open plan living room."[65]

The wooden toys made by LEGO and Swedish manufacturer BRIO, as well as the American toymaker Creative Playthings, had the abstract forms, natural material, and primary colors associated with the tools of progressive education.[66] Although today LEGO seems to have overcome its artificial nature, a 2013 article on a Japanese company with plans to make the interlocking block out of wood suggests that plastic still comes with a question mark. "Love LEGO but hate plastic?" asked the website Apartment Therapy, one of more than a dozen design blogs to feature wooden binding bricks, "the natural LEGOs," made by Mokulock.[67] Described as "handmade" and "all-natural," the 2-x-4-studded blocks had clear visual appeal, in a minimalist Muji way, and came packaged in a brown cardboard box, with an unbleached cotton sack for storage. But beyond the blocks' good looks lurked some very basic questions of function. A review in *designboom* noted a product disclaimer that "the pieces can warp or fit together imprecisely due to the nature of the material in different temperatures and scale of humidity."[68] Another commenter brought up sustainability and the possibility of deforestation, "considering the sheer number of Lego blocks produced a year, if they were made of wood." Do toys need to be as artisanal as our food? I understand why my child would want to make her own toy out of wood, but does someone else need to do it for her? And why wood?

This anxiety over "unnatural" plastic toys replacing "natural" wooden ones has deeper roots than we realize. In *Designing the Creative Child: Playthings and Places in Midcentury America*, design historian Amy F. Ogata explored how the baby boom restructured the American landscape, creating a demand for thousands of new homes and new schools. (We'll return to this in later chapters.) With this new construction came new thinking about how, where, and with which tools American children should be educated. As Ogata guides you through the playrooms, schoolrooms, and toy shops of the era, it becomes clear how much of the current aesthetic landscape of upper-income childhood—and specifically the contents of the toy chest—was constructed in the late 1940s and 1950s. One hears the echo of Froebel, Pratt, and Page urging the parent to let the child explore the toy on her own, to give the child tools for discovery and get out of her way. On the question of wood, Ogata writes, "Among the educated middle and upper-middle classes, wood became the material symbol of timelessness, authenticity and refinement in the modern educational toy."[69] She quotes Roland Barthes's *Mythologies*, where he characterized plastic and metal as "graceless" and "chemical," and argued that wood "is a familiar and poetic substance, which does not sever the child from close contact with the tree, the table, the floor. Wood does not wound or break down; it does not shatter, it wears out, it can last a long time."[70] No less an authority than Dr. Spock argued for the abstracted wooden train over the realistic metal one, while Creative Playthings combined furniture and toy in its Hollow Blocks: maple cubes, open on one side, that could be used for storage or fort making. In order to claim its place in those new suburban playrooms, LEGO had to prove it was up to those standards of authenticity and quality.

During this period, LEGO did two additional things that set itself apart from other plastic brickmakers and ensured its legacy. First, it improved the quality of the bricks after complaints that they did not bind as well as they should. As Page had anticipated, creating a better mold was key to maintaining a sense of difference and quality in plastic toys. They play-tested a number of different designs, and children preferred a brick with three cylindrical tubes on the underside, which up to then had been hollow. The studs fit between the hollow tubes and the side walls of the brick, which meant they would stay together under most circumstances yet were still easy to disassemble. LEGO calls this ability "clutch power."[71] The new tube-and-stud design was patented in Denmark in 1958 and eventually in thirty-three other countries. The new design allowed bricks to be combined in a much larger number of ways, leading to ever more complex sets. LEGO also created a sloped brick, which looked like a right triangle from the side and was ideal for creating slanted roofs, which allowed for more realistic buildings. In 1963, the company upgraded the plastic used to make the bricks from cellulose acetate to ABS, the material used today.

Second, Godtfred drew up the LEGO Principles of Play, which were distributed to everyone in the company in 1962. They ran as follows, and still guide the company:

1 LEGO—unlimited play potential
2 LEGO—for girls, for boys
3 LEGO—fun for every age
4 LEGO—year round play
5 LEGO—healthy and quiet play
6 LEGO—long hours of play
7 LEGO—development, imagination, creativity
8 LEGO—the more LEGO, the greater its value
9 LEGO—extra sets available
10 LEGO—quality in every detail[72]

The Principles of Play were used in LEGO advertising to set their toy apart from others, and they read like a branded version of Progressive kindergarten goals. In the 1950s, many consumers remained suspicious of plastic. Period magazines argued that plastic could never replace "good and honest" wooden toys, Lauwaert writes, because although the latter material may have been cheap, easy to clean, durable, and colorful, it was forever "associated with artificiality, superficiality, and fakeness."[73] "Part of Christiansen's genius was to make the new material feel almost as comforting, as domestically reliable, as wood itself," wrote Anthony Lane in the *New Yorker* in 1998.[74] Denmark was known for quality craftsmanship in design and decorative arts, and this turned out to be a transitive property when it came to playthings. LEGO continued to emphasize its production values for both wooden and plastic toys, and quality materials and manufacturing were used to justify higher prices. Good Toys tended to be classic playthings, simply designed, and made from traditional materials. Good Toys did not carry advertising or gendered messages. Good Toys were nonviolent and long-lasting. Good Toys sparked the child's creativity, and play with them could go on forever—all afternoon, throughout childhood, as long as the parent was willing to continue to add extra sets.

The beauty of the town plan as a sales pitch was that, like real-life cities, it could extend indefinitely. "The more LEGO, the greater its value," was right there in the Principles. American advertisements for LEGO from the 1960s, when it was newly introduced, indirectly call out other principles. A LEGO System ad from the November 1962 *Saturday Evening Post* (prime time for gift buying) shows a sister and brother standing and lying within a LEGO city of their own making. The copy says, "LEGO . . . the most creative adventure you can give a child," suggesting the romance of travel.[75] "Put magical LEGO into the hands of a five-year-old and she will make you a camel. A little boy will turn his LEGO into an airplane on Monday . . . Snap apart and it's a train on Tuesday, a skyscraper on Wednesday." Another advertisement, from 1967–68, makes the durability and duration of LEGO play even more explicit: "Lego, the toy they won't be tired of by Dec. 26th."

And yet, LEGO's marketing moves throughout the 1960s set up a tension between creative play and realistic architecture that continues to the present day. Page wrote that creators need to stand back and let children show them how to use a toy, but LEGO's numbered directions lead children by the hand. Early LEGO sets had come with drawings of completed creations, with just a few tricky connections called out in separate drawings. In 1964, directions became even more specific and began to use the thirty-degree isometric diagrams that are now intimately associated with LEGO. They took the guesswork out of the process but, as a by-product, created a one best way to build a set.[76] In 1978, the company moved further away from the free play associated with Good Toys, starting its present-day organization around "play themes." In order to survive competition from narrative-based toys, including Playmobil, LEGO had to reorganize. Castles, pirates, Westerns, and space (the particular focus of the childhood LEGO collection my brother and I shared), along with new city sets, took up the town plan idea anew. LEGO buildings had traditionally been closed, aping the solidity of structures in a town plan; now, new builds opened up like a stage set or a dollhouse, and an increasing array of minifigures served the purpose of the dollhouse family.[77] The narrative changed from quiet construction to character-filled action. More recently, LEGO has come under fire for its ever-expanding roster of commercial tie-ins, the ultimate mark of the Bad Toy. Where the original play themes included a generic castle, today a search for "LEGO castle" turns up one from *Frozen*, one from *Minecraft*, and one from *Ninjago* (an invented LEGO universe of ninjas, magic, and Asian rooflines). You can't buy a *castle* castle, and the branding makes it difficult to find one that reads as unisex, where both ninjas and princesses could live in harmony.

In 2014, a 1981 LEGO ad went viral. The advertisement shows a little girl with red braids, perhaps a subconscious reference to Swedish children's heroine Pippi Longstocking, dressed in jeans and blue sneakers and holding her latest LEGO creation, stacks of multicolored bricks on a green baseplate. What is it? Who knows? "What it is is beautiful," the copy reads.[78] Created by a female creative director, Judy Lotas, the ad was inspired by the Equal Rights Amendment, then before Congress, as well as Lotas's own two daughters. Although the ad had been memorable in its day, it went viral twenty-three years later as a form of protest. In 2012, LEGO had introduced LEGO Friends: LEGO for girls, in shades of primarily pink and purple, with curvaceous minifigs and a series of dollhouse-like settings in Heartlake City. In the new LEGO universe, girls didn't even get to name their own town. The imagination, the infinite possibility, and the unisex quality of the LEGO Principles of Play—skillfully evoked in Lotas's ad by the overalls and sneakers—had been overturned in favor of a narrower, narrative play pattern with simplified sets containing lots of custom pieces.

Free block play with LEGO is now associated with artistic projects, with adults, and with a lack of color. At the Louisiana Museum of Modern Art, just north of Copenhagen, the Children's Wing is stocked with bins of yellow LEGO, which children can use to build while their parents are looking at someone else's art. In 2005, Icelandic artist Olafur Eliasson initiated the Collectivity Project in a public square for the Third Tirana Biennale in Albania. The project consisted of bins of snow-white LEGO and a set of collapsible tables arranged in a ring. A decade later, the project returned as a temporary installation at the northern end of the High Line in New York, with two tons of white LEGO bricks and starter buildings by famous architects.[79] When I first read about the project I thought it sounded silly—why should LEGO be art?—but when I encountered the project in person it changed my mind. The bins of LEGO were sheltered by the scaffolding for the future headquarters of Coach, the first skyscraper to be built as part of the Hudson Yards redevelopment project. As white towers rose over the plateau of tables, a silvery tower rose above the builders' heads. To seed the creativity of the collective, High Line designers Diller Scofidio + Renfro and James Corner Field Operations, along with other New York-based firms, built an initial set of structures, including a branching tree, a city rearranged next to the city coming into being. After that, it was anarchy, or collectivity, as people came and built, transfixed by the opportunity to construct something in New York City, in public. The quantity of bricks, the lack of color, the anonymity of the busy park setting conspired to put adults and children into a state of creation. The desire to carve one's initials on a tree was transmuted into building lacy catwalks between mongrel versions of those initial architect-designed towers. Even in the middle of all that foot traffic, many visitors settled in for an hour or more of block play, screening out the imperatives of tourism—many languages spoken, none needed—to focus on their build. I was astonished at the concentration achieved. The whiteness turned the anarchy into art in the same way those the wooden Mokulock bricks seemed suddenly Zen. I could see why Eliasson chose monochrome, but I still wished that we might also participate in the freedom from taste embodied by that little red-haired girl in the ad.

•

BLOCKS HAVE BECOME the ur-symbol of childhood, used everywhere from the hand-drawn logo of Ann Martin's bestselling Baby-Sitters Club book series to the carved stone cenotaph on Friedrich Froebel's grave in Schweina, Germany. Though Froebel's method may have fallen by the wayside, it is rare to find a preschool or kindergarten classroom without blocks in some form, whether Caroline Pratt's unit blocks or LEGO's younger sibling, Duplo. As digital technologies enter children's lives earlier and earlier, it isn't surprising that blocks have become both a symbol of the Good Toy, as something beyond branding, as well as a bearer of meaning from the physical to the digital realm in toys, programming languages, and even games like the supremely popular *Minecraft*. Children's technologies count on our cultural familiarity with the block and the binding brick, and those technologies capitalize on the same ease of assembly and disassembly that made Froebel think blocks could show children the world.

"We have always been intrigued and inspired by the way children play and build with Lego bricks," write Mitchel Resnick, LEGO Papert Professor of Learning Research at the MIT Media Lab, and his co-authors in a 2009 paper on how they developed the Scratch programming language. "Given a box full of [LEGO, children] immediately start tinkering, snapping together a few bricks, and the emerging structure gives them new ideas . . . We wanted the process of programming in Scratch to have a similar feel."[80] And so it does: In Scratch, junior programmers are given a screen stocked with commands in color-coded "bins." Blue blocks are labeled with different motions, purple with looks, pink with sounds, and so on. By dragging a block out of its bin and into the Scripts area—the playing field—the child can make her sprite (initially a yellow cat) do something. Taking out more blocks and snapping them together creates more complex movements, as taking out more LEGO and snapping them together creates more complex structures. Tinkering offers the opportunity to build and test quickly, without excessive preparation, learning and planning as you go.[81] Cues in the shapes of the Scratch blocks show children which commands can be combined, and which can't; some have universal connectors and others are selective. Autonomy and creativity are central to the redefinition of some video games as Good Toys. In "Computer as Paintbrush: Technology, Play, and the Creative Society,"

Resnick lays out the argument for computers "not simply as information machines, but also as a new medium for creative design and expression."[82] Combining play, technology, and learning is not new, Resnick writes, citing Froebel as using "the technology of his time" to develop toys "with the explicit goal of helping young children learn important concepts such as number, size, shape and color." Technology marches forward, through the numerous iterations of the wooden block, to the plastic binding brick, and beyond.

The colors and the stickiness of the Scratch blocks build on the original insight of Page and Christiansen, that sometimes children want to make something that's both quick to assemble and has a rough permanence. In developing Scratch (and, later, Scratch Jr. for children ages five to seven), the MIT Media Lab team built on their experience in the 1990s developing LEGO Mindstorms, physical-digital hybrids that added robotics to the LEGO brick. It's not a leap but an iteration, from the building block that fell apart at a touch, to binding bricks, to adding levers, gears, and pulleys to get those bricks moving (really a hacked-together version of LEGO and the older, engineering-focused Meccano), and then finally to adding the circuits and the power to allow those machines to move without human effort. Tinkering, building, connecting, and debugging are all part of what legendary MIT Media Lab professor Seymour Papert called "constructionism." Child development and computer science professor Marina Umaschi Bers, who worked with Papert at the MIT Media Lab and collaborated with Resnick and Paula Bonta on the Scratch Jr. programming language, explains it this way: "Children learn better when making their own projects, constructing their own ideas, and describing their own solutions to the problems."[83] This sounds very much like the object-based learning strategies of Pratt, Hill, and Dewey, but with the computer as the primary tool. Papert's "constructionism" builds on Piaget's "constructivism," literally, by combining the idea of learning by doing with physical and digital products, and carrying hands-on learning forward into elementary and middle school education.[84] The current vogue for project-based learning is based in part on Papert's constructionist theory.[85]

Bers expands the physical-digital metaphor to playpens and playgrounds to describe the digital landscape that parents and children confront today. The Internet of chatrooms and public *Minecraft* servers is the forest, unbounded and unsupervised. The Internet of children's educational apps is the playpen, safe, colorful, adorned with cute cartoon characters, but typically commercialized and offering a limited range of toys, selected by the parent. Her ideal is the playground, a fenced world in which children can explore freely, touching and testing as is developmentally appropriate for their age, experiencing risk, and expressing their autonomy. On the playground, they aren't being fed education dressed up as entertainment—for prekindergarten children, preacademic lessons like ABCs and 123s aren't a fundamental developmental task—but making their own fun by playing pretend, trying the slide every which way, or scratching out a racetrack in the dirt. Blocks can serve a similar function. At the Eliot-Pearson Children's School, part of the Tufts University Department of Child Study and Human Development, kindergartners program with actual blocks, a sort of Scratch Jr. Jr. for children who can't yet read and are at the age when using their hands (not to mention their bodies) is their primary mode of learning.

This kind of digital-physical hybrid, pushing computer programming toward an ever-younger audience, isn't an unmixed good. Children of that age don't need the academic drill of run commands any more than they need to know the alphabet. And yet the category seems to grow each day. I bought the game Robot Turtles, a board game based on Papert's original Logo programming language for kids; other, block-based, and far more expensive products in the field include Cubetto, mCookie, and KIBO, created by Bers and KinderLab Robotics. In Bers's Developmental Technology (DevTech) Research Group at Tufts, she had been working on a developmentally appropriate product for kids younger than seven, a "digital manipulative" that she explicitly connects to the tradition of Montessori and Froebel.[86] They developed the Creative Hybrid Environment for Robotic Programming (CHERP), and eventually a cute little wheeled, robotic cart as their physical avatar, known as KIBO. To make their KIBO robot move, children snap together sequences of wooden blocks, labeled with colored symbols for different motion commands like "forward," "spin," or "shake" and locked in place with a green "begin" block and a red "end" block.[87] The design of the blocks means children can't make a syntax error, like putting "begin" in the middle of the sequence. Programming in the physical realm also opens the possibility for more materials: In her book, Bers describes a junk playground–like landscape of LEGO bricks, feathers, pipe cleaners, tissue boxes, straws, and Velcro used in the pilot stage, fun materials for a construction project on their own, but literally animated by the CHERP blocks and embedded robotic elements. "Children work on the floor, on the table, and on the computer and navigate among these physical spaces," Bers writes. "Children are physically busy. In the preschool years, development of motor skills is fundamental for later growing."[88]

Bers's hybrid approach also includes another element of playground play: socializing. She describes ways in which children can be encouraged to collaborate and help each other with programming projects via a series of simple organizational changes. Most robotics projects in educational settings give a presorted kit to an individual child or group (the same would be true in the home), but in her program she placed the materials for a given project in sorted bins in the center of the room, forcing children to negotiate for what they needed and introducing the idea of scarcity and desirability. The DevTech group also created what she calls a "low-tech tool": At the beginning of a day's project, children are given a printout with their photo at the center of an array of photographs of the other kids in the room. Teachers prompt kids, throughout the day, to draw a line between their own face and those of children with whom they have interacted. At the end of the day they write a thank-you note to the children they have collaborated with most. Studies have shown that children may actually interact more when using a computer together than when doing other parallel tasks like putting together a puzzle.[89] Bers sees this kind of social education as an essential part of the digital landscape, working against the stereotype of programming and computer games as isolationist and toward safe digital worlds that still offer the opportunity for developing online and offline relationships.

Olafur Eliasson's Collectivity Project offered a place where parents and children could play with all the bricks they wanted, in public, with the potential for communication and collaboration in person and over time. But there's another place, right at home, with almost all of the same characteristics. *Minecraft* is a video game created by Swedish game designer Markus "Notch" Persson and originally released by Mojang in 2011. It swiftly rose to become the second-best-selling video game in history, after Tetris. Microsoft purchased it for $2.5 billion in 2014, and it has sold more than 121 million copies as of February 2017. Cultural anthropologist Mimi Ito, who studies new media use and the history of educational games, has written that this unprecedented popularity for a learning game "rewrites the playbook . . . At its heart, *Minecraft* is about constructing and problem solving in a networked social world. The blocky indie vibe just contributes to the culture of DIY creativity in *Minecraft* and kids feel empowered to make it their own."[90] *Minecraft* is usually described as a "sandbox" game, meaning that, when launched, the user is presented with a crudely detailed environment—not the absolute blankness of a fresh sandbox, but grass and sky, a forest, or mountains—and she has to make something of it. The suggestion of a grid, not unlike Froebel's lined table, is clear, as the square pixels that make up the purposefully low-resolution graphics are visible, brown and green lines stair-stepping their way to make up a square of grass. I'll discuss the history of the sandbox in greater depth later, but suffice it to say that piles of sand, in empty lots, were late nineteenth-century reformers' first attempt to make playgrounds. Persson, and Mojang, have done something similar in their bounded digital space by offering an environment rich in raw materials but without verbal instructions or (at least at first) a narrative. The *Minecraft* player—learning the controls, finding her toy cupboard of materials in Creative mode or the actions that allow her to make materials in Survival mode—is like the child reaching out to touch the eight wooden cubes of one of Froebel's gifts, or Hilary Page tinkering with his giant woodpile. Equally important for *Minecraft*'s ultimate educational potential is that your sandbox can be shared with those of others: You can play alone, or you can join worlds and collaborate.

The relationship of *Minecraft* to the long history of building toys has not gone unnoticed. In a 2014 essay, "Teaching Tools: Progressive Pedagogy and the History of Construction Play," Colin Fanning and Rebecca Mir write, "*Minecraft*'s overwhelmingly positive reception relies on historically well-established ideas about play, building, and architecture, especially those promoted through the long-standing genre of construction toys."[91] In other words, the same "object lessons" that inspired the academically minded block play of Scratch and CHERP. Mojang seemed to explicitly acknowledge *Minecraft*'s place on a continuum of toys in a 2011 trailer, where the narrator says, "Let's go to a place where everything is made of blocks. Where the only limit is your imagination . . . With no rules to follow, this adventure—it's up to you." He might have been reading the copy from a 1960s LEGO ad. In interviews, the reclusive Persson has described playing with LEGO bricks. As a child growing up in Sweden in the 1980s, he was likely also exposed to classic wooden toys from BRIO and its competitors.

Fanning and Mir also find game developer Peter Molyneux making the offline/online comparison explicit and expressing common (if misplaced) LEGO nostalgia: "It is, in a way, a social LEGO, when LEGO used to be a creative toy, which I don't think it is so much anymore, it's much more prescriptive . . . LEGO used to be just a big box of bricks, and you used to take the bricks, pour them on the carpet, and then make stuff. And that's exactly what *Minecraft* is."[92] Like its sandbox predecessors SimCity (1989) and Spore (2008), both designed by Will Wright, *Minecraft* offered a virtual prepared environment, and its popularity has led to the use of the game as a medium for education. MinecraftEdu offers teachers an educational license and prewritten lesson plans to use the game to teach science, engineering, math, languages, and the humanities. One sample lesson has students building a house with walls that are half red and half blue, exploring the different ways "half" can be expressed physically and creating a narrative around the mathematical concept to demonstrate understanding. This lesson also suggests students go back and forth between the digital and the physical, building their construction in both realms, or at least planning it on real-world graph paper.[93]

The Chicago Architecture Foundation has run summer camps that combine real-world exploration of architecture with online building. "Campers pursue answers to questions such as: 'How was that designed?', 'What was the architect thinking?' and 'What stories can this building tell us?' "[94] Block by Block, a 2014 partnership between Mojang and

UN-Habitat, the United Nations human settlement program, endeavored to use *Minecraft* as a modeling tool for community participation in public-space design. If kids are building somewhere, the thinking goes, why not meet them where they are? If kids know how to use this tool, rather than costly professional 3-D-modeling software, why not speak their language? Fanning and Mir sound a note of caution, however: Ideas about creativity shift and slide with changes in culture. Just as plastic was "redeemed" by LEGO bricks, so has the language around digital realms attempted to assimilate the new, pixelated blocks into a larger narrative about educational toys.[95]

In a *New York Times Magazine* cover story, "The *Minecraft* Generation," Clive Thompson reports that he first glimpsed the complexity of *Minecraft* construction when he saw his sons, then eight and ten, use "redstone." Redstone acts like an electrical conduit within the game's blocky environment, allowing children to build not just static structures but active machines. "Persson ingeniously designed redstone in a way that mimics real-world electronics. Switches and buttons and levers turn the redstone on and off, enabling players to build what computer scientists call 'logic gates,'" Thompson writes.[96] Within the play world of *Minecraft*, children simulate the circuitry of a computer chip, the chain of *and*s and *or*s and *not*s that connects lines of code within the computer and, more prosaically, the physical connections required to power a simple machine. LEGO Mindstorms have been reabsorbed by the computer landscape, with the same potential for kids to explore "computational thinking" through ambition, failure, and renewed attempts to make their contraptions work. As with the sheer number of blocks, the freedom with which players can use "redstone," working out an idea through trial and error without fear of fire, flood, or waste offers an environment that can be better than the real world.

Patty Smith Hill, and later Caroline Pratt, came to understand larger-scale blocks as a means of fostering children's interactions with each other, and Hill specifically designed some of her pieces to be too large and unwieldy for a small child to move on her own. Cooperation, negotiation, and mutual narratives were essential parts of this conception of kindergarten, and one Bers and the DevTech group addressed with their preverbal "collaboration web." In the farms, forests, and oceans of *Minecraft* and other online multiplayer games there are no teachers, and few adults to set norms of behavior. A player or mob set on "griefing"—destroying or sabotaging others' builds—can drive novices out of the game and create online social drama, not unlike the cliques and social saboteurs of high school. Thompson reported on the Darien Library in Connecticut, which decided to host its own *Minecraft* server; getting a library card is the price of admission. "I'll get a call saying, 'This is Dasher80, and someone has come in and destroyed my house,'" John Blyberg, the library's assistant director for innovation and user experience, told Thompson.[97] "Sometimes library administrators will step in to adjudicate the dispute. But this is increasingly rare, Blyberg says. "Generally, the self-governing takes over. I'll log in, and there'll be 10 or 15 messages, and it'll start with, 'So-and-so stole this,' and each message is more of this," he says. "And at the end, it'll be: 'It's O.K., we worked it out! Disregard this message!'"

In 2015, Mimi Ito and partners Tara Tiger Brown and Katie Salen launched Connected Camps, an online summer camp and after-school program based "in our safe, moderated, kid friendly *Minecraft* server." Ito and her partners saw an opportunity to create a better online playground on dedicated servers: same kit of parts, better supervision. "Very few educational programs are really working with kids in virtual space and providing appropriate guidance," Ito told me. "Some geeky parents might be running their own *Minecraft* servers, but you don't really want to be sitting around the playground every day with your kids. That is the equivalent. You don't want to be that parent."[98] What the founders of Connected Camps have tried to create is "something more like an organic community with positive values, where you have older kids guiding little kids." Kids learn well from mentors who share their interests but aren't necessarily seen as authority figures, like a parent or teacher. Connected Camps trains and pays high school and college students to serve as counselors, providing them with moderator privileges for chat and scripts to use in case of conflicts. Given the speed with which technology and digital culture are changing, being an organic part of the community is key. "Kids who show up in *Minecraft* have never really been guided to how to interact with people in chat," Ito says. "That's not the only thing kids need to learn, but kids have to understand the rules of digital behavior and digital spaces, as much as they need to understand how to walk across the room."

When I first started looking into the digital aspects of block play, I expected to find claims for the ability of the digital to replace the physical, or for the obsolescence of wooden blocks in our networked world. But this didn't happen. It would be hard for prekindergarten children to skip object-oriented play, no matter how skilled they are with a smartphone. And online and adapted versions of the same, like *Minecraft*, Scratch, and LEGO Mindstorms, are really for older children, used in tandem with or in order to move beyond a mountain of LEGO. The physical and mathematical gains of blocks and construction toys have been absorbed, and the next steps in real life might involve more complex structures, movement, circuits, and collaboration. The next steps online involve the same, if you choose your digital paintbrush carefully. Defining educational potential solely around learning a mathematical skill or scientific principle is too narrow, and a wholesale avoidance of contemporary video games—either due to economic limitations or a misplaced sense that all video games are Bad Toys—may put children at a disadvantage. The digital toy aisles are much like the real-world ones, filled with flashing lights, cute characters, and gendered distinctions. Just as you shouldn't assume all blocks are the same, you can't assume all digital games are the same. The material is only one aspect of a larger play experience, which may or may not be moderated, scaffolded, or undermined by adults. To understand the roots of a toy—wood, plastic, pixels, or a hybrid thereof—you have to see its potential in a child's hands. To understand what children can do, you need to give them tools and experiences that are open-ended, fungible: worlds of their own making.

•

FROM FROEBEL CUBES to unit blocks to LEGO, the world of construction toys can appear to be a universe of straight lines and sharp angles. *Minecraft* seems to extend those design principles into digital space, but the future of toys might also take another shape entirely—not through the architecture studio but through the science lab. Consider Zoob, a "play system" created by artist Michael Joaquin Grey. Its name stands for Zoology, Ontology, Ontogeny, and Botany. The Zoob family has five members, each two and a half inches long and shaped like a miniature barbell. The central player has two spherical ends, dimpled like golf balls and called "citroids," and a notched middle. It is made of yellow plastic. Its opposite number, colored green, has ends shaped like open hands, called "orbits," the better to snap around the spheres, and a thick middle the same diameter as the notch. Other members of the set include hybrids, with one sphere and one hand, some notched and some not. The pieces come in five colors, with each color specific to one type of piece. The five

Zoob pieces snap together in twenty different ways. Building toys, one realizes, are the best illustration of the principle of theme and variation. From the moment the child puts her hands on them, they teach the principles of like and unlike.

Grey's great leap with Zoob was to think of the building blocks of life as something other than block-shaped. Blocks are based on the principle of stereotomic modeling, otherwise known as stacking, which aped the building systems of agrarian societies.[99] Whether made of stone, brick, or mud—or sand, wood, or plastic in toyland—such blocks go up and fall down. During the Industrial Revolution, new understanding of engineering, and a new ability to refine raw materials, brought about the creation of structural steel. Larger and taller buildings, with thinner walls made of less material, transformed the architecture of cities. Building sets reflected this new way of enclosing space with beams and girders: Meccano engineering toys, Erector Sets, and the triangular spans of Buckminster Fuller's domes all put these advances in children's hands. But with Zoob you can build *bodies*. Zoob was part of a wave of new toys from the 1990s based on scientific principles, including the Chaos Tower, K'Nex, and the Hoberman Sphere. Boxy and blocky were out, molecular was in. Grey was well aware of the history of building toys and, with degrees in sculpture and genetics, had the background to combine simplified form with the potential for complex, biological construction. I once left my then six-year-old son alone in his room with his 250-piece tub of Zoob for an hour and came back to find his carpet and shelves adorned with a Natural History Museum's-worth of dinosaurs, from a long-necked *Apatosaurus* to a two-legged *Velociraptor*. With LEGO bricks and Magna-Tiles he had built settings in which action might happen. Zoob, because of its obvious skeletal potential, allowed him to build actors, and his room became the stage for narrative play.

I thought he was pretty clever, but it wasn't until I visited Grey in his Chelsea apartment that I realized the full extent of what Zoob could do. A life-size Zoob cat, with glowing yellow eyes, hissed from one shelf while on a long table made of weathered boards sat a Zoob sea urchin the size of a pasta pot. Pick it up and the ring flexes, like a living creature. The illusion of life was so spooky I almost dropped it. In translucent plastic bins around the edges of the room were more models: Zoob as herringbone-patterned fabric, thick and heavy as a fur, that can be attached to create a Moebius strip; Zoob as space frame, with interlocking circles attached to form a curved, enclosing surface; gray Zoob as a skeletal hand and arm, accurate in number of plastic bones; green Zoob as a graceful branch with leaves that tremble when shaken. In a series of 2010 YouTube videos, filmed in the same living room, Grey manipulates a chain of three silver Zoob like a magician, demonstrating how the linkage transforms from one dimension to two to three.[100] But what I hadn't realized, until Grey showed me, was that Zoob can also model mechanics. The orbit-to-orbit connection is designed for movement, so it can be pushed in and out like a piston. It has give, while a set of interconnected triangles can flex without breaking, more like a shock mount. The rigid and static systems of previous building toys suddenly seem ancient and inelastic in comparison. The ball-and-socket joint, so similar to our own elbow, allows for a 360-degree range of motion. The two-and-a-half-inch piece reads as a skeletal extension of a finger or, when standing up on the orbit's two petals, a tiny person. In the hands of its inventor, Zoob aped an infinite number of other living things.

"Zoob is the perfect synthesis of all that thinking about complex systems and biology, condensed in a toy that could be used by children," says Paola Antonelli, the MoMA curator who brought Zoob into the Architecture and Design Collection at the Museum of Modern Art. "Playing with it allows you to become literate and familiar with those

ZOOB Play System, Michael Joaquin Grey. Manufacturer: Infinitoy, San Mateo, CA. ABS Plastic. 1993–1996. [Courtesy Michael Joaquin Grey]

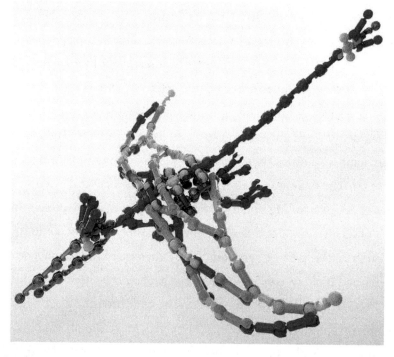

ZOOB Play System, Pterodactyl, Michael Joaquin Grey. Manufacturer: Infinitoy, San Mateo, CA. 1993–1996. [Courtesy Michael Joaquin Grey]

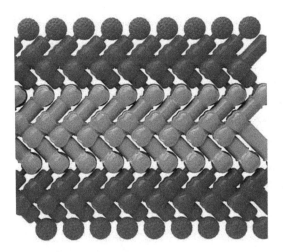

ZOOB Play System, Herringbone weave, Michael Joaquin Grey. Manufacturer: Infinitoy, San Mateo, CA. 1993–1996. [Courtesy Michael Joaquin Grey]

concepts without anyone teaching or preaching those things."[101] (When she was growing up, Antonelli adds, her European intellectual parents brought her to Scandinavian toy stores where wood was the only material. "All we wanted was something in shiny plastic. We always privileged plastic over everything else.") As with earlier construction toys that responded to building trends in the real world, Zoob reflects contemporary architects' interest in growing buildings, embracing natural processes as part of structural growth, says Antonelli. All that from an inexpensive, mass-produced toy: A seventy-five-piece set can retail for less than twenty dollars.

Grey's early investors were art patrons, and his early models were designed on the computer and printed out, in plastic, using rudimentary 1990s stereolithograpy—now known as 3-D printing, and instantly available. The aluminum die to cast a single piece cost $150,000 to create. "Once it becomes something that isn't just an artwork, it has not only to be made and reproduced but reproduced quickly, and at a price to make it affordable," Grey says. The first time he made the pieces they cost thirty cents per unit, but he had to get the cost down to pennies by reducing the amount of plastic and simplifying the design on the inside. "If you had a piece that was five cents instead of one cent and it was made of Delrin or Teflon or some combination, you would never have a problem with the jaw. It would never weaken. But it would end up being ninety dollars to one hundred dollars for 120 pieces. Your market is just so much smaller."[102] The two halves of each Zoob piece are sonically welded together after molding, which leaves a barely detectible seam down the middle. If you step on a Zoob, the petals will break off, which Grey says is a manufacturer error: The plastic is injected into the mold right at the center of one petal, leaving a tiny raised O. That O is a weak spot right where the toy requires the most movement. The connection between quality and price, always in the background when discussing wooden toys, permeated Grey's design process. And the need to keep reinventing a product he had designed with classic blocks in mind eventually soured him on life as a toy designer. "You have to educate people on what Zoob can do and not just make it pink and glitter."

Once people knew I was researching this book, I was often asked for my recommendations for the best building toys. My short list includes Duplo, LEGO's younger sibling, which is easier for toddlers to manipulate and is most commonly sold in unlicensed, multicolored bins; Tubation, a set of straight, L-, T-, and X-shaped tubes that can be connected into marble runs, musical instruments, and animal skeletons; the aforementioned Magna-Tiles; and Zoob. Once you've bought those, and maybe some LEGO for the over-fives, your best bet is to simply buy your children more pieces. The freedom of Eliasson's Collectivity Project lies partly in its sense of abundance, as do the well-stocked classrooms at City and Country for block play. Kids learn ingenuity, and negotiation skills, from running out, but you need enough to go tall or long or all the way around the room. But what, one father wondered, if all the sets could fit together? What if the universes of building toys were not separate but connected?

In 2011, Carnegie Mellon professor Golan Levin observed his son trying to build a car. "Aside from the minor inconvenience of being 4 years old, the younger Levin faced an engineering challenge," *Forbes* later reported. "His Tinkertoys, which he wanted to use for the vehicle's frame, wouldn't attach to his K'Nex, the pieces he wanted to use for the wheels."[103] Levin père decided to do something about it. Had he had this idea in the 1990s, when Grey was working on Zoob, the cost would have been prohibitive. But by 2011, the cost of 3-D printing had come down, making it possible for Levin and Shawn Sims to create a set of digital blueprints, free of charge, for more than eighty connectors to link Zoob, LEGO, K'nex, Bristle Blocks, Tinkertoys, and five other construction toys into one gonzo system. "Adapter Kit Lets Your Lego Bricks and Lincoln Logs Play Together," wrote Gizmodo, while *Forbes* referred to the project, called the Free Universal Construction Kit (abbreviate at your own risk), as aiming to "liberate Legos." The blueprints were the project, available for free digital download, with the printing-out at the discretion of the downloader. This method cleverly exploited a hole in the brave new world of print-on-demand. Had the partners tried to market the connectors in stores, they would have been sued for copyright infringement by any and all of the toymakers involved, as in the Tyco v. LEGO suit that turned up Kiddicraft's original patent. "This isn't a product. It's a provocation," Levin told *Forbes*. "We should be free to invent without having to worry about infringement, royalties, going to jail or being sued and bullied by large industries. We don't want to see what happened in music and film play out in the area of shapes."[104]

The digitally printed examples acquired by museums were made of the fleshy white thermoplastic that comes with your 3-D printer, deliberately generic and unstyled, marking them as different from the shiny commercial ABS plastic of the toys with which they intersected. In a post on MoMA's *Inside/Out* blog, Pamela Popeson viewed the connectors as a utopian project. "Call me a cockeyed optimist, but I'm convinced that the smallest effort toward compatibility goes a long way."[105] Compatibility and universality have been what the creators of blocks have always sought: a system that could explain the world, a kit of parts to make everything. The Free Universal Construction Kit is a geek dad's way of taking back the sandbox from the copyright bullies—that's embedded in the name—but Levin did it as an act of sympathy for his son, trying, like the rabbit in *Not a Box*, to escape the realm of the visible.

Golan Levin wanted to grant his son autonomy, to make him a bigger playground not by buying more but by doing more with the toys he already owned. Making the kit open source, and free, was another way of subverting the commercialization that has followed toys since they

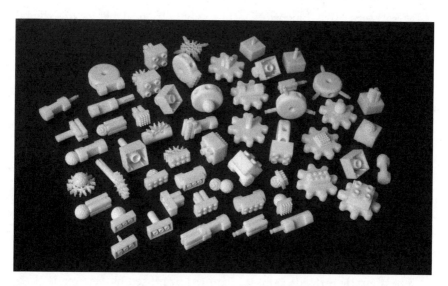

Free Universal Construction Kit, Golan Levin (F. A. T. Lab) and Shawn Sims (Sy-Lab). 2012. FDM-printed thermoplastic. [Courtesy F. A. T. Lab and Sy-Lab]

began to be made for children: to make a plastic brick without a tiny little trademark logo. A child trying to connect Tinkertoy to Zoob to ride on the back of LEGO might turn to masking tape or glue, testing and refining her solution according to her age and skills. Levin found a more elegant way to give his son more imaginative space, thinking beyond the walled gardens of copyright and instruction manuals toward a game as yet unschooled. The Bad Toy is one that just sits there, to be mashed and pulled in a set sequence, and is ruined once it falls apart. The Good Toy lets children stitch their own world back together, using the simplest of physical parts to conjure cities of imagination. The F.U.C.K. was included in a 2014 exhibition at the Cooper Hewitt, Smithsonian Design Museum in a section titled *Revenge of the User.* Curator Ellen Lupton writes, in the catalog, "Users are taking apart and reassembling consumer products, treating the world of manufactured goods as a kit of parts to be reworked and rewritten."[106] And all those manufactured goods? They come in cardboard boxes.

CHAPTER 2

HOUSE

"They? Who were they—exactly?"

"Homily, Pod, and little Arietty."

"Pod?"

"Yes, even their names were never quite right. They imagined they had their own names—quite different from human names—but with half an ear you could tell they were borrowed . . . Everything they had was borrowed; they had nothing of their own at all. Nothing. In spite of this, my brother said, they were touchy and conceited, and thought they owned the world."

"How do you mean?"

"They thought human beings were just invented to do the dirty work—great slaves put there for them to use."

—Mary Norton, *The Borrowers* (1952)

In Mary Norton's 1952 novel *The Borrowers*, we are first introduced to our tiny protagonists in passing, as seems just. Borrowers, the mouse-height Homo sapiens who live in the hidden spaces in our houses, are only glimpsed by accident, as a movement on a mantelpiece or a shadow on a curtain, their surnames derived from the rooms and furniture they live behind. Homily, Pod, and Arietty's surname is Clock, as they live under the grandfather clock in the hall. They think of what they call "human beans" as heedless giants who drop pins, matchbooks, spools, and crumbs, the better to provision the borrowers' homes nested within ours. It took me far too many readings of the book to figure out that borrowers are meant to be children: little people whom adults think of as insignificant to nonexistent, petite tyrants of the house. It was the quote above that tipped me off, with its echo of slight fuzz in transmission of words that leads to children's radical mispronunciations, as well as children's deep offense when adults laugh at the results. Children do identify with the Clocks, fascinated by their tiny world and the clever miniatures in it, but the book also casts a gimlet eye on the gap between children's and their parents' perceptions of the home. The book is deeply invested in the material qualities of the house, from the scruff of a front door mat to the softness of blotting paper. Adults grow used to these elements, and they drop from view. *The Borrowers* makes texture and textiles present again by the simple trick of making them enormous.

Size is the first consideration in understanding how the modern house is transformed by the presence of children, followed by questions about space and about stuff. Children are smaller than adults, but not merely small adults. They need furnishings couched to their frames but also to their abilities. Although children before the nineteenth century were provided with chairs modified to their dimensions, it wasn't until childhood came to be seen as a separate, even desirable, state of existence that those thrones turned into furniture that was both useful and fun. Useful, for containing children as nursery maids became a rarer and more elite resource; fun, as mothers began to see education as part of their role at home and bought furniture that was both plaything and seat. Yet kids' size, and their abilities, are typically temporary states. The baby's ExerSaucer (which I consider among the ugliest objects in existence) is outmoded when baby becomes a toddler; the toddler's walker is discarded for the scooter. Long before the "sharing economy," parents handed down and traded up for possessions needed for only a short period of time. Clever designers tried to build growth into objects made of wood or cardboard, rather than flesh and blood, or used cheap or recyclable materials that could be fitted to a child's exact needs without excessive cost. Small things, and small people, were seen as fertile ground for experiment, with their changing needs and inbuilt informality.

"Making do" was not associated solely with thrift but also with creativity, the same creativity fostered in children by box and block play. Doing it yourself is something the borrowers obviously excel at. They live, in one sense, in a preindustrial society, too isolated for the sociability of shops, though their most prized possessions were store-bought by the giants. Squares of blotting paper, matchbooks, and the fancy cigar boxes from which Pod crafts his daughter Arietty's majestic bedroom—"on the ceiling lovely painted ladies dressed in swirls of chiffon blew long trumpets against a background of blue sky"—are status symbols in their new setting. Cardboard boxes make yet another appearance as a conduit for the imagination, the materials of an afternoon's creativity and fantasy for a child. As American homeownership grew in the twentieth century, more and more adults wanted to recapture some of the hands-on skills of the past. Industrial production might have phased out craftsmanship, but adults turned nineteenth-century professions into hobbies, and the DIY movement was born. Families found that being given too much ready-made stifled the creative spirit, as well as taxed the budget. In the 1950s, manuals pointed fathers and mothers toward specific areas of the home, setting him up with power tools and her with paint swatches. In the 1970s, DIY manuals went back to basics, suggesting cardboard as a starting point for putting the play back in adult lives too by building your own kid-size furniture, storage, and toys.

The denouement of the book, and eventual discovery of the Clocks, comes when they get greedy and take some things that still have value to adults. The full-size boy who becomes the Clocks' accomplice is sick in bed, situated in a part of the house full of unwanted things (he is himself an unwanted thing, at least to the housekeeper). He sleeps in the old night-nursery and next to the schoolroom. When children were first given space in houses, it was usually upstairs or below stairs, and furnished with the outdated and past-its-prime, just like the Clocks' house. "The schoolroom, at that time," writes Norton, "was sheeted and shrouded and filled with junk—odd trunks, a broken sewing-machine, a desk, a dressmaker's dummy, a table, some chairs, and a disused pianola—as the children who had used it, Great-Aunt Sophy's children, had long since grown up, married, died, or gone away."[1] Childhood creates an alternate set of needs nested within adult ones. Each stage comes, at least for the middle-class family, with a new set of imperatives, as well as new clothes and books and objects that then need a place to store them. Old houses had attics and basements; modern architecture tried to eliminate those extra spaces in favor of smaller floor plans and efficient storage. A whole literature, and then a whole profession, sprang up around the proper accommodation of children and their things. The latter part of this chapter addresses the ways that children have slowly taken over the American home over the past two centuries, going from having no place of their own to having half the house. By the mid-twentieth century, children's rooms and playrooms, and even, in designer George Nelson's parlance, the multigenerational "room without a name," became the focus of animated discussion. Should they be colorful or plain, fitted out like workshops or decorated to suit a child's interests . . . that year? Storage, which starts out sounding like a dull topic, turns into a baroque one, exemplified by deluxe mudrooms and living room furniture made like giant toys. The expanding category of kid's stuff became another element in home design, one which, as UCLA social scientists found, threatens to swamp twenty-first-century domestic space.[2] Those small people have had an outsize effect on how we live.

•

RAISING CHILDREN CAN give even adults trained to observe human behavior new insights into the material world. Around 1972, young Thor Opsvik had grown too big for a high chair but was still too small for a regular one. The only chairs available in his size were little, for use at little tables, away from the adult action. His father, Peter Opsvik, noticed and, as an industrial designer, had the skills to do something about it. The result was the Tripp Trapp, two zigzags of lacquered beech joined by a pair of platforms that serve as seat and footrest: a chair for kids that is not kid size, that grows over time, and that never needs to be mothballed. Stokke, the company that manufactures the Tripp Trapp, has made more than ten million since the early 1970s. I should know: I bought a Tripp Trapp for my son when he was two and thought he could hand it down to his sister four years later. Nine years on, he's still using his (orange), and we had to buy a second one for her (plum). I had to consider them an investment. If you visit the café at the Museum of Modern Art, you'll see a rainbow lineup of Tripp Trapps awaiting patrons' use; I've also spotted them at the café in the Designmuseum Danmark, where my kids waved at them like old friends, hardly able to

Tripp Trapp Chair, Development sketch, Peter Opsvik. 1972. [Courtesy Peter Opsvik AS]

Tripp Trapp Chair, Peter Opsvik. 1972. Distributor: Stokke, Alesund, Norway. Beech, steel, 78.7 x 46.5 x 50 cm. [Courtesy Stokke AS]

distinguish between the chairs on the wall in the galleries and those in use at the café.

The Tripp Trapp's double ubiquity, in design collections and on many a kitchen floor, sticky with use, is a testament to the expansiveness of Opsvik's insight. He made a chair not for one child, of one age or ability, but for *children*, a level of adaptability designers have sought throughout the twentieth century in furniture, rooms, and houses for people with children of standard and exceptional needs. A 2012 MoMA exhibit titled

The Century of the Child included a five-foot-tall Tripp Trapp for adults to sit on in order to experience (again) the child's point of view. The vulnerability I felt dangling my legs from that maxi-chair—the museum's oak floor felt very far down—was a useful state of disembodiment. In the exhibition catalog, the curators characterize all design for children as "inclusive," a term more often applied to design for disability.[3] But this makes sense: Children, like many people with disabilities, don't fit much of the furniture of the industrialized world.

Since the mid-nineteenth century, kid-size has become a separate category, but it took more than one hundred years for inclusive and adaptive design to become its own profession. When designers James Hennessey and Victor Papanek wrote their do-it-yourself manual *Nomadic Furniture* (1973), they noted that there were no standard measurements available for children, or women, or the (sic) handicapped.[4] Creators of furniture for children sized it, by and large, from their own offspring, and many products for the disabled were homegrown. Legislation providing equal access to facilities and education, passed between the late 1960s and 1990, would change the imperatives for inclusive, universal, and assistive design. Activists sought the elimination of both physical and program barriers so that people with disabilities could lead independent lives; they also chose to describe themselves as "disabled," rather than the previously acceptable "handicapped," as an additional form of self-determination. "Designers who consider the whole child—and reject simply making miniature versions of adult products or rendering them decoratively juvenile— continue to contribute objects and environments that extend the ability of design to improve and transform everyday life," writes MoMA curatorial assistant Aidan O'Connor.[5] The museum had just acquired a therapeutic high chair, the Jockey by Krabat, which seats the child on an adjustable-height saddle, with an embracing back and footrests with straps. The aim of the Jockey is to provide lightweight, movable support for a child with disabilities in the classroom, allowing her to see eye to eye with her classmates. According to the product website: "The compact design draws attention to the child and not the chair."[6]

In Peter Opsvik's 2008 book *Rethinking Sitting*, he includes a drawing of the dining table as a datum line, showing the relative positions of a child growing from baby to teenager. "I started by drawing all sizes of people with their elbows at tabletop level," writes Opsvik. "Since the elbows and lower back are at the same level, the chair's backrest could be permanently fixed at tabletop height."[7] The platforms, broad and sturdy enough to be used like a ladder, are adjustable, so your child can chart her growth by moving them down a notch year by year. Facing forward, the chair brings the whole family's heads to the same level. Facing backward, the chair is a step stool, ideal for pulling up to the counter for cooking or to the pantry to forage for snacks. The long tail of the bottom zag, running along the floor, makes it almost impossible to tip over. Opsvik saw the Tripp Trapp as a tool for children's liberation, one adaptable to their growth rather than designed for inevitable obsolescence, and one that might make their participation in family life smoother. "My hope was that this would make sitting at the table more enjoyable and make it easier to perform activities there," writes Opsvik. "Mealtimes may become more relaxed, and children find it easier to concentrate on the activities taking place around the table when the physical environment has been adapted to their size and needs." Though the Tripp Trapp now comes with more binding accouterments to meet the high chair safety standards of the United States and the European Union (which differ), such containment was not part of Opsvik's original plan: "Why shouldn't children of that age be able to climb up and down from the chair when they want to?"

It's a telling question. The course of the centuries-long history of high chairs has mostly pointed toward containment and civilization rather than freedom. The high chair looks more like a cell than a ladder, and family meals sound more like a chore than an environment adapted for the child's needs. Its purpose was to raise the child up to the level of the adult, yes, but in order to learn the manners of their household and the proper mode of eating. The expectation for children in previous centuries was to conform, not to enjoy. The earliest existing high chairs, from the late sixteenth and early seventeenth century, closely imitate the style of adult furniture and are often elaborately carved or upholstered in leather in the style of parents' seats.[8] These chairs did not typically come with a bar across the front to hold the child in, but were pushed up to the edge of the table. Museum collections contain a whole range of tall, slim chairs with diminutive seats, reflecting the range of furniture fashion from pointed, carved Gothic arches to simple, curved Windsor comb backs, velvet-upholstered minithrones to cane-and-bentwood chairs with back wheels. In *The World of the Nursery*, author Colin White writes, "Windsor high-chairs, however, were a failure, for their disproportionately long legs gave them a giraffe-like appearance."[9] In the nineteenth century, when it became more common for the upper class to have matched sets of chairs in their dining rooms, children's chairs were ordered to match the rest of the set, acknowledging their presence and importance as members of the family circle.

It wasn't until the 1830s that the high chair became part of a typical upper- and middle-class household inventory. Childhood had become its own domain and started to acquire its own furnishings: Toys and books were first, furniture second, and eventually space would follow. The high chair became a place where children could be contained in order to be socialized—as well as a place simply to be restrained. Civil society was thought to depend on members' self-restraint and control, and it was never too soon to teach your children those lessons. For babies unable to control themselves, furniture had to fill in the gap, holding them up and slowing them down.[10] The furniture and organization of the schoolroom during this period taught a similar lesson: hard communal benches, recitations as a class or "form," an education in literal groupthink as well as in reading, writing, or arithmetic. Family values were promoted at mealtimes, as children were seated at the adult table. The "deportment chair," designed by surgeon and anatomist Sir Astley Paston Cooper in 1835, was a high-backed high chair with a small round seat and no footrest or arms, intended to ensure the child did not deviate from proper posture (or if she did so, she could be immediately corrected).[11] A frequent punishment was to make children sit in such chairs, in the corner of a classroom or nursery, for long periods of time. Other high chairs checked movement in other ways, creating an architecture of containment for the child when she was out of her own territory.

By the 1850s, manufacturers began to add kid-size dishes to the tabletop landscape. At first these were purchasable in the same patterns as adult dinnerware, but the didactic message of sitting at the table eventually made its way to the plate. Bible scenes, ministers' maxims, and illustrated quotations on the subjects of diligence or charity appeared at mealtimes. Bowls, cups, and plates were also painted with nursery rhymes or the alphabet, so eating one's porridge would reveal a message at the bottom of the bowl. The design of these dishes, like the interaction provoked by sitting at table, was intended to bridge the gap between children and adults, making them just comfortable enough, just amused enough, to behave. In previous centuries, and at higher income levels, servants like governesses and baby nurses had taught children how to hold a spoon offstage in the nursery, restraining them with their bodies and cleaning up messes out of sight. But middle-class access to servants decreased throughout the nineteenth and early twentieth century as industrial jobs attracted more young women.[12]

In addition, advice manuals stressed the importance of the mother's instruction: It was her manners and her level of education that ought to be transmitted to the child, using modeling and positive reinforcement.[13] Resorting to physical punishment was a sign the mother had failed. It wasn't only the children whose lives were contained and constrained by this new mandate. High chairs and their cousins, playpens and perambulators, became inanimate replacements for female servants, silent assistants for mothers who now had to cook, clean, and keep their children out of trouble, while also instructing them in good behavior. One early nineteenth-century expert believed that "children should be taught to sit down, and to rise from the table, at the same time; to wait, whilst others are served, without betraying eagerness, or impatience; to avoid noise and conversation, and if they are no longer confined to the nursery, to be able to see delicacies without expecting or asking to partake of them."[14] According to antiquarian Sally Kevill-Davies, the "more relaxed style" of American family life meant children spent more time in the presence of adults, and in the living and dining rooms.[15] While English upper- and middle-class children ate separately in the nursery, American meals were considered prime time for instruction on "etiquette and self-restraint." Children practiced their manners within the family in readiness for company meals, which should showcase how well those lessons had been learned—and how good the mother was at parenting.[16]

The nineteenth-century emphasis on manners, and their proper display, reminds me of some of the twenty-first century emphasis on healthy eating, and the many manuals (cookbooks) of family dinner. The importance of eating together as a family is emphasized in such books, as is the parents' modeling of eating a variety of foods, including the spicy, the green and leafy, and the unfamiliar. Children are not to be shamed into trying a bite but encouraged through repetition and exposure. And while training children to eat with company is not emphasized—it is more likely to be the restaurant meal that challenges manners and palates today—there is a type of competitive parent who likes to tell others about his child's consumption of chard, sushi, or lentils, often served atop a place mat printed with the alphabet, a world map, or other contemporary symbols of knowledge and culture.

As the nineteenth century passed, furniture makers' interest in children's comfort and adult practicality increased, and the degree of ornament decreased. New, industrially produced chairs were made of lightweight bentwood and cane, sometimes with wheels. Legs were splayed to guard against tipping and mitigate the "giraffe-like appearance" noticed in the Windsor high chair. Some had movable trays so that children might eat away from the table, as well as footboards upon which to rest the legs and feet.[17] The profile of these bentwood chairs, which would look right at home at a dining table surrounded by classic café chairs, begins to resemble the arrangement of the twentieth-century high chair: wide stance, lift-off or lift-up tray for easier cleaning, made for mobility. The chair's height ensured the child would be at eye level, while the tray separated the results of her attempts at self-feeding from the rest of the family's dinner. The wheels, or a lightweight construction with thin uprights and cane or rush seats, meant the chair could be easily moved from kitchen to dining room, either for cleaning or to keep the child within sight of the mother. Between mealtimes, spoons, teething toys, and wooden spools on a string might be tied to the tray or arm to keep an immobile baby occupied.[18] Manufacturers differentiated their products by offering multiple size options; by creating chairs that were convertible from high to low positions, and even into a rocking chair; by stenciling and carving the word BABY across the back; or by adding built-in abacus beads or "sanitary leather cloth" seats. The particular needs of the child, and her parent, began to drive the category in directions unnecessary for adult furniture. *The Cabinet Maker's Pattern Book*, published in 1877, included a high chair with an optional cutout seat, allowing the chair to be used first for eating, then for eliminating food.[19] The throne for the household's tiniest member was changing, becoming more of a center for immature activities and less of a corrective armature. The development of the high chair mirrors the transformation of children's space from something peripheral to domestic life to the organizing principle for the same, and from hand-me-down attics to spaces built to purpose.

Until the eighteenth century, children lived in what architectural historian Marta Gutman characterizes as a "generationally integrated world," where they could learn from adults as they worked beside them, and adults and children alike had few items beyond their clothes to call their own. Children used those adult spaces, from the private home to the public street, yard, or common, because they had no choice. "In 1500, it would not have been possible to find a house with a child's bedroom, a neighborhood with a playground, or a city with a public high school," writes Gutman.[20] In seventeenth-century America, Dutch and English colonists' houses consisted of two principal rooms, divided by function and formality: the hall and the parlor. In the hall, the family cooked and ate and performed most of their daily activities. The parlor held the family's finest things, including the best bed, in which the heads of the household slept.[21] Furniture, tapestries, tea services, even mirrors would all have been handmade and meant to be handed down between the generations. There was no margin for the useless, the temporary, or for childish accidents. Childhood was a period to be gotten through, not lingered within, as sixteenth- and seventeenth-century Christian adults believed children to be born sinful. Only through hard work and strict example could they be delivered to adulthood as morally upright beings. The sooner they began to contribute economically to the household, the better.

Ever since the publication of Philippe Ariès's *Centuries of Childhood* in 1960 (translated into English in 1962), a battle has raged among historians about whether his blithe statement "In medieval society, the idea of childhood did not exist" was in fact true.[22] Most subsequent scholars think not, but Ariès ushered in several decades of childhood studies that agree, at least, that there was a fundamental shift in the eighteenth century in attitudes toward children.[23] Locke, Rousseau, Pestalozzi, and the other early philosophers and educators who recognized the child as an individual, and childhood as a period adults might influence, set up a nineteenth century in which children received their own goods, their own rooms, and their own spaces. The child went from being an asset, as a worker, to being a dependent.

Looking at the material culture of childhood—kid's stuff—it isn't until the early to mid-nineteenth century that one sees a range of products and places, used by the middle and upper classes, that are recognizable in the twenty-first century, including wooden toys, nurseries, primary schools, and playgrounds. Even if human relations around these objects were different—more servants, fewer teachers—the roots of design for children start here. Children must be protected, not pushed out into the world. The upper classes had the means and now the moral obligation to provide a safe, engaging, and happy upbringing for their children. Although the lower classes had the desire, they rarely had the space: Urban reformers of the late nineteenth century were horrified by communal living conditions in tenement buildings that required families to share, fearing it might encourage "communistic modes of thought," according to University of Chicago sociologist Charles R. Henderson in 1902.[24] "Home, above all things, means privacy," said U.S. Commissioner of Labor Charles P. Neill in 1905. "It means the possibility of keeping your family off from other families."[25] Literature of the period often focused on saintly children who are able to teach their elders about the meaning of love and personal sacrifice. Other popular accounts told of adults saved from the evils of intemperance by the offices of a child.[26] To expose the child to unrelated adults was to open their lives to immorality; even sharing bedrooms with parents or siblings of the opposite sex—the way most families lived before 1800—was, by the 1890s, an invitation to sin.[27]

This new attitude toward children came about at the same time that new patterns in adult lives were altering the architecture of the public and private spheres. The separation of work and home life was spurred by the Industrial Revolution, as factory jobs drew men and women away from farms and other cottage industries. The authors of a new category of women's literature, the domestic guide, emphasize the need to separate public life, private life, and women's work within the house.[28] The bedroom for the heads of the household might still be downstairs, next to the parlor, but additional sleeping rooms for servants and children were tucked away upstairs.[29] The home, now a place of respite from work, also benefited from new, cheaper industrial goods and an economy in which people had the money to buy ready-made furniture, clothes, and toys. The formal front rooms began to acquire decoration: birdcages, shelves with platters and plates on display, rugs underfoot, and stenciled patterns on the walls. Children's furniture would still have been repurposed goods from attics and storerooms. Until the early twentieth century, house plans, and even apartment plans, waver between creating a private sleeping zone of bedrooms either upstairs or at the back of a domicile and placing a principal bedroom downstairs or up front as a sign of status.

The protection of the home, and the work associated with it, took more than children out of the city: Women found themselves isolated too.

Though the ennui of the suburban housewife is more commonly associated with the 1960s, as early as the 1860s the so-called materialist feminists critiqued women's dependent economic position, given that their work went unseen and unpaid, and argued against the wasted labor of each woman cooking, cleaning, and providing childcare for her household alone. Melusina Fay Peirce published critiques of women's dependent economic position in the *Atlantic* in 1868 and 1869, railing against the waste of women's education and their need to ask permission of fathers and husbands.[30] Her solution was "cooperative housekeeping," where women would band together to buy a building and outfit it with equipment for cooking, baking, laundry, and sewing, performing the work together and charging their husbands retail prices for the result. Once established in an area, families who were part of the cooperative could move into kitchenless houses, set in the center of an urban block rather than along its edge, creating a commonly held yard around the domicile. One in every thirty-six lots would be taken over for the cooperative building, the work engine of the reorganized domestic space. Peirce received a lot of attention for her writing and lectures and, in 1869, tried to launch the Cambridge Cooperative Housing Society in a rented building on Bow Street in Cambridge, Massachusetts. Peirce managed to establish the laundry and eventually the store, but never the kitchen. The husbands of her adherents struggled with the idea of their wives working for other men's comfort, and her own husband, a Harvard professor, undermined her by begging her to go on vacation. Peirce closed her cooperative, but she remained an important, if sometimes unacknowledged, influence on later thinkers such as Edward Bellamy and Charlotte Perkins Gilman. Bellamy's futurist novel *Looking Backward* (1888) envisions a Boston of the year 2000 where citizens eat in public kitchens, get almost instantaneous deliveries to their homes, and shop at centralized stores where everyone is given the same amount of credit (something like today's proposals for a basic income, regardless of profession). They also live in apartments as a means of achieving a more democratic (some would say socialist) division of goods.[31]

It was clear from the beginning of the set-aside single family home that it would be "more work for mother," but nonetheless, it remained the American ideal and only grew in isolation and complexity. Within this new architecture there were spaces set aside for children who should now be protected from the adult activities in which they had once been active participants. Colin White writes, "A nursery is a 'room of one's own' and this, by implication, means there must be other rooms in the house." There are no nurseries in American log cabins or industrial housing in northern England. Carved out of attics and furnished with castoffs, in the nursery children could eat bland foods and play with childish things away from the dirt, spice, fire, and conversation of the adult spaces in the home. "In this room, a child did not engage in any kind of productive activity that contributed to the family economy," Marta Gutman writes.[32] On the contrary, the child spent the family money. White credits architect A. W. N. Pugin with "inventing" the nursery as a luxury feature in his British homes of the 1830s and 1840s: Pugin's Gothicized mansions were seen as a ticket to respectability for Britain's newly rich manufacturers. In these houses, Pugin installed day nurseries and night nurseries, whose positions close, but not too close, to the parents' bedroom seemed to necessitate a nanny.[33] Such separate suites, attended by servants, were rarer among the upper classes in the United States, where children remained integrated into general family life at multiple economic levels. In the United States, the Victorian suburbs, built after the Civil War, advertised themselves as an escape from the problems of the city, and as protection for women and children. Available at a variety of price points, and located near train lines, these subdivisions attracted both owners and renters. During the mid- to late nineteenth century, domestic labor was cheap, so child-rearing and education could be accommodated at home. Early kindergarten advocates in the United States had to overcome the feeling, among middle-class mothers, that their children required the protection and nurturing only possible within the house. The decoration of the home itself was supposed to be educational, so women bought Greek statues and Japanese scrolls, filling their suburban retreats with goods purchased in, and imported from, cities around the world. The sprawling, anti-minimal nature of the Victorian home, with multiple levels and odd hideaway spaces, was actually ideal for combining family privacy with formal social life, and for leaving odd spaces for children to hide and for possessions to be stowed.[34]

The earliest nursery furniture was basic, adapted castoffs like the borrowers' salvage—adult-size tables and chairs with sawed-down legs—as befit the second-class status of both the children and the nurse. But over time, even as the Victorian Era introduced new ways of sequestering children in the private space of the home, it also devoted considerable energy to putting them on display as status symbols in their own right—a paradox that we still grapple with today. We begin to see bassinets, cradles with hoods made of wicker or basketwork; cribs, rectangular beds with slatted sides; and cots, bassinets suspended between two uprights so that they could be rocked from side to side.[35] The pierced or woven sides made the wood-frame pieces lighter and more moveable, as well as allowing babies to see out and minders to see in. Such small beds, which ranged in style from Renaissance elaboration to Windsor rectitude, would be handed down, as they were mostly used for daytime show. Their tiny users actually slept at night in utilitarian cribs. When perambulators came into vogue in the 1860s, as part of a ritual promenade in major cities' new public parks, their design took its cues from the bassinet: The first carriages that were pushed, rather than pulled like a wagon, were made of wood with fabric and leather hoods. The most elaborate had silver-plated trim and even tiny oil lamps. "The baby was the ultimate symbol of the family, the culminating product of the 'cult of domesticity,' the center of familial and cultural expectations. The pram was designed to draw attention to its occupant and show the baby off to best advantage, like a bright jewel on a dark velvet tray," writes historian Karin Calvert.[36] After 1880, many designs included a seat belt and were large enough to be used until the child reached the age of six. Where once parents had rushed their children on, ready for them to work, now they kept them specifically idle, enrobed in white clothes, needing books, games, toys, and a female attendant to give them something to do.

This push and pull between the nursery and the pram—between concealment and display, freedom and control—brings us back to the high chair, and to its position in the house. The emphasis on the dining room as the location of shared family life continued through the 1930s, when new ideas about children's place in the home, and the degree of formality required by society, began to literally tear down the walls of the typical two-story middle-class household. In the March 1931 issue of *Parents* magazine, home furnishings editor Helen Sprackling writes, "What an important place the dining room is when there are children in the home! There is so much more to it than just the purpose for which the room has been set aside. Its atmosphere of gracious dignity has so direct a bearing upon everyday life and manners, resulting in a greater refinement of living and higher standards of taste. Its charm, its feeling of congeniality make three meals a day there a pleasure and the family reunion at the evening meal a joy anticipated throughout the day."[37] The "colorful informality" of new spaces like breakfast alcoves cannot replace the "soft candle-lit charm" of the dining room, Sprackling says; the room teaches taste, in every sense.

And yet, a decade later, her magazine would do away with the dining room in its depictions of the "whole-family house." Between the wars, the emphasis on child-rearing shifts from children's place in adult spaces to rooms of their own, and from how they might fit—through appurtenances like the high chair—into adult rooms to how their rooms might fit their needs and interests. Sprackling extolls the importance of family meals, but her tone marks a shift from that of the nineteenth-century etiquette manual: It is not discipline and restraint that should be taught through dinner, but family cohesion and attitudes, as in Opsvik's home. The lessons of dinner are not for outward show but for interior growth, to the benefit of the child.

•

Home may be the family's castle, but people got tired of living in castles several centuries ago.

    —George Nelson and Henry Wright, *Tomorrow's House* (1945)[38]

Nurseries for children, and the kitchens and workrooms in which the lady of the house might actually get work done, were attached, like engines powering a yacht, to front rooms left beautiful and idle. But that idleness could not stand. Middle-class homeownership, and the increase in industrial and clerical jobs for women, meant houses grew smaller, and servants fewer. Parents—mothers—were doing the work of cooking, cleaning, and watching children, and a castle, with children in their own turret, really wouldn't do. Over the course of the twentieth century, the American home expanded its footprint and lost formality, placing children, their toys, and their needs at the center of the middle-class family home. Attics, basements, and dining rooms became playrooms, workshops, and open kitchens that were visually connected by design. To see this shift in action we turn, as generations of new parents have done, to the pages of *Parents* magazine, which published model homes under rubrics like "The Whole-Family House," "Best Homes for Families with Children," and "Homes Mothers Want Most." (These families, perhaps needless to say given the era, all have two heterosexual parents and no additional adult relatives living under one roof.) The ideal setup from the 1920s on is child-centered, reflecting just how far families had come from treating children as a temporary, potentially disruptive drain on resources. The presidential administrations of both Warren G. Harding and Calvin Coolidge wanted to create a nation of homeowners, with the underlying goal of beating back Bolshevism by mass ownership of property.[39] In October 1922, Vice President Coolidge published the essay "A Nation of Home-Owners" in the *Delineator*, a household magazine, endorsing the first week of Better Homes in America demonstration activities. The BHA campaign was headed by Marie Meloney, editor of the magazine, in collaboration with federal officials and home economics experts. Their efforts included local committees and model homes, displayed annually throughout the 1920s, and were intended to boost consumer spending. A replica of "Home Sweet Home" composer John Payne's colonial revival house was erected on the White House lawn, and a million people came to visit it, absorbing the idea of American style on the president's doorstep. Herbert Hoover, then secretary of commerce, said children were to be implanted with the idea of an owned home as the center of happy family life. Government loan programs, established after the Depression to deal with the nation's housing shortage, made homeownership possible for an ever-larger percentage of the American population.[40] While the Depression destabilized the nuclear family in some ways, as mothers entered the workforce and fathers lost their jobs, nostalgia for the era often enshrines family togetherness in the home, listening to the radio and playing popular board games like

Monopoly.[41] The family rooms incorporated into new postwar housing would give this type of activity a central place, and furniture of its own.

These loan programs, and the suburban developments supported by them after the Second World War, were available primarily to white families. As Dianne Harris writes in her 2013 book *Little White Houses: How the Postwar Home Constructed Race in America*, "Blacks, Asians, Native Americans, and Latinos were largely excluded from homeownership in most of the nation's new neighborhoods. The primary responsibility for this condition lies squarely on the shoulders of the federal government, which institutionalized racist housing policies and practices in the offices of the Federal Housing Administration (FHA) with practices initiated by the Home Owners' Loan Corporation (HOLC) in 1933."[42] Homeownership, promoted as an act of patriotism, was extremely difficult to achieve unless you were white. Less than 2 percent of the real estate financed through the GI Bill was available to nonwhite families, and thus, homeownership for nonwhite families lagged. In 1960, almost thirty-one million homes were owned by whites, compared with approximately two million owned by nonwhites. The model family dwellings I will discuss here need to be seen in this broader context: The families depicted are white, so the story they tell of the transformation of the home to accommodate the family is partial and would have been to many, for both racial and economic reasons, inaccessible.

Historians of the American family home, including Clifford Edward Clark Jr. and Gwendolyn Wright, have struggled with how to define the field of study given racial and economic restrictions, regional differences, and the great variety of American housing. I have followed their lead (and benefited from their research) in focusing for the most part on the ideal homes of the twentieth century—as seen in magazines, advertisements, and museums—as discussed for the benefits for the child. Clark says, "Whether they were able to live up to the ideal or not, most families could use it as a reference point, a lens thorough which they might view their own lives and measure their achievements and failures."[43] These projects remain fascinating records of inspiration and accommodation, as houses lose rooms, lose walls, lose attics and yet gain square footage, as architects, builders, and editors chase a floor plan that will fit always-changing everyday life. As Harris writes, these "ordinary houses were intended to transcend and even sometimes obscure middle-majority Americans' lower-economic, working-class, and ethnic or racial roots, and/or their efforts never to return to their prewar lives and conditions."[44] In the past few decades, for example, suburbs have become increasingly diverse, as African Americans, Latinos, and Asian Americans have bought houses in postwar communities.[45] The effect that these diverse populations will have on the interior design of houses has only been studied in a limited manner; the UCLA study of the twenty-first century family cited earlier didn't break out differences between family patterns based on race, though their sample did include nonwhite as well as nonheterosexual families. One interesting example is Arcadia, California, a 1940s suburb outside Los Angeles that has been remade to attract Chinese buyers. The new homes have multiple master suites to accommodate live-in relatives or visitors; separate wok kitchens for messy, high-heat cooking; and minimal backyards.[46]

Parents, founded in 1926 as *Children, the Magazine for Parents*, was established at a time of growing mainstream interest in child development, publishing articles on nutrition, education, and psychology as well as advice on home design and children's clothes (to buy and to sew). Editor Clara Savage Littledale, who ran the magazine from 1926 to 1956, also published articles on a wide array of public policy issues related to families and children, ensuring that her magazine did not have an exclusively consumer focus.[47] A May 1969 article covered the Berkeley, California, public schools' commitment to integration, lauding their first year of busing both black and white students to achieve racial parity across their system; an earlier issue had reported on one of the last one-room schoolhouses in the nation.[48] In an earlier era, the magazine ran articles promoting Progressive education, simple toys, and loose parts for indoor and outdoor play.[49] *Parents* was also very clear about a budget for home buying and home improvement, making its model homes a useful comparison to many more famous custom modernist houses built during the same period. The editors were versed in contemporary architecture but presented it differently than interior design magazines of the day did, emphasizing affordability and practicality rather than taste or style.

In 1929, the magazine began an ongoing feature titled "The Whole-Family House," with monthly installments covering everything from the ideal floor plan to heating systems to bathroom arrangements to furnishing

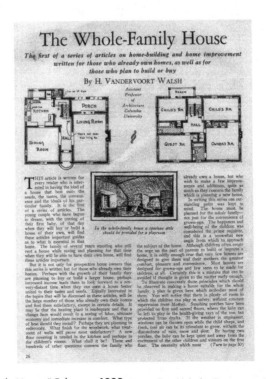

"The Whole-Family House," February 1929. [Originally published in *Parents* magazine. All Rights Reserved.]

children's rooms. The advice is highly practical and aimed at homeowners renovating piecemeal. The first article, by H. Vandervoort Walsh, an assistant professor of architecture at Columbia University and the author of several books on home design, shows plans for a compact two-story house with four rooms on each floor. A central, enclosed hall and staircase provides access to each chamber. "In writing this series one outstanding point was kept in mind," notes Walsh. "The house must be planned for the *whole* family—not just for the convenience of grown-ups. The happiness and well-being of the children was considered the prime requisite, and this is a somewhat new angle from which to approach the subject of the home."[50] At first glance, the accommodations for children look minimal: Each child has his or her own bedroom, but they are small and tucked away at the back of the house. Downstairs, the living room and dining room are surely no place for toys, and the kitchen has just enough room for Mother to move in a neat work triangle. A pass-through from kitchen to dining room saves more of her steps. Where exactly is the "plenty of room in which the children can play in safety, without constant supervision from Mother"? Their space, we find, is in a "spacious attic" above all the rooms, fitted out with child-size furniture and with plenty of empty floor space. An illustration of the attic shows it under the eaves of a gable-roofed house, with dormer windows added for light and air. The porches marked on the plan are also intended as children's territory. Covered spaces that were part of the house allowed children to play "outside" even on rainy days, or when Mother doesn't feel like pushing a baby carriage. The porches, as Walsh described them, also become a kind of swing space: extra rooms for when a baby needs to nap or a toddler to make noise and there's only one adult to supervise. Children need privacy too, Walsh asserts, so better to have the playroom separate from the domain in which the adults work and entertain. The necessity of room near, but not too near, Mother's command post in the kitchen is a recurring theme in the *Parents'* plans for family homes.

Manuals are filled with warnings about the nervous or smothering mother (what we would today call a "helicopter parent") who watches her child's every move, while scientific housekeeping manuals lay out a day's schedule with only a few hours devoted exclusively to childcare. A properly laid-out home, *Parents* suggests, can make all of this possible, even pleasurable: "Mothers need to play as well as children, but unless their work is made easy, the care of the youngsters and of the household will absorb all of their time." A lavatory on the first floor, as well as an array of "mechanical labor-saving devices," including electric refrigerators, washing machines, vacuum cleaners, and central heating, are there to help even if the "family purse" cannot extend to a maid.

As Ruth Schwartz Cowan ably describes in *More Work for Mother*, the time saved by labor-saving devices was not necessarily the housewife's time but that of her helpers. "The housewife was told, for example, that if help was scarce, it was easiest to serve children the same food adults were eating, although clearly it would be better for the former's digestion and your temperament if they ate with a nursemaid in the nursery."[51] Time study of housewives shows no reduction in time spent caring for the home between 1900 and 1920 or so. Instead, the childcare part of her portfolio expanded. Messages from government agencies like the U.S. Children's Bureau stressed combating infant mortality by breastfeeding, monitoring children's diets through daily weighing, and frequent visits to the doctor. Childcare no longer involved just teaching the basics and providing meals and clothing, now women were supposed to go to child-study meetings, read books and magazines about parenting (like *Parents*), supervise play, and take kids to lessons.[52] As Gwendolyn Wright notes, "The appeal of the suburbs had a great deal to do with anxiety about child-rearing, about giving one's children the space they needed yet controlling the people they met and what they did outside the home."[53]

A healthier interaction between parent and child was to be found in the basement, also left off the plans, which Walsh suggests be fitted out as a workshop for son and father. "In such a room as this, the creative powers of the boy are developed and a true bond of comradeship between father and son will grow."[54] The workshop, whether in the basement, the garage, or on a workbench in the corner of the family room, makes appearance after appearance in *Parents* home-design articles. By providing more to do inside the house's walls, parents could decrease outside influences and keep their children close. During the 1930s, hobbies became a means of displacement for unemployed or underemployed Americans. Modelmaking and carpentry workshops took over basements, garages, and attics. By the 1950s, the writers of those articles will nod to the fact that girls may enjoy building with tools or experimenting with electronics, but tinkering is generally considered a province of boys and men. Midcentury family room plans may include workbenches and sewing areas, along with open spaces for play with toys, but it is clear that Father is using the hammer and Mother the needle. The look of Walsh's house would not be amiss in any urban single-family neighborhood or streetcar suburb of the early twentieth century. The difference is in the assertion of the importance of children's happiness to that of the whole family, and in the emphasis on internal arrangements— of space, light, and appliances—to make such balance possible.

In the 1930s, domestic arrangements made a more substantial change, and *Parents* emphasized new materials and newly constructed homes as part of the transformation of family life. In June 1933, Douglas Haskell, who would go on to be the influential editor of *Architectural Forum* from 1949 to 1964, wrote an article titled "New Homes for Old," which included a photograph of A. Lawrence Kocher and Albert Frey's experimental

Aluminaire House in Syosset, Long Island.[55] "The object" of such experiments in lightweight, panelized fabrication, Haskell wrote, "is to enable the purchaser to order his home a good deal as today he orders his car." The dream of prefab family life had yet to be realized, but the ideal home Haskell describes has other futuristic aspects, most notably a one-story floor plan and a flat roof. On a roof deck, Haskell said, the family can enjoy meals in the open air, with storage not in the attic but down below, "where you neither have to climb ladders nor bump your head." The child's playroom is repositioned by the front door, with racks for hats and coats and large windows, because "doctors are unanimous in declaring that a growing child requires sunlight just as does a growing plant." In January 1934, the house plan in an article titled "Better Homes for Children" also placed the playroom just off the front hall, with its own closet and toilet, and a built-in window seat. The photo accompanying the article shows another plainly furnished room, with a small rug and graphic curtains; its main feature is a set of hollow wooden blocks, stacked to form a tiny playhouse with a doll waiting at the door to greet visitors.[56]

Educational experts held sway over the proper furnishing of the child's bedroom or playroom. Object-based learning did not occur solely at school, but could become part of home life if parents bought the right toys and gave their children an environment in which to pursue their own interests. Maria Montessori suggested blackboards hung at a child's height long before the mania for blackboard paint swept the nation, and other decorators suggested corkboards so that children could post their own artwork.[57] Most early twentieth-century child experts were united in the belief that children's environment had a great effect on their prospects. "Providing a proper environment for children became synonymous with good parenting," writes Bryn Varley Hollenbeck in her dissertation, "Making Space for Children." Décor, play spaces, and playthings for education and discipline all became the purview of experts. The commercial children's market, then in process of expansion, began to sell more to parents with a variety of messages of "success."[58] Demand for children's furniture grew in the first decade of the twentieth century, and by the 1920s and 1930s, when *Parents* was publishing this advice, department and furniture stores had set up rooms and floors exclusively selling juvenile décor.

Sprackling laid out a checklist for the modern nursery: "color that is clean and attractive but not too stimulating, space uncluttered and free from distracting and meaningless design, tables that are comfortable and correct in height, chairs that are sturdy and encourage good posture, chests and bureaus that stimulate order and self-help, surfaces that are durable and easily cleaned, no sharp corners to cause injuries, an absence of dust-catching ornament and device."[59] The nursery is the child's work space and, like the mother's kitchen, should be made as convenient as possible so there are no physical hindrances to play. "Every item in the room has been measured by the yardstick of health, fitness and need," Sprackling wrote of a 1934 "health-first nursery" along much the same lines: "Modernism in the nursery means the ultimate in sanitation, and functional fitness." The child-mortality rate remained a concern, though it dropped, between 1900 and 1920, from one in six children under the age of five to one in twelve.[60] The floors of the nursery were to be bare wood, cork, or linoleum, softened only with washable rag rugs. Armstrong linoleum advertised continuously in *Parents* throughout the early to mid-twentieth century, often showing nurseries and playrooms with gaily colored floors. Washable paints were used, "dead white" for the walls, powder blue trim for the windows, which were shaded with venetian blinds instead of curtains. There were no moldings or baseboards, traditional elements that were difficult to dust, and the furniture had an enamel finish that could be easily wiped down. More important, as Sprackling pointed out: "Nowhere in the room are there any frills, no cute gadgets with 'Baby' painted on them to become mere useless dust gatherers. The child's welfare should be the first design concern, the editors said, 'not pink-and-blue bows, fairies and toy balloons.' "[61] Health, ahead of beauty or educational value, was an effective method of attracting parents' attention to furnishings for their children, and simple lines, washable surfaces, and light colors, the so-called hygiene aesthetic, were seen as ideal for keeping clean and spotting dirt. Air was also considered an important element of child health. Popular magazines like *Ladies' Home Journal* suggested the construction of screened sleeping porches outside the bedroom, and manufacturers made sleeping bags that left only the face exposed. Other innovations included the window bed, which extended over the windowsill at night, protected by an awning, and the fresh-air tent, which attached to an open window, surrounding the sleeper's head but leaving the rest of his or her body warm and under the covers.[62]

Sprackling's design advice (if not her war on germs) still sounds entirely reasonable, and the photographs that accompany her story on the modern nursery, look far less dated than adult décor of the 1930s. She calls particular attention to the designs of Gilbert Rohde, originally made for his own children. Rohde, who went on to work for Herman Miller in the 1930s and early 1940s and introduced that venerable Zeeland, Michigan, furniture maker to the modern design for which it is now known, had also designed the interiors for the Design for Living House at the 1933 Chicago World's Fair (the theme of the fair was "A Century of Progress"). Children were getting the most advanced design not because they were connoisseurs but because it suited their needs. Open shelves and toy boxes should, according to educators, promote independence and neatness, encouraging children to take care of their own things. Rounded corners and hard-wearing materials originally intended for the kitchen, like linoleum, Bakelite, and washable wallpaper, made cleaning up easy. Color was kept simple, pale paint with contrasting handles, though Sprackling said the simple furniture goes just as well in a room with dotted wallpaper and chintz curtains. The important thing was not to overwhelm the child with detail: A pictorial frieze should show things with which the child is familiar—flowers, animals, blocks—because she can only recognize things from her own experience. In truth, this admonition is more important for toys, which the child can touch and manipulate, than for the walls of her room.

At the 1928 American Designers' Gallery exhibition in New York, which featured ten complete rooms, Ilonka Karasz was the only female designer given responsibility for full rooms: a studio apartment and a nursery.[63] The nursery was designed to be both functional and as a spur to creativity. Geometric, child-height furniture with large ball knobs made it easy for the owner to tidy her room, teaching independence. A marionette theater, building blocks, and a chalkboard running around the whole room at eye level acted as invitations to imaginative play. A rug on the floor, also designed by Karasz, included dots, squiggles, and swirls of the kind a child might draw on her walls. *Arts and Decoration* credited Karasz with "the first nursery ever designed for the very modern American child," and *The Arts* called it one "of the gayest, jolliest and most practical rooms ever designed for a child."[64] In an essay published in *House and Garden* in 1935, Karasz explained that modern design worked best for children because it left room for their own imagination. The child should be surrounded with elemental shapes and primary colors so that she could start to manipulate these elements on her own.[65] When Joseph Aronson designed playrooms for the Toy Manufacturers of the U.S.A. in the late 1940s and early 1950s, he subscribed to the same model: yellow walls, blue ceiling, red linoleum floor, and minimal decoration. "Whatever pattern a child sees every day he will tend to copy—to the detriment of his own creative development.

If you must have some decorative design, let it be strictly abstract, or something the child has drawn himself."[66]

Another 1933 *Parents* article, on awakening the spirit of scientific inquiry, made a related point: "Every child ought to have a place to work where he will not interfere with other household affairs and where other household affairs will not interfere with him." For the young child, that space is the nursery or playroom, but for Robert, the boy in "Science from Six to Sixteen," that space is his room.[67] His mother was distressed to see him bent over an old table strewn with electric wire, tire tape, thumbtacks, a candle, a penny, and a dime, not put away since Sunday, but author Ronald Millar describes such messes as essential. Robert is trying, so far without success, to make electric current. When his mother interrupts, he is deep in "an outbreak of curiosity." Children need space where they never have to put things away so that a question may be pursued over time. The parents' job is to provide the raw materials and answer questions when asked, or when a child is frustrated. "The incident of young Robert and his mother," Millar writes, "illustrates clearly a distinction between the desire of children to *make* and *run* things and their desire to investigate *how* things are made and *why* they run." When parents give children blocks and construction sets, they are fulfilling the first part of that desire; when they give children magnifying glasses and magnets, the second. Raw materials are essential to this inquiry, from the cardboard boxes of construction play to the wood, wheels, and tools of junk playgrounds. "Before long the child will have accumulated a boxful of assorted 'junk' that will seem worthless but to the child will be a veritable treasure chest containing more wonderful possibilities than a whole store crowded with ready-made playthings," Millar writes, sounding much like the makers of contemporary toys for so-called tinkerers, including Sugru and littleBits. In toys, in rooms, in playgrounds, one can see an ongoing tension between making things perfect—a modern nursery designed by Gilbert Rohde—and making things available—Robert's messy tableful of junk. It is to *Parents* magazine's credit that it promotes the low-cost dirty option alongside the hygienic one. In a 1935 article on a combined playroom-bedroom, the author writes, "if you provide your child with a workbench, be professional about it. Don't try to prettify such a piece of furniture."[68]

In the 1940s, *Parents* magazine embraced the postwar expansion to the suburbs. While earlier articles on the whole-family house had dealt with old-fashioned floor plans and traditional architecture, as well as the question of remodeling, the magazine's housing features now focused on new homes, making the assumption that their white, middle-class readers were in the market. During and just after World War II, popular magazines dwelled on Americans' pent-up desire to own a home. A ROW Window Company ad published in the October 1945 issue of *House Beautiful* shows a couple looking at their house plans with a castle floating over their shoulders. Down below, drawn almost like a play set, we see the single-family detached house of their dreams. "Are You Weaving a Magic Carpet?" the copy asks.[69] The *New Yorker* cover from July 20, 1946, shows a father carrying a blueprint and holding hands with a child in a sailor suit. His modishly dressed wife holds the child's other hand as all three are whisked upward toward their dream house in the clouds.[70] The dream became a reality for millions: More than 5 million houses were built in the United States between 1946 and 1949, and by 1959, 31 million of 44 million American families owned their own home. This rapid increase in ownership was largely thanks to the GI Bill, which offered veterans home mortgages with little or no down payment.[71] The *Saturday Evening Post* cover of August 15, 1959, continues the dream narrative: A young couple sitting under a tree envisions their future as constellations in the night sky—a house, a pool, a nanny pushing a pram, a girl playing piano, a boy playing baseball, plus a boatload of electric appliances, including a vacuum cleaner, a TV, an iron, and the Little Dipper of DIY, a drill. Electric drills were one of the first industrial tools to make their way into home toolkits: Black & Decker managers noticed that many of their employees were borrowing drills from work for weekend home-improvement projects and saw a new market, repackaging drills in bright boxes and distributing them through department and hardware stores. Kits and accessories soon followed, turning the workshop into another location for endless consumer additions.[72] Historian John Archer uses these images to illustrate the pervasiveness of the "dream home" in advertising, illustration, literature, and popular song. An important element of those songs, as in these magazine covers, was the presence of a child: The dream home came with a family.

For those who couldn't afford the dream, or who couldn't buy it outright, there was the drill and DIY. More leisure time, and more low-priced power tools, meant you could upgrade, personalize, and customize on your own. There's something wonderfully circular, as well as sinister, about buying a home and building in a workbench for your child, even as the home itself becomes your weekend project. Are you its owner or its servant? *Time* magazine's August 2, 1954, cover story, called "Do-It-Yourself: The New Billion-Dollar Hobby," depicted a Norman Rockwellian dad, astride a tractor, as a many-armed Shiva wielding table saw, paint roller, drill, chain saw, and buffer.[73] *Business Week* wrote, in 1952, "In any suburb on any weekend, the master of the house is apt to turn into his own handyman. He's painting the porch, patching a pipe, or building an open-air fireplace so he can roast weenies in the garden."[74] *Parents* magazine's articles and designs for ideal family homes reflect these interests, including spaces for Mother's sewing machine or an empty table in a son's room marked out for modelmaking. Like father, like son, the plans seem to say, and advertisements in the same magazines show moments of mutual concentration over projects like building a wooden table.[75]

Even though thousands of women had worked in the defense industry during World War II and taken care of home maintenance on their own while their husbands were overseas, postwar media and advertising reinforced traditional spheres for men and women. Work on the outside of the house was his responsibility, while the inside was hers. The cover of Sherwin-Williams's 1958 *Home Decorator and How-to-Paint Book* shows Mr. Homeowner in jeans, painting the exterior of a Cape Cod cottage, while Mrs. Homeowner—in heels and a frilled apron—paints the interior while discussing paint samples with her daughter.[76] If a couple is shown working together, he is up on a ladder, while she hands him supplies. A double-page Valspar paint ad from 1955 shows the whole family at work in a cutaway, two-story home and garage. The men and boys paint the garage, a boat, a tricycle—a professional in painter's overalls handles the exterior gable—while the mother and daughter paint a modern cabinet and an interior room. As Carolyn M. Goldstein writes in the catalog for the 1998 National Building Museum exhibition *Do It Yourself*, "A 1940s Luminall paint brochure suggested that women possessed the innate aesthetic ability—or even magical power!—required to properly choose paint colors."[77] It was not until the 1970s when a new generation of publications focused on women as do-it-yourselfers, responding to the feminist critique of gendered advertising and media. Skillful, confident home repair was presented as a form of female liberation, even as the same skills had been presented to the postwar man as a sign of masculinity and purpose.[78] The cover of Florence Adams's 1973 manual *I Took a Hammer in My Hand* depicts the Statue of Liberty in coveralls, her torch a hammer, her book two-by-fours, a wrench, lightbulbs, and a measuring stick. *In Christina's Toolbox*, a children's book originally published in 1981, depicts an African

American girl, also in overalls, repairing various things around her house using the contents of her toolbox . . . "just like her mother's."[79]

In March 1946, *Parents* published its first Expandable Home, designed by Ketchum, Gina & Sharp: a one-story, L-shaped ranch house with a low-pitched roof and a garage at the end of the L. A year later, in October 1947, the magazine visited two families who had built versions of that house, relaying their stories as proof of the house's adaptability to different sites and different family structures.[80] The Expandable rubric was intended to appeal to families of varying budgets, as more amenities could be added to the basic structure as funds permitted, and the interviews with the homeowners stressed DIY as a money-saving measure. The first family to embrace the magazine plans was the Bradleys, of northern Michigan, looking for a new home after Rog's return from the navy. Despite shortages of building materials, the family took out a permit for a home with a construction budget of twelve thousand dollars and ended up doing much of the work themselves. The interiors are simple, with natural plywood walls and a white-painted kitchen with decals, linoleum floors, and tilt-in windows. Provisions have been made for storage of the Bradleys' hunting and fishing equipment, and of Mrs. Bradley's supplies of home-canned fruits, jams, and pickles. When asked why they "fell in love" with the house, Mrs. Bradley says, "Because the house was planned for every member of the family—particularly the children. I remember when I was a child there never seemed to be a room or place in the house that truly belonged to the children . . . In this house the children can carry on no matter how much company we have—and when the children are older they will be able to have fun without disturbing us."[81] The Bradley children have their own bedrooms and a playroom, accessible off an enclosed yard with a climbing structure made by their father. The playroom has built-in shelves and drawers along the window wall, plus child-size tables and chairs. In a remarkable touch, the playroom is visible from the kitchen through a tilt-up door that is part of the kitchen cabinetry, but it and the children's bedrooms can also be closed off from the public rooms of the house via a large sliding door on a track.

The idea of an expanded kitchen as household command post resonates with us in the twenty-first century, as it remains the center of family activity. In *A Pattern Language*, the encyclopedic book on the design of cities, neighborhoods, and homes by Christopher Alexander and his colleagues at UC Berkeley's Center for Environmental Structure, he calls out the archetypal farmhouse kitchen as an essential "pattern" for anyone planning a house, an architecture that creates a set of desirable social relations. "The isolated kitchen, separate from the family and considered as an efficient but unpleasant factory for food is a hangover from the days of servants; and from the more recent days when women willingly took over the servants' role," Alexander writes. "But this separation, in a family, has

"Come Visit *Parents* Magazine Expandable Homes," October 1947.

put the woman in a very difficult position . . . Modern American houses, with the so-called open plan, have gone some way toward resolving this conflict."[82] Alexander argues that the open-plan kitchen doesn't go far enough: The mother is still on one side of the counter and the family on the other, separating the pleasure of eating from the chore of cooking. "Make the kitchen bigger than usual," they say, "big enough to include the 'family room' space."

Thirty years on, one can see the shadow of this idea in the "great rooms" that dominate builder houses, with kitchen flowing into dining area flowing into den. They aren't one room but a hybrid version of three, with the isolation of the kitchen reduced by the introduction of a full-height breakfast bar—those stools pulled up to the counter, and the television as a kind of counterweight to the refrigerator. The ever-increasing average size of a new single-family home in the United States, which was 983 square feet in 1950, 1,660 square feet in 1973, and 2,392 in 2010,

according to the U.S. Census, has come about not from the swelling of storage areas but from the swelling of room sizes: master bedrooms with sitting areas and en suite bathrooms, bed and bath for every child.[83] By 1972, 65 percent of new American homes had at least three bedrooms, and half had more than one and a half baths.[84] And yet the kitchen remains the heart of the house and, as recent research has shown, the one place everyone in the family comes to dwell. A study of thirty-two Los Angeles families conducted by the Center on the Everyday Lives of Families (CELF) at UCLA between 2001 and 2005 found that the kitchen, whatever its size, was the most used space in the house. Most of the families' houses were built before 1970 and had small, enclosed kitchens. And yet, in the three to four hours the two-career parents had with their children after work and before bedtime, the kitchen was where they met, with children doing homework on the kitchen table, phones charging at the island outlets, and piles of papers, backpacks, and lunch boxes on the counter.[85] Data from a larger study of 435 families in eight cities, surveyed by the Alfred P. Sloan Center on Parents, Children and Work at the University of Chicago, found the same thing: 42.3 percent of the time parents spent with one or more children was in the kitchen.[86] The mother's desk has moved out of the kitchen and into a shared home office, but the refrigerator remains the location of family planning: If there is a wall clock in the house, it will be in the kitchen, along with a physical calendar. (The UCLA study found an average of 5.2 calendars per family, a reflection, they believe, of the increasingly scheduled lives of adults and children.)[87] The refrigerator is a repository for invitations, prescriptions, phone numbers, and other paper messages, with a chalkboard or pin board besides it. "Materially, kitchen assemblages index a culture of busyness that has come to define middle-class families in the twenty-first century."[88] The researchers even found that the density of refrigerator clutter correlated with the relative tidiness of the house. Ironically, if families had remodeled their older houses, they did the master bedroom first, creating oases of little-frequented tranquility. In midcentury homes, the grandest spaces were the communal ones, connecting indoors and outdoors, food and play, while the bedrooms were typically small and utilitarian. In this organization, the architects were ahead of their time: This is how the twenty-first-century family lives, but many people still don't have architecture that fits.

In the 1950s, the *Parents* magazine houses took on a more explicitly modern look. In February 1955, the magazine's Fifth Annual Builders' Competition "Best Homes for Families with Children" included one of Carl Koch & Associates' Techbuilt houses in Concord, Massachusetts.[89] The patented Techbuilt system was one of the most successful American attempts at architectural semi-prefabrication. Twenty years after Douglas Haskell had first raised the idea of ordering up a home as easily as a car in the pages of *Parents*, here was a charming example, built with a wood post-and-beam frame and premade four-by-four-foot wall, floor, and roof panels, which Koch claimed could be put together in a few days, like a giant dollhouse kit. The blessing of Koch's system, according to the magazine, was its flexibility: "The interior can be finished one room at a time, expanded, improved or changed as family needs dictate." Like its predecessors, the Techbuilt house was not a fixed dream house, but a flexible one, intended to be accessible to the middle class and accommodating of the fact that children grow up. It cost $18,100 (appliances included) and was two stories, with a simple pitched roof and top-floor balcony. Upstairs, four small private bedrooms flank a large open area at the top of the stairs—a future bedroom, should the family expand. Downstairs, living, dining, and kitchen have at last become a single room, with the fixed stairs, chimney, and bathroom arranged in a tight cluster at the front of the house. Dotted lines mark another area adjacent to the kitchen as "future playroom," along with a second, downstairs bathroom. The dissolution of the walled, formal living room and dining room is complete. The only rooms with doors that shut are the bathroom and bedrooms tucked upstairs; the children's rooms have become so compact that downstairs is the only place to play.

In the January 1955 issue, *Parents* boldly stated "Every Family with Children Needs 2 Living Rooms." "Far from being a luxury, the second living room fulfills the family's needs for a really adequate activity space. Here's where the family can work and play together, where there's room for hobbies, a snack, rough and tumble play or quiet enjoyment of music."[90] Once children are out of the blocks stage, the family still needs an alternative zone, free from the formality of the official living room, where each member can act on his or her interests. The trick is to make it adaptable to both quiet and loud pursuits and separate from the other living spaces. In other stories, such spaces will be referred to as family rooms or rec rooms, but the materials and layout are generally the same: open floors, built-in furniture, fold-down and open-out cupboards with TVs and stereos, workbenches, and sewing machines. Rooms like this are what architects George Nelson and Henry Wright refer to, in their influential book *Tomorrow's House*, as the "room without a name." "We have all read articles about the family—its difficulties in the world of today, the inadequacies of parents, the waywardness of children," state Nelson and Wright. "Could the room without a name be evidence of a growing desire to provide a framework within which the members of a family will be better equipped to enjoy each other on the basis of mutual respect and affection?"[91]

The book, published right after the end of World War II, and just before the nation embarked upon the construction of hundreds of thousands of Cape Cod– and colonial-style homes, was intended to disrupt Americans' visions of their pitched-roof dream house with a hard look at how families really lived. It chronicles, in pictures, the most modern houses built in the United States in the 1930s and challenges, in prose, readers' preconceptions about what matters. "This book challenges not most, but all of the sweet-scented nostalgia on the domestic scene," Nelson and Wright claim in their preface. "Despite its persuasive manner, it is going to disturb many readers who keep their milk in the latest refrigerator, drive to business in the newest car, but persist in thinking that a Cape Cod cottage remains the snappiest idea in a home," they write, attacking as "fake" the weathered shingles and picket fences, hooked rugs and shoemaker's benches on, and in, houses with late-model Buicks parked out front.[92] They challenged their readers not to be afraid of change and to embrace the idea of a house that would fit the modern family's needs. Nelson, although trained as an architect, first achived fame as a writer, attracting the attention of Herman Miller's D. J. De Pree. Appointed design director, Nelson declined to do all of the design himself, bringing in the Eameses, Isamu Noguchi, and Alexander Girard. Tomorrow's house, like the furniture Nelson produced at Herman Miller, should be honest in its materials and honest about what family members like to do: running electric trains, listening to music, woodworking. The activities that would once have been accommodated in stolen spaces like garages, attics, and basements should now be combined into one multipurpose room for everyone. "It makes the first time a room *for the whole family* has appeared in the home since the days of the farmhouse kitchen," state Nelson and Wright.[93] This room expresses the character of that family and thus cannot be standardized. What should come standard is finishes that are easy to clean. Furniture should be tough but lightweight, so friends can gather around a game table or push the chairs against the wall for a dance party, and there should be lots of built-in storage where games and toys and tools can be kept out of sight. Their storage wall, illustrated in *Life* magazine in 1945, was a single piece of furniture that could hold 1,000 of the average family's 10,000 articles.

The exemplary houses in *Parents* magazine emphasize walls of shelves, particularly in children's bedrooms, as a way of increasing floor space and decreasing clutter. The kitchen always has a complement of cabinets and appliances, but that aesthetic, and those materials, creep outside the hygienic confines of the kitchen, until any room might benefit from cabinets, wipeable surfaces, and moppable floors. The increasing casualness of home life changes the materials away from high-maintenance draperies and upholstery, carved furniture, and surfaces covered in knick-knacks. Mary and Russel Wright's *Guide to Easier Living*, published in 1950, builds on suggestions in *Tomorrow's House*, offering greater detail and diagrams of individual rooms along with specifics on cleaning, entertaining, and scheduling. If Nelson and Wright's book was aimed at an architectural audience, and filled with small photos of houses that illustrated their ideas, the Wrights created a visually compelling manual aimed squarely at the woman of the house, updating earlier home manuals by Christine Frederick that spelled out the care and maintenance of the ideal home. The Wrights even recommend a number of books on motion study, the field pioneered by the Gilbreths, that are beneficial to the "housewife-engineer."[94] The tone is bracing:

> The first two years of a child's life are full of strenuous
> physical experiment: crawling, standing up, walking,
> climbing. To spare him bumps and frustrations, and his
> parents anxiety, have all furniture with flush or rounded
> corners, sturdy, and with nothing loose or hanging or
> unstable to be pulled down or overturned. Everything from
> floor to ceiling should be washable. This is an obvious first
> thought (too often it is also the last). But it does not have to
> mean a hospital look. There is no good reason for baby
> furniture to be always anemic white, pink, or blue. You can
> wash a bright-red chest or crib as clean as a pale one.[95]

Bassinets are soon obsolete, so buy a crib on wheels so the baby can be moved outside for airing. "Surely, you want no frilly curtains on the windows here." Chalk makes dust, crayons are preferred. Children need a corner of their own to "pile things in any order or none." And they, too, recommend hollow blocks. The advice is illustrated in clear, bird's-eye-view drawings of the various rooms in the house. A particularly effective sequence shows a large room, divided in two by a sliding partition, designed for a brother and sister.[96] We watch the children, and the room, grow up in place and in the same space. Walls of built-ins, installed in L shapes on the opposite ends of the room, morph from crib to bed to sofa. A writable wall for a toddler becomes a pinup wall for a teen. At first the furnishing is minimal so that the floor and low pieces made of hollow blocks can be used for open play. For the "rough-and-tumble" stage, the partition is pushed back and an indoor slide installed in the center of the room, with a dollhouse on her side and trains on his. For teens, the partition is fully closed. The L of the built-in becomes a desk for him and a vanity for her; he decorates with sports pennants and has a model plane in progress, she hasn't given away her dolls. She sits on an antique chair while his lounge chair is by Jens Risom, another modern furniture master.

Parents magazine illustrated the same space-saving idea with their "two-in-one room" in 1955.[97] A large room for a brother and sister close in age is divided by an accordion-style door into two private sleeping chambers. Because the room is converted from a garage, it has its own entrance to the outdoors, and it is at the opposite end of the house from the living areas and the parents' own room. The two spaces can be thrown together during the day to create more floor space for play, and the built-in furniture around the walls provides stations for different activities, gendered in what begins to seem like a very familiar way. "There's everything to satisfy a young lady's needs in Patty's half," including ample storage for toys and a drop-down door on a wall cabinet above her bed that transforms it into a sofa with a padded backrest for reading or entertaining friends. Her desk has a pullout typewriter shelf and a top that can be raised to become a slanted drawing board. Patty's side favors quiet activities and socializing, centered around giving her her own little living room, complete with phonograph and records. On her brother Clark's side, things are indeed more rough-and-tumble. The article emphasizes his "impervious" green-tinted concrete floor, a trundle bed for overnight guests, and storage for his many hobbies: "games, sports equipment and rock collection." The text notes that the room is now big enough for hosting children's birthday parties. Again and again in *Parents* home stories, the differences between boys and girls come through not so much in décor—though Patty has a rose-coral bedspread to inflect the maple built-ins in a feminine direction—but in contents. The boys' desks are littered with collections and the ephemera of making or scientific inquiry, while the girls' desks have clean books and

There's plenty of room for fun and an overnight guest in Clark's half of

THE TWO-IN-ONE ROOM

Plan shows how one room becomes two; Clark's half shaded.

"A Two-in-One Room for their Children," April 1955. [Originally published in *Parents* magazine. All Rights Reserved.]

writing materials or, in some cases, serve as dressing tables instead. She has a sofa and records, he has a train set and floor play. Even if the furniture and flooring are the same, the impervious nature of concrete is only emphasized in his half of the room.

Though all statistics point to Americans having larger houses and many more things now than they did in 1945, the anxiety, it seems, remains the same. Goods cost less than at any other point in history, and families in the United States buy 40 percent of the world's toys, spending $240 million each year. The result is that a family living in a 980-square-foot house has 2,260 visible possessions in their living rooms and two bedrooms.[98] The Center on the Everyday Lives of Families studied thirty-two families living "amidst sometimes extraordinary clutter." Only a quarter of the families studied could even park a car in their garage—the rest are filled with stuff. CELF psychologists Darby Saxbe and Rena

Repetti found such clutter was actually affecting the moods of the mothers in the study, making them more depressed in the evenings when they returned home. "Disorder exacts a psychological toll because it so clearly taxes family labor. Dusting, cleaning, upkeep, repair, straightening, reorganization—all these chores consume parents' time and energy. Merely *anticipating* such work almost certainly generates anxiety and stress, and carrying it out is a measurable strain on the household time budget," Jeanne A. Arnold writes about their research.[99] Despite family's investments in their yards, another important feature of California-style homes from midcentury on, few of the parents in the study ever use them, trapped in a cycle of spending their spare time managing possessions. Kondo suggests letting go and then finding ways to reduce the space that even your joyful possessions take up.

The dream embodied by these storage-heavy walls is of everything in the house having a place, children included. But in recent decades, the contents of those cupboards have exploded. Millions have turned to Marie Kondo, author of *The Life-Changing Magic of Tidying Up*, to #organizetheworld. Her method, nicknamed KonMari, has been reduced, in the popular press, to a few signature moves, most notably holding up each possession in your cluttered home and asking yourself whether it "sparks joy." But before you can individually assess those possessions, Kondo suggests piling books, clothing, papers, and sentimental items, in a massive, glorious pile in the center of the room. In an article on the Kondo phenomenon in the *New York Times Magazine* in 2016, Taffy Brodesser-Akner unearthed a divide among the organizational ranks: The (mostly) women of the National Association of Productivity and Organizing Professionals (NAPO) are less interested in letting go than in finding a place for everything. "Whereas Kondo does not believe that you need to buy anything in order to organize and that storage systems provide only the illusion of tidiness, the women of Conference [NAPO's annual meeting] traded recon on timesaving apps, label makers, the best kind of Sharpie, the best tool they own ('supersticky notes,' 'drawer dividers') and the best practices regarding clients who wouldn't offer their organization goals in a timely manner," Brodesser-Akner writes.[100] In this effort, they update and disperse the storage wall into hundreds of under-bed bins and behind-the-door racks. When the city of Toronto published its guidelines for designing for children in condominiums in 2017, they included a separate section on storage, with recommendations for built-in storage walls and entry closets in each unit, as well as communal storage rooms for strollers on the ground floor and lockers adjacent to parking spots in the garage.[101] The rise of two-career and single-parent families has, at long last, begun to reverse the American preference for more space and more suburbs: Women want less house and yard to take care of, less commute time, more of the socialization that living vertically can bring.[102] We'll return to this aspect of twenty-first-century family life later, but the main point for now is that shrinking your footprint doesn't necessarily shrink your stuff. What makes a house family-friendly may actually be storage.

•

THERE'S A PHOTOGRAPH of a Tripp Trapp chair on the wall of Alex Truesdell's office at the Adaptive Design Association (ADA), a closet-size space fitted out with a wall unit made of cardboard, a cardboard design, and a library of books on cardboard carpentry. "That's a chair we've worked with many times, many many many," she says, "because there have been many children who needed a little something to add to it. The seat was a little too wide, or they needed the back to be closer."[103] In the photo, a boy is sitting on a Tripp Trapp adapted with a tray and a cardboard cradle, curved to hold a guitar so that he can learn to play it even if he doesn't have the strength to hold it. If children's furniture helps to bridge the gap between the adult-size world and the typical child, cardboard makes customization affordable and (relatively) swift. People don't ask for Tripp Trapp modifications too often, though, because "as far as thoughtfulness, it's a winner," Truesdell says. In a world not sized for children, and not adapted for differences in ability, Peter Opsvik achieved his goal of designing for most and created something long-lasting and adaptable, if expensive. Truesdell's mission is not only to fill in the gap between the back and the seat, but the one between need and market, until every child is comfortable and capable of learning.

Truesdell, who was awarded one of the MacArthur Foundation's "genius" grants in 2015, is the founder and executive director of the ADA, a nonprofit that builds low-cost tools and furniture for children with disabilities. Her mission now is to teach as many other people as possible how to build such equipment too. Design for disabled children is no more and no less than an extension of the variability built into the best design for children: Disabled children may also require customization and variation, and they are even less easily held to an average or standard. The term "disabled children," used instead of "children with disabilities," is itself a commentary on the way the world does not meet their needs. The social model of disability holds that disability is not something people have, but the result of their relationship to an environment filled with barriers to participation.[104] Truesdell feels strongly that the word *disability* itself should not apply: What she seeks in her designs for her child clients is custom fitting, something many people who simply aren't standard size would find useful. "Humans have variability, that's everybody. But how are we different? That would be a far healthier conversation," she told TechRepublic.[105] As we speak she sizes me up, at a glance, as a little over five feet tall. "So, you're too short for all standard chairs, sorry. It's almost like you're responsible for not fitting, as opposed to, 'Let's make you comfortable so you can concentrate on writing your book.' "[106]

In stories from her more than thirty-five years of practice, which she illustrates via photos on her iPhone, Truesdell returns again and again to the intellectual and social transformations physical interventions can bring. A little girl provided with a wedge-shaped booster, one that doesn't even have a back or arms, is able to sit up and feed herself. A boy in a stander that supports him and gives him a built-in desk is finally able to turn the pages of a book himself. There are thousands of commercial products on the market for people with disabilities, but the ADA doesn't make anything you can buy. "We are not making a cheap version of a commercially made item," Truesdell insists. "Many families come here who have significant means. They still come here because what they need isn't made. If you say, 'Oh, it's expensive,' it completely derails the topic. Where will that money come from? Who will approve it? And, if we have so many that need it, don't we have to divide the costs?" Confronted with that great a need, Truesdell turned to a material and a method popularized for children in the 1960s: cardboard carpentry. The low cost and malleability of the cardboard box, the qualities that make it an ideal material for creative play, also make it appealing for the adult "play" of design, particularly when those designs have to be customizable and may be temporary. "The cardboard has been problematic because there's been the assumption you're doing it cheaper because you can't afford the wood," Truesdell says. But cardboard has its own strengths. Why buy something when you can make it? And why make something when you can share the plans with everyone?

Cardboard is her material of choice, though the design teams at the ADA also work with plastic, metal, motors, and whatever else is required to fit a child's needs. The most basic of these, in her view, is "a seat at the table." Twenty percent of the population, by conservative estimate, has a disability.[107] Without a chair in which a person with a disability can comfortably sit eye to eye with her doctor, her teacher, her employer, her sibling, "they're not at the meeting, they're not in the classroom, they're not at the workplace," says Truesdell. Truesdell herself never sits down in that office—like an inquisitive bird, she is constantly jumping up to show me something, talk to someone, or turn over the furniture prototypes that provide much of the seating in the ADA's two-story headquarters in Manhattan's shrinking Garment District. We perch together at a conference table surrounded by short stools, on half-round bases, with slanted tops. "The pelvic tilt is the magic of these," she tells me, "a ten-degree forward tilt. If you sit on something flat, it doesn't work, but somehow tilting the pelvis forward does magic." The stools, which are made of cardboard, have a thin cushion on top cut from yoga mat. As we talk, I am able to shift my position slightly and continuously, rocking imperceptibly in the manner recommended, I realize, for children with attention-deficit problems. I've just bought my fidgety son an exercise band to loop around the front legs of his classroom chair to give his feet something to do while his hands and mind are at work. But now I want to make him a rocking stool. And I could, because all of the ADA's designs are open source.

Truesdell gestures toward Bailey, a soft, child-size doll in a striped shirt who is sitting across the room in one of the ADA's most popular designs: a booster strapped to an ordinary chair that brings Bailey's elbows up to the table and supports his back. Fisher-Price sells something like this, in plastic, for children up to fifty pounds, but the back is lower and the armrests less substantial, and it is hard to imagine a child over four years old fitting in the seat. "So here he is, and you are I are meeting over here," she jumps up and we go over to symbolically include Bailey. In case he might be bored while the adults talk, she picks up a long narrow tray—cardboard—with raised sides and sets it in front of him. Now he can play with a ball without worrying about it rolling off the table, or keep other toys corralled within his reach. His hands are occupied and the adults aren't talking about him above his head or out of sight. When he grows, the ADA will make him a bigger chair or a bigger tray, and these will be handed down to another child. "Bailey's going to grow very fast, so if we make the booster out of wood or a permanent material, then the focus is on the money and permanence," Truesdell says. "He may need less."

Truesdell has an undergraduate degree in early childhood education, and a master's in teaching the visually impaired. Just six months into her career, her aunt suffered a spinal cord injury and her uncle, founder of Easystreet Cleaning in Poughkeepsie, New York, a paving and sweeping company, began to make over their longtime home to ensure his wife's continuing independence. "It was my uncle's capacity to modify, adapt, repair, replace, invent that was so mind-blowingly marvelous," she says. "It gave permission to my imagination, and then he gave permission to my use of tools." These skills, which we now see referred to in the tech sphere as tinkering or hacking, became key to working with her aunt and uncle to adapt their home to her aunt's new level of ability. "What would be the way that she could continue to live, essentially with two flippers at the end of her wrists as opposed to two normal hands?" Truesdell wondered.[108] Among the adaptations Truesdell and her aunt and uncle came up with was a way to open a dresser drawer: They attached pet collars to the handles so her aunt could hook her hand through and pull with her wrist. This reminds me of a work in progress I saw in the workshop at the ADA: a dressing device the team is working on for a four-year-old with arthrogryposis, a condition that causes stiff or locked joints. They've attached plastic hooks to a motorized arm made of PVC pipe. The arm will be attached to a chair, and a shirt looped over the hooks so that, if they are successful, the boy will be able to dress himself by threading his arms into the O of the shirt and pressing a switch by his knee. "His parents want him to be independent," a college student assembling a chair in the workshop tells me. Independence, Truesdell learned with her earliest experiments, is baked into her material.

On a trip to Maine to work at a school for the blind, Truesdell, on a hunt for a missing play station, found a cardboard chair in a storeroom. Made for an adult whose limbs were not symmetrical, the chair opened her eyes to the possibilities of the medium. The client, and the chair's maker, were long gone, but another teacher at the school remembered it came from a place called Learning Things.[109] Truesdell went back to Massachusetts and found Learning Things, then in Arlington, a workshop run by George Cope and Phylis Morrison that published the book *The Further Adventures of Cardboard Carpentry: Son of Cardboard Carpentry* in 1973.[110] That book was the first on her cardboard shelf, where it was soon joined by *Cardboard Carpentry: Making Children's Furniture and Play Structures* and many, many more titles. In the early 1980s, Truesdell says, American society was at "the tail end of the early human world of making. At that point, fast food wasn't quite as fast as it became, catalogues weren't quite as available. We weren't quite as consumer-driven," she told TechRepublic.[111] Her first constructions, made at the Perkins School for the Blind in Watertown, Massachusetts, in the 1980s, were activity trays and walls designed to keep musical instruments or lights, or blocks and cars, within the reach of a child with a visual impairment. "It would be like making a dashboard, where the cardboard worked as a way to hold fascinating, fun, curiosity-eliciting things," she says.[112]

The Adaptive Design Association's present-day work is deeply rooted in the recycled-paper, do-it-yourself tradition of the 1970s, one Truesdell is happy to see make its return via makerspaces and junk playgrounds. As with home improvement, a hands-on activity in the age of office work, it seems we have to come to the point of loss and estrangement from once-commonplace skills in order to value them again. Even manual training seems to be making a comeback. On a recent visit to the Blue School, an independent school in lower Manhattan, I admired the elementary school's carpentry workshop, a busy, dedicated space with a wall of tools and its own curriculum. First graders make number blocks, second graders make a yardstick, and so on, up to the sixth grade, where they make a wooden treasure box. The shop teacher, now called a STEAM specialist, for Science Technology Engineering Art and Mathematics, described to me the process of teaching kids to make a drawing—or at least a rough outline—before they start cutting, and to try to think about the time they have. "The design process is really fundamental to everything, from the first grade on up. Why are we even doing this? What's the point? What are our options? What material do we have? What can't we do? Those are good conversations for the kids to plan," Rob Gilson says.[113] Wood takes more strength and requires more tools, however, and much of what those kids are learning could be accomplished through cardboard in schools with a smaller budget or less space for a shop.

Truesdell caught the tail end of an American turn toward collective and inexpensive design, one that feels very far from contemporary children's consumer culture. Her project acknowledges that all children need furniture and space tailored to their every-changing needs, without buying in to cycles of planned obsolescence or denying children with disabilities a seat at the table. "People became less imaginative, because you bought the solution. And more helpless, because you didn't need to fix it, it was cheap to buy a replacement. And then, the people that could have repaired the clock, the chair, the whip, were fewer. And they needed to earn an income, so it was maybe more expensive."[114] As part of the ADA's emphasis on teaching, the nonprofit is also trying to pass skills on to its clients. The seat at the table is not merely for listening but for acting, so that children sometimes thought to be incapable of contributing can show what they are capable of do with the right tools.

The day before my visit, the conference table where we sat had played host to a class of elementary school–age children being taught to make small cardboard boxes by a class of high school students. "Winston Churchill apparently had a belief that there would be a lot more decency in the world if we shared," Truesdell says. "Our purpose is really to teach all of this. We've made lots and lots and lots of things, and we—as opposed to a network of trained cardboard carpenters—should not be making for that individual child necessarily." Unlike many MacArthur fellows who go on to TED Talks and the speaker circuit, Truesdell sticks close to her team and to the children who are her clients and lets others do the talking. "If it's going to outlast me, which it better, it means a whole lot of people have to be able to speak to it, in whatever way touches them."

CHAPTER 3

SCHOOL

The schoolhouse was a room made of new boards. Its ceiling was the underneath of shingles like the attic ceiling. Long benches stood one behind another down the middle of the room. They were made of planed boards. Each bench had a back, and two shelves stuck out from the back, over the bench behind. Only the front bench did not have any shelves in front of it, and the last bench didn't have any back.

There were two glass windows in each side of the schoolhouse. They were open, and so was the door. The wind came in, and the sound of waving grasses, and the smell and the sight of the endless prairie and the great light of the sky.

—Laura Ingalls Wilder, *On the Banks of Plum Creek* (1937)

There is a wealth of design information packed into this brief description of the Walnut Grove, Minnesota, schoolhouse where Mary and Laura Ingalls go to school for the first time in 1874. The family has recently moved from a sod house on the banks of Plum Creek (and before that, a log cabin) into their first home made of machine-sawed lumber, but most of their clothing and furniture and their few beloved toys remain homemade, by Ma and Pa. When Ma dresses the girls in their Sunday best that morning (blue-sprigged calico for Mary, red-sprigged for Laura), she is doing her utmost to make them blend in with the townspeople, with their store-bought clothes and dolls. Laura doesn't recognize chalk, the girls don't own a slate, and they share a single speller, saved from Ma's own childhood, so consistent has the curriculum been across the decades.

The school is as well built as their new house, its rows of benches made from more machined planks in a clever arrangement designed to save material by eliminating separate seats, and having the benches' backs double as a support for a shelf upon which to rest a book. Students are arranged by age and ability, so the unschooled Ingalls girls sit up front, Laura studying from the front of Ma's primer and Mary from the back. The single teacher calls students up, class by class, to recite what they have read. The rest of the time they "spell" themselves, studying a lesson in silence until they know it well enough to replay it. The windows let in the only light, and in winter, a stove at the front of the uninsulated room gives off the only heat. So rigid and repetitive was the arrangement of these one-room schools that nine years later, when Laura is in charge of one herself, it is considered a gala day when students are allowed to gather round the stove—lest they freeze in their seats.[1]

The design of this school—exactly the same as the design of every other school described in the Little House books, give or take a few benches— is a machine for a certain kind of education, transmitted without interpretation from a single adult to a room of any number of children. The literature of children's playthings is littered with construction metaphors and so, too, the literature of schooling is populated by attempts to quantify architecture's effect, often quoting Reggio Emilia founder Loris

Malaguzzi's statement that "environment is considered the third teacher."[2] And although "the little red schoolhouse" seems like a relic of the distant past, in 1913, half of American schoolchildren were still attending one of the country's 212,000 one-teacher schools. While the majority of these were in rural midwestern and western states—in 1936, 71 percent of Illinois schools were one-teacher—the last one-room schoolhouse in Connecticut was closed in 1957.[3] As nineteenth-century educators pushed for elementary schooling to become universal, rather than self-selecting, the school year lengthened and enrollments grew. New schools had two rooms, then four, a second story, and a central hallway. They took on the architecture of civic buildings, with porticos and columns, a sign that they were an institution as important as the post office or city hall. Children were separated into classrooms by age, and as individuals by furniture: By the mid-1870s, the desk with attached chair replaced the bench with attached shelf. Throughout this chapter, we will encounter various combinations of schoolrooms and school furniture, each molded to, as well as molded by, the dominant understanding of how best to teach. As children completed each primer, they would move farther from the teacher, so that everyone in a row would be studying the same book and could file forward as a class. In practice, this meant that the schoolroom was arranged from small to large, with the youngest children closest to the teacher and to the heat source. As the bigger children aged out of school in their early to mid-teens, the boys to farming, the girls to marriage or school teaching of their own, they moved closer and closer to the door, until finally they were free.

Pedagogy and architecture go hand in hand, as even the earliest American school reformers understood, and a new building cannot solve problems of disinvestment, segregation, and student performance. Innovations in education, as embodied by those buildings, have sometimes taken decades to transfer from private to public schools, from urban to rural locations, and from white to minority children. The housing discrimination discussed in the previous chapter has made school desegregation an ongoing challenge and has meant that most of the new ideas I want to highlight have been practiced on white children first. Access to equal education has been at the center of the twentieth-century civil rights movement, and buildings have been used as a bargaining chip. In this chapter, I will discuss both the thirty-five hundred Rosenwald Schools, built in the rural South between 1917 and 1932 and specifically designed to be lesser in appearance than white schools, and modernist schools built in New Orleans in the 1950s, specifically designed to be equal to, but still separate from, the city's white institutions. At the Rosenwald Schools, the curriculum included vocational training, seen as less threatening to white supremacy (which, before the Civil War, had kept many blacks illiterate). During the same period, public schools serving immigrant and Native American children were used as levers of assimilation, teaching English, Anglo American history and culture, and even in home economics classes cuisine. The school has to fit the teachers, and the teachers have to work with the school, so a history of American school design is inextricably entangled with politics as well as with fashions in education.

In 1968, *Parents* magazine took a "Last Look at the Little Red Schoolhouse" in Calaboose, Kentucky, and found that modern educators, some only two decades removed from attending such a school, were finding elements of the one-teacher education inspiring.[4] Nongrading, for example, which allowed children to be grouped by ability rather than age and to progress at their own rate, was a feature of a number of experimental school designs of the late 1960s. Bernard Ryan, the *Parents* photographer and reporter, also responded to the "affective tone" of the Calaboose classroom, where the teacher provided individualized and small-group learning and offered students autonomy to choose their own activities after they completed their work, in sharp contrast to the arrangement in Ingalls's day. Laura is taught, and teaches, by the recitation method, and never questions its wisdom.

Laura, it is established from that first day, is a quick learner, eager to catch on and catch up. Her greatest performance in the books, one of the few times she is allowed to be singled out for praise, is a cumulative recitation of American history, from Christopher Columbus through John Quincy Adams, in *Little Town on the Prairie*.[5] It is a feat of memory aided by the same kind of spatial structure as the schoolhouse, where *this* is learned at the first bench and *that* at the second. Laura marches forward through history, pointer in hand, guided by maps, illustrations, and each president's portrait.[6] This feat leads her to her first school-teaching job, a profession she accepts as her only option to earn a salary but never seems to love. The performance is intended to prove to the town that it needs something better than a one-room schoolhouse: a graded school, with classes for individual age groups, a symbol of its growing population and prosperity. As with children's toys and kids' rooms, the materials of educational space for children contain a message about cultural values. In Laura's childhood, obedience was paramount, a guard against the uncertainties of life outside the board walls. But education was also a value: Ma had been a schoolteacher, and she saw book learning as a hedge against the wilderness in which she was raising her children. (It was Pa who had the wanderlust.) The church, the school, the store, these marked a town on the vast prairies. School is both an actual structure and a civilizing one, teaching the girls reading, writing, and ciphering in the same manner it did generations of children across the American states.

•

IN THE ONE-ROOM schoolhouse, there are two pieces of design: the room and the seat. Moving forward through the history of American schools, these two elements, the container and its contents, become the object of invention and modification, transforming from anonymous patterns into patented, stylized, designer productions. In the one-room schoolhouse, the benches were fixed, the children moved: generations sitting on the same worn boards, learning from the same book. The lack of individuation in the system is baked into the design of the benches, where your desk is a board is attached to the seat back of the row in front of you and your chair is continuous with that of the child beside you. You and the others in your row are a "form," called up to recite for your teacher as a group, not as individuals. Even as the first patents were taken out on school furniture, in the 1870s, inventors maintained the interdependent relationship of the rows of seats and desks. The 1873 Cox and Fanning school desk model that is part of the National Museum of American History's collection has an iron armature decorated with pointed Gothic elements, an architectural style often associated with education due to its use in British institutions like Oxford and Cambridge.[7] A slatted wooden seat, with a curve that represents an early understanding of ergonomics, faces front and folds up, while a slanted wooden desk is attached to the back, for the use of the children in the row behind. Under the desktop, a shelf attached by more Gothic tracery gives the student storage for books. A groove at the top of the desk holds a pencil. The seat was intended to fold noiselessly, to cut down on classroom distractions when a form was called to the front. Nonetheless, the desk represents an advance in comfort on the benches in Ingalls's school, with its cupped seat and book storage; it also represents an advance in manufacturing, combining industrial ironwork and machined wood parts. The manufacturers' investment in design also reflects a new education economy: By the second half of the nineteenth century, many states had passed laws making schooling compulsory for children between the ages of eight and fourteen, with some variation. (Massachusetts was the first, in 1852, and Mississippi the last, in 1917.) By 1870—in cities, at least—every state had free elementary schools, which required equipment. Good-quality blackboards were installed at the front of the classroom and, by 1875, maps and globes had become standard.[8]

By the end of the nineteenth century, children started to move in more directions, and so did the furniture. From the long bench to fixed double desks, from desks to movable tables and chairs, from indoors to outdoors. In the 1880s, inventors patented the first desks that attached a work surface to the student's own seat, placing each child on a pedestal. John Glendenning's 1880 patent model design features slim iron uprights, grouped at the center to make a tulip shape, supporting a single chair and a boxed-in desk.[9] An iron rod along the floor attaches the two pieces front to back, and wooden supports keep it from tipping to the side. The top of the desk flips down for writing, and books (and surreptitiously passed notes) could be stored inside. The seat is made from a single piece of wood, again shaped for support, and the back of the chair is made from two boards angled to hug the lower back. This type of desk provides the template for most twentieth-century designs, which place each child on an island where all of their supplies—books, pencils, notebooks—should be ready to hand. It is these desks, in numerous iterations, that filled the classrooms of Progressive era and postwar schools, slowly improving in ergonomics but preserving essentially the same classroom organization: forward-facing, teacher-focused, largely immovable. Designers aimed to make the desks quiet, not light. In the 1950s, the elements of these desks became more streamlined, adjustable in height, and could be ordered in different colors, but the arrangement of seat and desk on two connected stalks remained the same. A 1957 American Seating ad shows a classroom

Sylvanus Cox and William W. Fanning's 1873 School Desk and Seat Patent Model. Oak, brass, 8¼ x 6¼ x 8dz (20.955 x 15.875 x 20.32 cm). [Archives Center, National Museum of American History, Smithsonian Institution]

transported outdoors, with the rows of desks, in Easter shades of pink and blue, surrounded by beds of flowers. "If your school furniture were on display every day like this . . . you'd buy American Seating furniture every time!"[10] One innovation, in the 1960s, was the rise of the wraparound desk, typically made with a plastic seat, metal frame, and laminate writing surface. The storage element moved to a basket below the seat, while the L-shaped top offered support for the arms of the right-handed— unless administrators were forward-thinking enough to order a few for the left-handed. These desks had the benefit of being light enough to move, so students could rearrange the classroom into smaller work circles and bring their writing surface with them.

In 2010, Steelcase, a longtime manufacturer of furniture for education, introduced the Node chair, designed by IDEO, which puts the student's all-in-one on wheels. Fast Company writes, of the context for the new chair: "If you've spent any time in a schoolroom in the last 15 years, you're

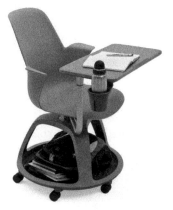

DSS Plastic Stacking Chair with Table Arm, Charles and Ray Eames. Manufacturer: Herman Miller Furniture Company. 1960-1961. Fiberglass, steel, plastic laminate, wood, nylon, 24½ x 19½ x 32 in. (62.2 x 49.5 x 81.3 cm). [Courtesy Herman Miller]

Node Classroom Chair with Wheels. Manufacturer: Steelcase. 2010. [Courtesy Steelcase]

familiar with the high-pitched whine of metal scraping against linoleum, as students rearrange their chairs and desks to whatever activity is going on. It seems like a minor annoyance, but it's a serious design problem: School furniture was largely designed 50 years ago for static, face-forward teaching. It isn't suited to the myriad forms of teaching that take place in the modern classroom."[11] With the Node, you can start to envision the slick classroom floor as a skating rink or dance studio, with the teacher as choreographer of chairs moving in concert into rows, circles, duets, and corralled into a corner at the end of the day. And you wouldn't be far off: The teacher, or team of teachers, in a school that embraces project-based learning is constantly shifting the activities and groupings within her classroom, from front-of-the-room instruction to small-group learning to individual meetings. Where once the students were fixed or moved in straight lines, now a well-run classroom requires flow. More dystopically, the curved lines and bright colors of the Node remind me of a 1960s aesthetic of the future, like the pods in which earthlings zip about their Starliner in the movie *Wall-E*, grown fat and blubbery because they never have to walk.

The Node chair mobilizes the seat, unfixing it from the traditional row. An alternative design disruption focused on the desk, merging the individual work surface into more collaborative tables. In 1930, philanthropist Edward Harkness wrote to the head of Phillips Exeter Academy in New Hampshire about how he would like his $5.8 million donation to the school to be used.[12] "What I have in mind," instructed Harkness, "is teaching boys in sections of about eight in a section . . . where boys could sit around a table with a teacher who would talk with them and instruct them by a sort of tutorial or conference method, where the average or below average boy would feel encouraged to speak up . . . and the teacher would know . . . what his difficulties were . . . This would be a real revolution in methods.[13] Learning, Harkness thought, should evolve from discussions, questions, and statements from all directions, rather than lectures delivered from the front of the room. The rigid system of rows that had allowed a single teacher to run a town school on the American frontier had now been adapted to consolidated urban schools, with classrooms separated by grade, but why should smaller groups of children be taught in the same manner? Exeter promptly hired more teachers—seminars require significantly more personnel—but it took longer to restructure the classrooms around a new piece of purpose-built furniture: a short oval table, made of wood, with twelve "slides" hidden under its protruding lip. The Harkness Table, still in production, proved to be a truly transformative technology, albeit one whose use is limited to schools that can offer small, discussion-based classes. Teacher and students were physically at the same level, sharing the same surface. There was a place for everyone at the table, with no bad seats and no back row in which to hide.[14]

School treasurer Corning Benton was the table's designer, and it took several prototypes to get it right. His first thought was the round table: nonhierarchical, where everyone was an equal, but set for twelve it also created a vast empty expanse in the middle. It was hard to dust, hard to communicate across, and hard to move around the room. The second version, a long table with curved ends, put the teacher at the head but made it hard for those on the sides to talk to one another. The final version was a narrower oval, curved all around, with no no-man's-land in the center. Slides—flat boards that could be pulled out from under the table—were used for quizzes, the one time when students need to turn their backs to each other. The first tables, too wide to fit through the doors of the school's classrooms, had to be built on-site. The wooden version was adopted at a number of American schools; the headmaster of the Lawrenceville School in New Jersey applied directly to Harkness to fund the tables, renovated classrooms, and new teachers. But the Harkness method of teaching through discussion had a much greater reach, radiating out from the table but not necessarily including the actual artifact.

Schools on a smaller budget broke down the oval into other, more modular geometric shapes. Once a Harkness Table is installed in a classroom, it fixes the room to that method and is as inflexible, in its own democratic way, as rows of desks. The trapezoidal tables of my open-plan middle school in the 1970s hinted at a brave new order, cellular rather than gridded. Creative Playthings catalogs of the 1960s included these tables among other school furniture. Copy for the Trapezoidal read, "Independent research and team studies will play important roles in the period ahead. We must develop in children resources for working independently, as well as in groups." In such groups, "children participate more actively and teachers relate better."[15] We held seminars around a hexagon. When we took tests we were assigned places, one to a side, around the trapezoid. We lined the trapezoids up, short side toward the teacher, for two-by-two direct instruction. The hexagonal tables created what little architecture there was within the large open volume of my school, one of hundreds constructed during the 1970s that reflected a broader interest in letting children shape the space of their own education, making the classroom itself a collaborative project described by a new vocabulary of pod, area, unit, and suite.[16] In my Quaker education, we all went by our first names, classes occasionally took the form of choose-your-own-adventure games, and we learned Greek mythology by acting out the gods. The trapezoidal tables provided a flexible platform from which physical, multidirectional learning could spring.

Open-plan schools questioned the very idea of a classroom, but flexible furniture entered the educational vocabulary much earlier. In the early 1950s, the Brunswick Corporation began to sell stackable, colorful chairs, in metal and plywood or plastic, that were unmoored from desks and intended to "[turn] your classrooms into *living rooms for learning*."[17] At a time when the living room was itself under scrutiny, with heavy and traditional furniture being replaced by the lightweight and modular, the classroom was to follow. A Brunswick ad of the era shows a cheerful modern classroom featuring large windows with built-in storage underneath, with student chairs arranged in a variety of learning modes: set at lightweight individual desks, around a circular table, and in front of the teacher's desk. The staging suggests three different learning events happening at the same time. Caudill Rowlett Scott, a firm that specialized in postwar school design, created a teaching-space divider for a school in Laredo, Texas, with modular four-foot square panels to hold shelves, easels, a chalkboard, or a pinup wall. As with so many childhood innovations, the divider was first tested at home, where architect William W. Caudill built a mock-up for his nine-year-old daughter.[18] These pieces were the forerunners for the open school's accordion-pleat walls and rolling cabinets, innovations embraced and then discarded, because who really does want to rearrange the furniture multiple times a day? While most American classrooms stuck to rows, the model for new postwar schools was taken from experiments by John Dewey in the early part of the century that were eventually adapted into modernist school designs by Richard Neutra; Perkins, Wheeler & Will; and Eliel and Eero Saarinen, all of which will be described later in the chapter. Photographs from a 1921 handbook on school architecture show a kindergarten with child-size chairs and desks in one area, a workbench in another, and a number of students playing with blocks and a doll on the floor in the center of the room.[19] In *The Child-Centered School* (1928), authors Harold Rugg and Ann Shumaker write, "Informality, flexibility, freedom, mark the use of the [physical] plant in the new school. A classroom, depending upon the interests of the children using it, may be successively a shop, a studio, a bank, a store, a farm, a whole city, or a place to cook and dine. Certain activities requiring the use of specialized tools, to be sure, are localized."[20] Classroom furniture no longer meant desks in rows but tables, chairs, easels, workbenches, storage, as complicated, in many ways, as furnishing the all-in-one room of a house. The classroom and school building will also transform, in the chapter that follows, from a simple, stove-warmed box to a complex organism, sheltering, spinning, and encircling the schoolchild.

•

In the United States today schooling is thoroughly identified with the special place in which formal teaching and learning occur. So intimate is the link between schooling and the schoolhouse that in the 1960s "schools without walls," where pupils learn while associating with adults in everyday environments, were hailed as revolutionary.

—William W. Cutler III, "Cathedral of Culture: The Schoolhouse in American Thought and Practice Since 1821" (1989)[21]

As EARLY AS 1838, one-room schoolhouses were under attack. Architects and educators worked in concert from the early nineteenth century on, believing school architecture could galvanize popular support for universal education, as well as improve the experience of students within a school's walls. Henry Barnard, secretary of the boards of education in Connecticut and Rhode Island, wrote in the pattern book *School Architecture* (1850) that the current buildings "are, almost universally, badly located, exposed to the noise, dust and danger of the highway, unattractive, if not positively repulsive in their external and internal experience."[22] Barnard proposed a design by Horace Mann, secretary of the Massachusetts Board of Education, as the model for future schoolhouses. In Mann's plan, the teacher sat at the front of the room on a raised platform in front of fifty-six separate desks. Windows lined the side walls, and there were two blackboards behind the podium. Connecting schooling to the design of schools made architecture a partner in the learning process and helped transform teachers—often poorly paid teenagers or young adults—into masters worthy of respect and funding. Mann believed that universal public education "would do more than all things else to obliterate factitious distinctions in society," bringing the country closer to its democratic ideals.[23]

In 1847, Mann and Barnard created one of the first graded schools in Quincy, Massachusetts. While other schools of the period included one or two large rooms with a seat for every child, the Quincy Grammar School was divided into a dozen classrooms, over three floors, allowing for more supervision and more direct instruction, with a gymnasium on top.[24] The whole school met only for "devotional services, and other general exercises." Graded schools, according to Barnard, created a quieter and less distracting schoolroom experience, with teachers able to vary their method, freed from hearing dozens of recitations in a day. Advanced students could move on to a different classroom with minimal disruption, slower students wouldn't hold back an entire grade, and teachers were insulated from burnout and high turnover. This experiment was so successful that by 1855 every Boston grammar school was divided by grades, as were primary schools by 1860. The standard classroom was twenty-eight feet square, with desks for fifty-six children.[25] Boards of education in Philadelphia and St. Louis also built graded schools in the 1840s and 1850s, and other major cities followed suit in the 1860s. Among cities, only New York continued to build schoolhouses with central study halls and separate recitation rooms.

Even as childhood was recognized as a stage of human development, deserving of protection and requiring an investment in education, its years were still circumscribed for families who relied on their children's incomes to survive. The U.S. Census Bureau estimated that 765,000 children ages ten to fifteen were "gainfully employed" in 1870 (one out of every eight children), 1,990,000 in 1910, and 1,061,000 in 1920.[26] During the post–Civil War period, attendance at public high schools was extremely low; by 1890, only approximately 6 percent of American fourteen- to seventeen-year-olds were enrolled in high school. Most of these children were middle and upper class, the only economic groups that could be spared entry into the workforce for another four years. The curriculum at high schools during this period was also fairly specialized, based on the classical model and eschewing the practical and vocational; job training was learned through apprenticeships.[27] Progressive reformers saw child labor as antithetical to this new conception of childhood and worked to get children off the job and into schools. Their efforts were linked to the work of settlement houses, like Jane Addams's Hull House in Chicago, which provided social and educational opportunities for members of the local community, particularly women and children. In the 1890s, different states adopted child labor laws limiting the age at which children could legally be employed and the number of hours they could work each day. These laws were often paired with compulsory-attendance legislation, which focused on keeping children in school until the age of twelve, fourteen, or sixteen. By 1918, most states had some level of mandatory attendance, leading to a vast increase in the number of students in public elementary schools during the first two decades of the twentieth century. The Keating-Owen Child Labor Act of 1916, a federal attempt to ban child labor, failed, and the country only passed the uniform Fair Labor Standards Act during the Depression.

In response to the influx of students, construction of new schools, with a civic presence and close attention to hygiene, accelerated after the turn of the twentieth century, and many proved to be so sturdy that they are still in use. My own children's Brooklyn school, built in 1921, follows a pattern set by the New York City Board of Education in the 1890s, when the department of school architecture was led by C. B. J. Snyder. Snyder, like his Chicago Board of Education contemporary Dwight H. Perkins, focused his attention on better light, air, and sanitation, creating a classroom whose plan was not unlike the one-room schoolhouse, but which could be lined up and stacked without loss of quality. Snyder said that he hoped "to make the school building itself quite as much a factor in education as the textbooks."[28] Classrooms began to take on a standardized format, designed to increase light and air quality. Individual desks were set in rows perpendicular to a window wall.[29] Daylight from over the student's left shoulder was found to be optimal to prevent shadows on their work and glare at the front of the room. Windows should cover 40 to 50 percent of that wall and start three and a half feet above the floor to avoid lateral glare, and the width of the room should not be more than twice the windows' height so that light would reach the inner wall of the room. Perkins typically handled this requirement with five vertical "ribbon windows," separated by narrow masonry piers, which he described as "factory-like."[30] A how-to article of 1916 set the ideal classroom at twenty-three by twenty-nine feet, with twelve-foot ceilings; a survey of schools in 1933 found the same result in practice, with variations of only a foot or so in either direction. Today, when architects and educators have so many more resources at their disposal, light and air quality, good acoustics, and an appropriate number of students per room still top the list of positive attributes for school design. The causal relationship between student achievement and other design factors is likely too complex to isolate.[31]

Alongside the improved classroom, these new schools added purpose-built rooms that spoke to the broader role of the curriculum and the school building's place in the community. William B. Ittner, official architect of the board of education in St. Louis, argued for the modern school as a civic monument, contributing to the "aesthetic development of the community." The Philadelphia Regional Plan of 1932 also referenced school buildings and grounds as "places of inspiration," reflecting a general belief in the elevating power of grand architecture.[32] Schoolyards were open after hours and on weekends. Evening lectures in the new auditoriums attracted adults. Libraries, gymnasiums, and auditoriums were part of new facilities, and they continued to be open after hours until the Great Depression made it difficult to fund the additional staff and programming. These community facilities were typically arranged symmetrically, flanking ceremonial lobbies and staircases, giving the schools the civic prominence of libraries, town halls, and churches. In the standardized plans Perkins developed for the Chicago schools, he placed the ground-floor auditorium across from the main entrance, making it easy to access after-hours; later, school libraries joined those assembly rooms. Vocational classrooms, used as workshops for manual training or labs for domestic science during the day, could be used for adult classes at night.[33] In subsequent schools, Perkins also moved kindergartens to the first floor, ratifying a pattern of minimizing the distance between the front door of the school and the classrooms for the youngest students that continues today. Recreation spaces including vegetable gardens and playgrounds with climbing equipment were also incorporated into his Chicago standards. In 1915 Perkins wisely suggested combining the Chicago park and school boards in order to more easily collocate facilities.[34]

Most schools built during the first decades of the twentieth century were dressed in historic architectural styles, with neoclassical columns, Gothic stone parapets, or mansard roofs. On urban sites, schools were built up to a maximum of five stories (deemed the highest people would climb without elevators). Snyder, the New York City schools architect, created the H-plan to deal with midblock sites, stacking classrooms against the party walls of existing buildings and connecting the school buildings across the center, but leaving two open courts for light, air, and play. Snyder also specified large windows, central heating, indoor plumbing, fireproof materials, and fire escapes. DeWitt Clinton High School (1906), one of his designs and the largest high school of its day, is a five-story building with an elaborate triple-arched entrance, leading to one of two midblock courtyards, and a cornice with elaborate, almost royalist points. Snyder believed in regulating health and safety, but he decried the sameness of school plans and facades, arguing that as schools are not factories, to standardize them would be "to standardize education itself," treating students as widgets.[35] He also introduced movable furniture into kindergarten rooms, recognizing that this stage of childhood, at least, required a different format.

Students in the new schools had ergonomic, silent-closing desks, a glare-free look at the chalkboard, and respite from the classroom in specialized spaces like science labs, machine shops, and domestic science kitchens. But most instruction was still highly regimented in content and activity. John Dewey, the educational reformer and founder of the University of Chicago's Laboratory School, and later associated with the Lincoln School at Columbia University Teachers College, described the traditional classroom in this way: "If we put before the mind's eye the ordinary schoolroom, with its rows of ugly desks placed in geometrical order, crowded together so that there should be as little moving room as possible, desks almost all of the same size, with just space enough to hold books, pencils, and paper, and add a table, some chairs, the bare walls, and possibly a few pictures, we can reconstruct the only educational activity that can possibly go on in such a place. It is all made 'for listening.' "[36] Rooms like these, in Dewey's view, treated all children as the same, and yet "the moment children act they individualize themselves." In order to break the rigidity of the traditional classroom structure, he saw the school as a node in a network of child-centered architecture including homes, parks, libraries, and museums. Learning should not take place only in the room, and it was not solely transferred from teacher to student. Within the classroom's walls, he wanted to break up the rows: Photographs of the Lincoln School in the 1910s and 1920s show rooms arranged as they would be in the modernist schools of the 1930s through the 1950s, with lightweight furniture, storage for learning materials other than books, seats by the window, and blackboards and bulletin boards ready for student work.

Dewey organized his students' day around "occupations"—the same language used by followers of Froebel—where children could cook, garden, carpenter, and weave. But unlike Froebel, Dewey provided play materials that were realistic, giving children real duties with tangible results.[37] The home became a particular area of study, with brooms, mops, irons, and dishes part of most classrooms. Children washed doll clothes and made snacks for their class, sweeping up the crumbs afterward. A sandbox, a workbench, puzzles, and painting easels also became part of the classroom furniture. Dewey's wife, Alice, wrote that in the early years of the Lab School, "people announced that the University was running a school for teaching children to sew and bake in order that their mothers might teach them to read at home."[38] In addition to giving children freedom to act, Dewey put the development of the school's course of study and administration in the hands of its teachers, writing, "The teachers started with question-marks, rather than with fixed rules, and if any answers have been reached, it is the teachers in the school who have supplied them."[39] Althea Harmer, textile instructor at the Lab School, used domestic arts and sciences to teach children history: "The child's understanding of the daily life of a people is vivified by reproducing their typical occupations," she wrote. "This realization of their daily struggles is insured by his use of the actual materials and methods of their time."[40] Dewey's ideas, promulgated through texts like *The School and Society* (1900), did eventually influence educational architecture.

•

WHILE URBAN AND immigrant children had the opportunity to attend school in newly constructed buildings, African American children in the American South in the early twentieth century still had extremely limited educational opportunities, attending school for a few weeks a year in old buildings with poorly trained teachers. Booker T. Washington, then principal of the Tuskegee Institute, concocted a plan to remedy that situation, based on his philosophy of self-help and aided by strategic philanthropy. Historically, African American communities had built their own schools and churches, without public funding. In 1912 Washington proposed to build six rural schools around Tuskegee, Alabama, with funding from Julius Rosenwald, who had made a fortune through his nationwide expansion of Sears, Roebuck and Co. stores and was a new Tuskegee trustee. Rosenwald initially proposed that the schools be standardized and sold as kits, like Sears's famous kit houses, but Washington thought local participation was key.[41] The Rosenwald Fund would contribute one-third of the cost; interested communities would raise another third in cash, labor, or building materials; and the final third would be contributed by the white-run school boards. Once the schools were built, they were to be handed over to the school boards. As architectural historian Mabel O. Wilson writes, "The fact that black Americans had to pay for even part of their schools was a stark reminder of the unequal distribution of state education monies."[42] The education students would receive at the so-called Rosenwald Schools was a practical one, intended to teach literacy and basic arithmetic, with vocational training for agriculture and trades for boys and home economics for girls. Many blacks at the time had mixed feelings about the structure of the program: It did not challenge Jim Crow laws or previous neglect of African Americans by the public schools but set up a parallel set of institutions, paid for by private funds but donated back to that white, public system.[43] Limiting the schools' curriculum to vocational education was also a strategy intended to make educating the African American population more palatable to white school boards. Six schools were built in 1912, and they proved successful enough for the program to continue; by the time of Rosenwald's death in 1932, which ended the building, there were more than five thousand schools across fifteen southern states, from Virginia to Texas. By 1928, one of every five schools in the South was a Rosenwald School.

It was important to the schools' planners that they achieve the same standard in school design as the white schools being built at the time. Professional architects and educators prepared plans that reflected current thinking on the correct environment for education and offered them free to community members. Robert Robinson Taylor, the first black graduate of MIT and the architect of more than twenty buildings on the Tuskegee campus, contributed to the 1915 booklet *The Negro Rural School and Its Relation to the Community*. A follow-up, *Community School Plans*, written by Samuel L. Smith and Fletcher B. Dresslar, was published in 1920 and updated thereafter. Dresslar emphasized utility in school buildings—simple vernacular construction with good proportions and a minimum of ornament. Since the schools were to be built remotely by a variety of hands, the plans needed to be clear and familiar. "The Rosenwald Schools may have looked traditional, but they incorporated many design innovations," writes architecture critic Witold Rybczynski:

> The classrooms were often separated by movable partitions so they could be combined into one large space. The most common arrangement was two classrooms, an adjacent "industrial room" for shop and cooking classes, as well as vestibules and cloakrooms. (So-called community schools had more classrooms, and included an auditorium as well as a library.) Classrooms had tall ceilings and exceptionally large double-hung windows, typically arranged in batteries for maximum daylighting, which was crucial since many of the sites lacked electricity. East and west light was favored and building orientation was emphasized. "It is better to have proper lighting within the schoolroom, however, than to yield to the temptation to make a good show by having the long side face the road," instructed the Tuskegee handbook. Cross-ventilation was facilitated by "breeze windows"—internal openings—and the buildings were raised off the ground on piers to facilitate cooling.[44]

Each classroom had a large blackboard and thirty to forty modern desks, with attached chairs and movable lids, along with separate cloakrooms for boys and girls. Walls were to have dark-painted wainscoting, to mask scuffs, but to be light-colored above to augment the daylighting from the windows. Historian Mary S. Hoffschwelle emphasizes the contrast students must have felt, in these light, up-to-date buildings, between their homes and schools. She also reports that one contractor, chair of the white school board in an Alabama district, ceased work on a school when he realized "it would be better than the white schoolhouse."[45]

The most famous Rosenwald School, architecturally speaking, is one that was never built, designed by Frank Lloyd Wright. Darwin D. Martin, Wright's longtime Buffalo patron, was a friend of Rosenwald's, and in 1928 he convinced Wright to design a school for a site at the historically black Hampton Normal and Agricultural Institute in Virginia. Wright designed a courtyard school with a swimming pool, a children's theater with an M-shaped roof and feathery detailing over the doors, and classrooms lit by pointed dormer windows, transforming one of the pattern book's standard plans. Fieldstone walls and shingle roofs added to the fairy-tale effect—the exact opposite of the brisk, functional style of the existing schools. In a letter to Martin, Wright acknowledged that the courtyard and pool would increase the cost, but he said it would "be worth it—Physical Culture should be 3/5 of 'Education.'"[46] Wright was familiar with the ideas of early twentieth-century educational reformers, both via his own Froebelian education and his Chicago milieu. John and Evelyn Dewey featured his Coonley Playhouse in their 1915 book *Schools of To-morrow*, and in 1926 Wright had designed a series of fieldhouses for Oak Park, called "kinder-symphonies," which combined playrooms and wading pools and were adorned with balloon-like light fixtures. The reaction to his school design, from Hampton, was negative.

The courtyard plan was fine, but the outside was deemed "an entire misfit." As Wilson writes, "The typical Rosenwald School was not only austere as disciplinary reinforcement, but its simplicity ensured the schools appeared inferior to ones for white children."[47] But their simplicity masked their technology, providing African American children with a layout, as a sort of educational minimum, that was equally conducive to learning. The Rosenwald Schools reflect the Progressive Era emphasis on healthy buildings through light and air, and the latest understanding of how to organize a classroom. Some larger schools did feint toward a greater public presence, albeit without Wright's drama: A "Six Teacher Community School," with a plan shaped like an H, had a central public auditorium and could offer that space plus a stage-slash-meeting room for public events. A broad front porch established the school as a welcoming place, with a civic presence, in rural areas dominated by small domestic structures.[48] These buildings did not have the monumentality or centrality of white schools and were not built in urban centers; they were separate and unequal, despite the decision in *Plessy v. Ferguson*. The ambitions for both container (the school) and contents (the curriculum) had been scaled down in order to pass, a strategy that did not diminish the effectiveness of the design and proved successful in extending public education to tens of thousands of children. After the *Brown v. Board of Education* decision in 1954, the Rosenwald buildings became instantly obsolete, and many, worn by decades of use, were torn down. Since 2002, however, the National Trust for Historic Preservation has provided assistance toward the preservation of the approximately eight hundred that remain, interpreting them as symbols of progress, however halting, rather than oppression.

•

By the 1930s, Dewey's "whole child" approach had become mainstream. He and other Progressive educators stressed that public education ought to pay attention to children's physical and psychological development as well as their academic success. Dewey's ideas about shaking up the internal classroom structure were reflected in new plans for schools and new theories about their buildings' architectural role in the city. Modern architecture, only recently introduced to America, came to be seen as part of the solution to the problem of authoritarian, one-size-fits-all schools. The new style, built around functional concerns about light, air, and cleanliness, seemed appropriate for children, especially given modernism's preference for low-to-the-ground buildings. The idea of an outdoor classroom, doubling the instruction space by pairing gardens with rooms, became a linchpin of innovative school design from the 1930s through the 1960s. The new buildings took advantage of steel frames and other twentieth-century building materials, resulting in lighter, larger structures. This change in materials and aesthetics—modern architecture was seen as more affordable and efficient—continued into the postwar school-building boom, where pent-up demand met a baby boom that brought ten million new children into the public school system from 1950 to 1960, and again from 1960 to 1970. In 1955, the editors at *Architectural Forum* wrote, "Every 15 minutes enough babies are born to fill another classroom and we are already 250,000 classrooms behind."[49] As the system scrambled to catch up, and architects looked around for models to replicate, no school's design was more influential than that of the Crow Island School in Winnetka, Illinois.

Carleton Washburne, superintendent of schools in Winnetka from 1919 to 1943, could often be found in the front row at kindergarten assemblies, seated in a child's chair with his knees up to his chin. When it came time to build a new school in his district, it was only natural that he wanted his architect to work from a child's perspective. "The building must not be too beautiful, lest it be a place for children to keep and not one for them to use. Its materials must be those not easily marred, and permitting of some abuse. The finish and settings must form harmonious background with honest child effort and creation—not one which will make children's work seem crude," wrote Frances Presler, director of activities for the school.[50] So their young architect, Lawrence Perkins, went out and learned from children. "I had to figure out what happened in a classroom, and why a normal classroom wouldn't work in Winnetka," he told an interviewer in 1987.[51] He went to classes at the town's two old three-story schools and new one-story schools, built in the early 1920s, which had outdoor access from almost every classroom. To attract the children's attention, he would draw characters from the popular Dutch Twins books written by his mother, Lucy Fitch Perkins, and then ask the kids questions. They hated that the classroom doors had windows, which allowed adults to spy on them. They hated waiting in line for the bathroom. They needed running water for art projects and a comfortable seat for story time. Perkins interviewed teachers, parents, and the maintenance staff too. The janitors wanted easy cleanup, including recessed lockers, flat skylights, and heating coils under the front steps to melt snow in winter. Washburne wanted each class to be an independent unit and to have its own yard. Presler wanted a separate room devoted to role-playing pioneer life, making candles, carding wool, and cooking in a working fireplace connected to the building's tall chimney (a school tradition for third graders that persists to the present day). Teachers needed a flexible classroom, as each day's work required six different conditions for learning, including sitting at a desk, listening as a group, doing individual or group activities, and performing basic physical tasks like hanging up coats or using the bathroom.[52]

When Washburne had taken over in Winnetka, although still in his twenties, he had restructured the elementary school curriculum, incorporating John Dewey's child-centered philosophy but adding an

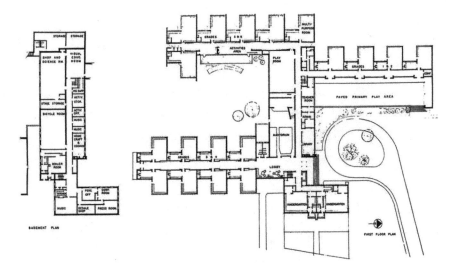

Plan, Crow Island School, Winnetka IL, 1940, Perkins+Will, Inc. with Eliel & Eero Saarinen.
[Courtesy Perkins+Will]

academic component that he thought more suitable for students out of kindergarten. After graduation from Stanford University in 1912, Washburne was hired by Frederic Burk, a San Francisco–based educator who advocated for an end to the grade system in schools, allowing children to learn at their own pace.[53] Washburne's so-called Winnetka Plan (by 1925, the Winnetka Educational Press had begun to publish the self-instruction books for other schools) had "common essentials" like arithmetic, reading, writing, history, and geography taught through workbooks and frequent testing. Passing grades would allow students to move ahead, a failure would require a return to the workbook for more explanation and exercises. While this regime sounds rather grim—a longtime teacher described the "brown arithmetic books" as "the most didactic things you ever saw"[54]—half of each day was reserved for more creative group activities around art, science, and social studies. In the early years at Crow Island, these were organized by Presler. Science classes did experiments, growing plants, caring for animals, taking field trips. Social studies classes built Native American structures like hogans and pueblos. There were creative writing exercises and a choral program. Each of these activities needed a different sort of space, whether in the classroom or in community rooms like the auditorium or gym. What developed, from an unusual partnership between architectural royalty like the Saarinens and Perkins learning on the job, was a classroom design and school organization that would influence American education for the next three decades.

The Winnetka school board had approved a bond to build a new school in the northwest corner of the district in April 1928, but the Depression put construction on hold until 1937, when a site on Willow Road was purchased and Washburne began his search for an architect. The site was mostly marshland, with one piece of high, dry ground on which crows would congregate, known as "crow island." Representatives of thirty-five firms visited Washburne at his superintendent's office during the search. His goal for the school, as he wrote to Perkins, a local architect with a three-year-old firm and an interest in education, was for "it to be the most functional and beautiful school in the world. We want it to crystallize in architecture the best educational practices we can evolve."[55] Washburne's willingness to meet with Perkins at all can be ascribed to Perkins's connections: His father, Dwight H. Perkins, had been the architect for the Chicago Public Schools between 1905 and 1910, and the younger Perkins had designed a house for a prominent publisher who was friends with a number of board members. Washburne could not, he wrote, entrust the task to "youngsters who have only built one house and one small church"— referring to Perkins and his partners, E. Todd Wheeler and Philip Will. Perkins argued that their young firm would give the school far more time and thought than an established one. Washburne acknowledged the point, but he had a suggestion: What if the enthusiasm of the young could be married to the skill of a legend like Eliel Saarinen?[56] At the end of their meeting, Perkins promised to get Saarinen, then promptly forgot his promise. A few days later he received a call from the president of the school board, who said he would be in Detroit and would like to meet Saarinen. Perkins called Saarinen—with trepidation—and explained the project. "I do not *do* Gothic or colonial," said Saarinen, then best known for his design of the Cranbrook Schools, north of Detroit, where he was also head of the architecture department. Perkins assured him that the Winnetka school board was interested in something original. Saarinen agreed to the meeting and, after further discussions, a fifty-fifty partnership to execute the commission.

Crow Island School opened in September 1940 with fourteen classrooms and almost three hundred students. While additions have been made over the years, the visitor's first impression is largely as it was seventy-five years ago. Before you even step through the doors at Crow Island, you know that the design is, as Presler would have it, "childlike—not what adults think of children."[57] A long stone bench built into the brick wall on the porch outside the kindergarten entrance is there for children who come early or stay late, visible from inside via the lobby and from outside via the circular drive. The three-pane glass doors bring the transparency all the way down to the ground, so there's no chance of hitting a small child with an emphatic push. The generous lobby beyond offers space to get your bearings: the kindergarten to your left, the auditorium to your right, and a long double-loaded corridor before you, leading to upper-grade classrooms. The lobby is furnished with comfortable chairs, like a modern living room, and has floor-to-ceiling glass on the east side, so it is flooded with light in the morning. On the brick wall on the south side of the lobby, just above a long sofa, you can see the only interior artworks not made by the school's pupils: terra-cotta bas-reliefs by sculptor Lily Swann Saarinen, a Cranbrook graduate who was then Eero Saarinen's wife, showing Noah, pairs of animals, and the dove carrying a green sprig in its beak, a symbol of hope. The reliefs, none bigger than an adult hand, are arranged asymmetrically on the brick wall, as if they grew there. In general, however, the building's materials are left to speak for themselves, as was Presler's request: "We suggested that there be no illustrative frieze decoration as the means of *presenting* the place to children . . . lest it designate too definite form of creation thereby inhibiting instead of encouraging child expression."[58] From the 1930s on, one sees in discussion of décor for children the repeated argument that adult-made illustration quashes child creativity, and an argument for plainness, or at least abstraction, in any added ornament.

Signs that the architects have taken their perspective from waist height are everywhere: The water fountain is low, the light switches are low, the door handles, low. The classroom doors are painted, as they have always been, in primary colors, so that preliterate children can find their way to their own yellow, red, or blue door. In the interests of safety and durability, the bricks at the corners where hallways meet are curved, and three wooden handrails curve with them, all the way down the hallway, providing a perfect place to line up or lean. Eliel Saarinen suggested exposing the brick, inside and out, as a gesture toward economy and practicality, copying the low-maintenance detail he had used at Cranbrook. At the base of the interior walls, a course of glazed dark red soldier brick sits below the golden, unglazed common brick. The glazed bricks do not absorb dirt from the water in mop buckets. The three wooden rails were also his suggestion, to soften the long masonry wall at child height.[59] The wall opposite the brick is faced in vertical wood paneling of ponderosa pine, soft enough to bear the staples of the ages with grace. Here is the frame for children's efforts and creations, here are the materials permitting wear, here is the childlike setting Presler imagined, not pandering but cradling.

The classrooms—the center of educational innovation—offer a more concentrated version of the same: wood-paneled walls waiting for artwork but now doing double duty as cabinets for supplies. Presler wrote, "The atmosphere of these rooms which particularly are the school homes, should give feeling of security. These are especially the places of living together and should express home-likeness."[60] The original classroom was L shaped, an organization Perkins credited to John Boyce, an employee at Perkins, Wheeler & Will. The ceilings were nine feet, rather than the more typical twelve. Materials were stored in cupboards, bins, and shelves that the children could reach, and the students could sit on those child-size Eames and Saarinen chairs. A long storage bench along the two-sided window wall provided a gathering place for story time or a work surface for children sitting on the floor. The L included a bathroom and washbasin, so children didn't have to use a large communal facility, as well as a sink and a wet bar to make experiments with food, paint, and mud easier to keep under control. Teachers now use these rooms for science experiments, large-scale building projects, or as technology centers. The classroom was meant to be able to serve, particularly in the lower grades, as the child's whole world, with the larger and communal school facilities there when needed.

The classroom was shown as a model, complete with miniature furnishings (some made of wooden blocks) at the Museum of Modern Art in 1942 as part of the exhibition *Modern Architecture for the Modern School.* Curator Elizabeth Mock wrote that the school should go further than providing space, light, and air: "It should be a place where the child can feel that he belongs, where he can move in freedom, and where he can enjoy immediate contact with the outdoors."[61] The schools in the exhibit, built from 1934 to 1942, were all chosen to illustrate, as she wrote, updated versions of "the little red schoolhouse of our forefathers." The sense of belonging Mock mentions was created, in the classroom setting, by the scale of the furniture and fittings and by the domesticity of materials. The same low-lying amenities here expanded to include child-size tables and chairs and a long storage bench along the two window walls. The bench, whose bins hold blocks and other toys, can be either a construction surface or a seat.

Kindergartners at the Crow Island School have their own entrance and their own playground, as well as a kitchen with a dairy counter set up to dispense glasses of wholesome milk. "One general principle weathered the strains of discussion and argument," Perkins wrote in 1942. "It was that children of primary-school ages are not ready for participation in groups larger than a class unit. They simply cannot comprehend and be loyal to a social setup of that complexity. Therefore, the class unit should be as complete a home as possible."[62] First and second grades cluster in one wing, with a broad, partly sheltered play terrace just across the hall from the lockers holding their coats and the door to the outside. Second and third graders are in a separate hall, closer to the library and auditorium, with access to a larger, undefined playground. The landscape was designed by Robert Everly and John McFadzean, who balanced lawn, plantings, and play structures in areas that included the first jungle gym. "But that is an ideal piece of school playground equipment. It can take care of many children in a small area. It satisfies every child's desire to climb. It exercises all the muscles," Washburne wrote in a memoir of his time as Winnetka superintendent.[63]

Crow Island was widely publicized in its day, both in periodicals like *Architectural Forum* and in exhibitions like the one at MoMA and another, a decade later, sponsored by the Henry Ford Museum and the Encyclopedia Americana.[64] Perkins credited the success of his firm, still in existence today as Perkins+Will, to his hiring of a publicist to promote the school, as well as procuring the services of the well-known architectural photographer Ken Hedrich, of Hedrich Blessing, to photograph it.[65] The principles of Crow Island were also distilled in the influential books *Space for Teaching*

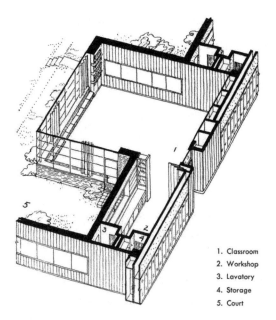

1. Classroom
2. Workshop
3. Lavatory
4. Storage
5. Court

Classroom diagram, Crow Island School, Winnetka, IL, 1940, Perkins+Will, Inc. with Eliel & Eero Saarinen. [Courtesy Perkins+Will]

Classroom, Crow Island School, Winnetka, IL, 1940. [Photograph copyright © Hedrich Blessing Photographers. Courtesy Perkins+Will]

(1941) and *Toward Better School Design* (1954), written by architect William W. Caudill, of Caudill Rowlett Scott. Caudill, whose firm would go on to design dozens of modern elementary schools across the United States over the next decade, pared Crow Island's luxuries down to their bones, emphasizing the L-shaped classroom, the walls of windows, the paired classroom and garden, and the child-size universe:

> Everyone agrees that the pupil should not have to tip-toe to reach the chalkboard or to sit in a seat too large or too small for him. But we still have schools, elementary schools at that, which are scaled to the adult. The child who uses them lives in a world constructed for adults. Doors he cannot easily open, stairs hard to climb, windows too high, coat hooks, drinking fountains, and shelves too high and furniture too big—these serve to remind him constantly that he is small and dependent in a world of watchful giants. He will move with more ease and more peace of mind when the spaces of the school, the equipment and furniture are all scaled to his size. He will feel that this place was created for him, and he will be more self-reliant and do more and better work.[66]

What Caudill most admired about Crow Island was the responsiveness of the architecture to Washburne's curriculum.[67] In *Toward Better School Design* he itemizes all the activities the new classroom must host in a day, breaking them down into individual design solutions, from a child-height hook for her coat and a cubby for her things, through a nook for one-on-one instruction, walls to tack up a mural, and a room large enough for the whole class to sit in a circle.[68] "Children must be challenged educationally, however the wisdom emanating from the building itself is explicit: children deserve and flourish in an atmosphere of love, community, mutual respect, beauty and a connectivity to nature," writes Eleanor Nicholson in an essay titled "The School Building as Third Teacher."[69] In alumni reminiscences about Crow Island, the architecture remains vivid in the adults' minds, affecting not so much for something specific that it taught but for the respect it offered them.

•

COLUMBUS, INDIANA, IS a small town known, since the 1960s, for its abundance of modern public architecture. Architects from both coasts, as well as from midwestern design centers like Chicago and Detroit, competed to build schools, libraries, post offices, and fire stations in Columbus, many of them paid for by a revolutionary philanthropic initiative called the Cummins Foundation Architecture Program. The shapes of schools have always reflected civic ambition and pedagogical change, and Columbus, a town like many others where the postwar population boom was a source of great pride and great anxiety, was quick to embrace new thinking about how children learn via progressive architecture. It serves as a case study in how the modern schoolhouse, based on Crow Island's homelike model, was adapted by various architects and adjusted to the next big thing in educational ideas. Columbus was famous as a town of design wonders, and the schools built with Architecture Program funds all received national attention. Many of their architects, with careers buoyed by Columbus exposure, went on to build educational structures elsewhere, just one of the ways the small town had an outsize impact on American architecture.

The prime mover behind the Architecture Program was J. Irwin Miller, the president of Cummins. Miller was the subject of an October 1967 *Esquire* cover story with the tagline "This man ought to be the next president of the United States." He was a businessman and a banker, a religious leader, a civil rights activist, and a patron of the arts.[70] Years later,

Miller would tell an interviewer, "The first two schools that were built
{after the war} were Clifty and Booth Setser, which were pre-fab schools.
And that really shocked me. I said we've got to do better than that."[71]
The metal-sided schools were not, in fact, prefab but pre-engineered, a
manufactured product that could be put up quickly and cheaply by a
municipality desperate to replace its previous school stock: one-room
schoolhouses, used well into the twentieth century without electricity or
indoor plumbing.[72] Miller had become friends with Eero Saarinen when
Saarinen worked, with his father, on Columbus's First Christian Church
(1942), a project under way in the office at the same time as the Crow
Island School. When it became incumbent upon the town to build
new schools, Miller wanted to make sure they were of good quality and
asked Saarinen for recommendations of architects to suggest to the school
board.

Miller, along with the executive vice presidents of Cummins, wore
many hats in the town. In the early 1950s, as head of the mayor's task force
on housing, he brought Harry Weese, a Chicago-based architect who had
been educated by Eliel Saarinen at Cranbrook, to Columbus for his first
commission, the Columbus Village rental apartments. These apartments,
built from 1953 to 1960, were on what was then the northern edge of town
and were intended to relieve a housing shortage that had begun in the
1930s. In order to attract the kind of young engineers and executives local
industry needed, Miller realized the housing had to come with additional
services, like new parks and schools. Dick Stoner, one of those Cummins
VPs, was then the head of the school board. As Weese was working on the
apartments, he was also hired to design a new elementary school across the
street. In public meetings about his plans, Weese emphasized that this was
no "bargain counter" building, referring obliquely to those two previous
schools.[73]

Lillian C. Schmitt Elementary School, which was completed in 1957, has a simple plan and a familiar gabled roofline.[74] (Earlier versions swapped the gables for barrel vaults.) Weese was commissioned directly by the school board, and the school was financed by a number of local businesses, including the Miller-controlled Cummins and Irwin Union Trust, as well as a loan from the Korean Veterans Memorial Building Fund. Schmitt was built before the official beginning of the Architecture Program, but it was its direct inspiration. The original Schmitt building had thirteen classrooms, with kindergarten and the younger grades to the west along a single-loaded corridor, with individual play areas accessible off their thirty-foot-square classrooms.[75] Older children's classrooms were to the east, with their own larger common playground. In between was a hexagonal "great hall," the physical and social focal point. The great hall could be opened up to the hallways or the adjacent cafeteria via sets of double doors. The hall was lined in wood, with exposed beams and boards on the ceiling, and an acoustic frieze made of different-size dowels over fabric wrapping around the vertical walls below the roof. The school was wood-framed, with concrete and brick infill and lots of wood details, including built-in cupboards lining the hallways and the classrooms' interior walls. In general, the materials were chosen to be low maintenance and usable as is: exposed brick, cedar beams, concrete floors, and glazed tile. The exterior walls were largely glass, frosted above six and a half feet to reduce glare. The exterior gardens, shown bordered with low hedges, would have provided privacy from passersby.

Weese's design even included a fireplace in the kindergarten classroom, a representation of the school as a new kind of home and hearth.[76] At Schmitt, where each classroom fitted under its own peaked roof, the effect was like a set of one-room schoolhouses all in a row—albeit with far larger windows. Familiar and yet new. The fireplace, the gables, the small scale,

Classroom, Lillian C. Schmitt Elementary School, Columbus, IN, 1957. HB-20950-C.
[Chicago History Museum, Hedrich-Blessing Collection]

Exterior, Lillian C. Schmitt Elementary School, Columbus, IN, 1957. HB-20950-E.
[Chicago History Museum, Hedrich-Blessing Collection]

and the warm materials were all adaptations of Crow Island on a slightly less luxurious scale. Miller, because of his close relationship with Eero Saarinen, and Weese, because of his Chicago home base, would both have been familiar with Crow Island and Washburne's revolutionary ideas. The transplantation of those ideas to Columbus, and the modern architecture of the whole, was a complete success. Today, the original Schmitt is so beloved that Columbus residents are still angry about an addition by architects Leers Weinzapfel Associates, built in the 1990s.[77] As Randall Tucker, a Cummins vice president and head of the school board in the 1960s, told me, "If Schmitt had not been acceptable when it was done, the whole program would have been impossible."[78]

In December 1957 Miller sent a letter to the school board proposing what would become the Cummins Foundation Architecture Program: If the school board chose from a list of at least six first-rank American architects, chosen by a panel, the foundation would pay the architect's fees for any new school building.[79] No architect could build more than one foundation project, and the list would be revised each time. After a few years, the program was expanded to include other public buildings, like the post office and fire stations. Rapid building of schools was inevitable—Columbus had data that reflected a need for one new school every two years through the 1960s—but by employing the country's best architects, the schools could become a lifetime asset for the town and its employers. Eero Saarinen and Pietro Belluschi, then dean at the Massachusetts Institute of Technology's School of Architecture and Planning, suggested the first few rounds of names. Weese, after completing Schmitt, also graduated to the panel. In this way, Miller maintained some level of control over the result: He and his Cummins colleagues solicited names of up-and-coming architects for the list from the country's leading designers and educators, ensuring that the results would be modern (and later postmodern) and the practitioner excited by a Columbus assignment.

Schmitt set a precedent in another way as well: Each school would be named after a longtime Columbus educator, a method of honoring teachers that provided the town with the rare opportunity to name public buildings after women.

The first official Architecture Program building was Mabel McDowell Elementary School, commissioned in 1958 and completed in 1960. John Carl Warnecke, a Harvard-trained, San Francisco–based architect, was recommended for the first architects' list by Saarinen and found out about the potential commission unofficially from the same source. In the Columbus archives there is a letter from Saarinen, dated March 1958, summarizing the program for Warnecke and telling him to expect an inquiry from the school board.[80] Warnecke had recently completed the Mira Vista Elementary School in Richmond, California, which had achieved some fame for its gabled roofs and its outdoor orientation stepping down a sloped site. Warnecke sent a photograph of his proposed scheme for the Columbus school to Saarinen, who wrote back, "I liked the initial thinking very much."[81] Through the early 1960s, the building blocks that shaped schools remained the same: They were typically single story, surrounded by open space, with a large central room that might serve as gymnasium, cafeteria, library, or all three. There were individual classrooms for each grade, sometimes differentiated by domestically scaled roofs. The kindergarten was always closest to the front door and typically had its own playground or garden. Flow between interior and exterior was encouraged. Within classrooms, desks were not arranged in rows, but instead classrooms were open plan so that teachers could create areas for different activities with child-size furniture. Sinks, if not bathrooms, were a must for hands-on art and science activities.

Mabel McDowell Elementary follows the same model as Mira Vista, albeit on a flat site adjacent (as most subsequent schools were) to a new public park. The school is designed on a symmetrical cluster plan, with four sets of three-classroom clusters at the corners of a square garden, which centers on three larger, communal facilities. All of the buildings have peaked, shingled roofs, with the central roof rising a full story above the classrooms. The design brief included the wish that "the atmosphere be warm and friendly, the scale should be small and intimate, and the child must be able to develop a feeling of his identity and importance," all of which echoed Washburne's philosophy. The stylized roofs have heavy overhangs, as well as additional steel trellises (now painted red) that connect one building to the next. Steel-framed, with black-and-white brick-and-glass walls, the overall effect is of a Japanese village dropped on a flat Indiana field. In an August 1962 *Architectural Forum* article on the school, Warnecke noted that the grouping was inspired by the grouping of the gabled Victorian house, barn, and silo on local farms, surrounded by groves of trees. He said he hoped to give the school a similar sense of enclosure, while being part of the greater community.[82] In its initial conception, the clustering was intended to deal with the town's teacher shortage: A senior teacher could supervise less experienced ones within each set of three classrooms. When Lady Bird Johnson visited the town in 1967, a reception was held for her in the courtyards between the classroom clusters at McDowell. In 2001, the school was named a national historic landmark, the only school among Columbus's seven landmarks.

•

THE SINGLE-STORY, FINGER-PLAN schools built on the Crow Island model seem necessarily suburban, built on open sites that didn't need to be exploited for maximum classroom potential. But in New Orleans, an ambitious young Tulane professor named Charles Colbert spearheaded a postwar effort to upgrade urban public schools, in historic, tight-knit neighborhoods, with design suited to the hot climate and new teaching practices. Like the Rosenwald examples, these new buildings embodied progressive ideals and were designated for African American children, yet they were built in the last, contested years of the Jim Crow South. Modern architecture was used as a way of warding off deeper change— desegregation—by finally providing equal facilities, complicating the narrative I've sketched of interlocking improvements in facilities and pedagogy. As Nikole Hannah-Jones has written, even as white southerners accepted the desegregation of parks, restaurants, buses, and libraries, "schools were different. Nearly every American child, then and now, attended a public school. Schools were intimate. For hours each day, students sat next to one another, learned with one another, influenced one another."[83] As twenty-first century artifacts, these schools have proven to be controversial, provoking some of the same conversations about preservation and representation as the Confederate memorials built in the twentieth century.

In 1948 Colbert organized a studio for his second-year students to design schools, and then organized a public exhibition of the results, which was attended by thirty thousand people.[84] Helena Huntington Smith covered the exhibit for *Collier's* magazine, noting: "They went away all steamed up over such items as modern, soft-finish, non-glare desk tops; light-absorbing, easy-on-the-eyes green chalk boards instead of old-fashioned blackboards; glass wall blocks which filter light and produce a soothing indirect illumination in the classroom; windows on two sides; 'orientation' toward prevailing breezes—and all this at a smaller cost per foot than is usual for conventional school buildings."[85] New Orleans had not built any new schools in the 1940s, and, following a comprehensive study by Colbert, appointed supervising architect and director for a new school planning office for the parish, went on to construct thirty new schools during the 1950s, plus eighteen additions. Most were built as neighborhood schools, designed to fit on small urban lots, but Colbert also came up with the idea of a "school village," building three schools on a rural lot and busing students to that location. The most interesting architecturally, however, are those that adapt the single-story modernist model to the city, and to New Orleans's humid climate. These new institutions took their cues from residential structures specific to Louisiana, that is, not the features of the midwestern farmhouse but the raised floors, open corridors, and cross-ventilation of local wooden architecture. Colbert and the colleagues he recruited transformed gracious homes into crisp, boxy buildings in concrete, glass, and steel.[86] Named for African American historical figures, these schools represent a rare example of midcentury public architecture built in black neighborhoods—built while the local chapter of the National Association for the Advancement of Colored People was filing lawsuits to desegregate the city's schools.[87] One of those suits would eventually reach the Supreme Court, consolidated into *Brown v. Board of Education*.

Colbert designed the best known of the schools that followed from his plan, Phillis Wheatley Elementary School, completed in 1955 and an American Institute of Architects (AIA) award winner the same year. Phillis Wheatley resembled a box kite, with harlequin-patterned panels at either end, though some contemporary articles referred to it as a tree house. Historian John C. Ferguson writes that Colbert "produced a building that seemed to be about to take flight."[88] Elevated eleven feet above the ground on V-shaped concrete piers, the building invited students to enter by climbing a staircase into its open center. A bridge at the top of the stairs led to the classrooms, which were cantilevered thirty-five feet out over the ground level, leaving the first floor shaded for play. The walls of the classrooms were floor-to-ceiling glass, crossed by the diagonals of the supporting steel trusses.

The 1954 Thomy Lafon School, designed by local modernists Curtis and Davis (architects of the Superdome), was also raised on concrete pilotis, with a long, boomerang-shaped volume housing classrooms all on the upper level. Playrooms at the end of the long V were reached up a ramp from the checkerboard playgrounds on the ground. Classrooms were daylit on both sides and accessed via an outdoor corridor shaded by an overhang. Period photographs show their extremely simple design: glazed block walls, linoleum floors, movable metal and laminate furniture. There was no gym, as the raised section allowed most of the site to be used for recess, and a boxy building on the ground held the school offices and cafeteria. A tile mural near the entrance on the ground floor included world and local maps, the ABCs, and a child-oriented biography of Lafon, who left his real estate fortune, a *Life* magazine story noted, "to men of all races."

Phillis Wheatley Elementary School, New Orleans, LA, 1955, Charles Colbert. Frank Lotz Miller, photographer. [Southeastern Architectural Archive, Special Collections Division, Tulane University Libraries]

Life published an illustrated feature on the school in 1954, also reporting that the Lafon School was the first built for African American children in the city in thirteen years, while three were built for whites. "But, with five other Negro schools going up this year and plans for seven more," the *Life* writer noted, "it was making a start toward redressing the balance."[89] The Lafon School received an AIA Honor Award in 1954, one of a record number of New Orleans and Louisiana projects recognized nationally in the mid-1950s. "The California architect is responsible for the pavilion type of school which, because of its open, spreading plants, used up land at an alarming rate," write Edward and Elizabeth Waugh, authors of the 1960 architecture survey *The South Builds*, referring to people like Richard Neutra and John Carl Warnecke. "The school board of New Orleans and some school architects are taking a realistic view of the population expansion in the United States by raising their schools above the ground

Thomy Lafon Elementary School, New Orleans, LA, 1954, Curtis and Davis Architects. Frank Lotz Miller, photographer. [Southeastern Architectural Archive, Special Collections Division, Tulane University Libraries]

so that the areas beneath the schools may be used as playgrounds."[90] In architectural publications, the race of the students the school served was not mentioned, with the focus completely on the sensible nature of the design, as it responded to the baby boom, limited space in the city, and the New Orleans climate.

Only one of those thirty schools remains today, McDonough 36/ Mahalia Jackson Elementary School, designed by Sol Rosenthal and Charles Colbert in 1954 and renovated by John C. Williams in 2010. Time had not been kind to the 1950s schools, and urban reconstruction following Hurricane Katrina took out those that remained. Both Phillis Wheatley and Thomy Lafon were demolished in 2011, despite being spared major hurricane damage by their elevated designs, and an international outcry by organizations including the World Monuments Fund. Lafon could not be restored because it sat over a historic cemetery, protected from redevelopment by state preservation laws enacted in the 1990s and 2000s.[91] Although the architecture press represented the schools as innovative and advanced—more than equal to the facilities built for white children—some contemporary local leaders viewed them solely as symbols of segregation. To continue to educate African American children in what they perceived as substandard buildings was, in their view, to compound that ongoing inequity. Equal funding and equal access to public schools is not just a problem of the past. New Orleans public schools did not desegregate until 1960, under duress, with U.S. Marshals protecting the four African American girls selected to attend McDonough 19.[92] Phyllis Montana-LeBlanc, who went to Wheatley in the 1960s and early 1970s, told the *Times-Picayune*, "Once Wheatley is gone, another part of our history, of African-American culture in New Orleans, is demolished . . . If we're going to worry about a history of racial struggle, let's remove the plantations. Let's remove the slave quarters."[93] Better to have renovated and relaunched the schools as integrated community institutions, celebrating their innovation, explaining their past, and demonstrating that the future can be different—the approach taken, at long last, with the remaining Rosenwald Schools—than to obliterate them.

By and large, black children were educated in hand-me-down schools. Old, unmaintained buildings of the previous school-building boom of the 1920s were still in use in poor and African American communities and urban areas, while new schools sprang up in the empty fields next to the newly built suburbs from which minority families were explicitly excluded. As middle-class whites left cities, immigrant and later African American children occupied the schools, built for an earlier era, that they left behind.[94] When, in the 1970s, many urban schools were closed due to declining enrollment, parents protested their loss, recognizing the importance of proximity in the creation of neighborhood ties. "They did not want to abandon a familiar educational place. Their schoolhouse was special, after all. Not only was it nearby and well known. It was very important—a critical partner in the education of the young and the most tangible link between the child and society," writes historian William W. Cutler III.[95] The contentious dialogue around the attempt to save the Phillis Wheatley School reflected this narrative: Adults who had been students at the school spoke of it as a hub for the Treme neighborhood, and of their deserved pride in the school's outstanding design.[96]

•

IN COLUMBUS, GUNNAR Birkerts (1967) and Eliot Noyes (1969) would receive the next two school commissions, and John Johansen the one after that, for the L. Frances Smith Elementary School (1969). But the difference between Johansen's compatriots on the foundation's 1965 list and those on the 1966 list is instructive. It reflects a break in architecture, and the end of modernism as America's house style. Farewell Noyes, Ulrich Franzen, and Craig Ellwood; hello, Robert Venturi, Charles Moore, and Romaldo Giurgola.[97] The building Johansen produced was also a break. The architect was best known in the 1950s for elegant, single-story houses in Connecticut, where he and four of his architecture school classmates had moved to New Canaan and were known, collectively, as the Harvard Five. In monumental public commissions of the 1960s, Johansen abandoned the box, producing, for Columbus, a building called a "cubist grain elevator," a "freaked out soybean factory," and even a "slaughterhouse," with educational spaces on nine levels connected by brightly painted industrial tubes fitted with ramps. In an interview about his design for the Oklahoma City Mummers Theater (1970, demolished 2014), Johansen described his approach as "ad hocism," and the building as being "like a bubble diagram brought to life."[98] His architecture was not about form only, but for the theatergoer (or student) to become part of the process, and part of the performance. Children, as you might expect, got it immediately.

L. Frances Smith Elementary's architectural eccentricity reflected a different, if not entirely new, educational model: Smith was to be a "continuous progress" school, in which children move through instruction at their own pace rather than one mandated by the state.[99] Washburne's Winnetka Plan had allowed children to advance this way, but the architecture of Crow Island was still rigorously organized by grade. At Smith, three sets of classrooms fed off double-loaded corridors, with windows on one side and blackboards on the other. Movable partitions allowed for classrooms to be combined, but these were reportedly rarely used. Each complex (like the McDowell school's clusters) had its own teachers and set of 180 pupils. The tubes, so confusing to adults, were easy for the children to read. The first exit off the ramp was for the youngest children, the second for midlevel learners, and so on, up to the rooftop aeries for the administrators and the school library. Although it seems counterintuitive to put the principal's office far from the front door (and when Smith was remodeled a few years ago, this was changed), it made symbolic sense: The school administration was watching over you, albeit through slit-like windows. The spiraling configuration also created an outdoor space at the heart of the school, accessible from multiple points. (Johansen compared his plan to the petals of a flower.) Many of the single-story schools based on the Crow Island model include versions of its stepped agora; this is Smith's. Today, that central yard is one of few places from which the whole ensemble can be understood. The classrooms and hallways form a sort of levitating constellation in which children make upward progress toward enlightenment (or middle school). The pinwheel plan of the Crow Island School achieves liftoff at Smith.

When the school opened in 1969 it was quite controversial, resulting in many letters to the editor. What shut down the discussion was a letter published in the *Republic* in September 1969 from J. A., then a Smith student. "It's about time the children started giving their opinions," wrote J. A. "The ramps are great. We had a fire drill and got out two times faster than we would on stairs. We don't feel like cattle or hogs! We feel safe because we don't fall when we are pushed. And as for the carpets, we can sit on the floor, play games, and not make half as much noise as on a regular floor. We, the kids, love it!"[100] If Smith reflected a gradual shift in thinking, Columbus's next two schools, Fodrea and Mt. Healthy, reflected a revolution. Both return without nostalgia to the one room/one roof idea of the one-room schoolhouse but treat that large room more like Crow Island teachers treated their L-shaped classrooms: as rapidly changing stages for almost any educational activity. Enter the open plan.

A 1973 *Architectural Record* story on Mt. Healthy Elementary School heralded it as an important "experiment" in open education, the first of its kind in Columbus and a model for other communities considering a change to this form of pedagogy.[101] As the article notes, the architects of Mt. Healthy, Hardy Holzman Pfeiffer Associates, and those of the Fodrea School, being built concurrently by Caudill Rowlett Scott, were the first to design in Columbus for team teaching and mixed-age classes. Until the late 1960s, the Bartholomew County school board had resisted new approaches to teaching and thus the buildings, up to and including Smith, reflected the postwar architectural emphasis on light, space, and belonging. Whereas postwar schools had emphasized flexible classroom design, the open-plan schools operated as "schools without walls," separating groups and functions through level changes and other sectional architecture or by adaptations of Johansen's cluster idea, where semi-enclosed classrooms would feed into a common area. Since 1969, 50 percent of new American schools had been built for open education, but no consensus on form had yet been reached.

In open education, the hierarchical classroom disintegrates: Mt. Healthy has blackboards and desks, but the idea of a permanent front and back, or even of a class in an enclosed room, disappears. As Mildred F. Schmertz writes in the *Architectural Record*, "The classroom has become a workshop stocked with fascinating materials, but the children are not just doing their own thing. They educate themselves while participating in projects which interest them, and thus the learning grows out of their own interest." This description closely resembles both that of the "affective" Kentucky one-room schoolhouse visited by *Parents* magazine (albeit blown up to a larger scale) and one of the newest models for public education today, "project-based learning," a movement in contemporary education that, like the open plan, is an attempt to reform a school system many fear has become overly focused on teacher-led education, high-stakes testing, and rote learning. Yes, this was precisely the problem the Progressive-influenced midcentury school design was supposed to solve. But by the 1960s it, too, was perceived as overly didactic and inflexible. Education historian Larry Cuban writes, "Open classrooms' focus on students' 'learning by doing' resonated with those who believed that America's formal, teacher-led classrooms were crushing students' creativity. In that sense the open-classroom movement mirrored the social, political, and cultural changes of the 1960s and early 1970s. The era saw the rise of a youth-oriented counterculture and various political and social movements—the civil-rights movement, antiwar protests, feminist and environmental activism—that questioned traditional seats of authority, including the way classrooms and schools were organized and students were taught."[102]

Mt. Healthy, like many of its open-plan compatriots, was likely influenced by Dutch architect Herman Hertzberger's 1966 Montessori school in Delft, a widely discussed project by a respected designer and theorist. At Hertzberger's school, a wide central hallway meanders between four large L-shaped classrooms, each one divided into three zones by a few steps and turns. On both the interior and the exterior, each classroom has a separate presence, like a tiny house, which registers in the staggered roofline. Children would be able to identify their classroom easily, and the articulation of the entrance to each classroom operates almost like a front porch. Aesthetically, it is the stagger that American architects like Hardy Holzman Pfeiffer often copied, setting classrooms in a stair-step relationship to one another to avoid the long, double-loaded corridors of the previous two generation of schools. Hertzberger's central hall has sittable steps of its own that enable its transformation into a theater for all-school events. Such staircases are now so ubiquitous as to have become clichés, used to symbolize gathering everywhere from schools to tech offices to libraries, but open-plan schools were the first to bring them indoors. Hertzberger also tinkered with school furniture, making his own play on building blocks: a square, recessed section of floor, termed a "sitting-hollow," in which sixteen hollow blocks, with cut-out handles, could be stored. When taken out, they become campfire stools or the makings of a tower, and the pit becomes a secondary play space.[103] For another school he devised a learning banquette with a low L-shaped sofa, high walls, and a built-in desk. On the exterior, the area underneath the sofa serves as storage cubbies. The changes in height that pieces like the blocks or banquette create insert pockets of privacy within the large, open schoolrooms without building actual walls. The meandering central hallway also recalls some of the nostalgia, during this period, for the unplanned irregularity of the Italian hill town. Open-plan schools really want to be villages, with a main street, a few landmarks, and tidy front doors marking each class's domain. "These pupils are not yet of an age to go into the city and explore the life of the city but they should explore life through the school," Hertzberger said.[104]

At Mt. Healthy, the youngest children nest close to the front door in a multilevel classroom space that includes a set of sittable steps, used for story time or as desk space, as well as more enclosed places for individual or small-group learning. The kindergarten has its own entrance from the parking lot and its own outdoor play area. The area is marked by alphabet supergraphics on the overhanging wood-clad balcony. The little children go down to reach their classroom, while larger children go up to balcony A, B, or C to join their "cluster" of 180 students. To reach any of the communal facilities, like the gym or cafeteria, classes walk along the building's diagonal spine, less a central hallway than a street with many shops defined by what's on either side. In the initial design, the principal's office was at the top of the tree, at the end of the hall, one of the many peculiarities of Hardy Holzman Pfeiffer's stepped, nonhierarchical plan that only makes sense in three dimensions.

I went to an open-plan middle school myself, Carolina Friends School in Durham, North Carolina. Our building was a giant rectangular prism with metal siding and metal trusses overhead, the better to provide a vast, undivided, and underheated room. The carpet was orange and the interior walls were minimal, classrooms separated on at most a single side by a thin wall with a blackboard. A couple of woodstoves tried, ineffectively, to warm the place in winter. (If we complained of the cold, we were told to put on another sweater.) The design was meager because we were supposed to fill it ourselves: with theater and song and dance, with giant silent Quaker meetings and smaller discussion circles on the floor, with research from the library housed on rolling carts. I don't remember it being loud, but it must have been—one hundred kids, no boundaries—the saving grace being the woods and fields all around us. The only rooms with doors were the bathrooms, the teacher's lounge, and the computer room, stocked with Commodore 64s. Schools built this way embodied a new freedom in education: Work at your own pace, call your teacher by her first name, write a poem instead of a book report. We had no report cards and no standardized tests, and you took the math class at your level, regardless of age. I loved it until I realized, as I approached college, that I was years behind the standard in calculus and French (albeit years ahead in creative writing and feminist theory and exposure to the brilliance of Zora Neale Hurston).

Writer Laura Lippman recently published her own memories of open-plan education in Columbia, Maryland, in the 1970s. Columbia, like Columbus, is a community known for its modern architecture: Developer James Rouse imagined it as a contemporary utopia where classes and races would mix, and the planning would foster the community typically lost in

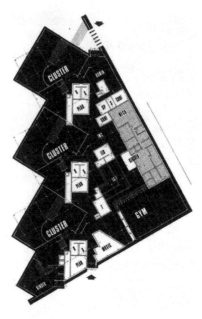

Plan, Mt. Healthy Elementary School, Columbus, IN, 1972, Hardy Holzman Pfeiffer Associates. [Courtesy H3 Hardy Collaboration Architecture LLC]

Interior, Mt. Healthy Elementary School, Columbus, IN, 1972, Hardy Holzman Pfeiffer Associates. Photograph by Norman McGrath. [Courtesy H3 Hardy Collaboration Architecture LLC]

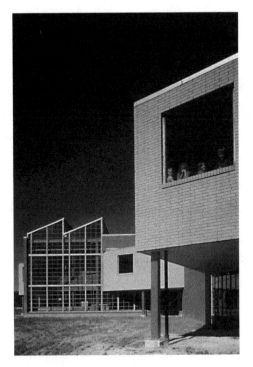

Exterior, Mt. Healthy Elementary School, Columbus, IN, 1972, Hardy Holzman Pfeiffer Associates. Photograph by Norman McGrath. [Courtesy H3 Hardy Collaboration Architecture LLC]

the suburbs. The school was no different. Lippman describes it as looking, from the outside, "like a space station." Design attention was all focused within, with the outside merely a container drawn around the activity plan. On her first visit, Lippman writes,

> the school was hushed and serene out of term time; it would
> be the last time I ever experienced it that way. There was
> a constant, low humming, sometimes shot through with
> a teacher's authoritative voice. Open-space education was
> literal: on the second floor, where most academic classes
> met, there were few walls, just utilitarian dividers carving
> subject areas into smaller areas. Going clockwise from the
> front door, there was history and social studies, literature

and composition, foreign languages, [math,] and science.
The last two were increasingly taught traditionally, unless
a pupil was a certified genius.[105]

By the end of the decade, the free plan and free curriculum had gotten
chopped up into more manageable segments. By the end of the next decade
the school was gone, replaced by a traditional one with windows and
internal classroom walls.[106] But as she looked back on her years at Wilde
Lake High School for a novel, Lippman found something strange. "Yes, it
was crazy to expect adolescents to make sound decisions about how to
allocate their time. However, students who were motivated could soar at
Wilde Lake. It was a great place to be an outlier. There were quite a few
success stories, now that I began to take notice."[107] My middle school and
high school classmates are musicians, magicians, designers, novelists,
and software engineers. What you lost in book learning, you gained in
autonomy and creativity, independence and motivation, just as the
open-plan proponents said you would. The transition to college was
rough for me, as it sounds like it was for Lippman and her classmates,
but we recovered.

Mildred Schmertz, who wrote the article on Mt. Healthy for *Architectural
Record*, astutely anticipated many of the problems that would plague that
school and its contemporaries. While the open classrooms are still at work
today, the hallways and cafeteria have become more enclosed to mitigate
the noise of moving bodies. Who thought it was a good idea to put the
cafeteria and library next to each other? One parent of a recent graduate
said that before the renovation, her children often had to sit through "silent
lunch." Other work has been done to improve the air quality, balancing
heating and cooling across those multiple levels, as well as ensuring that
some spaces are, in fact, quiet. When Schmertz points out that "there is

no quiet room as such for the child who may be tiring of interacting with his peers, suffering from sensory overload, and wishing to make a total commitment to his book,"[108] I thought of more recent articles on introverts versus extroverts. No one educational philosophy is right for every child.

Open-plan schools, and the educational philosophy behind them, were doomed by three factors. The first was design-based: They were simply too loud. No matter how many soft surfaces architects designed, noise levels in an undivided room with hundreds of children remain distractingly high, with the unscreened movement of other children, and other classes, as a secondary disruption. Although architects attempted to modulate the acoustics with carpeted floors, padded nooks, and level changes, most open-plan schools still had high ceilings and many hard planes. Teachers' speech bled from one area to the next, as did movement and chatter from other classes moving around the school. Distraction, annoyance, and straining to hear were the result, though some studies have found children in open-plan schools can become habituated to the noise.[109] In new semi-open school settings, as children pursue individualized lesson plans on an iPad or laptop, they may wear headphones, not an option for previous generations. Glass walls replace open sides so teachers can see students in other rooms without broadcasting every word. I visited one new school where "acoustic clouds"—blob-shaped cutouts of absorptive material painted pretty colors that I imagined siphoning the words from my lips like a vacuum cleaner—were hung from the ceiling in each stair hall.

The second factor was pedagogical: To teach in an open-plan school, teachers had to teach differently. You are not the mistress of your classroom but a part of a system. Such spaces live and die by the organization and energy of teachers who can spend one period lecturing from the front of the room, the next organizing a field trip, and the last providing individual guidance to students at different stages of projects on a range of topics. In the 1973 book *The Open Classroom Reader*, Charles Silberman spoke frankly to early adopters: "By itself, dividing a classroom into interest areas does not constitute open education; creating large open spaces does not constitute open education; individualizing instruction does not constitute open education . . . For the open classroom . . . is not a model or set of techniques, it is an approach to teaching and learning."[110]

The final, and most decisive, factor for the disappearance of open plan was performance. How do you measure the effectiveness of a program intended to encourage such ephemeral things as creativity, engagement, and enthusiasm? Through standards, as measured by testing and as practiced in a traditional, teacher-directed classroom. In a short history of the open-plan experiment, "The Open Classroom," Larry Cuban describes the 1980s backlash: "The national crisis gave rise to a perception, amplified by the media, that academic standards had slipped, that the desegregation movement had failed, and that urban schools were becoming violent places. This time the call was not for open education but for a return to the basics, again mirroring general social trends—namely, the conservative backlash against the cultural and political changes of the 1960s and early 1970s."[111] Schools built in the 1980s and 1990s had closed classrooms. States set standardized tests and competency requirements for all high school graduates. Today we have the Common Core, which sets an educational norm for students from K through 12 across the states. But I think we may be on the brink of a 1970s-style revolution, and for the same reasons: The skills children need for the economy of the future don't come from writing down what a teacher says but from research, discussion, exploration, and tinkering, skills children can only learn by doing. The Silicon Valley entrepreneurs trying to disrupt education say nothing has changed in a hundred years, which, if you've read this chapter, is patently wrong. They are also focused on technology—what's inside the container—rather than on the container itself. In order for schools to transform, architecture and teaching have to change together.

•

WHAT IF WE went back to fixed furniture but instruction moved? That's the theory behind the toy-like educational landscapes created by Rosan Bosch, a Dutch-born, Copenhagen-based designer whose practice focuses on the art, design, and architecture of learning. Bosch is best known for the Vittra Telefonplan school, which opened in Stockholm in 2011.[112] In Vittra Telefonplan, and in the dozen schools Rosan Bosch Studio has completed since, archipelagos of furniture in bright, attractive colors work in concert with café tables, cubicles, and lab surfaces to divide high-ceilinged white rooms into zones. (The aesthetic is echt Scandinavian and not unlike many tech-company offices.) A wave of publicity followed the opening of Vittra Telefonplan, sparked by photographs that show children hanging out on a giant green upholstered island, running up a set of blue mountain stairs, and sitting with a teacher in a village of picnic tables, each contained within a three-dimensional structure that looked like a child's drawing of a house. STOCKHOLM'S SCHOOL WITHOUT CLASSROOMS, read one headline. IS SWEDEN'S CLASSROOM-FREE SCHOOL THE FUTURE OF LEARNING? SWEDEN DEBUTS FIRST CLASSROOM-LESS SCHOOL. As usual, this was design media hyperbole: The layout of Vittra Telefonplan is more like a series of classrooms without walls, not unlike the 1970s. The furniture pieces, while abstract in form, are intended to suggest the relationships and postures children adopt in school—or would adopt if not confined to chairs and desks—and hence to provide better support, literally, for the different interpersonal interactions that make up the school day. The pieces don't replace the teacher but suggest that a teacher's time is not best spent managing bodies. In interviews, Bosch often cites the Malaguzzi quote that environment is the "third teacher," but with a novel interpretation, far from the Reggio Emilia model, of what an instructional environment might look like.

Instead of making containers for children, Bosch creates magnets, each with an evocative name inspired by futurist David Thornburg's ideas about learning communities.[113] "The show-off," for example, is that blue, stepped mountain, a space where teachers and students can explain their work to an audience of their peers, and the whole school can gather. "The cave" has the opposite purpose: a red, carpeted nook under the mountain to get away from it all, have a private conversation or a private moment. Concentration niches, also coded red, provide private work space, while a child looking for interaction might head to "the watering hole," adjacent to more benches for

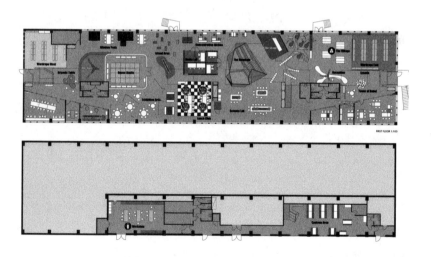

Plan, Vittra School Telefonplan, Stockholm, Sweden, 2011, Rosan Bosch Studio.
[Courtesy Rosan Bosch Studio]

two, or to the village of tables for small-group work. The last two magnets are "the campfire" and "the laboratory." The second is self-explanatory, a zone of metal-topped tables ready for hands-on science or cooking experiments on the working set of appliances. The former represents the tightest of groups, a seminar discussion in the round. Bosch updates the Harkness Table (or its hexagonal offspring) as an organic archipelago with three lobes and two cutouts. Kids can arrange themselves around the perimeter or draw closer around a lobe, even sit themselves within one of the cutouts, like a prairie dog, for the full frontier effect. They can *move*— which, if you are a fidgety child, feels like a godsend—and array themselves on the floor, on a lounge chair, or, indeed, at a desk, depending on what suits them best. The physical autonomy relates to a degree of educational autonomy as well: Students in a class are not all learning together all the time, facing a teacher at the front of a classroom with walls—that's what time in the show-off is meant for. Instead, they are working on individual assignments, as well as longer-term projects, in various smaller groupings, at their own pace. In the United States, versions of this kind of curriculum are known as project-based or inquiry-based learning: Students are set a question as a class and given time to research answers in a variety of ways, from readings to experiments to interviews. At the end of the cycle, students present their work as a paper, a poster, a presentation, or a PowerPoint, learning from each other as well as collaborating along the way. It's a model that has been embraced by public, private, and charter schools as a mode of twenty-first-century education less about learning facts and more about what you do with them. But like so many of the previous disruptors to American education, it requires buy-in from teachers and parents and a radical redevelopment of space within the classroom.

Bosch began this work, like so many designer parents before her, out of frustration with her own children's early experiences at school: They went in as "wonderfully curious beings," she says. "They like to learn from everything, and then you bring them to school and you suddenly have to commit to this huge compromise, which in a way you feel is damaging your child. Worse, it's actually damaging their ability to learn and develop. That just felt so wrong."[114] This is a refrain heard from Dewey on: that school is crushing children's natural desire to learn. Bosch makes the critique physical, beginning by mostly eliminating the upright, individual chair, but first she had to find a school that would let her in.

Bosch's first school intervention was structured as a provocation: In 2010, she convinced Vittra, a Swedish education company, to let her office do a six-week takeover of a school of 750 students, serving ages six to sixteen. She and her staff moved in, and every morning the teachers would walk by the design team's temporary office and Bosch would give them a task. "We had bought this very cheap carpet and cut it out in organic forms," she says, by way of example. "We would give each teacher a roll of carpet and tell them to set the kids out on group work in the building. They could freely go wherever they wanted with a little carpet, in small groups doing some kind of assignment, and come back after forty-five minutes." The children colonized the whole school: the halls, the gym, outdoors, but the kids were respectful of one another's carpets, stepping around other groups and speaking quietly. "It took away the fear of letting them move freely," Bosch says. That became the campfire.

On another day, Bosch's team got permission to turn off the harsh overhead lighting and gave each classroom five small table lamps, provided by IKEA. The teachers put the lamps on the tables, put the tables in groups, and, according to Bosch, the kids' levels of concentration completely changed. That became the cave.

On a third day they gave everyone Post-It notes, the kids one color, the adults another. Everybody had to write a note with an observation about a particular spot in the school. "I like this space because it's cozy, or I hate this spot because it's always very noisy or it's cold or ugly or whatever," she says. "It was like insects. You would have corners covered in Post-Its. It was an eye-opener for the adults to see how the children experienced the space." Because of Bosch's physical prompts, she says, the teachers gained a greater understanding of what the children thought about the school and how they might react to different design elements. She saw three basic types of learning spaces: spaces for small-group dialogue, spaces for concentration, and spaces for public presentation. She went back to her office determined to transform those patterns into fixed pieces, buoyed by the teachers' changes in attitude. Her Post-Its and table lamps changed teachers' minds about what was possible, both in terms of the enclosure of the learning environment and in the amount of physical autonomy children could be allowed. If you put a class of kids in a room with one adult, she says, you'll revert to one-directional teaching. "Change is a little like grass which is bending. If you don't actually finish it off with a physical design, it will bend back."

The Vittra schools, and others Rosan Bosch Studio has completed, might seem like mere fodder for design blogs or for the aesthetic utopia that is Scandinavia. But Bosch is now working in Chicago, collaborating with architects Studio Gang on the design of the public charter school Academy for Global Citizenship (AGC). AGC was founded in 2008 by Sarah Elizabeth Ippel, an idealistic twenty-six-year-old who spent three years applying, and reapplying, to the Chicago Board of Education to start her school, where more than four hundred and fifty kindergartners through eighth graders learn in Spanish and English, raise chickens, grow vegetables and eat their harvest for lunch cooked by an on-site chef in a zero-waste organic cafeteria, practice yoga in classrooms lit by on-site solar panels, and, she hopes, learn to become leaders in their community and the

Island Area and Media Lab, Vittra School Telefonplan, Stockholm, Sweden, 2011, Rosan
Bosch Studio. Photograph by Kim Wendt. [Courtesy Rosan Bosch Studio]

Science Lab and the Mountain, Vittra School Telefonplan, Stockholm, Sweden, 2011, Rosan
Bosch Studio. Photograph by Kim Wendt. [Courtesy Rosan Bosch Studio]

world.[115] (The school is part of the International Baccalaureate system and will eventually include a high school.) Articles on Ippel tend to start with her looking for eggs in the school's chicken house—it's almost too easy a metaphor for a young woman with four hundred and fifty children under her wing, searching for a collaborative, healthy, and communitarian environment in order to nurture them to adulthood. The school currently occupies two rented buildings, separated by a busy street, in the Garfield Ridge neighborhood on Chicago's Southwest Side, a low-income and minority community. The International Baccalaureate curriculum emphasizes inquiry-based learning, with six-week cycles in which children as young as kindergarteners investigate transdisciplinary questions, Ippel says, "about local and global food systems, or inventions and innovations over time, often using technology to research, to Skype with sister schools, to create a PowerPoint or a documentary."[116] When I query the technology, Ippel assures me, "I've had first graders invite me for their PowerPoint presentation." Ninety percent of the students are minorities, and Ippel has said that while she was developing the school's program, many people suggested that the student-led model could not succeed with low-income children. "It was very disheartening for all of us to see that these expectations and these beliefs were held in some people's minds, that not all children have the capacity to learn and that maybe we should focus our energy on kids who have a more promising future," she told the *Chicago Tribune* in 2013.[117] In 2015, as the school prepared to graduate its first cohort of students, Ippel and her team began to process of creating a model campus, one that would support her goals for Chicago *and* be affordable enough for other public schools to replicate.

If Ippel and AGC can reach their fund-raising goals, a new thirty-five-million-dollar school will be built on a former brownfield site at the corner of West Forty-Fourth Street and South LaPorte Avenue, next to

LeClaire-Hearst Park. A three-acre urban farm, including lightweight hoop houses, designed in partnership with the nonprofit organization Growing Power, sits at the northern end of the site. Farm activities will be part of each day's curriculum, and the intention is that the year-round harvest will provide a significant amount of the produce for breakfast and lunch each day. South of the farm, a C-shaped building, with one- and two-story sections, embraces a central, south-facing courtyard. Each section has a sloped roof, tilted toward the sun and covered with photovoltaic panels; the goal is for the building to become a net-positive producer of energy. On the shady sides, a clerestory window between the building's solid wall and the edge of the slanted roof will let cool northern light filter into the classrooms. Gutters running along the low points in the roof collect storm water, to be used for flushing toilets and irrigating the gardens. Operable windows under the eaves allow for natural ventilation, and a greenhouse sandwiched between the classroom wings will create a sort of thermal-blanket effect in the winter, capturing sunlight, heating the air, and warming their neighbors. "The whole thing is really all about growing a power- and food-conscious community and designing a replicable system that can be used by other schools in the future," Studio Gang told the *Architect's Newspaper* in 2016.[118] The school has written a guidebook about its design, and it will be constructed with accessible materials and prefabricated systems, so that, while the arrangement is unique to the location, future schools could reproduce the model with changes reflecting their own climate, program, and site orientation. The lessons of stewardship, the connection to the outdoors, and the emphasis on healthy eating are all manifest at a glance.

Students of all ages will move from space to space as their curriculum dictates and following what the designers call the Wonder Path, an updated version of Hertzberger's village streets. "It's a flipped relationship with circulation space," Ippel says. "Rather than breaking learning spaces up with hallways and walls, and asking each educator to stay in one space with one group of students, teachers circulate around the shared entire learning space throughout the day depending on the activity and learning needs of our students."[119] Paired grades will cluster in "neighborhoods," like a city in microcosm, outfitted with the same kinds of differentiated furniture as in Bosch's Vittra schools. Ippel describes the neighborhoods using natural terminology: Every neighborhood will have a forest with worktables for small groups; a farm-to-table area, where even the youngest can make a snack; a beehive with little nooks for one or two people; and a mountain with stepped seating for larger gatherings.

The plans for the Academy for Global Citizenship are the most architecturally ambitious I've seen in the United States in the way they transform the school into a landscape of inquiry and abandon the old vocabulary (verbal and physical) of classroom, desk, and chair. But Ippel, Gang, and Bosch are far from alone in their quest to restructure public education in America. At the P. K. Yonge Developmental Research School in Gainesville, Florida, a K–12 public school run by the University of Florida that admits students from thirty-one cities across that state, a 2012 redesign of their elementary school by Fielding Nair International was the result of a long collaborative process that also restructured the way teachers taught. The approximately four hundred students in grades K through 5 are grouped into three sections by ability and subject, not just by age, and assigned a team of seven teachers. Those groups may change during the year or change for a single topic, depending on students' needs. The outside of the one-story school is largely brick, with symbolic pedimented porticos supported by blue columns marking the entrance and giving it a retro-village-like feeling not unlike Weese's homestyle roofs in Columbus. Inside, classrooms bleed into hallways, and hallways into classrooms, everything linked by internal windows and wide apertures: Teachers have set-aside spaces for collaboration, and a cluster typically includes at least one classroom with a door, but the hallways are stocked with soft comma-shaped ottomans that are in a state of constant rearrangement. In fact, you can find pretty much every type of furniture you could imagine in the school's rectangular rooms: those ottomans, plus pie-shape tables that reminded me of the trapezoidal tops of my youth, two-person tables on wheels, outdoor café tables, indoor camping-style floor seats with backs, and so on and so on. Rather than a narrow corridor with closed cell-like classrooms, the hallway seems to sprout petals of different shapes and different levels of transparency and sociability. The architecture is less stylish, the colors more cacophonous than those in the Scandinavian examples, but the school design represents the same thinking about choices: choices made by students, not just teachers, about how their bodies need to be situated to accomplish a given task. Because it's Florida, the classrooms include outdoor porches adjacent to the class clusters.

Fielding Nair has become a leader in the push for opening up learning environments, both as architects and as educational consultants, using rhetoric that recalls that of Progressive educators of a hundred years ago. President Prakash Nair has called the classroom "a relic, left over from the Industrial Revolution, which required a large workforce with very basic skills." He economically describes the vision for schools like P. K. Yonge as "enclosed spaces for direct instruction, but perhaps these could be adjacent to a visible and supervisable common space for teamwork, independent study, and Internet-based research."[120] Separate areas for art, science, and performance can be shared by clusters but don't need to be set aside for one class's exclusive use. I see the same principles at the Booker T. Washington STEM Academy, a magnet school that opened in a predominantly African American neighborhood in Champaign, Illinois, in 2013 in response to a state desegregation order. The K–5 school, designed by CannonDesign and Bailey Edward, which serves 425 students, puts students in "learning studios," three to a grade, which share a common work space with a sink and demonstration counter. The "STEM studio," a souped-up lab space, is next to an outdoor courtyard where the raised beds are irrigated with rainwater, which can be used by the whole school for more-elaborate, hands-on experiments. This school, too, has solar panels, and a wall-mounted readout so that students can track how much of the school's energy is being generated above their heads. But architect Stuart Brodsky, the partner at CannonDesign in charge of the Booker T. Washington school, argues that encouraging movement marks the greatest change from the former "factory model" of American education (even if he is ignoring previous generations of education architecture, from Dewey to the open plan).[121] "Students need to move. There's a direct connection between physical activity and a hormonal physiological response in the brain. It turns on the right part of the brain," he told me, and research backs him up.[122] That's why Steelcase came up with the Node, and every new school I look at seems to have chairs on wheels, or tables that stack or nest. Furniture, which was once the heaviest and most fixed feature of the learning environment, becomes more like an indoor, perpetual playground, harnessing children's natural tendency to fidget, bounce, and touch and building physical activity into the school day beyond recess.

As Bosch warned, however, the architecture is only as good as the adults' commitment to the project. Curriculum and design have to work together, or things fall apart. The Henderson-Hopkins School in East Baltimore opened to great fanfare, and an architecture review in the *New York Times* in 2014.[123] Envisioned as the linchpin of a redeveloped neighborhood in one of Baltimore's most challenged communities, the school was a joint venture between Johns Hopkins University and the

Baltimore City Public School System and received funding from a variety of education-related nonprofits. The design, by Rogers Partners, placed shared school and community facilities including a library, auditorium, and gym on a main urban thoroughfare, in front of classroom pavilions mixed with open courtyards. One hundred years ago, in Chicago, architect Dwight H. Perkins argued for, and designed, the same kinds of integrated amenities for adults and children, so that schools could become open neighborhood centers rather that exclusive pavilions for children, open only from 8:30 A.M. to 2:30 P.M. The classrooms at Henderson-Hopkins were designed for team teaching: Combined grades were assigned to a "house," with a two-story commons, an exclusive outdoor space, and what was intended to be a fluid arrangement of big classrooms, smaller seminar rooms, and shared teachers' offices, just as in the other project-based plans. Each house would hold approximately 120 students, close to "Dunbar's number," the maximum number of people you can really know, as theorized by anthropologist Robin Dunbar.[124]

But in March 2017, a *Baltimore Sun* story reported that the school was struggling, after multiple changes in leadership, and was planning to change its curriculum and redesign some of its three-year-old classrooms.[125] Socioeconomics undoubtedly play a major role in the school's travails: Henderson-Hopkins was intended to be a magnet school with economic and racial diversity, factors known to improve educational outcomes, serving both low-income students from its East Baltimore neighborhood and the children of Hopkins faculty and staff. But in response to neighborhood pressure, and the desire not to turn away students without other good public school options, school leaders increased class sizes. Those open learning spaces were jammed, making it difficult to teach and to maintain discipline. The *Baltimore Sun* noted, "The building's open spaces, meant to spark creativity, proved more distracting than helpful for teaching." There wasn't enough staff to cover the commons, intended to be used as intimate eating spaces, so three were closed. In its first three years, the *Sun* reported, academic performance was well below the state average, and out-of-school suspensions tripled. "Because teachers have found the school's open spaces difficult to teach in, [new principal Deborah] Ptak purchased six-foot-high partitions," the *Sun* reported, with plans to eventually divide each grade's "house" back into standard-size classrooms with permanent walls. Mariale Hardiman, vice dean of academic affairs at the Johns Hopkins School of Education and the liaison to Henderson-Hopkins, says the goal for the new renovations is to allow each class to have its own dedicated room for teacher-led instruction, with those rooms arranged around shared common spaces for additional child-led creative inquiry.[126] The pressure of high occupancy and high educational need forced the architecture to bend back to a familiar patterns: one teacher, one room, a fixed set of students. The scheduling and collaboration required for teachers to share the tiered rooms didn't work, Hardiman says, because of a lack of professional development before and during the move to the new building. Administrators, teachers, and students will have to learn to use the newly modified school together. "Open space schools were considered a failure back in the day," she told me. "My question for the architectural world is what was the catalyst" for making open plans again? Architect Rob Rogers is pained by this outcome, given the long planning process his firm went through with the Johns Hopkins School of Education and the first set of teachers and administrators at the school. "If you try to make stew in a skillet, it is not going to turn out so great," he said. "The school was not built for one teacher at a desk with thirty kids in the classroom."[127]

Even AltSchool, founded by ex-Googler Max Ventilla and funded by investors including Mark Zuckerberg and Peter Thiel's Founders Fund, has built classrooms. Initial coverage of the education start-up, founded in 2013, focused on its "personalized learning platform," tablet-based technology that was supposed to invisibly and constantly assess student learning. In its early years, the start-up needed students on whom to test iterations of the platform and from whom to gather data. Classrooms were recorded, student performance was tracked, and a teacher might take out her phone at any moment to document signs of learning, like a field scientist documenting baby animals in the wild. Stories about and photographs of the classrooms seemed to always include children sitting in beanbags with laptops or tablets, alone together. In 2016, *New Yorker* writer Rebecca Mead described the school's Brooklyn Heights location as rooms of minimal (as in minimally thought-out) design: "The space has been partitioned with dividers creating several classrooms. The décor evokes an IKEA showroom: low-slung couches, beanbags, clusters of tables, and wooden chairs in progressively smaller sizes, like those belonging to Goldilocks's three bears."[128] All of the attention seemed to be going into the platform—which AltSchool could sell to as many educators as it wanted—rather than into the students' environment. In its current iteration, AltSchool's Portrait software stores a record of each child's work and progress that can be passed on from teacher to teacher, and teacher to parent, managing test scores, teacher evaluations, and snapshots of physical projects like posters or cardboard creations; Playlist is the student home, an online collection of curriculum units that teachers can stock and sequence for each child.[129] With its focus on a platform that was both personalized and didactic, AltSchool reminded me a bit of Carleton Washburne's Winnetka Plan—where the children spent their afternoons in physical and communal activities after mornings spent hunched over a workbook.

But as the history of education design shows, how children sit, where they sit, and how far they can roam within their school environment are all key parts of learning. You can't play with online blocks until you've first played with real ones, and you can't learn the lessons of the digital playground without experience in a real one. AltSchool used their data—How do educators break up the day, the week? Where do students like to work? What kinds of instruction need which kinds of spaces?—and developed a physical plan. In September 2017, AltSchool opened its first purpose-built space and its eighth lab school, a middle school located in a turn-of-the-century masonry building in Manhattan's Union Square. Enrollment for the first year consists of just thirty students, but the school has the capacity for one hundred (Dunbar's number again). The design, by A + I, incorporates the elements of the other project-based learning environments I've described. You enter down a hallway, lined with a pin-up board and bench, into a large commons, with a "mountain" of sittable steps and an open "design lab" with space for fifty students to have lunch or work on a big group project. Classrooms, visible through glass partitions, have a variety of nooks and crannies, including window seats and upholstered benches (their version of "caves"), as well as more easily recognizable tables for eight. Tiny glass rooms, like phone booths, are set up for solo work or student-teacher conferences, and another small seminar room can also be used by students from any class. It's a campus in miniature, but it includes the same mix of small, medium, and large learning spaces, visually and physically accessible to each other, and is populated by the same motley mix of furnishings as at P. K. Yonge, Booker T. Washington, and Henderson-Hopkins. Kids and adults alike have a personal cubby but no dedicated desk, and they are intended to float as instruction requires.

I was intrigued by the way the urban setting's tight spatial confines pushed AltSchool to connect to the physical environment beyond its walls. The East Village AltSchool uses the local parks for PE for their elementary school students, and the Union Square location will be using the gyms and pool at the local YMCA for recreation. Students do neighborhood walks and interview local politicians and business owners—just as Caroline Pratt described in *I Learn from Children* in the early twentieth century. In *A Pattern Language* (1977), Christopher Alexander and his colleagues at Berkeley suggested Shopfront Schools (pattern #85): "Around the age of 6 or 7, children develop a great need to learn by doing, to make their mark on a community outside the home. If the setting is right, these needs lead children directly to basic skills and habits of learning," he writes.[130] Alexander's answer to the problem of maintaining a physical connection between home, neighborhood, and school is to decentralize the school, inserting it into the neighborhood fabric in a storefront or other small-scale commercial space on a pedestrian street, near adult workplaces, and within walking distance of a park. Here was another Progressive educational model, updated for the twenty-first century, but ultimately, that wasn't the area AltSchool wanted to innovate.

The Manhattan middle school, executives announced soon after the 2017 opening, will be the last they build.[131] "I believe effective learning can take place anywhere," says Devin Vodicka, the former Vista, California, schools superintendent who joined AltSchool as chief impact officer that May. "Learning should transcend the classroom. Microschools are helpful in informing our strategy, but we are now focused on using the platform, which makes the best education the most accessible."[132] AltSchool's primary goal is not to create a better school as a place but to be a player in all types of schools, private, charter, and public. Change via real estate is slow and expensive, and available to a limited number. "There is a discussion among educators on how to design physical environments to promote personalized learning," Vodicka says. "There are not many models at the moment that school leaders can draw from. Hopefully AltSchool and the Union Square site can be one of those examples." It is hard for me to believe, however, that those who seek to disrupt education won't end up rediscovering the lessons of the 1960s (not to mention the 1910s) and finding that classrooms aren't interchangeable. Without some control over the spaces in which their software is deployed, how will AltSchool even know that it is working? Small class sizes, creative teachers, hands-on activities—these physical manifestations of curriculum contribute to learning as surely as platforms and playlists. In a Bloomberg article on AltSchool's change in direction, current parents reported "their children benefited more from the extensive attention of talented teachers and small class sizes. There are multiple instructors per class, and the school places a premium on interdisciplinary projects, like building a model house that can withstand different weather—a task that incorporates current events, science, engineering and budgeting."

Alex Ragone, head of school for AltSchool Union Square, says that the schools and districts interested in the AltSchool platform are probably already moving in a progressive direction and have left the rows of desks behind.[133] AltSchool may not need to franchise their phone booths and steps because they are already part of the design vocabulary of the twenty-first-century school. Instead, Ragone sees AltSchool's software as a support for teachers working in less-than-ideal circumstances, allowing them to organize and track kids so that a big class can operate more like a small one. The benefits he ascribes to AltSchool's software are a kind of shorthand for good teachers, those individuals with a preternatural ability to remember, anticipate, and connect with each kid in their room. With the intelligence gleaned from students' data—and sufficient support to learn how to use it—the question AltSchool now explores is how, and whether, software can make more good teachers. The real test will be at scale, when performance can be tracked across a wide variety of schools, public and private, large and small, rather than just boutique environments. While AltSchool's founders seem happy to use their children as guinea pigs, will other parents see it as a choice? Would funding be better applied to creating replicable school architecture, as the team behind the Academy for Global Citizenship hopes to do? The lesson I draw from history is that curriculum and its container must ever be complementary. Beware those selling a fix in an app, as well as in a shiny new building. The best students—the Laura Ingallses of the world—can learn by rote as well as by following their bliss. To teach everyone else, the physical and the intellectual must be in sync, building on the foundation of the simple needs identified for the early twentieth-century classroom: light and air.

CHAPTER 4

PLAYGROUND

Marian called it Roxaboxen.
(She always knew the name of everything.)
There across the road, it looked like any rocky hill—
Nothing but sand and rocks, some old wooden boxes,
cactus and greasewood and thorny ocotillo—
but it was a special place.

—Alice McLerran, *Roxaboxen* (1991)

Roxaboxen was just that: rocks, boxes, thirsty desert plants, and a road curved like a river that Marian, the mayor, named River Rhode. It was an empty hill, too rocky for gardens, too steep for houses. But to the children in the neighborhood, it became a city. Currency: round black pebbles. Construction materials: white stones, desert glass, "bits of amber, amethyst, and sea-green, a house of jewels." Furniture: wooden boxes. Transportation: sticks (horses), "something round for a steering wheel" (cars). If you broke the speed limit, you had to go to jail. There were rules in Roxaboxen, taken from the adult world: You had to pay for ice cream, you were safe in your fort, there was a cemetery for dead pets. All these details are outlined in Marian Doan's diary, written in 1916, and the basis for daughter Alice McLerran's 1991 illustrated book *Roxaboxen*. The story of Roxaboxen had been passed down as oral history, from Marian to her children. As adults, the citizens of Roxaboxen would find themselves thinking of the place, triggered by a black pebble or called to return to a dusty corner of Yuma, Arizona, by the white stones and sea glass, which remained long after Main Street was dispersed by wind and sand. McLerran's version is poetic and painterly, setting a scene with a few bright strokes and letting children's imaginations fill in the rest, as her mother must have done before her.

Roxaboxen has undergone something of a revival in recent years. After the book came out, children in Yuma realized that the place still existed, and a private group bought the land and gave it to the city—just as it was. A companion volume, including Marian's original diary, was published in 1998, filling out the story of the site's before and after.[1] In 2015, Jon Mooallem wrote in the *California Sunday Magazine* about his own pilgrimage, as a new father, to that rocky hill at the corner of Eighth Street and Second Avenue in Yuma: "It didn't look like much: a steeply sloping, empty lot in a weathered subdivision. But as soon as I climbed the hill, I saw the shrine-like arrangements of rocks and desert glass. Some of the newer ones still glinted; the orderliness of others had eroded over time. They'd been deposited there by readers on pilgrimages, or mailed to the site, via a local art museum, with notes or dedications, from around the world."[2]

I read *Roxaboxen* as part of an ongoing oral history of outdoor play, one that watches children at a distance, provides tools and refreshments when needed, and leaves their invented structures alone. The first spaces in America called "play grounds" were created in Boston out of piles of sand, providing the raw material for imaginative play Marian and the other children found wild(ish) in Yuma. Since then, parents, educators, social workers, and designers have debated what the baseline materials for a playground should be: sand and water, wood and cardboard, or equipment and activities. If the answer is wood, is it a pile of scrap like the ones that inspired Caroline Pratt and Hilary Page, or precut panels like those that inspired the Eameses? If there is an "apparatus"—what we would now call a climbing structure—should it look like a Western fort or a rocket ship or a simpler, older form, like the wood pyramids children held in their hands at a Froebel kindergarten?

Playgrounds are places made by adults, for children, always with the hope of harnessing their play to a specific location. This is what architectural historian Roy Kozlovsky calls the "paradox of the modern discourse of play": As society sets aside space and time for childhood, through kindergartens, public schools, and, in the early twentieth century, playgrounds, "it is subjected, just like education, to the social and political designs of others."[3] Playgrounds were seen first as grounds for assimilation of diverse immigrant populations around a common goal (sports!), but later as an antiauthoritarian tool, an area where kids could rule. Once lawyers got involved, the playground began to seem more like a playpen, with rules on how high kids could climb and how soft the ground needed to be beneath their feet, limiting what had been a fruitful project for designers in the decades after World War II.

Roxaboxen's appeal is part of a more general feeling, over the past decade, that the regulators and narrators have grown too powerful. The 1959 United Nations Declaration of the Rights of the Child state, "The child shall have full opportunity for play and recreation, which should be directed to the same purposes as education."[4] *Great!* you think. And then, *"directed"?* What McLerran saw in her mother's stories of that place was a truth commonly acknowledged by child-development experts: Children require their own spaces, stocked with simple, manipulable objects, not just in the classroom but outside, in the world. Children can only understand risk if they are allowed to experience it, whether in the confines of a playground or on the way to it. Navigating the city solo engages some of the same senses, and can bring the same satisfaction, as finally climbing to the top of the jungle gym. Junk playgrounds, created in the aftermath of war, have been revived in a time of overdesigned peace. One can find them in residential neighborhoods in Tokyo, or on an island off the coast of Manhattan, or as part of the facilities run-up to the 2014 Commonwealth Games in Glasgow. Designer playgrounds created by artists or architects seek to provide the same freedom as block play, without moving parts. The beauty of Roxaboxen was partly in its particularity: Nowhere else could you find that combination of pebbles and sand, desert glass and ocotillo, that gave the kids just enough material to build their own playground. The best playgrounds have a mood of their own, but I believe there are many ways to achieve that end. A natural setting is by no means required.

On a recent trip to Copenhagen, I visited Traffic House, recently renovated by GHB Landskab and architects MLRP. Situated in the large, green Faelledparken, Traffic House is mostly paved, an asphalt wonderland painted with road markings in which children are literally in the driver's seat. Bicycles and scooters, available for check-out, allow children in one of the most pedestrian- and bike-friendly cities in the world to experience the other side of transportation, driving on miniature roads, obeying traffic signals, signs, crosswalks, and roundabouts. On a weekday afternoon, it was mayhem, but the park offers workshops on the weekend as an addition to the traffic safety curriculum all Danish students are taught in primary and secondary school (45 percent of them bike to school). The original traffic playground opened in 1974. The architects had updated it for the fortieth anniversary, but the goal remained the same: teaching the laws of the roads through hands-on-the-handlebars experience.[5] In 2016, another "traffic garden" opened in Seattle, modeled on the Copenhagen version.[6] There's no way of knowing what city the children are driving through on the windshield of their minds, and that's the beauty of even a park made of pavement: It's a site of autonomy, where you as a parent can sit on a bench—in the shade, if you please—and watch them go.

•

THE FIRST AMERICAN playground had no climbing bars, no seesaws, no swings. In 1885, a group of female philanthropists decided that the immigrant children of Boston's North End needed somewhere other than the increasingly crowded and dangerous streets to play. They paid for a pile of sand to be poured into the yard of a chapel on Parmenter Street at the beginning of summer.[7] "Playing in the dirt is the royalty of childhood," said Kate Gannett Wells, chair of the Massachusetts Emergency and Hygiene Association. The idea came from Germany, where such "sand gardens" were introduced in Berlin's public parks in 1850 as an offshoot of Friedrich Froebel's emphasis on the "garden" part of kindergarten.[8] The success of the first sandpile spurred subsequent summer installations on Parmenter Street and Warrenton Street, each supervised by a matron. By 1887 there were ten sand gardens, mostly located near the settlement houses that served recently arrived immigrant families. Country children had plenty of dirt, while wealthier city children likely had yards; it was poor children who needed access to free, communal play spaces.

As the number of such gardens increased, they began to be located in schoolyards and eventually became the property of the school board and parks department. A ten-acre "outdoor gymnasium," with aboveground play equipment like swings and seesaws as well as sand opened in the West End in 1889, as well as twenty other playgrounds in Boston. One opened in New York that year and another, in Chicago, in 1892 at reformer Jane Addams's Hull House. The Hull House playground was more elaborate, with sandpiles, swings, building blocks, a giant slide, and ball courts for older children.[9] When Boston mayor Josiah Quincy VI was inaugurated in 1897, he proclaimed every ward should have a playground, and the city followed through. In 1907, neighboring Cambridge opened its own gardens, using local schoolyards. Older children were sometimes turned away due to fears that they might get bored and cause trouble, but superintendents found that one in three would soon come back with a young relative, asking to "mind baby in the sand."[10] The repurposing of urban schoolyards for out-of-school use echoes more recent efforts, in New York among other cities, to open these spaces as weekend parks, installing trees, painting lines, and thinking about equipment to serve the needs of neighborhood adults and children. Play, once thought of as the exclusive province of children, is now seen as a lifetime need, while open space remains at a premium.

What were children doing in the sand? G. Stanley Hall, the psychologist who pioneered the study of child behavior, grew fascinated by the societies that spring up around sand play. In 1888, friends of Hall's, the Rev. Dr. A. and his wife, Mrs. A., decided their boys did not have enough to do at their summer cottage twenty or thirty miles outside Boston. Mrs. A. decided the solution, "not without some inconvenience," was to have sand brought in from a faraway beach and dumped in their yard, steps from the back door. Hall wrote of their experience in *Scribner's Magazine* as keenly as any naturalist: "The 'sand-pile' at once became, as everyone who has read Froebel or observed childish play would have expected, the one bright focus of attraction, besides which all other boyish interests gradually paled.

Wells and tunnels; hills and roads like those in town; islands and capes and bays with imagined water; rough pictures drawn with sticks . . ."[11] The first summer or two are for excavation and discovery, with primitive shelters made of propped-up boards and bricks. After a time of treating the sandpile like wilderness, the boys begin to introduce rural civilization. A knot of wood becomes a horse, men are whittled from sticks, and gradually hunting and gathering is replaced by agriculture, new farmhouses dwarfed by elaborate barns, miniature fields planted with real beans, wheat, oats, and corn. The sons of the As are joined by friends from other cottages, who build houses and barns of their own. Slowly they reinvent the plow and the wheel out of wood, wire, tin, and leather, then start stamping money out of felt. The key is the availability of "loose parts," elements children can pick up and transform into environments themselves, rather than having places to jump, hide, and tunnel set out by unseen designers' hands. Children are the designers here and, even though they are under adult supervision, they have more autonomy than within the fenced and labeled precincts of fixed equipment.

Sand was also a material of choice at the first Progressive schools. The Horace Mann School at Columbia University compensated for lack of open space by creating a rooftop playground, stocked with a small garden, a sandbox, art materials, and woodworking tools, along with an aquarium and cages for animals.[12] The teachers there integrated indoor and outdoor play, while creating indoor and outdoor curricula: a more directed version of the loose parts model that still allowed children freedom to explore. At John Dewey's Laboratory School at the University of Chicago, children gained hands-on experience with indoor and outdoor sandboxes, using them to learn about landforms and erosion, or as a relief map base for building twig forts and log cabins of previous civilizations. "On their sand table the whole class may make a town with houses and streets, fences and rivers, trees and animals for the gardens," write Dewey and his daughter Evelyn in *Schools of To-Morrow* (1915). "In supplying the needs of the dolls and their own games, they are supplying in miniature the needs of society."[13] Back at the As' sandpile, "Why do you have no church?" the boys were asked. "Because," they replied, "we are not allowed to play in the "sand-pile" on Sunday, but have to go to church." "And why have you no school?" "Why," said they, exultingly, "it is vacation, and we don't have to go to school."[14]

But eventually adults enter the Eden. Once it is known that Hall will visit the sandpile in the fall, and may write about it, the miniature community spruces itself up, as if for a state visit. A young lady adds decorative paint to roofs and walls. A carpenter makes tools for show and not for use. Some boys age out of their immersion in the parallel society and become self-conscious. Fall comes, school and sports call, and the sandpile quiets down, though some residents spend the winter making new inventions indoors for summer use. The parents of the boys are happy with their experiment, estimating that eight months of schoolwork have been covered in a summer in the sand. The boys have solved their own problems of administration, carpentry, industrialization, sewerage, and monetization. They have cooperated and rarely been idle, even as they played in the yard under observation and minimal intervention. "Here is perfect mental sanity and unity, but with more variety than in the most heterogeneous and soul-disintegrating school curriculum," Hall writes. The boys have created a unified and ideal curriculum out of the sandpile and one which, he believes, prepares them for adult lives of action and imagination. Today, the sandbox has become so familiar that, as Jay Mechling writes in the essay "Sandwork," "playing with sand in its various states is so universal that the play has become nearly invisible to us, so taken-for-granted that it bumps up against what Brian Sutton-Smith

(1970) called the 'triviality barrier' of children's play," and falls below adult notice.[15] Yet while the digging and sifting are invisible, the tame little sandbox itself has been demonized as unclean, visited after hours by vermin or used as a litterbox by cats bearing toxoplasmosis. Like its early playground neighbors, the merry-go-round and the seesaw, equipment that was once trivial has become an endangered species in the urban environment. Once upon a time sand was a little bit of freedom, especially for children whose summers never included a trip to the beach.

Even as the number of real sandboxes has dwindled, the term's reach has expanded to the point where it designates any limited environment offering ultimate freedom to explore without consequence, smash and build, and smash and build again. Today the sandbox is as likely to be the rectangular space of the computer screen, where digital sand, in the form of *Minecraft* cubes or Scratch block commands, are used to explore building, civilizations, and geography. The "Good Toys" narrative in *Minecraft* is most deeply embedded in the terminology used to refer to the game's Creative mode. "May 10, 2009: From the beginning, *Minecraft* was a sandbox creative building game," reads the time line in the official *Minecraft* wiki. Video games played in sandbox mode, or purpose-built sandbox games, allow the player access to the whole world (the box) at once, and allow her to change that world at will (the sand). There is no preset narrative to force the player to run, hide, or shoot, and no marauders to destroy what she has built. Time is her own. The pleasure is in the creation, as it was for the As' young sons with sand and twigs and other scavenged materials.

Sandbox has taken on a pacifist and constructive meaning in games, but it could have gone the other way. Tabletop sandboxes were used as educational tools for small children in Dewey's era, but long before, they were military tools for diagramming war strategy. A plan of attack might originally have been sketched on the ground of the battlefield with a stick, but even during the Roman Empire, sand tables would have been set up within military encampments, with tokens representing soldiers and units in the coming battle.[16] *Minecraft* is probably the most popular sandbox game of the moment, but earlier hits like *SimCity* and *Spore* demonstrated a market for open-ended game play, and before them 1990s games like *Lemmings 2: The Tribes* and *Railroad Tycoon* had modes in which players could explore the game at will. In a detailed history of sandbox games published on the website Gamasutra, Steve Breslin unpacks the metaphor in terms of its relationship to a preindustrial childhood: "It implies that it is a *young child* in the sandbox (and a pre-videogame child at that, with no toys), and assumes an idealized childhood imagination, an unlimited creativity. It is a good metaphor, and a useful one, but the metaphor is also a little misleading, insofar as it suggests a sort of dream-world imaginative capability of the audience, which is not always justified."[17] Breslin sees adults as less capable than the child of coming up with a new world from scratch and describes games based solely on "leveraging the player's imagination" as "ambitious, and more than a little risky." The freedom of mind that early childhood experts seek for children in the sandbox is lost by adulthood, he implies, except for adults who make games. "Game design itself," Breslin notes, "is, undoubtedly, the ultimate sandbox game: you the designer get to determine the game's objectives, and not only that, but also create and assemble the artwork and other presentation elements, balance the game as you see fit—create a whole world to play in."

As a result, he argues, such games may actually require more care to create than those with a short-term goal represented in coins or other in-game prizes: "The great risk of the sandbox is that it can be boring," writes Breslin. The care goes into design work that is behind the scenes, as in the prepared environment of the Froebel kindergarten or the stocking of a playground with sand, wood, or junk. In *Minecraft*, the wide array of

materials at the Creative player's command, as well as the implicit competition and explicit community created by YouTube videos, photos, and
blog posts of other players' creations, spurs players on.

There are two different things happening in the sandbox, as there
were two different games being played at Roxaboxen. First, there was the
discovery of materials and the building of the place, set off by Marian's
naming of the River Rhode. Next, there is the narrative, the unfolding
intersection of story and making that turns the box into a stage. The
original sandpiles were framed by the walls of the city; later inventors of
equipment, like Aldo van Eyck, would use colored pavement or geometric
shapes in concrete to give children a territory for invention. Sand is a
material that lends itself to sharing, making, and remaking. In either the
digital or real-life sandbox, the player has to create her own intrinsic
fun. Maybe sandbox games are the playground adults don't realize they
still need.

•

THE PLAYGROUND ASSOCIATION of America (PAA) was founded on
April 12, 1906, and sought to organize the efforts of reformers in cities
across the United States to get public financing for outdoor recreation. They
were lucky in their patronage. President Theodore Roosevelt was elected
honorary president of the PAA and received the organization's leaders
at the White House the next day. In a 1907 letter to Cuno H. Rudolph,
president of the Washington Playground Association, Roosevelt wrote:

> City streets are unsatisfactory playgrounds for children
> because of the danger, because most good games are
> against the law, because they are too hot in summer, and
> because in crowded sections of the city they are apt to

be schools of crime. Neither do small back yards nor
ornamental grass plots meet the needs of any but the very
small children. Older children who would play vigorous
games must have places especially set aside for them; and,
since play is a fundamental need, playgrounds should be
provided for every child as much as schools. This means
that they must be distributed over the cities in such a
way as to be within walking distance of every boy and
girl, as most children can not afford to pay carfare.[18]

In 1887, settlement house leader Charles B. Stover, an activist who also
advocated for public ownership of the nascent subway system, proposed a
New York City law allowing the city to spend up to one million dollars a
year on small parks and playgrounds, but the city didn't spend the money
until 1901.[19] Instead, private funders created the Outdoor Recreation
League, which sponsored the opening of a few small play spaces, typically
little more than a sandpile bordered by three building walls, or a ball court
with a few pieces of play equipment such as seesaws, slides, and horizontal
bars. The most famous of these was Seward Park, on the Lower East Side,
which the city finally adopted in 1903, making it the first of what are now
seven hundred New York City playgrounds. In taking over, and taking on,
Seward Park, the city changed its nature: A limestone and terra-cotta park
pavilion included marble baths, an indoor gymnasium, and meeting
rooms, as well as a broad porch where mothers could sit in rocking chairs
with their babies. A running track encircled the park, with areas set aside
for a children's garden and outdoor play equipment, divided by curving
paths and plantings.[20] Stover, who had badgered the city to invest in play
and transportation, became parks commissioner.

In Chicago, architect Dwight H. Perkins, whom we met earlier as a
designer of Progressive era schools, and sociologist Charles Zueblin argued
that public space was the key to developing civic spirit, and that children

needed more options for play than vacant lots and the existing parks, which were designed for passive recreation. Perkins was appointed to the Special Park Commission of Chicago in 1901 and went on to design a number of parks, playgrounds, and field houses for the city over the next decade. As architectural historian Jennifer Gray writes, the design of playgrounds in the early twentieth century rapidly became a formula.[21] From above, the parks resembled a textile pattern, with facilities radiating out from a central building housing changing facilities, an indoor gym, and sometimes classrooms for adult education. Close to the building, you were likely to find ceremonial spaces, like decorative fountains or a paved concert promenade or grove. An open ground bordered by trees and paths would be provided for games, and smaller zones—also set off by planted beds, tracks, or low walls and benches—would be provided for children's play equipment and a sandbox. Separate exercise spaces were set aside for men and women, plus a pool. The most important contribution of the playground reformers was making play into policy: Setting aside space within rapidly built-up cities became a municipal priority, no longer dependent on individual charities or tied to the settlement movement.[22] The anarchic and self-built nature of the sandpile was replaced by Beaux-Arts planning: symmetrical, geometric, with a place for each activity, and every activity in its place.

The architecture, with its fussy separations and organized agenda, reflected the ideology of the child-saving movement, adopted as urban policy. Children were genuinely in danger on the city streets—in 1910, traffic accidents were the leading cause of death for children ages five to fourteen, and in 1908, five hundred children marched up Eleventh Avenue, known as "Death Avenue," carrying a coffin lid to protest the predations of the New York Central Railroad—but well-meaning adults also feared the effects of too much freedom to roam.[23] The streets were dangerous because of traffic but also because of the corrupting influence of, and competition for space with, adults.[24] "What the boy's play has to do with building character in him Froebel has told us," wrote reformer Jacob Riis in in an 1899 essay for the *Atlantic* titled "The Genesis of the Gang." In the city, "that prop was knocked out. New York never had a children's playground till within the last year. Truly it seemed . . . as if in the early plan of our city the children had not been thought of at all."[25] As with the Progressive era push to outlaw child labor and make primary education mandatory, there was a paternalistic and nationalist side to the playground movement's positive effects. A mural painted by children's book author Lucy Fitch Perkins, at the University of Chicago Settlement House designed by her husband Dwight H. Perkins and built in 1904, is emblematic of the underlying purpose of the new playgrounds. Lucy Perkins used children from the Back of the Yards neighborhood as models for her "May-Pole Dance, Children of All Nations," which showed children in a variety of national costumes coming together to dance around a maypole, with mothers and babies looking on.[26] On the playgrounds, participating in games and exercises devised by professional play leaders, these American children would form a more perfect union. In order to do so, they needed a program of "directed activity," rather than "scrub play," focused on specific skills, sports, and the building of a healthy mind and body.[27] Henry S. Curtis, a student of child psychologist G. Stanley Hall and the founding secretary and treasurer of the PAA, had looked at recreation in England and Germany and found their organized gymnastics "individualistic and militaristic."[28] Team sports were the order of the day, as they forced children from disparate backgrounds to work together toward a common goal and elevated group effort over individual achievement. On the playgrounds, children of all levels of experience would be absorbed into a new collective. As Curtis wrote, "There is no more rich and poor in a scout patrol than there is in a baseball game. You have to deliver the goods to get preferment . . . Play is the most democratic activity we know."[29]

The sturdy field houses that were part of these new parks grew to house branches of the public library, as well as offering classes in infant welfare, music, painting, drawing, and dancing. Pasteurized milk was on tap, along with professional nurses and day nurseries. Alongside saving children from the streets, Progressive era reformers were deeply interested in reducing infant mortality; providing safe food and training mothers in proper baby care and hygiene slashed the rate from 100 per 1,000 live births in 1915 to less than 50 per 1,000 live births by 1950.[30] And all of this was supervised by professional "play directors" who were expected to be knowledgeable about sociology, physiology, psychology, and child development, as well as being athletes.[31] The supervisor of the South Park (Chicago) playground system described the play directors' role as "thoughtful managers, interpreters of child and adolescent life, chemists of human desires."[32] The Oakland superintendent of recreation claimed the play director should have the same qualities as a corporate manager or army officer. And John H. Chase, headworker at the Goodrich House in Cleveland, Ohio, contributing to the PAA's monthly journal the *Playground* in 1909, wrote, "Our first great hope is to have our playground become a place where hundreds of children may play. We want a play factory; we want it to run at top speed, on schedule time, with the best machinery, and with skilled operatives. We want to turn out the maximum product of happiness, to utilize all the space, to be awake to new inventions, to use our minds for planning and our hearts for enthusing."[33] Historian Dominick Cavallo quotes this description of a typical day at a New York playground run by the board of education: "It is one o'clock. The pianist has struck a welcome chord, and all the children assembled fall in line for the grand march. At a signal, the flag is saluted; then two or three patriotic songs are heartily sung, after which the order is given to 'break ranks.' "[34]

Despite this emphasis on the melting pot nature of the playground, not every child received the same training. Women's exercises, typically held on smaller, sex-segregated outdoor gymnasiums, avoided competitive sports and were considered good for developing the figure. Because playgrounds were highly tuned to their own neighborhood, housing and income segregation limited the diversity of the populations who used them, as it did freshly built public schools. African American children were largely excluded from the marquee urban playgrounds. In another parallel to the early public school system, they were provided with inferior facilities and left with the earlier generation of play spaces, like vacant lots and closed-off streets.[35] In 1921, of 3,969 municipally operated playgrounds and recreation centers in the United States, only fifty-six reported having a playground available for black children, and only fourteen cities ran integrated playgrounds.[36] Emmett J. Scott, secretary-treasurer at Howard University and former secretary to Booker T. Washington wrote an editorial in the *Playground* in 1925, titled "Leisure Time and the Colored Citizen," pointing out the lack of playgrounds for black children in the urban North, as well as playgrounds for any children in the South. "The negro child," wrote Scott, "through lack of encouragement and sometimes through definite prohibition, is practically and completely left out of consideration in both city planning and municipal maintenance of recreation centers in many sections of our country . . . The negro child must have the facilities for recreation to the same degree as the white child, if he is to develop into the healthy and right-thinking citizen that the country needs and the nation requires."[37] Playground advocates felt that play was an activity of assimilation and strength building. Scott built on that to argue, as Washington had for schools, for separate but equal facilities. He cites a previous article by Ernest T. Attwell, hired by what was by then known as the Playground and Recreation Association of America to do outreach in the black community, who pointed out that the health and well-being of African Americans was necessary to the overall health and well-being of the "body of the community." A "play factory . . . turn[ing] out the maximum product of happiness" is a far cry from the sandpile or Creative mode. As playgrounds were taken over by government they, like schools, became instruments of assimilation, backed by arguments about the common good for adult society, rather than a place where children were in charge.

•

ALONG WITH AN emphasis on organized activities, these playgrounds featured an abundance of equipment: architectures built purely for play. Period photographs of Seward Park in New York show a vast metal climbing frame, with hooks for ropes and swings, and boys perched on the corners, twenty feet off the ground, as if in a treetop. But reformers were divided over whether use of equipment did children any good. One described the psychological effect of swinging as "similar to getting drunk," while Curtis derided it as "unsocial." "It gives very little training to the eye or the hand or the judgment."[38] For girls, the swing was seen as a potential source of "voluptuous excitement."[39] Nonetheless, early twentieth-century playgrounds typically included an area for the "apparatus," metal- and wood-framed equipment installed over a bare patch of sand, grass, or dirt. Brenda Biondo's 2014 book *Once Upon a Playground* includes a number of period postcards showing gymnasiums across the United States. One in Rochester, Minnesota, from 1918 shows a metal frame hung with rings and ropes, plus a ladder and a high slide. Playgrounds in New York and Akron in 1914 had arrays of wooden seesaws in long rows, while one in Milwaukee, shown in a 1910 postcard, included a wooden rocking boat, like a precursor of amusement parks' pirate ship rides.[40] By the early 1930s, playgrounds had started to lose their staff, and their agenda. The apparatus, freely used by children, became the center of play, and manufacturers advertised their products simultaneously for their safety and their thrills. Many of these structures look terrifying to us today and in fact, in 1912, New York City removed gymnasiums from its parks because they were considered too dangerous.[41] Metal merry-go-rounds, wavy slides twenty-five or thirty feet high, tilting ladders set five feet in the air, poles ringed with ropes onto which children clung, jumped, and spun: Dislocated shoulders and broken bones seem inevitable. A 1931 advertisement for the Karymor, a spinning wheel surrounded by an eight-sided bench, reads, "You can't keep children from climbing all over a piece of apparatus. Karymor is so constructed that there is no place about the device for a child to get caught in a pinch or jam. Several State Institutions for Blind Children have installed Karymors because of the many safety features."[42] The popular Giant Stride, which had short ladders suspended from a central pole, promised ACTION! THRILLS![43] Despite manufacturer claims for safety, there were no federal regulations specifically addressed toward playground apparatuses until the 1970s. The creation of the Consumer Product Safety Commission in 1972, and the publication of 1981 guidelines for public playgrounds, changed the allowable height and distances between apparatuses as well as the type of surfacing material recommended for use underneath.[44]

The jungle gym has the most fascinating origin story, intersecting with the career of superintendent Carleton Washburne in Winnetka, Illinois. Physical play was an important part of the Winnetka curriculum, and the public schools shared a full-time physical education teacher. A local patent attorney named Sebastian Hinton had grown up in Japan playing on a multicube bamboo frame created by his mathematician father. It was originally built to teach three-dimensional geometry, but the children preferred climbing around on it "like monkeys." Hinton met Washburne at a dinner, and the two worked with Perry Dunlap Smith, the headmaster of the North Shore Country Day School, on a prototype made of iron pipes that was installed at the school in 1920 and patented as a "climbing structure" by Junglegym Inc., Hinton's company, the same year.[45] "But that is an ideal piece of school playground equipment. It can take care of many children in a small area. It satisfies every child's desire to climb. It exercises all the muscles," Washburne wrote in his memoir of his time as Winnetka superintendent.[46] An improved version was made for the playground at the public Horace Mann School nearby; when that school was demolished in 1940, the climbing frame was reinstalled at Crow Island, where it was in use until 2010. A 1948 advertisement for a "Junglegym" made by the J. E. Porter Corporation claims the structure has "more than ONE HUNDRED MILLION child-play-hours without one serious accident . . . It is called the 'Magnet of the Playground'" and was designed to meet the requirements of the Federal Housing Authority.[47] By the end of World War II, the standard playground was well-enough established that it had started to become dull, and the baby boom provoked a second expansion of public facilities for children, in both the city and the new suburbs. While many public officials were content with the four Ss— sandbox, slide, swing, seesaw—postwar focus on controlling and improving the lives of children, and rebuilding cities, led to an explosion of new forms for outdoor play.

•

IN THE SUMMER of 1920, children themselves constructed Squirrel Hall at the King Alfred School in North London. This enormous roof partly supported by the branches of an oak tree sheltered them in all weathers, while students as young as six helped to build an open-air theater.

Readings, plays, and science experiments were also conducted outdoors, and the education was based on the teachings of Pestalozzi and Froebel, as well as American educator Helen Parkhurst. Boys and girls were taught together, and from the first days, students were allowed to choose their own plan of study. Founded in 1898, the King Alfred School was a parallel experiment to Dewey's Laboratory School and Pratt's City and Country School, and it is hard to imagine a more exemplary pupil than architect Aldo van Eyck, who studied there until he was 14.[48]

Van Eyck has always seemed a Zelig-like figure in postwar architecture history, rebuilding Amsterdam after World War II, popping up in seminal collectives like the Congrès Internationaux d'Architecture Moderne (CIAM) and Team 10, and anticipating the cellular experimentation of the 1970s with projects like the Amsterdam Municipal Orphanage (1955–60).[49] There, van Eyck used a limited array of simple geometric shapes to create the interiors, which combined to make a gridded, nonhierarchical structure from what look like egg crates. Circles and squares, circles in squares, hexagons in circles, carving out and building up an interior landscape that would challenge the orphanage's inhabitants at every stage of their development.[50] In the infant quarters, a set of stacked cylinders of diminishing diameter became an indoor mountain. Through a plate-glass window, the infants could look at older kids digging outside in a covered circular sandpit, the valley to their hill. In the house for ten- to fourteen-year-old girls, residents would eat at a central communal table, a terrazzo hexagon ringed with cylindrical stools. To create a sense of enclosure, van Eyck added metal lamps on uprights and a tiny interior roof. An open kitchen in the same space encouraged group preparation of meals.

The materials for all of these installations were concrete, terrazzo, and stained wood—sober finishes for high-traffic areas. Van Eyck added a bit of shimmer via glass, water, and inset mirrors. In the loggia outside the house for two- to four-year-olds, there was a play pool that was half covered by the roof, half open to the sky, and ringed with seats. On a sunny day, pink-tinted glass set between the concrete backrests caught light and reflected it onto the surface of the pool, where the water bounced colored reflections up to the underside of the loggia. In an interior party room, funhouse mirrors were set into the top of a concrete platform intended for use as a campfire-like sitting area, creating an object of interest that also suggested a view to another world. That glimpse proved to be too distracting, even disturbing. Van Eyck later said, "The children very much appreciated the distorting mirrors—they saw all sorts of things in them—which is why they were removed!"[51]

Squares and circles and hexagons are mainstays of the preschool design vocabulary, but you rarely see children's architecture today, even in contemporary schools, in gray and brown, without carpeting, without imagery, without the tiresome palette of primary colors. One school of playground design offers up a cartoon of the child's interests, via stagecoach climbing structures or rocket ship slides. Van Eyck adhered to the minimalist school, where the architecture is a backdrop and armature for children's creativity. Imaginary animals don't belong in the city, he said in a 1962 lecture. They shut imagination down rather than stimulating it. "A play object has to be real in a way that a telephone box is real because you can make calls from it, or that a bench is real because you can sit on it. An aluminum elephant is not real. An elephant ought to be able to walk. It is unnatural as a thing in the street."[52] Van Eyck's influence can best be measured through the more than seven hundred playgrounds he designed between 1947 and 1978 as an employee of Amsterdam's town planning department. Architectural historian Liane Lefaivre writes, of the playgrounds, "The architectural profession was not capable of perceiving them because they were so immaterial, built out of thin air, as it were."[53] Van Eyck often sketched them in crayon. For years they were such a fixture of Amsterdam's streets that they went unseen, and many were torn out. A 2001 survey found 370 demolished and 237 drastically altered, with only 90 as they were originally designed. A 2016 survey found that only 17 in the city center remained intact; a small book, titled *Aldo van Eyck: Seventeen Playgrounds*, was published in their honor and as a spur for preservation of the van Eyck pieces that remain.[54] The reason for the decay, especially in neighborhoods built during the city's postwar expansion, is the aging population. New housing and new playgrounds were built for young families in postwar Amsterdam, but now those parents are senior citizens and the equipment has no audience.

In 1946, van Eyck was hired by Cornelius van Eesteren, head of Amsterdam's new City Development Department, and assigned to work on the design of new children's playgrounds with Jacoba Mulder, van Eesteren's second-in-command. Van Eyck's first playground was at Bertelmanplein, a twenty-five- by thirty-meter public square with mature trees, surrounded by housing built between the wars—housing where Mulder lived. One day, on her way to work, she saw a little girl digging in the dirt near a tree and making mud pies. But then a dog came and peed in the tree planter, and that was the end of the play. Mulder decided that a playground was needed, and van Eyck volunteered for the job.[55] A neighbor walking by saw that playground and wrote to van Eesteren, requesting one in his neighborhood. And the same thing happened again, and again, until it became a policy. Any neighborhood in the city that wanted a playground could request one, and the planners pinpointed abandoned and war-damaged sites within the historical fabric of the city as prime locations, along with spaces in the new housing developments being built on the city's periphery. After they were built, the letters kept coming, some with complaints about sand blowing in houses and being used by animals, others with complaints about overcrowding and youths "petting" after dark. But still, the majority of letters were requests were for more playgrounds.[56]

At Bertelmanplein, van Eyck established his basic vocabulary. In a small park, surrounded by trees, he placed a rectangular sandpit with a low concrete wall in the northwest corner, with cutouts in the curb to make it easier for small children to enter. In the sand he placed four round concrete play tables and a single steel climbing arch. On a diagonal from the sandpit, on the pavement, he added a set of three tumbling bars. Around the edge of the park, under the trees, there were five benches for parents. And that was it. The benches and the edge of the sandpit gave a sense of enclosure, but the park, like all that would follow, was open. His second playground, built at Zaanhof in 1948, was in the courtyard of a large housing structure, with trees at each of the four corners and the center of each side. Van Eyck absorbed that square geometry, creating four play areas, one with a large circular sandpit, one with seven concrete cylinders, one with steel somersault frames, and the fourth with a triangular steel merry-go-round. The paving of the play areas was white, with benches for adults staged on the ordinary brown.

Van Eyck never said whether the concrete cylinders that pop up in his playgrounds, placed in grids, were forest, columns, or rocks. Are "somersault frames"—bent half rounds of steel—tunnels or stepping-stones, solid or void? The most recognizable equipment are the "igloos," domes of steel rods that are a climbing challenge for larger kids, and a convenient playhouse for smaller ones. That's for the children to decide. It may be that the Amsterdam playgrounds do too little. It's hard to tell whether neighboring buildings give them a sense of privacy or merely channel the wind to whip through.

The most fascinating of van Eyck's playgrounds is the one tied most closely to the idea of reconstruction. On Dijkstraat, in 1954, he was given the narrow footprint of a demolished house, right in the center of Amsterdam and flanked by three- and four-story buildings. The site, open at one end, could feel dark and threatening, but van Eyck introduced diagonals, slashing it with white concrete tile and brown brick to form triangular stages and inserting a rare triangular sandpit. Somersault frames near the street act as a portal, with activities becoming more intense, and more dense, as you head to the back of the site. He was searching for a modern language that would sit back, allowing the children to take center stage. Even if children were in the city, that didn't mean their movement or imagination should be circumscribed. Robert McCarter, author of a recent

Dijkstraat, Amsterdam, the Netherlands, c. 1950. [Courtesy Amsterdam City Archive]

monograph on van Eyck, writes: "In making his designs van Eyck drew on his collection of photographs of children at play in Venice, Amsterdam, London, and other cities around the world, for he understood that children find ways to play with everything built in the city, whether they were intended as children's playthings or not."[57] Even as the numbers of playgrounds he designed mounted, van Eyck never standardized the elements, asking that existing walls be left as is and not smoothed over and placing the parts afresh on each site, sandpit first. Lefaivre writes, "Peter Smithson compared them to grains of sand introduced into an oyster (the present-day city) that caused irritation and thereby led to the growth of pearls (a renewal of urban life)."[58] I thought of this when New York had a

Playground at Dijkstraat, Amsterdam, the Netherlands, 1954, Aldo van Eyck.
[Courtesy Amsterdam City Archive]

January blizzard and bike advocates responded on social media with images of children playing in the car-free streets. Van Eyck was ahead of his time in this, too, celebrating "those rare times, such as after a heavy snowfall, when the children take over the spaces of the city, and the entire city becomes a playground."[59] In the classic 1962 children's book *The Snowy Day*, Peter finds his city transformed by the snow into simple shapes, an outside world devoid of adults and primed for experience—author Ezra Jack Keats's interpretation of the same sense of freedom.[60] Van Eyck didn't have that power, but for thirty years he seeded an old city with slices of modernity that offered children stages for play, separate but not sequestered from the business of adult streets and sidewalks.

•

THE SOUND OF hammering rings down the street. Walking past the supermarket and the indoor snowboarding facility, I hear the whip of trains on the Nambu Line every five minutes. Round a bend, past whatever the Tokyo equivalent of a bodega might be, I see the curving roofline of a concrete building, ornamented with black-and-white graffiti like an ancient frieze. There's a hand-painted sign on the gate, and lines of bikes and strollers baking in the October Sunday morning sun. The building, a former concrete factory, is a showcase for the material's possibilities, with curving overhangs and open, California-style walkways. But the architecture I'm actually here to see is still in progress, a street of what will be tiny, open-air booths currently laid out on the dirt in chalk lines.

The people wielding tape measures, paintbrushes, and saws are kids, thirty of them, between the ages of five and thirteen. On an industrial edge of Kawasaki, a city that is part of the greater Tokyo metropolitan area, they are building their own high street. Two weeks from now the carpenters will become shopkeepers, selling wares of their own making from the shops they are now building. Pancakes, *pachinko*, handwoven bracelets, slime, bought and sold with actual money. Because the yen will be real, the playworkers at Kodomo Yume Park (which means "children's dream") had to ask parents' permission for the exercise—and request that they not contribute funds. Ordinarily, everything that happens at the thirteen-year-old park is decided by the children and the workers who run it, paid for by the education department of Kawasaki City. There are no waivers, and no dress code; babies were wandering barefoot near the fire pit, and boys were hammering in flip-flops and bike helmets.[61]

PLAY FREELY AT YOUR OWN RISK, reads a sign at Hanegi Park, Tokyo's oldest adventure playground, and all three elements—play, freedom, risk—are in ample evidence here at its younger cousin Yume.[62] Beyond the open space where the village is taking shape, there is more secluded area with a permanent fire pit, water slide, and hammock swing. A mesa of dirt, donated by a construction company that was excavating nearby, is now riddled with canyons and holes, the marks of shovels and buckets of water. When Kodomo Yume Park opened in July 2003 it was hot and humid, and the children spent most of their time huddled in its one air-conditioned space. After a week of that the playworkers had had enough and cut the power. "We told them the air conditioning was broken," says my guide, Hitoshi Shimamura, director of the organization Tokyo Play. *"Then* they started playing with water." At every adventure playground I visited, at some point a child poured a bucket of water down a trench, just to see where it would flow. As architect Richard Dattner says, "Sand and water will give you eighty percent of what a playground can do."[63] Though accounts of junk playgrounds tend to focus on the fire and tools, for urban youth simply mucking about can be a pleasurable way of spending an afternoon. I was reminded of my own younger brother, who never found a stream or puddle too small to fall into. Had we had a Yume Park down the street, he would never have had to go looking for mud.

By happenstance, my Sunday visit to Yume coincided with the publication of "The Anti-Helicopter Parent's Plea: Let Kids Play!" in the *New York Times Magazine*, a piece that annoyed the nation's parents so powerfully it reached a symbolic 2,016 comments before the function was shut down.[64] Yume, Hanegi, and the dozens of other junk playgrounds in Tokyo offer, as a public amenity, what Mike Lanza (said "anti-helicopter parent") created in his private Menlo Park backyard: a challenging and unscheduled place for physical play, largely free of parental supervision, open to any kid who shows up. Lanza's yard, and his self-published book, *Playborhood: Turn Your Neighborhood into a Place for Play*, were born out of memories of his own childhood spent outdoors, with him and his friends refereeing their own made-up games. Melanie Thernstrom, the author the *Times Magazine* piece and a neighbor of Lanza's, sets up a conflict between her conception of risk and Lanza's: He reads the statistics and dismisses low-probability events, like falling off a roof; she reads them and thinks her child will be in that minority. She also highlights the sexism in Lanza's particular conception of play: It is boys who seek risk, and mothers who stop them. Lanza would later deny this gendered reading of his play crusade. Lanza is far from alone in believing American children have a play problem. (And indeed, in his book on the playborhood, Lanza describes the play problem as social and spatial.) At the temporary junk playground set up by the nonprofit play:groundNYC on Governors Island during the summers of 2016 and 2017, a sign on the fence read, YOUR CHILDREN ARE FINE WITHOUT ADVICE AND SUGGESTIONS. Lenore Skenazy's *Free-Range Kids* blog is peppered with reports of cops and child-protective services being called when parents do leave their kids to play unsupervised.

Without broader community support, such attempts are doomed to fail, to become the exercises in vanity—my kids are more resilient than yours!—that the *Times Magazine* article portrays. The answer is providing a greater range of activities so that parents can observe their children building the skills needed to climb roofs and use trampolines, as well as creating safe routes from home to play spaces so that children can get there on their own.

The overprotection of the lives of (some of) America's youth is the result of a nexus of changes to work life, home life, and street life that have made child-rearing into a series of consumer choices, from unsubsidized daycare forward. It is the public realm—where the Tokyo playgrounds operate—that needs to change for American children to have unstructured afternoons and weekends, for them to bike and walk between school and the playground, to see packs of kids get together without endless chains of parental texts. Kawasaki City, where Kodomo Yume Park is located, created its own Ordinance on the Rights of the Child in 2001. It includes an article promising to make "secure and comfortable places for the child." But independence requires infrastructure. Japanese adventure playgrounds can trace their roots back to the junk playgrounds of postwar Denmark. In one such playground, landscape architect Carl Theodor Sørensen set up an enclosed area of slightly more than an acre, stocked with scraps of wood, bricks, mud, and basic tools, supervised by an adult play leader. Sørenson later wrote, "Of all the things I have helped to realize, the junk playground is the ugliest; yet for me it is the best and most beautiful of my works."[65] The playground, in the Copenhagen neighborhood of Emdrup, might have remained a local phenomenon but for a 1945 visit by Marjory Gill Allen, Lady Allen of Hurtwood, a British youth advocate. Allen went back to England and published an illustrated article titled "Why Not Use Our Bomb Sites Like This?" in the *Picture Post* (a magazine similar to America's

Life).[66] Two photo-heavy spreads showed Danish children painting, shoveling, and building (including a replica of a tank), mostly dressed in shorts and sweater vests. Her text began by critiquing the traditional playground—which at that point meant asphalt and an apparatus—as "a place of utter boredom . . . It is little wonder that they prefer the dumps of rough wood and piles of bricks and rubbish of the bombed sites, or the dangers and excitements of the traffic." More than fifty years after the dawn of the child-saving movement, reformers were still trying to get children off the streets, replacing delinquency with activity. Except here, the activity is dirty, constructive, and child-led. Two junk playgrounds opened in the United Kingdom in the next decade, with more to follow. Allen saw the junk playgrounds, which she eventually rechristened "adventure playgrounds" to make them more palatable to local planning councils, as a tool of bottom-up reconstruction for European cities. As with van Eyck's designs in Amsterdam, or even the original sandlots, the new playgrounds could be woven into existing fabric.

Junk playgrounds had a brief postwar flourishing in the United States. The first one opened in Minneapolis in 1949, a one-year experiment called The Yard sponsored by *McCall's* magazine, which published a 1950 cover story about the experiment: "The idea behind THE YARD is simple—to give children their own spot of earth and plenty of tools and materials for digging, building and creating as they see fit. Instead of ready-made playground equipment, THE YARD is stockpiled with tools, used lumber, bricks, tiling, paint, nails, secondhand materials of all kinds. There's an old railroad boxcar too, a 1934 jalopy and a milk truck body the youngsters turn into anything they like."[67] By then, President Truman had paid The Yard a visit, in honor of the Midcentury White House Conference on Children and Youth, to be held in Washington that year. Allen traveled to the United States on a lecture tour in 1965, even meeting with Lady Bird

Johnson at the White House and speaking about playgrounds at the Guggenheim Museum. The American press called her the "no-nonsense dowager" and the "filler-in of gaps."[68] By 1977, there were twenty adventure playgrounds, most about a decade old, operating in Roxbury, Massachusetts; Eugene, Oregon; and Milpitas, Irvine, and Huntington Beach, California.[69] The oldest continually operating American iteration opened in 1979, on the Berkeley Marina, but it is one of only a handful today outside Europe and Japan. There was even one in New York, supported by the Vincent Astor Foundation, which also funded several of the most advanced architect-designed public playgrounds built circa 1970. The next year, the *New Yorker*'s Talk of the Town column paid a visit to one of them run by the Lenox Hill Neighborhood Association, on the corner of First Avenue and East Seventieth Street, shown around by a young woman named Beverly Peyser, dressed for play in "sunglasses, a long print dress, and high-heeled sandals." "The whole idea of this playground is a 'happening,'" Peyser said. "It's the idea of not staging anything. There is a feeling of chaos as you look around, but out of the feeling of chaos comes something."[70] Kids start dancing on top of an old Con Ed spool. "This is a *real* adventure playground," Peyser said. "These children are not supervised. They improvise. They'll build tunnels. They'll build their own slides. The whole theme of the playground will change from day to day . . . One thing is certain—this is not going to be a *tidy* playground."

When journalist Hanna Rosin went looking for adventure playgrounds in 2014, she headed to Wales, where The Land opened in 2012 at the edge of a housing estate outside Wrexham.[71] The story she tells tracks closely with my experience in Tokyo, and with the short documentary, also called *The Land*, made by Erin Davis around the same time. Fire, mud, hammers, wood: The experience is universal. It can also be hard for adults to watch. Sometimes it seems as if a child is in grave danger, sometimes it seems as if nothing is happening. The effect is cumulative. The "adventure" can be with water, with tools, with real fire, or simply with pretend kitchen equipment, allowing the parks to appeal to a much broader spectrum of children, and over a longer period of time. What this means, in practice, is a range of activity over days, weeks, even years. In the morning, the parks become settings for an urban version of a forest preschool, where small children learn the basics of getting along outdoors. In the afternoon, they become a place to let off steam between school and homework; many communities in Tokyo play a public chime at five P.M., a mass call that it is time to go home. On the weekends, Yume Park might ring with the hammers of children, but for teenagers there were other options: a recording studio with padded walls, a wooden shed piled with bike parts for the taking, a quiet, shaded place for conversation. As John Bertelsen, a Danish supervisor for Sørensen's junk playground, wrote in his diary:

> Occasionally, complaints have been made that the
> playground does not possess a smart enough appearance,
> and that children cannot possibly be happy playing about
> in such a jumble. To this I should only like to say that,
> at times, the children can shape and mould the playground
> in such a way that it is a monument to their efforts and a
> source of aesthetic pleasure to the adult eye; at other times
> it can appear, to the adult eye, like a pigsty. However,
> children's play is not what the adults see, but what the
> child himself experiences.[72]

There has been a resurgence of interest in adventure play over the past five years—play:groundNYC, the nonprofit behind the Governors Island project, would like to see mainland, year-round playgrounds in the city, but land values are against them. They are also sensitive to the politics of urban services, where even a junk playground has the potential to spur gentrification. "In New York, any time you put in an amenity for families, you are drawing in higher-income people," says Reilly Bergin Wilson, a member of the board of directors of play:groundNYC and a research associate with the Children's Environments Research Group at the Graduate Center of the City University of New York. "Even if you have the best intentions, even if you put it into a low-income neighborhood."[73] The Sallie Foster Adventure Playground opened in Omaha, Nebraska, in 2015, on donated land next to a community garden, and its prime mover, artist Teal Gardner, hopes to do it again, now that she's moved to Boise, Idaho.[74] Assemble, a London-based design group that unexpectedly won the Turner Prize, named for painter J. M. W. Turner and traditionally given to a single visual artist, in 2015, built a new adventure playground in Glasgow in 2014 as a public art commission for the Commonwealth Games. Citing Lady Allen, they argued that a permanent playground for underprivileged children was a better use of funds than a static art installation. (A year later, they re-created a van Eyck–esque brutalist playground, in foam, at the Royal Institute of British Architects. Play is, once more, avant-garde.) Artists, journalists, and enthusiasts are all responding to the same ennui over public play spaces that Allen described. They have become too circumscribed, too safe, too easy, and the past seems to hold the promise of escape. As Allen wrote, "Children are great explorers, continually discovering and testing the world around them. This is part of growing up and few things are more important, both to the children themselves and to society, but one could hardly say that the world around them does much to help in this vital process."[75]

What happened? It is no coincidence that American adventure playgrounds peaked in the late 1970s, because the 1970s brought lawsuits. Rosin writes, "It's hard to absorb how much childhood norms have shifted in just one generation. Actions that would have been considered paranoid in the '70s—walking third-graders to school, forbidding your kid to play ball in the street, going down the slide with your child in your lap—are now routine."[76] In 1978, a toddler named Frank Nelson was climbing a "tornado slide" in Chicago's Hamlin Park (followed closely by his mother) when he slipped between the railing and the steps and fell to the asphalt below. Seven years later, a judge awarded him a minimum of $9.5 million for severe head injuries.[77] The Chicago Park District, as well as the manufacturer and installer of the slide, had to pay the damages. Subsequently, the park district planned to remove all the twelve-foot-tall tornado slides, reducing the maximum slide height to six feet. In the *Chicago Tribune* story on the outcome of the lawsuit, I was fascinated to read that the twelve-foot slides had remained in use during the seven years since Nelson's injury. The park system's chief engineer, Maurice Thominet, also pushed back against the allegation that the district should install soft surfacing on playlots, or hire park attendants to monitor children. "I can't imagine a mother letting a 1- or 2-year-old go up a 12-foot slide," Thominet said. "That sounds preposterous. What good would it have done to have a supervisor there? What do you think a mother would have done if a supervisor had told her she could not go up the 'tornado'?" Rosin writes that

> Theodora Briggs Sweeney, a consumer advocate and safety consultant from John Carroll University, near Cleveland, testified at dozens of trials and became a public crusader for playground reform. "The name of the playground game will continue to be Russian roulette, with the child as unsuspecting victim," Sweeney wrote in a 1979 paper published in *Pediatrics*. She was concerned about many things—the heights of slides, the space between railings, the danger of loose S-shaped hooks holding parts

together—but what she worried about most was asphalt and dirt. In her paper, Sweeney declared that lab simulations showed children could die from a fall of as little as a foot if their head hit asphalt, or three feet if their head hit dirt.[78]

Today, it is difficult to imagine a twelve-foot slide or a playground without soft surfacing below, and standard play equipment comes with a label stating the ages for which it is appropriate. All of these changes are the result of lawsuits like Nelson's, which resulted in the publication of the first *Handbook for Public Playground Safety* in 1981, under the auspices of the Consumer Product Safety Commission. Those guidelines, as well as technical requirements by the American Society for Testing and Materials, became insurance industry standard. Manufacturers rushed to create equipment that fell within the guidelines, allowing municipalities to limit their risk and resulting in a mass-market playscape where children encounter the same equipment wherever they go. In December 2016, the *New York Times* ran an article showing children playing on one of the city's last seesaws, at the River Run Playground in Riverside Park.[79] Current guidelines suggest seesaws can be used safely if there is a tire installed beneath the seats and a buffer zone around them in case of falls, but the result has been the slow disappearance of the apparatuses, which were on 55 percent of American playgrounds in 2000 but only 7 percent by 2004. The New York City Department of Parks and Recreation said they had not installed a new one, except by special request, in thirty years. Twenty years before, the *Times* ran a similar story about the disappearance of monkey bars, most of them installed when Robert Moses was parks commissioner from 1934 to 1960.[80] It was the height of the bars that doomed them— up to ten feet—as well as the number of bars a falling body might hit on the way down. Teresa B. Hendy, a playground consultant who helped to write the 1980s safety standards, often works with park districts training workers to inspect and maintain their equipment. Soft surfacing reduces the likelihood of head injuries, Hendy told me, but only if it is properly maintained. Classic equipment with moving parts—swings, seesaws, merry-go-rounds—require more frequent checks and replacement of parts, which not every municipality has the capacity to do.[81]

Makers of the play equipment used in the majority of American playgrounds push back against the idea that it is the apparatus that infantilizes. Jeanette Fich Jespersen, international manager of the KOMPAN Play Institute (KOMPAN's research wing) showed me a YouTube video of the Saturn Carousel: a curved arm, attached to a center post, with two one-string swings dangling from the ends. Kids can sit or stand on the seats, holding on to the rope or attached handlebars, and get spun around in tandem. It's social, it's useable in multiple ways, it lets kids balance and spin using both their upper and lower bodies. It looks like a workout. But Jespersen says most American park systems won't buy it or its cousin, the Giant Swing with Birds Nest.[82] "There are some things in the regulations that are very important," says Hendy. "Head entrapment, a movement that could crush or shear a finger, things that project out-of-play equipment that could poke out an eye or cause internal injury. But you can design to avoid those hazards without being design proscriptive." She likes equipment that gently separates children by ability, like the Richter log climber on Governors Island, which layers a rope net over a bed of wood chips below multiple layers of horizontal logs. Small children insinuate themselves between the webs of the net, while older children crawl, walk, or run across the logs above, depending on their balance and confidence. Each account of disappearing equipment describes a real fear but also triggers a kind of instant nostalgia. Parents realize what is lost even as they clutch their children tight. Playground injuries are real:

Approximately two hundred thousand preschool- and elementary-age children received emergency room treatment for such mishaps between 2001 and 2008. Fifteen percent of those were classified as severe, but only 3 percent led to hospitalization.[83] Broken bones were the most common injury, at 36 percent. It is more likely that a child will die in a car accident driving to a playground than while playing there. As the story on The Yard in *McCall's* noted, "After a year of operation, injuries consist of some banged thumbs and small cuts and bruises for the entire enrollment of over 200 children."[84] When play:groundNYC applied for liability insurance, they described every dangerous thing they could think of happening on the playgrounds. The insurance company representative asked whether they were planning to have a bouncy castle, and whether they would ever install a swimming pool. When the organizers said no to both, they were charged approximately seven hundred dollars per year. It would cost seven times that if they wanted to hire a minibus to pick up campers.[85]

Making playgrounds safer has also made them less challenging, and children need challenges to grow, both physically and emotionally. Seesaws, merry-go-rounds, and other disappearing equipment of the past developed the vestibular system, which senses the body's relationship to the ground, improving children's balance and coordination. Monkey bars offered a graduated reward, allowing children to dare themselves to climb higher and higher, from year to year, difficult to do when each apparatus is designed for a specific age cohort. Helle Nebelong, a Danish landscape architect, has even argued that excessive regularity creates its own problems: Children used to all stairs being the same height are more likely to tumble when confronting the irregularities of nature.[86] The new buzzword around children's play is *risk*, popularized by Ellen Beate Hansen Sandseter, a Norwegian professor of early childhood education. Sandseter's 2009 article "Characteristics of Risky Play" sorts such play into six categories: 1) great heights, achieved through climbing, jumping, swinging, or balancing; 2) high speed, via swinging, sliding, running, cycling, skiing; 3) dangerous tools, either with sharp edges or potential for strangulation; 4) dangerous elements, or the unknown, like cliffs and deep water; 5) rough-and-tumble, like wrestling or other forms of play fighting; 6) disappearing or getting lost.[87] Sandseter's categories cover most of the activities of childhood, and it is hard to imagine insulating your child from every one of them. Education programs that teach children how to swim, bicycle, or use the road safely implicitly accept the dangers of those activities while helping children to better manage the risk.[88] Sandseter argues that children are born with an instinct toward risk, because once upon a time their lives were filled with real danger. Exposing themselves to risk, and coming back unharmed, is an essential part of psychological development. Direct experience may, in fact, teach children about which risks are worth taking. "Adults should therefore try to eliminate hazards that children cannot see or manage without removing all risks, so that children are able to meet challenges and choose to take risks in relatively safe play settings," Sandseter and Leif Edward Ottesen Kennair write, a fine description of the rules of the adventure playground.[89]

In *The Science of Play*, playground scholar Susan G. Solomon summarizes similar conclusions reached by other branches of science. Neuroscientists also believe that risk taking is part of typical child development. "Kids have to take chances, to constantly experience risks, if they are going to adapt to the world around them. We can tell from the gleeful yelling and screaming that they are finding it pleasurable."[90] Sandra Aamodt and Sam Wang write, "Play may be practice for real life. Risk taking in children's play may be an important developmental process. It tests boundaries and establishes what is safe and what is dangerous. In the United States, playground equipment has been made very safe, leading to the unanticipated problem that children lack experience with such distinctions, which may lead to trouble later in life."[91] The long-term benefits of children being allowed to challenge themselves, on the other hand, include resilience, self-reliance, adventurousness, and entrepreneurialism.[92] But, as Tim Gill points out in his extended essay *No Fear*, it is far easier to quantify danger than add up benefits, to compile injury statistics than capture creativity. He points to a 2002 statement by the British government–sponsored Play Safety Forum as a sign of change. In the statement, the group noted that safety could not be the overriding objective in playground design, and that providers needed to weigh risks and benefits using knowledge of child development as well as engineering considerations. Spaces should be designed with hazards kids can see, like heights, not those they may not, like nets or uprights that can trap heads or limbs.[93]

On the adventure playground, the do-it-yourself rule puts a limit on the potential danger. Towers built with simple tools are shorter than those ordered from catalogs. At Yume Park, there's a rope hammock big enough for twelve, handwoven by children and parents, rather than a trampoline. I saw plenty of children up on roofs—the rule was, if you can climb up without a ladder, relying on your own strength and ingenuity, it's okay. Journalism on adventure play tends to emphasize the danger, but these spaces actually need to be seen as exceptionally porous community centers in which lots of types of social activities, for parents and children, occur. One playworker told me he had sessions for parents in how to use tools, because their fear derived from their own lack of experience. It isn't only children that need a sense of ownership. Kids also take time to ease into that freedom and figure out which activity most appeals to them. If adventure play becomes permanent in New York, it would do better embedded in a neighborhood (in Tokyo, many of the parks were on former industrial lots) than as a weekend destination, as it is on Governors Island, which has no permanent housing.

The road to Kodomo Yume Park was narrow and winding, and there was no sidewalk for much of the way. And yet it was safe, because the drivers knew to look for pedestrians and cyclists and thus moved at slower speeds. There were people in the houses and stores along the route, and few of the buildings were more than three or four stories tall, offering "eyes on the street" as well as adults who might be appealed to for help. The neighborhood, like the adventure playground, operated as a safety net, ready in case of trouble but not often deployed. A mother who was camped out at Yume Park with five children, the youngest a three-month-old, told me a story—hilarious for her—that would have been a nightmare for me. Her two-year-old, who had observed his five-year-old brother being sent to the corner to buy bread, decided he could do the same and turned up at the shop with an empty wallet. This impromptu journey recalls the popular TV show *Hajimete no Otsukai,* or "My First Errand." On the show, which has been broadcast for more than twenty-five years, children as young as two or three do simple errands in their neighborhood, discreetly trailed by a camera crew. I looked around at the protected bike lanes, the publicly funded playground workers, and the houses where people are home in the afternoon. In Tokyo, a low crime rate and a society accustomed to community ownership of public space has created a city where there is more room for innocent error. Sandseter's final category—getting lost— seems much less fraught than it does in Brooklyn. Do I wish that my kids, aged seven and ten, could roll on their own after school to the park, meet friends, and appear on the doorstep at five P.M., muddy, damp, and full of play? I do, but then I remember my lived experience: Saturdays dominated by sports schedules, empty and windswept winter playgrounds, kids hit by cars in crosswalks, crossing with the light. It isn't the idea of my kids holding a hammer that scares me but the idea of sending them off to make community alone.

•

WHAT STRIKES YOU first is the scale. Moerenuma Park feels like it was meant to be seen from the moon, not explored on a tiny bicycle. Pyramid, mound, pyramidal mound, circular fountain, tripod, triangular bosque. The playground has become the size of a town, an exhilarating surface to experience and explore for children of all ages. You don't always realize what shape you're in (literally and figuratively) until you reach the top and can look back over the ground you've traversed. When I reached the peak of Moere Mountain, breathless and buffeted by strong winds, I couldn't believe I had made it up the stairs. Down below, my bike keeled over in a gust. A plaque at the center with a map of Sapporo read, in one corner, GENERAL SUMMIT FOR IMAGINATION. G.S.I. [GEOGRAPHICAL SURVEY INSTITUTE] DEDICATE IT TO MR. NOGUCHI. And I did feel my imagination start to run a little wild. Moerenuma is artist Isamu Noguchi's last work, a four-hundred—acre public park, completed in 2005, that includes mountains, rivers, beaches, and forests of play equipment. It combines Noguchi's greatest ambition, in terms of scale, with his smallest, in terms of audience. It marries Noguchi's highest aspirations as an artist with a deep engagement in children's play. And yet, children had no hand in its creation, and few elements can be moved. We are solely in Noguchi's hands. In any chapter on the designer's desire to shape children's space, Moerenuma is the end point, but to what end?[94]

In looking at playground design in the twentieth century, the makers ultimately divide into three camps. There are the manufacturers, providers

Moerenuma Park, Sapporo, Japan, 1988–2005, Isamu Noguchi. © 2018 The Isamu Noguchi Foundation and Garden Museum, New York / Artists Rights Society (ARS), New York. [Courtesy Moerenuma Park]

Play equipment, with Octetra at lower left, Moerenuma Park, Sapporo, Japan, 1988–2005, Isamu Noguchi. © 2018 The Isamu Noguchi Foundation and Garden Museum, New York / Artists Rights Society (ARS), New York. [Courtesy Moerenuma Park]

of the colorful, wood-and-plastic-and-metal apparatuses that today conform to all known design standards and are installed over what's called "safety surfacing," one of the costliest parts of a playground installation. Then, the junkologists, who believe the best playground is the one built by children and spend their money on materials and supervision. Finally, the abstractionists: architects, artists, and designers who want to give children the freedom of junk but haven't relinquished the desire to design. Aldo van Eyck was one of these, stripping equipment down to its essentials and providing a theatrical frame for children's games. Isamu Noguchi was another, practicing both on the equipment and on the ground plane, seeking a different kind of elemental landscape. Between the junk and the abstract lies a fourth type, an overlap in the Venn diagram: the so-called adventure playgrounds, built in Central Park in the late 1960s and early 1970s, that have sand and loose parts but also pyramids and slides.

Noguchi's first designs for play were executed in 1933. His *Play Mountain* includes a stepped pyramid-shaped hill, a curving access ramp, a pool, and a sitting rock, all elements that would recur as he designed and redesigned playgrounds and playscapes over the next fifty years. Through a social connection, Noguchi got a meeting with Robert Moses, then the city's new parks commissioner, who had a mandate to increase the number of playgrounds. Noguchi had no prior experience designing for children—his work at the time was primarily in portrait sculpture, and he had just begun to design stage sets and costumes for modern dance choreographers, including Ruth Page and Martha Graham. Moses, who would go on to open four hundred playgrounds using standardized equipment—the four Ss, plus monkey bars—was dismissive of the young sculptor, setting up a conflict that would last for decades. In 1939, Noguchi tried again, creating the prototypes for play equipment that was spidery and delicate rather than earthy and solid for Ala Moana Park, attempting, as van Eyck would a decade later, to improve upon the apparatus.[95] The equipment remained unexecuted, but a photograph of his maquette was published in *Architectural Forum.*[96] The inspiration may have been those tense and lightweight sets Noguchi designed for Martha Graham. She was developing a new vocabulary of movement and needed complementary armatures. Children's play is a kind of dance they make up as they go along, aided by curbs to traverse and walls to climb. In 1941, responding to critiques that his stepped swings and seesaws were too dangerous, Noguchi tried another tactic, modeling the *Contoured Playground* entirely of mounded, channeled, and hollowed earth, implying, subtly, that children can't fall off the ground. When Noguchi was included in the influential group exhibition *Fourteen Americans* at the Museum of Modern Art in 1946, a model of the *Contoured Playground* was displayed alongside paintings by Arshile Gorky and Robert Motherwell and drawings by Saul Steinberg.[97] In the 1947 Rita Hayworth movie *Down to Earth*, Noguchi's spiral slide and angular swings appear in an end scene, uncredited, and Noguchi sued Columbia Pictures for copyright infringement.[98]

In 1950, Audrey Hess, the wife of *ARTNews* editor Thomas B. Hess, asked Noguchi to design a playground for a site near the United Nations Headquarters, then under construction. The UN had agreed to set aside the one-acre plot as a way of giving back to the community, and Hess, whose philanthropic interests included both art and children's causes, thought Noguchi would be able to combine the two.[99] Noguchi prepared a plaster model with architect Julian Whittlesey, combining a contoured ground plane with his jewelry-like metal equipment. One end of the rectangular site digs into the earth, creating a spiral stepped pool, while the other end is mounded up and hollowed out for tunnels. A metal climbing dome provides more height, while an area of triangular concrete pavers, stacked up and spread out, suggests a rocky landscape. The forms, and the activities proposed by the forms, suggest nature, but shrunken down and smoothed out so that it might fit into New York City. The effect isn't unfamiliar if you have ever been to Heckscher Playground or the Ancient Playground in Central Park—designed by architect Richard Dattner in the late 1960s. Those projects are among those Noguchi was referring to when he wrote that his ideas "ha[ve] already been exploited by others, and I must go on to fresher fields."[100]

In their second encounter, Parks Commissioner Moses rejected the Noguchi and Whittlesey design and the United Nations went along with his decision. The Museum of Modern Art exhibited the model in 1952, and Thomas Hess wrote an editorial in his magazine mocking Moses's taste.[101] The model was widely seen, and, as Susan G. Solomon writes in her book *American Playgrounds*, it planted the seed of the idea that abstraction provided a more stimulating play environment than traditional equipment, and that children could learn about space and form through such a place.[102] Today, the notion seems almost commonplace. Landscapes from the High Line to the Madrid Río, from Millennium Park on Chicago's lakefront to Olympic Sculpture Park on Seattle's waterfront, combine transportation, environmental mitigation, public programming, and the highest level of architectural design—and a playground too. Noguchi was one of the first designers of any background to elevate play through urban intervention, seeing children not as lesser consumers of aesthetics but as the first and perhaps most important ones. Hess wrote of the unbuilt UN project that the playground "instead of telling the child what to do (swing here, climb there), becomes a place for endless exploration."[103] "Noguchi had a really good concept that playgrounds should not be designed like military exercise equipment for a cheaply executed boot camp," says Dakin Hart, senior curator at the Noguchi Museum in Queens. "He thought kids should experience the environment the way man first experienced the earth, as a spectacular and complex place."[104]

Noguchi would try one more time in New York City. In 1960, a neighborhood group was formed to try to upgrade a hilly, unsafe stretch of Riverside Park, on Manhattan's West Side near 103rd Street. The group contacted Audrey Hess, and she in turn contacted the artist on their behalf, assuring him that this time the local community and the new parks commissioner, Newbold Morris, would support an innovative design. The completed park would be named for her aunt Adele Levy. As the scale of the project became clear, architect Louis I. Kahn was brought in as Noguchi's collaborator.[105] Kahn made sense, both for his recent prominence and for his past interest in making playgrounds; in 1946 he had designed a multilevel play space for a tight urban site next to the Western Home for Children, in Philadelphia, that had included swings and climbing frames alongside platforms, sculptures, and a miniature, winding path. The two men had similar ideas about integrating topography and activity, as well as not dumbing down design for children.

Kahn and Noguchi presented their design to city officials in January 1962, showing a clay model as well as drawings. The designers used the site's topography to its fullest, embedding a semicircular nursery school into an upper slope, creating a round sandbox and pie-shaped amphitheater, and turning another rise into a slide hill. Despite Hess's assurances, the reception was chilling. Morris wrote to one of the neighborhood sponsors, "The very imaginative design which your people presented to us is in our opinion entirely too expensive in construction, too large in scale and too dramatic in conception to be suitable for neighborhood use by mothers and small children." He could not support "an unjustifiable architectural monument" that would only appeal to out-of-towners and the "avant-garde."[106] Despite this reception, the designers kept on working, seeking, through design changes, to please both their patrons and the parks department. Noguchi later recalled, "Each time there would be some objection—and Louis Kahn would then always say, 'Wonderful! They don't want it. Now we can start all over again. We can make something better.' "[107] In 1963, a group of neighbors filed suit, claiming the design would destroy open green space and picketing the homes of Hess and other committee members. They echoed Morris's assessment of the design as "largely vainglorious, rather than useful."[108] The *New York Times*, on the other hand, described it as a "fanciful wonderland for children—to be carved and molded out of a slope in Riverside Park" and endorsed it in an editorial, noting that (as had been true from the beginning) none of the project's pyramids and hills rose above the height of Riverside Drive.[109]

It was not to be. A new mayor, John Lindsay, was voted in at the end of 1965, and he and his new parks commissioner, Thomas Hoving, were not enthusiastic about the project. Kahn would never attempt to design another playground, but Noguchi would, far from New York City. Just pieces at first. *Octetra*, installed near Italy's Spoleto Cathedral in 1968: stacked, freestanding concrete play shapes, a beehive waiting for a swarm. In Atlanta's Piedmont Park, *Playscape*, an installation of his previously unexecuted metal apparatus, set in a verdant, wooded green to celebrate America's bicentennial. *Slide Mountain* turned into a series of *Slide Mantras*, black-and-white, visually monolithic sculptures, first executed for the Venice Biennale in 1986.[110] These pieces have undergone a recent revival: The San Francisco Museum of Modern Art installed one of his bracelet-like climbers in an alley next to the museum in 2017, and renderings of Washington, D.C.'s planned 11th Street Bridge Park were festooned with Noguchi equipment, used as shorthand for creative playgrounds.

Only in Sapporo, in the last year of his life, did Noguchi get his chance to realize the totality of his play dream. When the city first acquired the Moere Lake site bordered by marshlands in the early 1980s, they envisioned it as part of a "circular greenbelt concept" that would eventually create a ring of parks and open space around the center. In January 1988, in New York, Noguchi met Hiroyuki Hattori, the president of a Sapporo-based tech company. As they walked around his Long Island City museum, Noguchi stopped at his bronze models for the *Play Mountain* (1933) and *Monument to the Plow* (1933). "My best things have never been built," he said.[111] In March, Noguchi visited three potential sites with Hattori and Sapporo's mayor, who was happy to have an internationally known artist work in the city. Noguchi was in fine form on this trip. Biographer Hayden Herrera reports that Noguchi dismissed one forested site as needing no improvement, and a local art park as a "graveyard of sculptures." "Finally they went to Sapporo's municipal dump," she writes, "surrounded on three sides by a loop in the Toyohira River, and it had a broad hill where garbage had been piled. Noguchi was immediately taken with it and wanted to turn the whole 400-acre space into one large sculpture—the biggest of his entire career."[112] Noguchi returned to Sapporo two more times that spring and fall, making drawings and a model of the park at large scale. His last drawing includes *Play Mountain*. Noguchi died in New York in December 1988, knowing that the park would go ahead. Seventeen years later, it was finished.

Because it was off-season when I visited Moerenuma in October 2016, I was all alone amid the rustling leaves of the playground. Formal paths between the cherry trees lead from one circular clearing to the next, and each opening contains an array of Noguchi's play equipment, much of it executed here for the first and only time. The first, with the pyramid, an angular double slide, and a set of *Monument Valley*–like walls and stairs, is an easy on-ramp, ready for big, up-and-down movements. One in back, with a set of three swings bracketed by wedge-shaped walls, seemed like a place for flying high and then nesting in a set of stacked *Octetra*. Only when you've explored them all do you come upon the unique *Slide Mountain*, a cone-shaped stone mass with two arcing slides down and one narrow set of stairs up. So I did what any investigative play journalist would do. I slid down the slides, I swung on the swing, I climbed inside *Octetra* and looked up at the sky and thought for a bit. They were cozy and comfortable and could easily have served as a space pod or cocoon, Thumbelina's flower petal or Peter Pan's hideout. There's a valid line of criticism that modernist playthings are only an adult designer's idea of fun. But Noguchi's elemental shapes seemed to offer enough risk and enough options. I couldn't decide what to do on the wavy striped caterpillar rings. Should I run along the top or ride the apparatus like a groovy spaceship? I knew I wanted to bring it home and install it in my own backyard just to look at. The ambiguity suggested the form was a success, even if I couldn't shake the sense that Noguchi had, despite his and his team's best efforts, built another "graveyard of sculptures." Moerenuma is a monument to imagination, but whose?

•

"THE NEXT BEST thing to a playground designed entirely by children is a playground designed by an adult but incorporating the possibility for children to create their own places within it," architect Richard Dattner writes at the beginning of his own case history for the West Sixty-Seventh Street Adventure Playground, one of five he would eventually design at the periphery of Central Park.[113] Where Kahn and Noguchi failed, Dattner and landscape architect M. Paul Friedberg would succeed. New York was not to be without a park with slide mountains, underground tunnels, sand and water and ancient geometry, integrating topography with play rather than setting equipment out on a cushioned tabletop. In the late 1960s, Dattner and Friedberg, aided by several New York–based family foundations, designed and built a series of public playgrounds in New York City that have become beloved examples of how to play differently, even as they have faced their own preservation challenges.

After the Second World War, thanks to a donation from philanthropist Kate Wollman, the world's largest outdoor skating rink was completed north of the park's Fifty-Ninth Street lake. Parks Department architects and engineers would build new structures for the carousel, the Chess & Checkers House, the Loeb Boathouse, and so on, in a style condemned by *New Yorker* architecture critic Lewis Mumford as "crassly utilitarian."[114] The park's original designers, Frederick Law Olmsted and Calvert Vaux, had been at pains to minimize the architecture in their landscape, and most structures had a fantastic appearance. In 1956, Moses had decided to expand Tavern on the Green, the restaurant on the park's west side, and to build an eighty-car parking lot north of the building—on the site of a children's playground. Roselle Davis, wife of painter Stuart Davis and a park regular, noticed men with surveying equipment and checked out their blueprints with the title "Detail Map of Parking Lot."[115] She organized a petition, drafted by novelist Fannie Hurst, which attracted the attention of the *New York Herald Tribune.* Moses refused to meet with the petition's signers, instead sending in the bulldozers on April 17. When supporters Elliott and Eleanor Sanger woke up and saw the work going on from their apartment at 75 Central Park West, Davis, Eleanor Sanger, and the other mothers quickly rallied, forming a cordon of women, children, and baby carriages in front of their playground. As Jane Jacobs and Shirley Hayes would later find in their own fight against Moses to maintain their playground and open space at Washington Square, the smallest protesters are often the most photogenic.[116] The confrontation went on for weeks, until the mothers returned to the site one morning to find park workers had toppled a maple tree. The group sued for an injunction against Moses, and the sympathetic judge, State Supreme Court Justice Samuel H. Hofstadter, commented that, there being no dearth of nightclubs in the city, it wasn't necessary to have one in the park. A half acre of Central Park was a small thing in the abstract, he wrote in his ruling, but "no foot, or even inch, of park space is expendable in our teeming metropolis."[117]

Moses ultimately backed down, defeated by the mothers, and the playground remained next to a smaller one that was intended to be its replacement. Six years later, both had fallen into disrepair and a new group of users petitioned Newbold Morris, so unyielding on Kahn and Noguchi's plans for Riverside Park, for improvements, like adding a rubber safety surface under the equipment. He said yes, though it took him about four years. But in 1965, John Lindsay became mayor and replaced Morris with Thomas Hoving. Thirty-four years old, with a PhD in art history, Hoving saw parks as part of the city's cultural life, not just as recreation facilities, treating them as stages for public performance and "happenings," including child-friendly exhibitions with the Museum of Contemporary Crafts.[118] Hoving (who would later direct the Metropolitan Museum of Art) was far more receptive to the mothers' pleas for improvement and, once a donor was found, to a design that presented play itself as a daily happening. The Estée and Joseph Lauder Foundation offered to support the construction of a new playground north of Tavern on the Green. Leonard Lauder, speaking for his parents, said that "the family had first wanted to do this several years ago when many of our friends were fleeing the city because they thought New York was not the place to bring up children. We decided to build several of these to give the city just this little lift."[119] The reconstruction required in New York in the late 1960s was not in response to war, as in the playgrounds built in Amsterdam and London, but in response to an erosion of public amenities, outdated, undermaintained, and insufficient for the new generation of urban children.

At the time, Dattner had a small architectural practice. One of his first commissions, a Long Island laboratory, factory, and warehouse for Estée Lauder with Sam Brody, had been on the cover of *Architectural Record* in 1965, and the Lauder family was pleased with their architect. Despite his lack of experience, they selected him to design the park. Dattner told me, "The Lauders said to me, 'You want to design a playground?' Which I knew nothing about. My attitude ever since I opened my office was, 'Anybody asks anything, say yes.' Meanwhile, my wife was a young graduate student in psychology at City College. She steered me to the books that are quoted in my book, Piaget, Bruno Bettelheim."[120] In *Design for Play*, Dattner recalls the controversy over the Kahn-Noguchi park without mentioning it by name, and it may have been on the Lauders' minds as well. "Although never built, this playground had a considerable influence on subsequent playgrounds, including the Adventure Playground," he writes. "In addition to its outstanding design, the doomed project yielded one very important lesson: the community must be fully involved in a project from its inception."[121]

Logically, then, Dattner's foray into Central Park began with a community planning process. After presenting rough sketches to the most active members of what was now known as the Committee for a Creative Playground, Dattner created a scale model of the design out of sticks and clay that could be shown to a larger group. A second meeting, for seventy people, was held to look at the model. At the end of this meeting, the Lauders made a request: Would the community raise funds to pay for a full-time playworker, since they were paying for the architect and cost of construction? The act of fund-raising ended up being an important glue holding the community together during the process of design and construction. Asking for funds for the playworker increased outreach about the park and underlined the fact that parks have to be maintained, not just built. Dattner also presented his designs to children at the local elementary schools, showing them before and after scenarios that, he reported, were met with *oob*s from his young audience.[122]

But what was the design? The finished plan shows a series of linked play elements built of concrete and stacked cobblestones, most of them curved, arranged around a racetrack-shaped oval. Outside the elements is a paved path ringed with benches, intended to be the domain of the parents (who don't like getting sand in their shoes). Inside, the surface is sand, split down the middle by a long sculptural water trough, reminiscent of some of the garden designs of Italian modernist Carlo Scarpa. There are circular labyrinths and truncated cones, slide hills, and a fountain encircled by steps. A jungle gym made of logs and horizontal steel bars offers one high vantage point, and a treehouse built around one of eight existing trees offers another. There is also a boat with a burlap sail that children could maneuver, a departure from other playgrounds that had no adjustable elements. "The main thing wrong with playgrounds is that kids can't change them," Dattner told the *New York Times Magazine*. "A child must feel he has an effect on his environment. I really think that's why some kids destroy things. If they cannot create, they must destroy."[123]

The many levels offer degrees of difficulty, of protection and openness, of hideouts and public stages, just like the park that surrounds the playground. Unlike that park, the whole ensemble can be circumnavigated via a continuous path atop thirty-inch-high walls. What's different is that these mountains, streams, and valleys are man-made, but their symbolism is obvious to even the smallest child. The south end is designed for physical activity, running, jumping, climbing, and tunneling, while the north end is intended for digging, building, painting, and playing with water. Because of the successful fund-raising for a trained playworker, the playground was designed for supervision, with activities administrated from the hollow stepped pyramid, which contained a storeroom for all

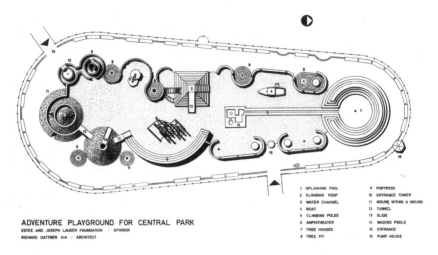

ADVENTURE PLAYGROUND FOR CENTRAL PARK
ESTEE AND JOSEPH LAUDER FOUNDATION · SPONSOR
RICHARD DATTNER AIA · ARCHITECT

1	SPLASHING POOL	9	FORTRESS
2	CLIMBING ROOF	10	ENTRANCE TOWER
3	WATER CHANNEL	11	MOUND WITHIN A MOUND
4	BOAT	12	TUNNEL
5	CLIMBING POLES	13	SLIDE
6	AMPHITHEATER	14	WADING POOLS
7	TREE HOUSES	15	ENTRANCE
8	TREE PIT	16	PUMP HOUSE

Plan, Adventure Playground for Central Park, New York, 1967, Richard Dattner Architect.
[Courtesy Richard Dattner]

the supplies the supervisors might need, along with changing rooms and electrical outlets.

Painter Julia Jacquette, whose own father designed another adventurous Central Park playground in the 1970s with his firm Ross Ryan Jacquette, published a graphic memoir in 2017 that skips from playground to playground and includes realistic drawings of the West Sixty-Seventh Street play space.[124] She told *Urban Omnibus*, of Dattner's design,

> I remember entering that playground for the first time.
> The utter thrill of seeing this interconnected waterway;
> the amphitheater-like structure, with the sprinkler in the
> middle, which then fed into a channel, letting the water
> flow down to a geometric wading pool. It was so obviously
> built for us, kid-sized kids, to be able to walk in, and put
> stuff in. The canal had very low walls. And children were, as
> I noticed immediately, putting rubber duckies or sailboats

at the top, watching them go down this thirty-foot-long channel, and then retrieving them as they bobbed around in the wading pool.[125]

Each element was carefully considered for its play possibilities for both older and younger children. Take the climbing poles, as one example, an improvement on the metal jungle gyms over asphalt that the playground replaced. A fall from the jungle gym had been part of the mothers' original complaint to then commissioner Morris. Dattner says the sanded redwood uprights are better to look at and to touch than steel, and the design varies the spacing of the rungs so that small children can more easily climb below, but only as far as safety allows. The poles are surrounded by sand, in case of falls, but falls are few because there are plenty of places to step on or grab. During less active moments, the poles become easels, with large sheets of paper stapled on to form a mural-size painting surface. This use reminded me of the soft pine paneling along the walls at the Crow Island School: a material that doesn't hide wear but embraces it and is not marred by decades of tacks and staples. Friedberg, whose woodsy Billy Johnson Playground (1985) is still a rustic respite in Central Park, would eventually design and license, through the company TimberForm, a modular version of such log-and-steel climbers, making them accessible to playground planners across the country. He wanted to allow park supervisors to customize their climber to their site but found that most customers wanted prearranged models from which to choose, overwhelmed by the tyranny of choice.[126]

Thinking about design that would work for children of different ages led Dattner to consider playgrounds for children of different abilities. *Design for Play* includes a set of designs for "Playgrounds for Handicapped Children."[127] The disabled child's physical and mental development must also be accompanied by an increase in territory, in challenges, in options,

West 67th Street Adventure Playground, Central Park, New York, 1967, Richard Dattner Architect. Photograph by Norman McGrath. [Courtesy Richard Dattner]

and Dattner shows a series of examples of modern play spaces that have been made more accessible with simple changes. At a vacation camp for the blind in Spring Valley, New York, Friedberg and architects Samton Associates inserted curved sections into straight horizontal railings to indicate changes in direction or level. Dattner himself designed a fully wheelchair-accessible version of the adventure playgrounds for the rehabilitation unit of the Bird S. Coler Hospital in New York City. Like the Central Park designs, this unexecuted playground was to be largely built of concrete, with areas for different activities distributed among a series of geometric enclosures, arranged on a flat piece of ground and shaded by trees and a few pavilion roofs.[128] Almost all of the children who were clients for the project used wheelchairs, crutches, or wheeled beds, so a wide, even

Play Panels, West 67th Street Adventure Playground, Central Park, New York, 1967, Richard Dattner Architect. Photograph by Norman McGrath. [Courtesy Richard Dattner]

concrete pathway ringed each activity area. There was a circular wading pool, with a chair on a boom to assist children who couldn't climb steps, and a rusticated concrete tower, a stepped amphitheater and circular ramp that led to a bridge, creating a series of covered and parallel tunnels like those at Dattner's Ancient Playground. Sand, water, and dirt, which can gum up wheelchairs and prosthetics, were corralled in raised concrete beds with a projecting edge. Wheelchairs could be pulled up to and under the beds, so children could reach the sand, tend the plants, or place boats in the channel of water that wraps around the entire perimeter of the park. Dattner would realize a Rehabilitation Playground for the Rusk Institute of Rehabilitation Medicine at NYU with many similar design features in 1969–70, later demolished.

It's fascinating to compare Dattner's forty-five-year-old design to contemporary guidelines and products for inclusive play. Playworld

Systems, a Pennsylvania manufacturer of playground equipment, published an *Inclusive Play Design Guide* in 2015 in consultation with an array of professionals, and the landscape the guide proposes is very different from Dattner's.[129] Since 2010, the U.S. government has required that public play areas be accessible to people with disabilities, but that can mean one flat route, or a few elements like swings with full body support and a ski lift– like harness. Yet less than 5 percent of today's children with disabilities have a mobility challenge, so elaborate and expensive ramps, the design guide argues, are not a good investment: The guidelines emphasize ground-based equipment, with bars to grab or molded plastic saddles to climb or crawl up. Eighty percent of children on the autism spectrum become runners at some point in their lives, says Ian Proud, market research and inclusive play manager for Playworld, so inclusive playgrounds should have a clear, controlled perimeter for caregivers' peace of mind. "If you don't welcome the parent, you don't welcome the children," he says. "Just as if you don't welcome the typically developing child, you won't get their siblings with disabilities. That's why the levels of challenge are important."[130] For the same reason, it is important to arrange equipment into a quiet zone and a noisy zone, so children who may get overstressed can find a calm nook within the park. There's also a reason domes figure so prominently and permanently in both architect-designed and mass-market playgrounds—they are a great way to combine physical play at different heights, and they provide a sense of enclosure for imaginative play. Playworld's Unity Dome updates van Eyck's igloo climber by creating its surface out of two sizes of metal tubular circles linked with straight pieces, and rigging a circle of rope ladders through the center. While younger children use the small, fixed circles, older children can challenge themselves on the larger ones or on the ladders, whose rungs bend and shift under the weight of one (or many) climbers. A few of the circles are filled with manipulable panels, a half measure toward loose parts. KOMPAN, which bills itself as "the world's no. 1 playground supplier," manufactures a series of products that unwrap the dome, stretching out a series of challenges below an arch of metal tubing. On the Altair, for example, children can climb on, up, and across elements including plastic swings, rope nets, and flat footholds using arms or legs. "A ramp for the sake of a ramp is no fun," says Jeanette Fich Jespersen of KOMPAN. "You made it accessible, but did you make it playful?"[131]

Playworld has a line of playground electronics called NEOS 360 that provides challenge games with lights and touch pads. When I expressed some dismay at gadgets for the great outdoors, Proud vigorously defended their use: "If I am in a chair, my notion of play is going to be based on fine motor skills. Also, we have become a largely sedentary and indoor culture, and true believers are advancing the idea that we need to reconnect children with nature. Which is not untrue. But there is more than one way of doing that. If a child is used to interactivity, it becomes bait, it becomes a reason to get out and then look at that tree, look at that bug. They've become our biggest sellers." Spinning elements are also coming back into vogue. Children with sensory disorders often crave the feeling, and smaller cups and vortexes can be used by a single child and have a smaller fall zone than the old merry-go-rounds. Jespersen echoes Proud's defense of the digital playground component, particularly for sites where children go often, like schoolyards and housing estates. "The circumstances of play have changed—we have no free-range kids today," she says. That means kids don't have the time to get absorbed in play, and they need more instantly gratifying, and instantly sociable, play equipment. This sounds like a bit of a chicken-and-egg defense, making playgrounds more like video games rather than, as noncommercial playground makers would argue, an antidote to video games. But Jespersen has a point: The way many children approach playgrounds now, with parents, with siblings of different ages and abilities, with limited time, makes a visit more limited and instrumental, for exercise of the body and not necessarily of the imagination.

For his Central Park Adventure Playground, Dattner also designed a kit-of-parts system, based on the Eameses' modular house. The so-called Play Panels, which were made of half-inch plywood and came in two sizes, 24 x 32 inches and 12 x 32 inches, could be notched together to create walls, houses, vehicles, and platforms. The two sides were painted with diamonds, triangles, circles, and stripes in a variety of bright colors, giving completed structures a harlequin effect.[132] Short matching ladders could be propped against the sides to access the roofs of structures built above the children's heads. The pieces were large enough to build forts and houses, while still being light enough for children to lift on their own. The notches meant that no additional tools or pieces were needed for assembly, unlike Patty Smith Hill's similarly scaled outdoor block system from the beginning of the twentieth century. At the end of the day, the pieces were gathered and compactly stacked inside the storage pyramid by the playworker. The panels didn't look like junk, or even off-the-shelf lumber from the hardware store. They looked like toys made for a giant's children, and as such, offered something that kids probably wouldn't have had in their own homes. For toddlers, there were nesting wooden boxes and wooden blocks that could be manipulated by small hands and from a seated position. Dattner never marketed the Play Panels beyond the walls of Central Park. He would try for greater reach with the glass-reinforced polyester PlayCubes, recently reissued, which resemble a lighter-weight version of Noguchi's *Octetra*.[133]

Dattner's Play Panels fall into the category of "loose parts," a term invented in 1971 by architect Simon Nicholson in an essay called "How Not to Cheat Children: The Theory of Loose Parts."[134] Inspired by the junk playgrounds of London, Nicholson writes that "in any environment, both the degree of inventiveness and creativity, and the possibility of discovery, are directly proportional to the number and kinds of variables in it." Children's environments, he goes on to say, "are clean, static, and impossible to play around with. What has happened is that adults in the form of professional artists, architects, landscape architecture, and planners have had all the fun playing with their own materials, concepts, and planning-alternatives, and then builders have had all the fun building the environments out of real materials; and thus has all the fun and creativity been stolen."[135] Nicholson argues that children need to be put back in the driver's seat as active consumers of recreation. He points out that, during the 1960s, educators had emphasized "the discovery method" as central to new curricula. Children learn most easily in a laboratory environment, finding things out for themselves via physical trial and error. If this sounds like Progressive education at the beginning of the century, it should, as all of the education reformers, from Froebel on, emphasized the hand as well as the head. Nicholson makes an important connection, however, between the indoor classroom and outdoor playgrounds. He envisions a future in which the boundary completely dissolves: "In early childhood there is no important distinction between play and work, art and science, recreation and education . . . Education *is* recreation, and vice versa."[136] He proposes extending the flexibility of early childhood to all of childhood, which means scaling up the parts and complexity of the educational environment.

The idea of an outdoor toy that works like cleaned-up junk has proven to be a fertile one, more marketable, in many cases, than just playing with junk. Charles and Ray Eames's The Toy could be used outside, but it wasn't really made to get dirty or for the wear and tear of public use. Patty Smith Hill's blocks required cooperation, but also some small specialized parts. More recently, architect David Rockwell teamed with play-advocacy group KaBOOM! to create the Imagination Playground in a Box: big blue parts made of lightweight foam in shapes ranging from long bendy poles to round cogs, stackable bricks to scooped-out channels.[137] One can see the shadows of many previous building toys in their array of forms, from Tinkertoys to unit blocks to marble runs and Erector Sets. Rockwell came to the project as a frustrated parent. As Rebecca Mead writes in the *New Yorker*, just before the first Imagination Playground opened, on Manhattan's Burling Slip in 2010, "like many first-time parents, particularly those belonging to the urban upper-middle class, Rockwell was nostalgic about the free play of his youth, and lamented the more constricted opportunities that were available to his offspring." She even nods to the Eameses' Carton City, and the discovery that "the box in which a toy is delivered is often of more interest to a child than the toy is."

At Burling Slip, the blocks are kept in an oval-shaped head house, with a bathroom inside and adult-size stairs up to a viewing platform. The site is managed by playworkers who were initially trained by Penny Wilson, author of the *Playwork Primer*. Without the blocks, the playground, also designed by Rockwell, can feel rather desolate, like a stage without players. But play is a delicate thing: I've been to the park several times with my own children, and the experience varies. Once there were no blocks, and no sign of life within the house. Once the playworker doled out the blocks in dribs and drabs, frustrating the kids who wanted a whole pile to work with. Once the playworker watched as teams and raiding parties developed, undoing the work of my eight-year-old and his temporary friends as fast as they could build. Should he have stepped in? As a parent, I thought yes, as tears persuaded my son to leave the broad, wood-floored building plain. As a historian I thought no; kids need to work things out between themselves. Since their introduction, I've seen the blue blocks at children's museums and pop-up parks; a set was purchased by the PTA at my children's school and another set donated to their preschool. For the children of the urban upper-middle class, the blue blocks have become ubiquitous and, in their ubiquity, boring. Junk, like the weather, is always changing, but the blue blocks remain the same, putting them at the same risk as a fixed playground of becoming static. Reilly Bergin Wilson, of play:groundNYC, says there's something wonderful about working with loose and inexpensive materials. It need not only be productive—that's our makerspaces talking—since sometimes kids just need to wreck.[138] Loose parts theory arises out of an interest in anarchy rather than order. Whether designer loose parts actually fulfill this mission is unclear. The Toy, the Play Panels, the Imagination Playground blocks are perhaps too clean, too easily lofted and joined. In the adult design world, constraints are a creative opportunity, but these loose parts intentionally minimize the degree of difficulty.

In Nicholson's loose parts essay, he points to the community involvement of parents in organizing new forms of recreation as an unintended, highly positive consequence of the adventure playgrounds movement. "In terms of loose parts we can discern a natural evolution from creative play and participation with wood, hammers, ropes, nails, and fire, to creative play and participation with the total process of design and planning of regions of cities."[139] The process of learning about, proposing, funding, and finally playing in these new parks becomes an exploration of administrative loose parts for adults. Liability insurance isn't really that expensive. How do you collect enough junk to last a summer? The adventure playgrounds of Central Park provide just one example of this, from their inception in a request for better maintenance to their recent rehabilitation for a new age, spurred by kids who grew up climbing the pyramids and now have kids of their own. Baby carriages lined up to save the playground at West Sixty-Seventh Street from demolition echo those lined up downtown to save the Washington Square Arch—a protest that helped spur the book about looking at cities from the ground up, and watching where people want to be: Jane Jacobs's *The Death and Life of Great American Cities*.

•

IN NEW YORK City, there's one place where you can experience the full sweep of playgrounds: the molded, abstract topography, the challenging (and safety-tested) equipment, the junk. The roads are free of cars so anyone can ride her bike. The fountains aren't just for looking, but operate as splash pads. The slopes are dotted with slides, faster and longer than any others in the city. Even the curbs are molded for play, in subtly patterned white concrete, ramping up and dwindling down to provide a path like no other. This is by design: Dutch landscape architects West 8 were hired in 2007 to turn the flat, uninhabited southern half of Governors Island, a seven-minute ferry ride from the southern tip of Manhattan, into a contemporary pleasure park. They did it by building the Hills: Outlook Hill, from which you can gaze across the harbor to Liberty Island; Discovery Hill, more heavily wooded, home to a site-specific sculpture by the British artist Rachel Whiteread; Slide Hill, whose fifty-seven-foot slide terrifies adults; and the lolling Grassy Hill, with a greensward intended for picnics and play, all set atop a combination of landfill, demolished Coast Guard buildings, and carefully calibrated soils.[140] Working with Leslie Koch, the president of the Trust for Governors Island, the park's designers and programmers seem to have reviewed the whole modern history of play and actually learned from previous mistakes. "If you create a park-like environment and people feel really free, adults hang out and participate like children do," said Adriaan Geuze, director of West 8. "Early on we said we didn't want to have playgrounds, but we didn't say what that meant," Koch told me in 2012.[141]

Four years later, I got to go back and see. Governors Island's regular ferry was in drydock for its biennial tune-up ahead of the site's opening, on Memorial Day 2016, so the vessel that picked up a dozen families for a test run at the Hills was a party boat, with a blue-glass, LED-lit dance floor and a top deck with café chairs and tables. It seemed right for a day off, with babysitters, parents, and offspring sprung from their desks and playdates. One set of kids pressed their noses to the window, pointing out the steady stream of helicopters rising from the downtown-Manhattan heliport, while others went to the top deck to take in the view. When the boat reached the island, the pack took off on the long walk from the pier, in strollers, on scooters, on bikes. "Where's your helmet?" one mother asked, glancing at her spouse.

The group swept around the west side of the island, passing between one end of Liggett Hall and a school. Beyond those buildings, the island opened up, with no structures except for a restroom trailer. Before us was the Statue of Liberty, same as she ever was, and something new: a tall, tan hill, terraced like a ziggurat, with a rockfall zagging down the north side. "Jonas, we are going to have to climb a mountain today," my then eight-year-old remarked to his best friend. As we walked closer, the fall resolved itself into large, *Minecraft*-like chunks, a frozen river of patinated granite recycled from the island's seawall, tough and gray against the hill's surface. "Can anyone tell me what this hill is made of?" Koch asked. No one answered. "A building that blew up!" The kids were not impressed— as daughters and sons of architects, some of them had been witnesses to the implosion. "Yes, we blew up a building that was right here," Koch said. "The rocks you are going to climb on were in the ocean for a hundred years. It's up to you to tell us if they are tough enough for New York."

With that, the children were off, the first time that feet under a size seven had touched the rocks of the stone scramble, sorting themselves by size order as they jumped, hopped, and bounced up the hill. In the olden days, one might have reached for a mountain goat metaphor; today, these kids had probably all taken a class in parkour. Before most of the adults

Outlook Hill and the stone scramble, Governors Island, New York, 2016, West 8 with Mathews Nielsen Landscape Architects. Photograph by Timothy Schenck.
[Courtesy Timothy Schenck]

had reached the foot of the hill, the big kids were up top, standing on the rocks that mark the hard-won height of seventy feet, looking across the harbor at Lady Liberty's face. They could barely be persuaded to pose for a photo before they were down, up, down again. An older child ran up, panting: "Vera found a wobbly rock!"

When the toddlers started digging in the dirt of what will soon be a grassy apron in front of the Hills' high spot, it was time to leave. By the time the island opened to everyone, there would be space for them to dig at play:groundNYC's junk playground near the historic yellow clapboard houses at Nolan Park. If they needed to cool off, they could try Liggett

Slide Hill, Governors Island, New York, 2016, West 8 with Mathews Nielsen Landscape Architects. [Courtesy WEST 8]

Terrace, behind McKim, Mead & White's vast barracks, where food trucks, café tables, and ovoid fountains sit cheek by jowl. Heading from the terrace to the Hills, they could first ascend a rope climber, or pretend to be crossing the river on a traverse of logs. The slides were ready to roll, made more pleasurable by the many ways to the top of Slide Hill—with nary a ladder in sight. The landscape was the playground, the playground was the landscape. As we walked down the hill back to the flats, Koch noted with satisfaction the kids running along the curbs. She wished that she could find the woman who had come up to her after one of the first planning workshops, in 2008, and whispered, "Don't tell anyone, but I let my kids run free here."

CHAPTER 5

CITY

As soon as Betsy got out of school, she and Tacy and Tib headed for the Big Hill behind their house to hunt for violets. It was a warm April day, and the three girls took off their stocking caps and unbuttoned their coats and sang, making up new words to "The Battle Hymn of the Republic" in honor of Betsy's birthday. It was tomorrow, and she was the last to turn ten.[1] They passed the Ekstrom house, the only one on the Big Hill, where once, when they were eight, they had pretended to be beggars and asked for milk and cookies. They went down the Secret Lane of beeches and past the Mystery House, now only a foundation. They marched so far they went through a fold in the Minnesota hills they had never encountered before. There, below a rocky ridge, they saw the cottages of Little Syria, a neighborhood of immigrants they had only driven through before. "Little Syria belonged to Deep Valley but it seemed as foreign as though it were across the ocean."[2] The rest of this classic children's book by Maud Hart Lovelace, *Betsy and Tacy Go Over the Big Hill* (1942), concerns their exploration of this new territory, so close and yet so far from their previous experience, through a friendship with a Syrian American girl who is just their age. Small-town geography and international geography coincide in a story about extending a child's range and opening a child's mind, and it is (almost) all achieved without the interference of parents. Lovelace's semiautobiographical books, published between 1940 and 1955, are set in her own remembered childhood, circa 1900 in Mankato, Minnesota.

When they were five—and they didn't even know Tib yet—Betsy and Tacy had only been able to go as far as the bench at the base of the Big Hill and play mostly in Betsy's backyard. When they were eight, they had to ask permission before they went up the Big Hill, but now their only rule was to be back by supper. At ten they have free range over the rural landscape that abuts their dead-end street, a zone between town and country. When they are twelve they will finally be allowed to explore in the other direction, downtown Deep Valley, where a new library is under construction and Front Street holds Schulte's Grocery Store (for candy) and Cook's Book Store (for inappropriate dime novels). It is there that they see their first car—a horseless carriage—owned by Mr. and Mrs. Poppy, who live, in a fit of exoticism, at their own Melborn Hotel. Read as an adult, the books show Betsy's evolving independence through an ever-widening geographic radius, from bench to hill, street to downtown, and eventually farm to college. Her circle of friends, and her knowledge of the world, grows with each increase in range, as the titles reveal. First she meets Tacy, then Tib. On the Big Hill she first encounters people unlike herself and learns to respect rather than fear their differences. When she goes downtown, she finds the automobile, the sumptuous Opera House, but most important, the library (a Carnegie library), where she charts her course toward her own career as a writer. In every book, there is an extension and a reversal, an attempt at growing up that leads to minor tragedy. But Betsy picks herself up and tries again, gaining competence and achieving mastery, in the language of child psychology. The books embrace the rapid changes in society and technology of the early twentieth century, even as they grow up, in level of difficulty, with their readers, culminating in *Betsy's Wedding* (1955). Never fear, our heroine keeps writing after marriage.

The first thing I noticed about Deep Valley, Lovelace's fictionalized Mankato, was that there are women at home in every house. When the girls go high on the hill for the first time without a basket, and Betsy (always the imaginative one) decides they must bedraggle themselves to look like beggars, Mrs. Ekstrom is home to receive their visit with a twinkle in her eye. Mrs. Ray, Betsy's mother, does not work outside the home and has a hired girl to help around the house. She has freedom, too, to go out in the afternoons without Julia, Betsy, or Margaret, knowing there will be someone at the house or the house next door to deal with any of the usual difficulties. When the girls canvass for votes for May Queen, their tally is from the women and children on their street during the day, and from fathers coming home at night. The houses are watchful, helpful, and embracing rather than closed and dark. Roger A. Hart, director of the Children's Environments Research Group at the Graduate Center of the City University of New York, applies the concept of "social capital" to this kind of loosely organized community supervision, where the parent isn't required to be present at all times and other adults are around going about their own business—at home, exercising at a park that has equipment for all ages, working in a community garden. "It is important to note in this discussion that children are not just passive beneficiaries of the creation of a cohesive sense of community," he writes, "they are also agents. Their use of public space helps to foster interaction between adults and this can easily lead to other forms of cooperation."[3] My own deepening interest in public life and its provisions for children and families grew out of parenthood, so I can easily believe this claim: Parenthood makes you see your city in a different light, but it also increases your time on the street. Saturday mornings mean not sleep but the playground at eight thirty A.M. with a toddler who's already been up for three hours. Architectural historian Dolores Hayden has commented on the need for "public space for parents," writing, in the early 1980s, of small interventions, like Danish banks with children's furniture and toys, New Zealand department stores with childcare, and IKEA ball rooms, that give parents back some of the access they lose. Her research also delves into larger ideas about planning that bridges public and private life in order to rescue women and children from the age- and gender-segregated suburb, and their isolation in the private house.[4]

Part of the significance of the girls' visit to Little Syria is that it is the first time they need to explain themselves to strangers. The women on their street know who they are, but over the Big Hill they are strangers. At ten, they suddenly see themselves from the outside and understand difference. Later in the book, they defend the same Syrian girl, Naifi, who is being teased by their male classmates when she ventures into "their" part of town. Tib's mother, Mrs. Muller, expresses her pride in their actions, telling the girls, "Both of Tib's grandmothers came from the other side. Perhaps when they got off the boat they looked a little strange too." Betsy's father's commercial role as owner of the town's one shoe store also proves a blessing; his business cuts across the lines of class and race, and he ends up serving as a broker and translator between the children and adults, native-born and immigrants. In a later young-adult book, *Emily of Deep Valley* (1950), Lovelace would make her heroine, Emily Webster, just graduated from high school in 1912, an advocate for the Syrian community after she witnesses an incident in which white boys tease and harass a Syrian boy.[5] A moment of personal heroism opens a new world within the town Emily thought she knew and, the novel implies, provides her with the passage to adulthood her friends may be finding at college. Geography and maturity can be linked, if we let them.

When, in the next book in their series, Betsy and Tacy do go downtown, their interactions with the librarian and bookseller are again among their first with adults outside the circle of parents and teachers—the experience of the children in the Japanese television show *Hajimete no Otsukai*, or "My First Errand." It is not greater self-sufficiency but "group reliance" that allows this freedom of movement. As cultural anthropologist Dwayne Dixon told the *Atlantic*, Japanese "kids learn early on that, ideally, any member of the community can be called on to serve or help others."[6] It isn't just neighbors that are part of the network, but shopkeepers, cyclists, conductors. To grow up is to engage with more people, in more places. In the United States, there is little expectation that other adults will help children, or families in general. Lenore Skenazy, founder of the blog *Free-Range Kids*, calls the expectation that mothers will supervise their children at all times, or pay someone else for the privilege, "backdoor antifeminism."[7] Material feminists in the late nineteenth century also railed against the movement of women and children into the suburbs, understanding that once out of sight, women would never be fairly compensated for their work.[8] A community designed for families can be seen as an adjunct to easy access to childcare—and indeed, in most successful contemporary examples schools and day care are part of the agenda—taking the pressure off the mother, and the family income, to provide 24/7 coverage. In Deep Valley, Mrs. Ray is far from alone.

The second thing I noticed was the streets, where there are no cars—at least in the first three books—because there were very few private cars in early twentieth century. Going downtown is coupled with Betsy, Tacy, and Tib seeing their first car, as each visit to new territory builds upon the next. By the time the girls get to high school, the Ray family will have their own motorcar, and Betsy will learn to drive, though she is more often to be found dreaming in the driver's seat of a horse and buggy. But in these early days, Hill Street is quite empty and traffic is at the speed of a trot, meaning the children have little to fear from traffic. Drivers (of buggies, wagons, and carts) are out in the open and available to make eye contact, moving at much slower speeds than their automotive equivalents. It was the advent of faster-moving traffic, first horsed, then not, that moved children's play off the streets. In the late nineteenth century, when avenues on the Lower East Side were first paved and the speed of vehicles increased, boys spread glass on the streets to keep carriages from disrupting their games.[9] The earliest playgrounds, including the sand gardens, were intended to siphon these same boys into age-separated play spaces. Many of the early car accident victims in New York were kids, and the playground movement developed to provide pockets of space—of softness, via piles of sand—for children outdoors in the city.

But segregating children's play from the flow of urban life creates its own problems. The playground, like the playpen, eventually becomes constricting. Junk playgrounds allow children a greater range of self-directed activity, but they are still bounded by adult intervention and supervision, however lightly applied. As cartographer Denis Wood wrote in the provocative 1977 essay "Free the Children! Down with Playgrounds!": "A playground only makes sense if adults know better than kids where, when, and with what to play. But if kids do know best—and everything suggests they do—than the adult construction of playgrounds is senseless."[10] Betsy, Tacy, and Tib only use a playground when they are at school; the rest of the time, the built and natural environment of Deep Valley is there for their use. Present-day movements, like Families for Safe Streets, advocate not for separation but for design improvements, like lower speed limits, that put pedestrians first and make them more likely to survive being struck by a car. Busy streets are unplayable, and they also form moats, cutting children off from parks that are geographically near. Hart argues that the solution is not more spaces for children but fewer: Cities should be building places where people of different ages, speeds, and abilities can mix. The Dutch *woonerf*, or living street, is one design possibility. On these streets, pedestrians, bikes, and cars all share the road, one without sidewalks, curbs, or traffic lines; the road is often curved and may include play equipment adjacent to the roadbed. Width, proximity, rough paving, and an awareness of each other create an environment of slowness, even softness, one much closer to the streets of turn-of-the-century Mankato than contemporary cul-de-sacs. In Mankato, most children had a backyard, but front yards, hitching posts, and the public hills were where they came together, in a boundaryless common ground.

The description of Betsy's late Victorian childhood conjures the idyllic situation invoked by today's free-range-parenting movement. Then, children played outside until dark and there were no playdates, no afterschool activities, and parents were not arrested for leaving a child alone at a playground or for an instant in a car in the parking lot. Betsy's parents watch from afar, largely without interference, giving her and her sisters the rope appropriate to their ages. Research supports my sense, upon returning to the fictional hills of Deep Valley, that children's domain is shrinking.[11] HOW CHILDREN LOST THE RIGHT TO ROAM IN FOUR GENERATIONS was the headline of a 2007 article that went viral, dramatically documenting the change in territory granted to an eight-year-old in 1926 (six miles from home) and that of his great-grandson in 2007 (three hundred yards from home, the end of his quiet suburban street).[12] The result has been a rise in childhood obesity, damaging effects on mental health resulting from limiting self-directed experience and peer interactions, and even physical apprehension of geography. Children driven in cars have far less ability to map their surroundings and connect places they have visited than those who have walked or biked the routes. Skenazy, labeled the "world's worst mom" for letting her nine-year-old son ride the New York City subway alone, focuses her advocacy on parents' understanding of what the real risks are in leaving children unsupervised, and in changing the regulatory environment to accept their choice. "The hope is to get a critical mass of kids playing outside, so it becomes normalized again," she told the *New Yorker* in 2015.[13] To reverse this trend may require not only a change in policy, as the free-range-parenting movement advocates, but physical intervention—redesigning cities for children—which would have equity-building implications. Cities built for children shouldn't have to be an individual parent's decision, as that framing makes autonomy into a consumer choice, available to those with the resources to choose their neighborhood, or to choose to fight the system. A space-oriented response gives children the reins, by creating an environment in which they decide where they want to go and what they want to do. "A space-oriented response to children's well-being would place a strong emphasis on easy access to welcoming, accessible parks, squares and public spaces," writes childhood researcher and advocate Tim Gill. "It would encourage child modes of transport like walking, cycling, and public transport over the car. Barriers placed around children's institutions like the school would be less rigid and more permeable allowing, for example, for school playgrounds to be freely available to use when the school day finished."[14]

Mrs. Ray practiced free-range parenting, but within a built and natural environment and as part of an implicit social structure that provided plenty of other adults on watch, and plenty of room in which to fail. In the contemporary city, segregated by use and speed, it can feel like there's no room for failure. But what if softness could be designed in, not because we feel nostalgic for days of visiting on porches, but because a city with some give, as well as safer streets, shared outdoor space, libraries overlooking parks, and parks for every age and ability, would be better for all its residents? Wouldn't that, in fact, be in everyone's interest? In 2011, I published an essay in the magazine *GOOD* called "The Moms Aren't Wrong: Why Planning for Children Would Make Cities Better for All."[15] As I wrote then, in response to a new initiative to make New York more "age friendly," with longer walk lights, more public restrooms, and perches in stores on which to take a break:

> When urban parents, particularly mothers, complain about the public realm they are often caricatured as whiny and overprotective. Your child was burned by the climbing domes at the new park? Kids are too coddled. You can't carry your stroller and child down the subway steps? Make him walk. You can't find a public bathroom? Stay at home. But what if the mothers, in many cases, are right? . . .
>
> Kids don't have cash, but their parents and grandparents certainly do, and more families staying in the city would have general economic and social benefits. Seniors and juniors aren't the only groups whose interests align, but are balkanized in their advocacy. Children could lead cyclists, developers, school officials, and health nuts to their more perfect city, if only we would listen.

In that story, I looked at a series of design proposals that addressed different problems that were all part of the same problem: making stairs more appealing to combat the obesity epidemic, getting children out of cars to protect them from accidents, subsidizing family-size housing units to increase urban density. I proposed a supra-agency combining departments of planning, transportation, education, and health in order to restructure the physical planning of the city to promote these ends. As it happens, Vancouver had already done this and, in the ensuing years, more cities would follow. My title, though I didn't realize it yet, echoed a quote by Enrique Peñelosa, the pioneering urbanist mayor of Bogotá, Colombia, that child rights advocates love to repeat: "Children are a kind of indicator species. If we can build a successful city for children, we will have a successful city for all people."[16]

City serves as a placeholder term, in this chapter, for not rural. Smaller cities, exurbs, and even suburbs can also be redesigned for greater connectivity and autonomy. Radburn, New Jersey, and Lafayette Park, Detroit, early- and mid-twentieth-century developments I describe below, are suburban in setting, but their interest and influence lies in the way they upset patterns of private life and private property inherent in the creation of late nineteenth-century suburbs, to forge a communal and family-oriented public realm. A variety of twentieth- and twenty-first-century urban planning initiatives attempt to re-create the early twentieth-century idyll, designing and legislating a network of homes, community centers, and schools linked by safe streets, public transportation, and parks—a softer city, built not for the working man in his automobile, like Mr. Ray in his buggy, but for families of different compositions living in homes that, increasingly, a parent may work from.

•

ONE FEBRUARY MORNING, Adrian Crook looked down from the twenty-ninth floor to see four of his five children running for the bus. Crook had spent a year teaching the four, then ages ten, nine, eight, and seven, to ride the city bus between his rented downtown Vancouver apartment and their North Vancouver public school, but his training couldn't possibly cover every eventuality and, at that height, there was no point in yelling. He would have to wait until they made the reverse journey that afternoon.

Meanwhile, it was time for him to take his youngest, age five, to day care via the city's elevated SkyTrain. He would then rent one of the city's public Mobi bikes to make the ten-minute trip back to his apartment, where he works as a game-design consultant and blogs at 5kids1condo.com. In the afternoon, he would make the pickup on his own bicycle, fitted with one of the few ride-along seats made for kids up to fifty pounds (his five-year-old just fits). He looked into lightweight seats that could have been attached to a Mobi bike, but designers have yet to grapple with public bike options for those with kids in tow.

If this seems like a lot of effort, it was. The training period, when he made the bus trip to North Vancouver with the four kids, took four hours out of each day (his kids spend two weeks each month with their mother in North Vancouver, where she lives within walking distance of their school). But that effort was for what he thought would be a limited period, and it had an educational mission: teaching his children independence along with maps, money, and problem solving. Crook considers most of his parenting decisions from the perspective of data. "The number one killer of kids ages five to fourteen is car accidents," he says. "The safest thing you can do for your kids is get them out of the car."[17]

The rest of what Crook's family needs is within walking, scooting, or Aquabus distance. After their bus commute, the kids can attend an afterschool program at the Roundhouse Community Arts and Recreation Centre, a few blocks away. The neighborhood public elementary school— wildly overcrowded, for reasons I'll explain shortly—sits across the street from the community center, so children are walked over at the end of the day. The school's playground opens onto a large, green waterfront park, so the equipment is available for climbing on the weekends, and the fields are available for recess. The greenway along the seawall extends for seventeen miles, up to the wilder, wooded Stanley Park on the north side of the

Vancouver peninsula. On weekends, the family will bike south to Science World, a science museum housed in a Buckminster Fuller–inspired dome left over from Expo 86, or take one of the short Aquabus ferries to Granville Island to the east, which has its own community center; the candy-stocked Kids Market, with a padded romper room, an outdoor water park, and the grand, food-focused Public Market. Crook's oldest loves to take the Aquabus, riding it solo to camp in the summer or to meet the rest of the family at Science World. Crook gives him packs of ten tickets for his birthday, "which to him feels like a massive deal." There's a rideshare minivan at the end of the block, for the rare family car trip, and two full-size supermarkets within blocks, as well as a Costco a little over a half mile away. One of Crook's neighbors, Rachel Jonat, who blogs as the Minimalist Mom, bemoans that store's ten A.M. opening time. She drops her seven-year old off at a private school a block away, and her two- and four-year-olds off at a day care just past Costco. If the store opened at nine, she could get her food shopping done on the same walking trip.

Crook and Jonat live opposite one another in a pair of condominium towers linked by a car court and built over an underground garage. Because Crook doesn't own a car, he rents out his designated parking space to a friend who commutes in from the suburbs and works downtown, a short walk away. On rainy days, the underutilized garage has become an indoor play space for the buildings' fifty to sixty resident children, while in fine weather, when a trip to the playground feels like too much of a production, parents drag a net into the court for ball hockey—it is Canada, after all. It's a shame so much of the ground level is devoted to one of Vancouver's ubiquitous water features (seriously, every building has one) where there might otherwise be a small lawn.

What does he lack? In a word, stuff. Crook's apartment, technically a two-bed, two-bath plus a glass-walled "solarium" without a closet, is a scant one thousand square feet. To prevent it from feeling cluttered, Crook has taken fairly drastic action. A single bookcase in the minimally furnished living room—sectional sofa, picnic-table-style dining, spectacular view—holds a smattering of reading material; the rest is on Kindle or checked out from the library. (The main branch of the Vancouver Public Library, which has a children's floor and toddler play space, is five blocks away.) His television, DVD player, and game console are on a wheeled cart, which can be moved from room to room as needed. His children's art supplies and other toys are in a forty-square-foot windowless room with a linoleum floor, where they are free to make messes. His two girls share the solarium, sleeping on a bunk bed whose lower bunk converts to a restaurant-style booth during the day. His three boys share one of the two bedrooms, sleeping on an IKEA-hack triple bunk bed. Crook has a queen-size Murphy bed in the back bedroom, with a desk that cleverly folds out from the bottom. He can work from home during the day with a view through the floor-to-ceiling glass windows—an oasis of quiet in the middle of the city—before the five kids come home.

Crook thought he had it all figured out, but it only took one anonymous phone call to upset his plan. Someone had reported the kids riding the bus without an adult, and the Ministry of Children and Family Development had to investigate. They interviewed Crook as well as each of his children, visited the apartment, and interviewed character references. While the investigation continued, he had to sign a release saying he wouldn't let the kids ride the bus alone, and he returned to chaperoning them to and from school daily. When the Ministry came to a decision, it was worse than he had feared: Not only could the children not ride the bus to school, but children under ten years old could not be alone, inside or outside the house, for any length of time. (In Manitoba and New Brunswick, that age is twelve; in Ontario, sixteen.) Only his oldest could, legally, run to the store across the street, visible from his twenty-ninth-floor window, and only his oldest could, legally, take the family's garbage to the trash room thirty stories below.[18] Crook could risk his joint custody if he left the other four alone to do that chore. Since his family is on the Ministry's radar, his kids can't even join their peers in common practices that flout the under-ten rule, like walking to school when they are staying at their mother's house or riding bikes with friends. "All it took was one report from a stranger to shrink our world beyond everyone else's," Crook wrote on his blog in September 2017, launching a crowd-funding campaign to mount a legal challenge to the Ministry's ruling, and strike a blow for children's freedom.[19] His data, and his rights as a parent, were no match for what he calls "superstition," and what we might call culture: a culture that says terrible things happen if you aren't paying attention to your kids every minute. As Crook points out, that culture also had a lot to do with class: He has the means, and the time, to drive or bus his children to school or hire a nanny to do it instead. Most single parents aren't as privileged.

Vancouver had seemed to be set up for a twenty-first-century version of Betsy and Tacy's expanding territory, making the irony of Crook's predicament more acute. The physically connected, publicly mandated, free to low-cost amenities of which Crook took full advantage were planned with the idea of keeping families from moving away from downtown. Vancouver was one of the first cities in postwar North America to wrestle with the idea that families might not all choose the suburbs. Its planning principles, adopted in 1978, updated in 1992, and now undergoing a twenty-first-century reevaluation, created the template for most of what the Crook family uses every day. Planner Ann McAfee co-wrote those principles with architect Andrew Malczewski, who also provided the charming illustrations that make their report, *Housing Families at High Density*, a relatively accessible read, should your interests lead in that direction.[20]

9.   CHILDREN SAFETY AND SUPERVISION

A.   THE DWELLING UNIT SHOULD BE CAREFULLY CONSIDERED IN
RELATION TO EASY SUPERVISION, SPACE REQUIREMENTS
FOR CHILDREN'S ACTIVITIES, AND SAFETY FOR CHILDREN
WITHIN AND AROUND THE UNIT.

Units should be planned so that children do not
disrupt adult activities and vice versa (i.e.,
a children's domain, and adult domain and a
common domain). Cabinets, stairs, balcony railings and electrical outlets should be child-proof.
(See page 72).

B.   FAMILIES WITH CHILDREN SHOULD BE ACCOMMODATED
ON THE FIRST THREE STOREYS OF AN ABOVE GRADE
DEVELOPMENT.

Reducing the separation between playing children and parent is the most complex problem
posed by increasing density. Parents should
have easy visual and physical access to
children's play area. Children should be
within easy reach of their homes. Attention
should be given to the movement of bulky
and/or heavy children's equipment to and from
the unit. (See pages 50-53).

21

Ann McAfee and Andrew Malczewski, Housing Families at High Density, 1978.
(drawings by Malczewski). [City of Vancouver Planning Department, R. J. Spaxman, director]

The cover shows the proverbial shoe, except this time the old lady, shown sweeping her front porch, lives not only with so many children but with so many families, shown sitting down to dinner with a baby in a high chair, hanging out the laundry from the shoe's tongue, watching TV in a living room, and sunning on a balcony. Why live in your shoe, alone and overwhelmed, the cover says in the visual language of a picture book, when you can have friends all around you to share work and play? "At the time in the 1970s, most of the public housing in North America was in the United States, and Pruitt-Igoe [in St. Louis, a towers-in-the-park development that opened in 1954] was being demolished," McAfee says. "There was nothing available in the literature that suggested you could build housing at higher densities and make it work. The private market said to city staff, 'No families with children are going to want to live downtown!' We said there had always been housing close to downtown in the West End, which had a lot of families in the early years."[21] The West End, close to Stanley Park, is a charming neighborhood of mixed-height, mostly modern apartment buildings, ranging from a few units to dozens. Its appeal is fairly recent, however: 1970s literature described the West End as a wellspring of "alienation and loneliness in the midst of thousands of people," rhetoric similar to that used by single-family homeowners today to keep such architecture out of their neighborhoods.[22]

The West End illustrates what planners today call the "missing middle" in housing—between single-family homes and tall glass towers—that can range in form from rowhouses in Brooklyn or Boston to courtyard apartments in Los Angeles to duplexes or small apartment buildings elsewhere. This type of higher-density housing is a much easier sell to families because it tends to come with outdoor space and even your own front door. In a 2016 story on the "missing middle," journalist Amanda Kolson Hurley writes that the decades between 1870 and 1940 were the "heyday of medium-scaled housing in American cities."[23] Chicago built two-flats, purchased by immigrants who lived in one apartment and rented out the other. Boston had triple-deckers. Bungalow courts were the solution in cities with more land area, setting small, separate houses in a U formation back from the street, with a communal lawn in the center. It's less of a leap from the "dream house." What is lost in square footage is made up for, ideally, with the perks of increased density: access to mass transit, public parks, and retail, as well as shorter commutes to jobs. A 2015 National Association of Realtors and Portland State University community preferences survey found that most respondents wanted walkable neighborhoods with access to public transit, and 25 percent would be willing to give up their detached house for a shorter commute and places they could access on foot.[24] Today, such buildings represent only 19 percent of America's domestic architecture, thanks to the postwar Federal Housing Administration loans that made it easy to buy single-family homes. Even now, when there's a demand for walkable neighborhoods and houses of more manageable size, the limited number of options and cost of construction push prices up. You see that in central Vancouver, where what the developers thought would be a second choice has become an increasingly out-of-reach investment; families find more affordable housing in suburbs far from downtown, forcing long commutes.

Because of the quirks of the topography, most buildings in the West End have an expansive view, and you're never far from water or trees. One of the best qualities of that neighborhood is that many of the units are "ground-oriented." In the Vancouver guidelines, Malczewski illustrated this ideal with an image of a mother calling "Joey, supper's ready" from the third floor of a building with stepped-back balconies. Her son is on the ground, in what could be a building's courtyard, on a bicycle. On the second floor, a mother plays with a toddler and a baby on her balcony. On the lowest floor, a childless man reads the newspaper under the shade of the building's overhang. According to the guidelines: "Parents should have easy visual and physical access to children's play area. Children should be within easy reach of their homes."[25] If Crook lived in this building, he would have been able to yell at his running children to slow down in the moment, not at the end of the day. This was just one of twelve key principles McAfee and Malczewski called out for their audience of architects and developers. The first was that multifamily developments should be no more than a quarter mile from day care, transit, an elementary school, shopping, and playing fields, and no more than a half mile from a secondary school, a swimming pool, and other sports facilities. As developers began buying up industrial land in Yaletown, Coal Harbour, and other neighborhoods on the downtown peninsula, they were required to provide such amenities, building parks first in order to get their building permits, establishing sites for day care or other community facilities within the body of the building, and setting aside land for future public schools. "These are all standards the city has, so you don't have the option of saying you're not going to do it," says McAfee.[26]

Over forty years, whatever the political slant of the city's mayor and city council, the city left the planning principles and the planning department in place. "You don't get to develop here if you don't want to do it," she says. "We could be choosy." Larry Beasley, who was codirector of planning for the City of Vancouver with McAfee from 1994 to 2006, says that, even when residential projects increased in size in the 1990s, "developers had very few rights, and to be given the right to develop was seen as a privilege by the city. Big developers knew they were going to make vast profits once we gave approval. They did argue that they didn't think families would come," but they were required, nonetheless, to set aside at least 20 percent of apartments for low-income people and build 25 percent of apartments with two bedrooms or more.[27] A 2010 audit of higher-density areas found that 29 percent of the units downtown were lived in by families, with 5,100 children under the age of fifteen, whether the space was designed for them or not. For a resident of New York City, where developers are constantly crying poor and asking for density bonuses in return for building open space or setting aside square footage for schools—the very amenities that are attracting the homebuyers who will eventually overrun them—the breadth of the ask in Vancouver's guidelines is astonishing.

The first 1970s developments at False Creek South, a waterfront community south of downtown Vancouver and across the inlet of the same name, were limited to twenty to thirty units per building, considered the optimal size for knowing your neighbors and developing the kind of "social capital" that creates neighborhood cohesion, using the same Dunbar's number as school designers.[28] The neighborhood proved extremely attractive to families with children, with 40 percent of the units occupied by families in 1981. McAfee said they later realized they could have developed False Creek South more densely had they planned larger projects with clusters of twenty-five to thirty-five units. Buildings on False Creek have "territoriality," just as the guidelines suggest, a layering of exterior spaces from the private (like a small terrace or balcony) to the public on the streets or in citywide parks. In between the housing units are the recommended semipublic spaces like courtyards, shared activity rooms, or garden allotments, used and maintained in common. As I talked to residents of all sizes of Vancouver multi-family buildings, many brought up those activity rooms: When you have a small apartment, access to a free, big room, for a birthday party, a book group after the kids have gone to bed, or an organizational meeting, makes a difference in whether your lifestyle feels cramped. Similarly, open space around buildings needs to be zoned for different ages, with passive recreation space, active recreation space, and a sandbox or climbing structure, overlooked by the apartments, for the smallest community members. The 1978 guidelines even get down to the granular level of unit design. A small, enclosed kitchen and large living/dining room is to be avoided. Rather, McAfee and Malczewski suggest either an eat-in kitchen and separate living room, or three rooms, with the kitchen just off the dining area. Otherwise, activities by different members of the family will come into conflict. These guidelines, while operating at the scale of city planning, take the time to look at what happens when families lose the privacy afforded by a detached home with a yard, a garage, or a two-floor separation. Just as outdoor space has to be zoned for different levels of activity, so does the home.

Some things have not gone as planned. First, the explosion of real estate prices in Vancouver has made it increasingly difficult over the past decade for young Canadians to buy in, and for owners to buy up (for families) or downsize (for empty nesters). Most residents I spoke to seemed to feel their home was the wrong size but that there was little they could do about it. A 15 percent tax on foreign buyers, executed in August 2016, caused only a temporary drop in prices and volume of sales. (It is also being challenged in court.)[29] Meanwhile, owners of single-family detached homes have resisted zoning changes that would have added density—even the "gentle density" of duplexes or rowhouses—to their Vancouver neighborhoods, pushing new housing to towers on the downtown peninsula or distant suburbs. In the original design guidelines, planners assumed families would want to live close to the ground, either in the middle-density courtyard housing of False Creek South or in the town houses that ring the base of the tall, slim towers. The Vancouver version of towers typically have three-story structures at the street, with a retail podium and rowhouses, and the thirty-story shaft pushed to the middle of the block to preserve views and light at ground level. The guidelines suggest no more than twelve units grouped together on the same hallway, so that people know their neighbors, as well as semiprivate outdoor space that can serve as a communal backyard. But the town houses have proved popular with empty nesters and dog owners, making them too expensive for many families with children.[30] Brent Toderian, chief planner for the city from 2006 to 2012, lives in a downtown tower, choosing to raise his family many more than three stories off the ground: "It's a block-sized assembly of two midrise podium buildings, and two high-rise towers, interconnected and sharing amenities, attached to a transit skytrain station and creating multiple street frontages. In many ways it's typical of the 'podium & point tower' building type that has become part of the Vancouver Model internationally," he says. "In between the two towers and midrise is an elevated courtyard also partially framed by rowhouses, one of the best designed private courtyard spaces in the city in my opinion."[31] These semiprivate courtyard spaces, either at ground level or on the developments' podiums, were supposed to create safe spaces for children to play while parents (mothers) took care of the house. But post-occupancy reviews suggest that the outdoor spaces aren't visually linked to most apartments, and many of them are either unsecured or underdesigned. The square footage of those set-aside two-bedrooms has shrunk over the years, from a generous 1,500, to Crook's 1,000, to 700 square feet in some newer developments. Bedrooms in such apartments aren't large enough to accommodate both beds and floor space, forcing children's toys and children's play into the living room.

Another guideline set aside sites for community centers and childcare facilities, intended as second homes for the children in the towers. Both the day cares and community programs are now running over capacity, forcing parents onto waiting lists or out of the neighborhood for childcare. Lastly, there are the schools. Public schools in Vancouver are run by the provincial government, not the city, and so adding new schools to accommodate the projected new child population downtown fell to a different political system. In the early 1990s, the provincial government didn't believe the projections for the number of children downtown and insisted they wouldn't build capacity until they saw the growth. Thus Elsie Roy Elementary School, completed in 2004 near the greenway, was the first downtown school built since 1975, and it was at capacity when it opened. In March 2017, downtown finally got a second school, called Crosstown

Elementary, located on a plot of land next to a pair of residential towers, an existing day care, and a public park. It reached capacity when a full cohort of students enrolled in the fall of 2017. Francl Associates, the school's designers, even added another floor after the design process was under way. I toured the school with Alvin Martin, the project architect, and found it to be light, bright, and thoroughly up-to-date from an educational standpoint, with movable classroom furniture, pastel, ovoid "acoustic clouds" affixed to the hallway ceilings to cut noise, a community room on the ground floor, and a shared flexible space outside the kindergarten classrooms. The playful interior design extends outside, where architectural frames around the streetside windows glow with color, and rainbow fins shade the park side. Many find the glassy greenish architecture of the point-and-podium buildings built in the 1990s monotonous. As I stood on the sidewalk looking at the school with Martin, a woman came up to us and said, "I just love the colors. It looks different than everything else." "I didn't pay her to say that," he said, with a chuckle.[32]

•

To SEE A planned community I would like to live in I had to cross the Cambie Street Bridge from the downtown peninsula to the south side of False Creek, where the east-west waterfront park has a perfect view of the downtown towers from a very different type of multifamily, mixed-income housing. My rainy tour of False Creek South was led by Zoe, ten, Cyrus, twelve, and a bunch of grown-ups, including their father. He'd taken them out of school for the morning, thinking it would be educational for them to show me their world. In False Creek South, children can safely roam block upon block, up to a two-thirds of a mile, and still never have to cross a street. The through streets around the developments are essentially *woonerfs*—narrow, curved fire lanes flanked by grass and bike paths, where everything slows. It doesn't feel dense, but the overall coverage, aided by a few taller towers attached to courtyard housing, is forty-five units per acre, higher even than in the "missing middle." They show me the elements of their neighborhood, large and small, with precision and articulation. The planter boxes set up between the public bike- and footpath and the school? The grown-ups tell me they have made some with low sides so schoolchildren can access the plants on their own, but Cyrus demonstrates how great they are for tag, feinting back and forth between the aisles and leaping gracefully over a box, careful to step only on the wooden rim and not the planted interior. We approach a waterfall, a miniaturized version that emerges out of a suggestive stand of redwoods, illustrating the Japanese principle of borrowed landscape in a rugged idiom. The trees are planted along the berm that screens False Creek South from highway noise, but for a moment, in the middle of this scrap of forest, you might be lost in the Pacific Northwest. The adults describe summer picnics by the water, children wading and digging in the sand. Cyrus describes the landscape as a scene of battle, waged by action figures dying on the sands or hiding behind craggy rocks. The battle being waged in real life is between parents and dog owners—largely the older generation—between those who want to keep the sand and water clean enough for bathing and those who see it as a dog run. Such generational conflict wasn't anticipated by the original planners. They thought the families would be self-renewing, moving out as children went to college and careers shifted. But many of the original and second-generation owners stayed because they loved the lifestyle: the communal gardens, the cheek-by-jowl barbecue terraces, the easy access to the water and not-quite-as-easy access to wheeled public transportation. The desire of retirees to age in place is, in some sense, a testament to Peñalosa's ideal. Today, as the city-owned ground leases under 60 percent of the False Creek developments approach their expiration date, the city has initiated a "replan" that will likely add thousands of units to the current 3,200, utilizing open space like a parking lot near the Olympic Village transit station and bringing greater population to the area.[33] The residents created a set of new planning principles to guide future development, including providing affordable options for the residents of the 1,172 nonmarket units once their leases expire, increasing housing for families and low- to middle-income workers, offering smaller units for seniors ready to downsize, and not ruining the historic and somewhat idiosyncratic fabric of the place.

The individual developments at False Creek South have a variety of funding structures. Some are market-rate condominiums, some are subsidized rentals, a few are low-income housing, but most enclaves are designed in a similar high-1970s manner: arcs of attached units, up to four stories tall, create a long oval open space at the center and are separated by narrow, crooked paths. To children, these paths create a porous structure, secret routes between one courtyard and another. If early life is confined to one's own courtyard, in sight, increasing age brings increasing territory, annexing the next one over, then the next, then the next, for ever more elaborate play wars. Some of the paths have lockable gates, but their inconspicuous size provides its own sort of security for the courtyards. Had I not had my band of guides, I'm not sure I could have found my way in. The units step back, via balconies, either facing the courtyard or facing the water, to give lower units a piece of the view. This gives them a distinctive mountainous shape that, combined with the picturesque up-and-down topography and palette ranging from brown to gray to tan, recalls postwar architecture's love affair with the Italian hill town. As Cory Verbauwhede writes in a short history of the area, "One observer described it as a Greek mountain village with Belgian architecture in the heart of a North

American town. My father claims that for every minute that you walk along its windy streets there is a unique vista to greet you." Verbauwhede's father, Jos, worked for Thompson, Berwick, Pratt and Partners, the multidisciplinary firm that won the competition to develop the first part of the False Creek site in 1974, before the high-density housing guidelines were in place. In order to keep the site design from becoming repetitive, the firm laid out a roll of paper on the floor of their office and invited different architects to participate. "In the morning, one person would draw in a desired pattern, only to have it changed with eraser and pencil by someone else in the afternoon."[34] The result was a plan that replaces the urban grid with an urban web, and right angles with donut shapes, winding paths, and sloping curbs. Their original proposal for the site, then called False Creek Area Six, emphasizes the picturesque at every turn, using illustrations to call out the pedestrian waterfront, shared streets for bikes and cars, and the balance of buildings and trees. The designers even argued down the city's legal department in order to have a seawall without a high railing that might have blocked the view, a perfect example of the kind of zoning that robs residents of risk and reward.

The design elements in False Creek South reflect a particular sensibility, most prevalent in the 1970s, that embraced ancient, nonarchitectural models for creating new civilizations. A foundational text for many of these planners and architects is *A Pattern Language*, written by Christopher Alexander, Sara Ishikawa, and Murray Silverstein, colleagues at Berkeley's Center for Environmental Structure, and published in 1977, as well as its predecessor, "Cells for Subcultures," circulated in 1971.[35] Alexander and his colleagues' "patterns," all 253 of them, are observed particulars of the built world, described and illustrated, from the most intimate room in the house to the scale of a city. Returning to a text I first encountered in architecture school, as an adult, I found it riddled with resonant ideas about family life as part of urban life—patterns I ignored before I had my own children. By assembling your favorites, you might be able to build a pretty wonderful house or neighborhood. The most relevant pattern to False Creek South is #68, Connected Play. "Children need other children. Some findings suggest that they need other children even more than they need their own mothers," Alexander writes.[36] And indeed, one of the chief difficulties of contemporary parenthood is connecting your children to others in healthy ways. Even Crook, living in a complex with fifty or sixty other children, has difficulty finding playmates for his younger children on weekend afternoons. He went so far as to take the low-tech step of posting a flyer in his building's laundry room—PLAYDATES WANTED!—with his cellphone number on slips of paper at the bottom. The slips disappeared, but no calls came. In my own childhood in Cambridge, Massachusetts, children of the neighborhood massed on the sidewalks, and occasionally in the street, linking up with what I remember as ease and tunneling through centers of blocks by leaping the fences between adjacent yards. We needed an adult escort to go to the park three blocks away, but our yards, the quiet street out front, and the corner store at the end of the block were all within our domain. Alexander's Connected Play pattern has this covered: "Since the layout of the land between the houses in a neighborhood virtually controls the formation of play groups, it therefore has a critical effect on people's mental health. A typical suburban subdivision with private lots opening off streets almost confines children to their houses. Parents, afraid of traffic or of their neighbors, keep their small children indoors or in their own gardens: so the children never have enough chance meetings with other children of their own age to form the groups which are essential to a healthy emotional development."[37] A key word here is *chance*. In the age of activities, even casual interactions between children often get scheduled, but the dream for parents and children is to be able to

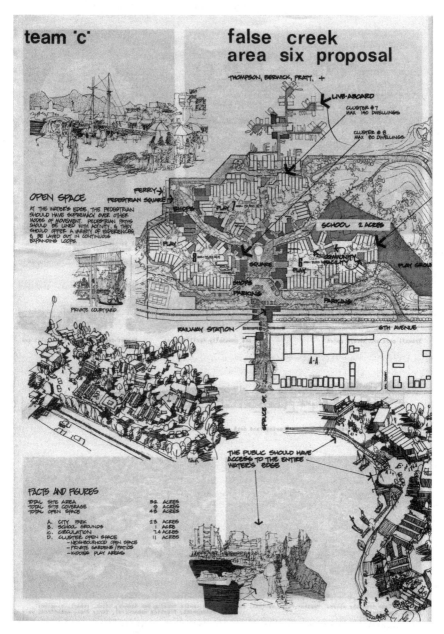

False Creek Area Six Proposal, Team C (Thompson, Berwick, Pratt and Partners), 1974. [City of Vancouver, Archives, PD158.]

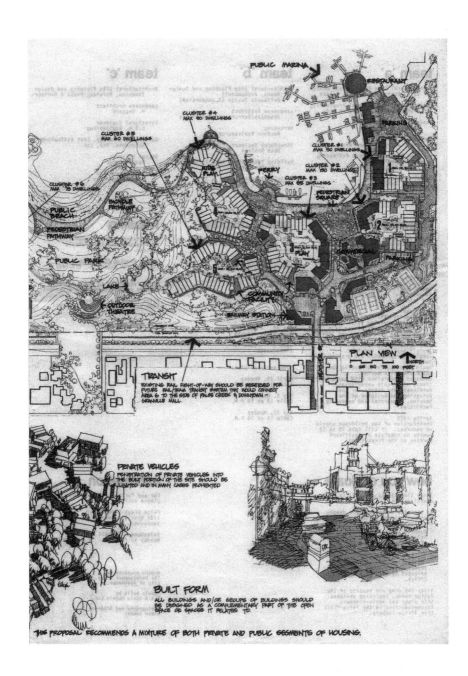

PUBLIC MARINA

RESTAURANT

PARKING

CLUSTER #4
MAX 50 DWELLINGS

CLUSTER #5
MAX 60 DWELLINGS

CLUSTER #6
MAX 75 DWELLINGS

PUBLIC
BEACH

PEDESTRIAN
PATHWAY

PUBLIC PARK

LAKE

OUTDOOR
THEATRE

BICYCLE
PATHWAY

KIDS
PLAY

FERRY

CLUSTER #1
MAX 50 DWELLINGS

CLUSTER #2
MAX 150 DWELLINGS

CLUSTER #3
MAX 65 DWELLINGS

PEDESTRIAN
SQUARE

PLAY

COMMERCIAL

PARKING

COMMUNITY
FACILITY

RAILWAY STATION

PLAN VIEW

0   25   50   75   100 FEET

NORTH

TRANSIT
EXISTING RAIL RIGHT-OF-WAY SHOULD BE RESERVED FOR
FUTURE RAIL/TRAM TRANSIT SYSTEM THAT WOULD CONNECT
AREA 6 TO THE SIDE OF FALSE CREEK & DOWNTOWN
GRANVILLE MALL.

PRIVATE VEHICLES
PENETRATION OF PRIVATE VEHICLES INTO
THE BUILT PORTION OF THE SITE SHOULD BE
LIMITED AND IN MANY CASES PROHIBITED

BUILT FORM
ALL BUILDINGS AND/OR GROUPS OF BUILDINGS SHOULD
BE DESIGNED AS A COMPLEMENTARY PART OF THE OPEN
SPACE OR SPACES IT RELATES TO

THIS PROPOSAL RECOMMENDS A MIXTURE OF BOTH PRIVATE AND PUBLIC SEGMENTS OF HOUSING.

step outside and play—wherever, with whomever. This is the plea for autonomy reflected in Denis Wood's cry "Down with Playgrounds!" and in Colin Ward's *The Child in the City* (1978), in which he writes, "I don't want a Childhood City. I want a city in which children live in the same world I do."[38] This type of planning has also been seen as feminist, freeing up time for the mother who, even when fully employed, performs more housework and childcare. Women-Work-City, a housing complex built in Vienna in 1993, combined midrise apartment buildings with landscaped courtyards, private balconies, and an on-site kindergarten and doctor's office, all close to public transit. It was developed as part of that city's gender-mainstreaming project—an attempt to provide equal access to city resources for men and women by taking a careful look at how men and women use cities differently.[39] Connections, and safe connections, turn out to be a major part of that effort, as does a focus on family life.

Research on children's lives done contemporaneously with the building of False Creek South indicated that greater housing density allowed children to use home as "home base," a place to rest and refuel between bouts of outdoor play. Children living in such environments had an expanded idea of friendship and learned to play with whomever was around, rather than with carefully chosen friends whose parents have to ferry them over for playdates.[40] The neighborhood setting puts much less pressure on individual peer-to-peer relationships, because the best-case scenario is a sort of morphing, elastic mob of kids into which yours might be absorbed, as Iona Archibald Opie and Peter Opie noticed in their pioneering 1969 study of street games.[41] Alexander's design solution is to make a purposeful version of that two-block assembly of street, sidewalk, store, and yard that I had in Cambridge. Each household, in his design, would open onto a safe and connected piece of common land, free of roads and overlooked by up to sixty-four households. (He arrives at the number sixty-four by calculating that each child is best entertained by at least five children of his or her own age.) This land might contain clusters of houses whose owners have some closer relationship, tending a common garden or other cooperative activity, or include an adventure playground, a water feature, or animals. The water is for swimming, with a shallow end for those learning to swim and an active set of pools and streams for pretend play. Having landmarks that children walk to, from their earliest years, would allow them to create a cognitive map of their world. Being walked, and then walking, from home to friend's home and school to playground allows a child first to understand his world and then to move about it independently. "The right setting for a child is the community itself, just as the right setting for an infant learning to speak is his own home," writes Alexander.[42]

An indoor gathering place should be adjacent to this connected outdoor space. Alexander calls it a Children's Home, #86, a day care/community center/play space open to its members 24/7 for babysitting and activities. Alexander saw this space as a replacement for the care once available within a child's extended family: childcare with minimal payment, and without a schedule, in a domestic environment. He felt it was important for the home to be actually in a house, within walking distance of its members' residences. (Alexander's attachment to traditional architecture can be a stumbling block for many modern readers, perhaps less enamored of the craftsman-style architecture all around him in Berkeley than he was.)[43] Several staff members would work there most days, and at least one would live there so that there could be services at night. Adults could use the Children's Home too, as a meeting space and coffee klatch, overlapping with their children but not there only in their service. The Children's Home operates as a pressure valve for the family, a nonjudgmental third parent to fill in the gaps and allow parents to get away from their children for an evening (even if they stay in). The Children's Home is one of those third spaces, more often discussed for adults as an alternative to home and work. Alexander's patterns for the private house, like his patterns for the city, treat the happiness of all members of the family democratically. The House for a Small Family, #76, should have a children's realm, an adult realm, and common space between the two—most likely a farmhouse kitchen. Without private space, Alexander counsels, the whole house becomes swamped with children's goods, pleasing no one.

In the courtyard of their own market-rate condominium, which centers on a fountain made of large, smooth rocks, Zoe and Cyrus, my False Creek South guides, show off tiny villages they have made on the turf, poaching the garden designer's ornamental stones. It is not lost on me that their villages, with their rampart-like walls and green interior spaces marked with tiny stick structures, are influenced by the layout of their own courtyard home, updating the traditional gable-roofed house that appears even in the commercial play structures residents have bought for those same courtyards. The form of their housing is still so radical it can't appear in a commercial product—they have to make it themselves. The century of anarchists, educators, and theorists who wanted to give children back the city through design also believed that children should have input into the city's structure, sparking a series of continuing experiments in gathering their kid-size view of the world. Urban95, an ongoing project of the Bernard van Leer Foundation, takes the average height of a three-year-old, just above three feet, as the vantage point for a new set of planning principles for healthy child development. The project is "premised on the belief that if we want to make a city livable for everyone, planning from the vantage point of a toddler is the best place to start."[44] Caroline Pratt included city exploration and city building in her educational plan from the earliest days of City and Country School. The corner of Manhattan's West Fourth and West Twelfth Streets, where she set up shop with six students in 1914, proved to be a perfect jumping-off point for what she called "our journey, none so long as to tire young children." Pratt writes, "The river traffic, endlessly fascinating, brought good simple questions to their lips, but they were too shy at first to ask the tugboat men and the bargemen and the wagon drivers for the answers. When they saw that I would not do their asking for them they plucked up courage to make the first move, and met with such friendly answers that their diffidence vanished quite away!"[45] The children sat on the docks by the hour, watching wagons getting loaded with goods and questioning the drivers about what they were carrying and where. But, Pratt writes, the accumulation of knowledge was not her purpose; the children were being taught to think. "After we had discovered some new facts on our trips, we hurried back to school to put them to use." To use, she means, in developing their own city and their own play. At first they push a block across the floor, aping the bargeman's path and the load's journey. But some children want a block that looks more like a real boat, and they learn to use tools to carve one. Then they want a train to bring the loads to the river, a cart, a dray, even a derrick, all eventually made of wood and paper. To build is to capture one's environment for oneself. Children in the 7s, from Pratt's day to the present, have as their year's central task the building of a play city, made of large open blocks and small solid ones, plus paper and a variety of other found materials for color and texture. The children read newspaper items about New York City, share information gleaned on their weekly class trips, and research how different elements they add to the cityscape actually work. When a boy adds a water tank, it sparks a discussion of how water gets to the top of buildings. " 'The science teacher was eventually called in to help us work out an experiment and so arrive at a satisfactory solution,' " Pratt notes, quoting from an account by one of her teachers, Bertha Delehanty.[46] Over the years, the children take more and more extensive trips, engineered to find out the answers: They go to a powerhouse to find out how electricity gets into their house, and some become "so electricity-minded" that they install working electrical systems in the play city, a task after today's STEM teachers' hearts. As a result, the 7s (or second graders) are "better oriented in their own environment geographically and socially than children who are introduced too soon to the remote and therefore less comprehensible primitive civilizations of Indians or Eskimos or ancient pastoral people," Delehanty writes. One day, a boy comes in full of an article his father read at the breakfast table, about then parks commissioner Robert Moses building new playgrounds on the Lower East Side. The class decides to write him a thank-you note, with a nudge to improve the facilities in their own Washington Square neighborhood. Did the playgrounds that were built, in due time, come about from the children's advocacy? Pratt doesn't know, "but they had done their duty as citizens, far better, indeed, than most adult citizens ever do."[47]

When the Vancouver kids described the landmarks of school and corner grocery, the edges of seawall and highway berm, the nodes where paths come together at the playground, the difference between the hill for sledding in the winter and the hill for birthday parties in the summer, they unconsciously replicated the language of architect and teacher Kevin Lynch. In his 1960 book *The Image of the City*, Lynch asked his subjects (first adults, later children) to make mental maps of their neighborhoods, through drawing and description, sifting them for elements of "imageability."[48] He came up with five: landmarks, edges, nodes, paths, and districts (that would be False Creek South itself). Another father on my kid-led tour had even asked his daughter to circle for me the key places in her False Creek on our tour map, a sort of reversal of

Lynchian technique. In 1975, Robin C. Moore, an expert in children's environments, did his own Lynchian urban study with ninety-six children, ages nine to twelve, in three cities in the United Kingdom. He asked each child to draw a map of their favorite places on an eighteen-by-twenty-four-inch sheet of paper, then followed up with child-led tours.

Moore's first guide is Heather, who lives in Notting Dale, who takes him to a "wasteland" behind a corrugated metal fence. He soon realizes she has found an oasis, a place ignored by adults where she can dig for "buried treasure" and discover a "lost civilization."[49] She picks a bouquet for her mother of weeds or wildflowers, depending on your perspective, and brings it back with pride to their "dingy" basement flat. Her mother, a street cleaner, accepts them with pleasure, telling Moore that Heather asked for a biology book for Christmas. Heather represents an ideal: Her spirit of inquiry has not been limited by poverty or urban life but allowed to flourish, aided by her mother's comfort with her playing in spots not marked as "for children." Moore contrasts Heather's freedom with that of Gill, a girl of the same age whose mother would only allow her to be interviewed, awkwardly, in her presence and who was only allowed to play on the windswept concrete playground of their housing estate. "The wellspring of competence may be seen as a natural striving by the young child to acquire knowledge and skills," Moore writes. "As the child develops biologically, new play opportunities must become available to support the growth of competence."[50] Moore describes the educational value of wandering in much the same terms as experts describe block play in kindergarten, or risky play for elementary school students: Children strive toward competence, but they can only achieve it if they have the opportunity to practice, failing and trying again, until they have mastered that tower, that jungle gym, or that route between school and a favored playground. Many of the children Moore talks to use local parks as meeting spots, particularly the swings, but as pretext. Their play veers off from specific pieces of equipment, and it is important, he notes, for the equipment to be presented as an ensemble within a landscape that is also playable.[51] The children also show him a variety of made-up games based on street furniture, including lampposts, retaining walls, stairs, and railings. For the child, the path between places can be as exciting as the place, if they are allowed to make the journey in their own time. Folklorists like Iona and Peter Opie, he writes, revealed the "child-to-child social complex . . . fully capable of occupying themselves under the jurisdiction of their own code." What if children playing in the streets isn't a sign of a problem but a solution? "There is a danger that children in the West are becoming passive receivers of predigested messages from secondary sources, instead of being agents for self-initiated interaction with the living world around them."[52] His ultimate goal is participation by children in making their own environment. If play is important, it must become the business of government.

More recently, researchers have used digital tools to harness the inquisitive nature and enthusiastic questions of children. In 2014, Norwegian designer Vibeke Rørholt was commissioned by Norway's Agency of the Urban Environment to encourage Oslo's forty-four thousand students to walk or bike to school. But first she had to figure out why they weren't doing so in the first place. The agency's question came as part of a larger initiative, by the Oslo city government, to improve the sustainability and ban private cars from downtown by 2019. Putting homes and workplaces closer together, and getting families to stay in the city, are a key part of that initiative. As of 2007, 50 percent of new homes in Oslo have to have three bedrooms. "I was supposed to make a traffic report on all roads in Oslo. That's a big job," Rørholt told the *Guardian* in 2016. "So I thought, why don't we ask the children how they feel on the street?"[53] Her solution was the creation of an app, called Traffic Agent, that turned the city's smallest residents into "secret agents" of road safety. Children using the app are tracked by GPS (though their data is anonymized), and can send real-time reports of problems along their path to school or afternoon activities. As with adult-oriented apps like SeeClickFix, part of the pleasure of using it is rapid results. "I received a telephone call from the mother of a little boy who had reported some bushes that meant he couldn't see when he was crossing the street. And two days later the bushes were cut. She phoned in saying he's so happy that he could make this happen," Rørholt said.

On the opposite side of gamification, in 2017 the Toole Design Group published what they said would be the first in a "kid's-eye view" series of children's books focused on safe street design—self-promotion with an illustrated face. *How I Get to School!* shows separated bike lanes, with rows of trees or bioswales as buffers between bikes and pedestrians and bikes and parked cars.[54] Dedicated traffic lights for cyclists "make it safe for everyone," reports the child. "There's a nice park on the way and sometimes we stop and play," she chirps from the front of his father's cargo bike. "My teacher says that helps make me do better in school!" The planted strips shade pedestrians and bikers, as well as absorbing rain- and storm-water runoff from the streets. On rainy days, she takes the bus with Mom, from a bus stop on its own traffic island, ensuring faster loading. On cold days, father and daughter wear matching scarfs. It's goofy, and definitely low-fi, but makes its point: Planners need to consider the city through the eyes of the child.

•

CHRISTOPHER ALEXANDER AND the 1970s planners who followed his lead were not the first to include connected open space, streets with limited traffic, and a common set of public buildings at the heart of a community. What can sound like a countercultural idea about shared space is actually part of a century-long reconsideration of land use, in cities and suburbs, around the needs of families. At the turn of the last century, playgrounds, compulsory schooling, and settlement houses were all architectural means of keeping lower-class children off the streets, while middle-class children would already have spent most of their time between home, school, and yard. Streetcar suburbs, built outside major American cities from the 1870s on, created a new model for domestic life: the detached house, with a garden on all sides, physically removed from its neighbors and from the real diseases at work in urban areas. "The new idea was no longer to be part of a close community," writes historian Kenneth T. Jackson in *Crabgrass Frontier* (1985), "but to have a self-contained unit, a private wonderland walled off from the rest of the world. Although visually open to the street, the lawn was a barrier—a kind of verdant moat separating the house from the threats and temptations of the city."[55] In the city, the backyards of rowhouses had most often been the site of privies, garbage heaps, and back-alley dwellings. Improved public sanitation, as well as indoor plumbing and other utilities, would eventually clean those out, but in the meantime, it was in the suburbs that children had the ability to roam. But while Ralph Waldo Emerson thought, "There is no police so effective as a good hill and wide pasture in the neighborhood of a village, where the boys can run and play and dispose of their superfluous strength of spirits," architecture critic Lewis Mumford saw the suburbs "only as a nursery for bringing up children."[56] In separating family life from city life, from work, from shopping, from institutions, the suburb created a land of perpetual childhood. "In reacting against the disadvantages of the crowded city," wrote Mumford, "the suburb itself became an over-specialized community, more and more committed to relaxation and play as ends in themselves . . . Such a segregated community, composed of segregated economic strata, with little visible daily contact with the realities of the workaday world, placed an undue burden of education on the school and family." As in Alexander's world of patterns, Mumford felt there was something unhealthy about the way children and child-rearing dominated home and social life. The green space was a blessing, for a time, but when children reached the age to explore, mentally and physically, there was nothing more within reach. The image of the suburb as a nursery, a clean, soft, bounded space for those of limited ability is a compelling one: The nursery is fine for a while, but then you need to learn to walk.

Progressive designers of the 1930s, attempting to create better, semi-urban settlement patterns, had earlier arrived at the idea that dissolving the fences between peoples' yards, throwing that space under a collective watchful eye and establishing a network of community facilities and retail within a set of bounded distances, could improve families' lives. The most important built example of this thinking is Radburn, New Jersey, located approximately fourteen miles from New York City, and constructed from 1928 to 1934. Planned by Clarence S. Stein and Henry Wright, and funded by the developer Alexander Bing's City Housing Corporation, Radburn was intended as a demonstration "new town," illustrating how best to plan residential settlement in the motor age, and backed by the influential Regional Planning Association of America. Radburn's building block was the neighborhood, and the neighborhood was specifically sized to be large enough to support its own school.[57] Stein and Wright were influenced by the neighborhood unit formula created by Clarence Perry for the Russell Sage Foundation, another affiliate of the Regional Planning Association, in the early 1920s. A diagram of the neighborhood unit, developed by Perry in 1929, shows a trapezoidal area bounded by major arterial highways and streets and centered on a set of community facilities including a school.[58] Narrow streets crisscross the interior, some surrounding residential streets and others, small parks, which should make up at least 10 percent of the total area. A circle a half mile across is inscribed over the trapezoid, indicating that no part of the neighborhood should be more than a five-minute, or quarter-mile, walk from the center. At the outer corners, near the major intersections, Perry proposed groups of shops or houses of worship.

The residents of Radburn were expected to be families, so planning for children—their safety, education, and amusement—was paramount. The most radical element of Radburn was the way it dealt with circulation: Single-family houses were arranged around U-shaped cul-de-sacs that served as service roads for driveways and trash pickup. These cul-de-sacs nibble into the edges of twenty-three acres of open space spread across three parks—the interior of Perry's ideal trapezoid, but with the houses confined to the edge and the park collected in the center. The houses all fronted small private yards and had immediate access to a central park and pedestrian walkways. The negative space between the backs of houses in a typical subdivision was collected into a continuous park, through which children could walk and bike to the included elementary school, swimming pools, play equipment, and friends' houses. This was the superblock. Between two of these superblocks, separated by a busy access road, the planners included a sunken underpass; two others were initially connected by a footbridge. Access roads were segregated to the outside of this block, so residents could drive in and out of Radburn but not within it. Advertised as a "Town for the Motor Age," Radburn nonetheless kept cars at the periphery.[59] Landscape architect Marjorie Sewell Cautley designed the parks and plantings in the naturalistic landscape style familiar from Frederick Law Olmsted's New York City parks, choosing species of plants and trees native to northern New Jersey. A high street was included in the plan so that basic shopping could also be done within the pedestrian confines of the neighborhood. Stein and Wright originally planned three neighborhoods, each with its own services and central green space, but after the Depression caused the financial collapse of the City Housing Corporation in 1934, construction along Stein and Wright's plan stopped. At that time, a single neighborhood and part of a second had been built, with approximately two hundred houses; when construction picked up later, the homes were built in a conventional suburban orientation, facing the street, with wide front lawns and individual driveways.

The so-called reverse-front houses have front doors facing the park and living rooms adjacent to their private yards and the open view. Kitchen, laundry, and garage were typically located at the back. The houses were built in a variety of sizes, from two to four bedrooms, and some are semidetached, sharing a wall with a neighbor. Most are built in either the popular colonial revival style or Tudor revival, in brick or frame with siding. Two three-story apartment buildings, originally known as Abbott Court, create a courtyard between their L-shaped wings and contain ninety-three apartments. These, like a set of duplexes on another street, were intended to provide lower-cost and rental options for residents within the overall development. Everything is ground-oriented, and great attention was paid to landscaping to ensure the connection between the apartment buildings and the park. As the nation's, and the funder's, financial situation worsened, the planners and their architects added more attached, terraced houses, influenced by their previous work in Sunnyside, Queens, as well as historic brick rowhouses in Philadelphia and Baltimore.

Radburn has proved to be one of the most influential residential developments of the twentieth century, both in the short and long term.[60] During the 1930s, it provided a template for towns built under the federally backed New Deal, including Greenbelt, Maryland, and Baldwin Hills Village in Los Angeles, as well as postwar new towns. Baldwin Hills Village (now known as Village Green), was planned by a group of architects led by

Town plan, Radburn, NJ, 1929, Clarence Stein and Henry Wright, planners; Marjorie Sewell Cautley, landscape architect. [Courtesy Regional Plan Association]

Reginald D. Johnson on a property owned by E. J. "Lucky" Baldwin, on sixty-eight acres of relatively flat land located within the city limits.[61] Construction began in 1941 on 95 buildings, containing 627 units with 16 different floor plans. Forty-four acres were left open for communal greens and garden courts, giving the project a density of 9.2 units per acre—low for inner-city housing. Johnson and his fellow architects adopted the superblock idea, keeping all through traffic at the edges of the site and orienting the housing units to the interior.

In postwar America, government loan programs subsidized the construction and purchase of new homes in suburban settings for white families, making that the preferred, and publicized, mode of family life for

Airview, Radburn, NJ, 1935. Photograph by Carl Mydans. [The Library of Congress, LC-USF344-000872-ZB]

generations. In 1954 *Fortune* estimated that nine million people had moved to the suburbs in the past decade, suburbs growing at ten times the rate of central cities. Between 1946 and 1956, about 97 percent of new houses were single-family dwellings, as the rowhouse, as well as other attached, missing middle–style housing, fell from favor. More of the area between those houses was left to streets and open space as well: Levittown, on Long Island, was half as dense as the streetcar suburbs built in places like Westchester County fifty years before.[62] Midcentury homes, more likely to be one story, with open kitchens adjacent to outdoor play areas, linked the indoors and the outdoors and established the private backyard as another room of the house. As early as 1960, observers had begun to notice the effect that suburban space was having on children, in books that attempted to do for kids what Betty Friedan's *The Feminine Mystique* (1963) would attempt to do for their mothers: free them from the isolated prison of the detached house with lawn. "It all began to register with me one sunny Sunday afternoon near the North Shore Railroad tracks in Highland Park, Illinois. I had my two boys aged ten and eight with me, and we were doing something quite extraordinary. We were walking," writes Peter Wyden in *Suburbia's Coddled Kids* (1962), citing a litany of lost urban skills observed among his neighbors' children.[63] A teen not knowing how to get on an escalator, having never seen one; a newspaper boy driven around to deliver the papers in his parents' station wagon on a rainy day; a girl crying at the sight of a drunk passerby on a rare trip to the city. By 1950, eleven million Americans under twenty lived in suburbia; by 1960, nineteen million, 28 percent of U.S. children and adolescents. And these suburbias were different. Streetcar suburbs were accessible, and dependent on central cities. Children could, and did, get on streetcars and buses and go into downtown. But sprawling suburbs, greater self-sufficiency, and dependence on the automobile pushed families and their children farther out. The result was that the white children of the baby boom were living in a monoculture where friends, activities, and experiences were essentially preselected by their parents. Writes Wyden, "A mother said: 'There's no place here to make a mess. Everybody keeps the yard just so. There's no place where kids can go dig a hole, no sidewalks to ride on, no fences to climb.' "[65] Nonwhite families, particularly those unable to buy in segregated new towns, still lived in cities, and in places like New York the Parks Department embarked on a robust program of playground building to meet the need. But in both urbs and suburbs, the spaces of children were only that, spaces of children, and the rest of the city remained the domain of adults. It wasn't until the 1970s that African Americans moved in significant numbers to the suburbs; Jackson reports that by 1980, 23.3 percent of the black population was living in suburbs, despite attempts to limit new residents via upzoning, increasing minimum lot size, and gating communities.[64]

When modern architect Mies van der Rohe designed the seventy-eight-acre Lafayette Park in Detroit with planner Ludwig Hilberseimer and landscape architect Alfred Caldwell, he also looked to Radburn's idea of the superblock as an organizing principle, setting a series of low, single-story courtyard houses, bars of attached town houses, and three twenty-story slab apartment buildings in a network of private, semipublic, and fully public parkland, along with an elementary school, pool and bathhouse, and shopping center.[66] Although the architectural language of Lafayette Park is radically different from that of previous garden cities like Radburn—steel, floor-to-ceiling glass, long straight lines and sharp edges—the idea of a garden within the city, a stretchy green network in which residents and their children can move freely and without cars, remains. Lafayette Park, considered the most successful urban renewal project in the United States, nonetheless required the demolition and displacement of Black Bottom, a 90 percent African American community on the east side of the central business district. The neighborhood was one of the few places in Detroit where African Americans could live, due to discriminatory deed restrictions, and it had some of the oldest housing in the city. A historic, functioning community was destroyed to create a modernist ideal on a very different plan. Targeted by city planners as a slum, the site was purchased by the city in 1951, giving them access to federal Title I funds. Developers were wary of the site because of its previous history and adjacency to low-income housing, while the city pushed for a mixed-income, medium-density development. It wasn't until 1954, when United Auto Workers president Walter Reuther pressured the city to do something with the vacant site, that plans moved forward. A citizens' committee, appointed by the city, wrote that the land ought to become "an integrated residential community of the most advanced design, of the highest possible [construction] standards; a community that on a purely competitive basis, can attract back to the heart of the city people who are finding their housing in the outlying sections of the city and its suburbs."[67] To illustrate their point, the committee hired a team of leading modern architects, including future Twin Towers architect Minoru Yamasaki and leading shopping center designers Victor Gruen Associates. The team produced a striking plan for 4,400 units in twenty high-rise towers, twenty to thirty town houses, and a grand boulevard in a green landscape, with 25 percent of units set aside as low-income housing. This plan, while unexecuted, spurred Chicago developer Herbert Greenwald to make a bid for the site, bringing Mies as his architect.

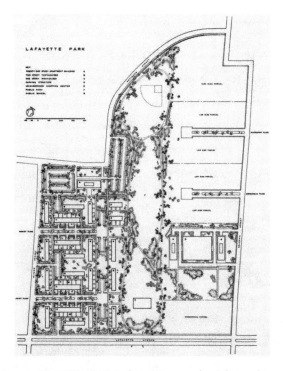

Lafayette Park, Detroit, MI, 1958–1965, Ludwig Mies van der Rohe, architect. [Edward A. Duckett Collection, Ryerson and Burnham Archives, Art Institute of Chicago. Digital File #198602.LaPk_final1.]

As with previous new towns, the planners made an effort to mix sizes of apartments and types of ownership (rentals and co-ops) to achieve economic diversity. An increase in construction costs meant that low-income housing was not part of Lafayette Park, though it was racially integrated, highly unusual for the period. The first building to fill up at Lafayette Park was the Pavilion, which was 98 percent rented by May 1960, while the town houses took longer to sell. A 1959 *Detroit Free Press* article on the community says many new residents are former suburbanites, and lists their professional qualifications: "Twenty-six physicians and dentists, 13 attorneys, seven architects, five securities brokers, 31 business executives, seven bank executives of at least vice presidential rank, six engineers, four certified public accountants, 12 merchandisers, 13 advertising, radio and television personnel, numerous college and university personnel."[68] Another article notes, "Perhaps the most obvious distinction the residents of the Park have over residents of more conventional suburbs is the high incidence of career wives and mothers. At least 14 have full-time careers, and many more work part time."[69]

The towers at Lafayette Park, which bookend rows of town houses on one side, and the open 14-acre Lafayette Plaisance on the other, are rentals, with units ranging from studios to two-bedrooms. The towers, far higher than any built at previous "new town" projects, were intended to make the public open space economically feasible. Many other urban renewal projects of the same era included just towers, or just midrise buildings, and arranged them evenly across the resulting superblocks, creating chopped-up open spaces and a sense of monotonous exposure. At Lafayette Park, the combination of housing types, and the arrangement of intimate landscaped areas near the ground-oriented town houses, creates a better balance. Small children can play together at their own doorstep, while larger children can play in the wide open Plaisance (an adaptation of an archaic French word, meaning "pleasure ground"), where their parents can't see them, but know them to be safe from traffic. The 162 two-story attached town houses, whose floor plans fit together like L-shaped cookies, giving one unit two bedrooms in front and the next two bedrooms behind, have front doors onto a common, tree-lined green, with open grassy spaces and the occasional piece of play equipment. Each unit has a private backyard that extends six feet from the building line—just enough room for a grill and chairs—and then access to either the Plaisance or a second semiprivate green zone. The town houses are also linked underground by an ingenious system of subterranean alleys; trash pickup and servicing of utilities can all be handled out of sight, adding to the parklike atmosphere with a density of almost twelve units per acre. The twenty-four attached court houses, housed in four separate buildings, have small, walled private gardens in the rear. Cars are exiled to the perimeter of the block, parked in sunken lots, cut in like Radburn's cul-de-sacs, that can hardly be seen from the housing. You drive in, you drive out, but you can go to school, play, and shop at an attached shopping center on foot and without crossing a street. As *Architectural Forum* wrote in May 1960, "the camera . . . cannot convey the deftness with which Detroit's own strident contribution to the world's landscape, the automobile, has for once been digested into a city street scene, instead of being allowed to dominate it."[70]

Construction on Chrysler Elementary School, designed not by Mies but by a local architecture firm in a complementary style, did not start until 1961, when residents had already begun to move into the complex. The Detroit school board wouldn't set up and staff a new school until there were enough school-age children. The developers, who didn't want to see those families go elsewhere, offered one of the newly completed town houses to the Detroit Board of Education as a modernist "one-room school."[71] According to a special section on the complex in the *Detroit Free Press*:

Aerial view, Lafayette Park, Detroit, MI. Photograph by Michelle and Chris Gerard.
[Courtesy Michelle and Chris Gerard]

Nicollet Place, Lafayette Park, Detroit, MI. Photograph by Michelle and Chris Gerard.
[Courtesy Michelle and Chris Gerard]

A one-room schoolhouse in the middle of a multimillion-dollar ultra-modern apartment development in the heart of Detroit sounds like a throwback to the 19th Century—until you talk to Ruth Belew.

Miss Belew is well equipped to run Detroit's only one-room schoolhouse.

"I can't sing, but we should be able to work something out," said the vivacious brunet who has been a Detroit schoolteacher since 1941—with time out for Red Cross service in Africa and Europe during World War II.

Miss Belew was an "old-timer" at the development, one of the first to move into the Pavilion. "This is a development designed to attract families," she told the *Free Press*. "If the children were forced to cross busy streets like Gratiot or Congress and Larned to get to existing schools, some parents would balk at moving in." After cramming all summer, Belew planned a child-centered curriculum focused on projects in which all grades might participate. She had hoped to set up a basement woodshop for the boys at the school (girls could get their manual training in by cooking native dishes from the newest states, Alaska and Hawaii), but thought better of unsupervised carpentry.

Belew's ideas about how to run her school are remarkably forward-thinking, anticipating the organization of the open or mobile classrooms. "We have the entire downtown area as our classroom," she said, as well as parent volunteers ranging from artists and musicians to a circuit judge. "In some ways, this is like a small town. We can be close to each other. But, unlike a small town, we don't pry into the private lives of others." Belew changed her own lifestyle upon moving to Lafayette Park: Where once she drove eighty miles a day, now she barely had to drive at all. She had also put her 1957 pink convertible up for sale.

The story of Belew's urban conversion hits all the high points of new town planning—walkability, community, freedom, DIY, even feminism, with those workingwomen. On the page, it is surrounded by ads for Lafayette Park and its makers, including millwork, paint, ceramic tile, and electrical wiring. A small article next to the profile of Belew says that Detroit motorists drive only twenty miles per hour during the afternoon rush hour and spend twenty-seven minutes commuting in the morning, and thirty-two and a half minutes at night. Robinson Furniture invites readers to visit their model unit at 1352 Nicolet Place, while Michielutti Brothers ask and answer, SUBURBAN LIVING—DOWNTOWN DETROIT? YES, LAFAYETTE PARK IS ALL OF THAT AND MORE. "Now Detroiters can buy not just a house but a new concept of carefree, gracious 'downtown' living," reads an ad from the Realtors, which includes a drawing of father, son, and dog strolling the grounds. "We provide extra time for relaxation, for reading, for enjoying the company of your family. (Save a half a day or more of commuting time per week!)" Having it all, family-style, wasn't terribly different in this version of 1950s lifestyle coverage.

•

WHEN YOU THINK of the most child-friendly outdoor environment you've experienced, what comes to mind? For many people, it may be Disneyland, where Main Street is car-free, and places to eat, play, and rest abound. This is not by accident but by design. Walt Disney was once a bored parent, trying to figure out what to do with his daughters on a weekend afternoon, sitting on the sidelines as they tried the rides at a local fair. On trips to Europe, he visited Tivoli Gardens, Copenhagen's historic amusement park, where he admired the beautiful landscaping, quality restaurants, activities for everyone in the family, and general cleanliness, in stark contrast to American midways. At Madurodam, in the Netherlands, he saw an amusement park that also served as a history lesson, with miniatures of the landmarks of Europe. He went home determined to build his own version, a permanent world's fair, with glimpses of the future and autobiographical structures from his past, with a train running around the outside edge and a high berm screening out the ugliness of Los Angeles as it was. In 1954, in an ABC special, Uncle Walt showed the television audience what he planned to build in Anaheim.[72] You would enter Disneyland through the front gate, leaving the sea of cars in the parking lot behind you, and stroll down that Main Street. Behind old-time facades that looked like narrow, separate shops was actually a huge single structure, punctuated by a doorway every eighteen feet, some fake. A strip mall in Victorian costume. Disney's Imagineers (for *imagination* + *engineer*) used forced perspective, making the upper stories of the Main Street shops successively smaller to make the buildings look taller. At the end of Main Street was a compass rosette with radiating paths to the park's attractions. You could never get lost, because you always had to return to the rosette. In front of you, the castle, with the Matterhorn behind. On the left, water features, patrolled by Mississippi riverboats and overlooked by a lakefront café. On the right, pale shapes and rounded lines indicated Tomorrowland, its outline indistinct.

World's fairs had long been a site for advanced childhood technology, as children's welfare was seen as integral to mankind's future. Froebel blocks and the kindergarten debuted, for many Americans, at the 1876 fair in Philadelphia, while the Children's Building at the 1893 Chicago fair had woodcarving workshops, an international display of toys, and an indoor gymnasium with rings, bars, and trapezes.[73] The 1933 Chicago World's Fair included a neighborhood of Houses of Tomorrow, with glass walls and individual airplane hangars, and the Golden Gate International Exposition in 1939 showed the domestic tomorrow of ranch-style houses, including one by Kem Weber (who worked for Disney) with the latest in linoleum, laminates, and an Isamu Noguchi sculpture in the living room.[74] Fairs criticized the status quo by showing us how good we could have it, and Disneyland was no different. "By forcing his guests to walk along Main Street, by banishing the automobile from his domain, Walt was suggesting that something was amiss in the car-mad culture outside the park," writes historian Karal Ann Marling.[75] While the family car and the new Santa Ana Freeway were key to the success of Disneyland, Disney saw the park as offering an urban alternative, and he was always tinkering and upgrading the intrapark transportation (as he tinkered with the miniature railway that encircled his own Los Angeles home on Carolwood Drive). In June 1959, Disney added the first working monorail in the United States, which went straight to Tomorrowland to visit the MIT-designed Monsanto House of the Future, a bulbous white mushroom with giant glass windows, a push-button phone, and built-in furniture. In 1967, the park would get a people mover system, intended for downtown business districts. It was fake, it was commercial, it lacked housing, but the park still gave people what they wanted, many of the things whose absence urban planners of the era had already bemoaned: cohesion, connectivity, street life, public transportation. He wanted to create an amusement park for the entire family, a place "where parents and children could have fun—*together* [emphasis mine]." This quote now appears on the plaque below the statues of Walt and Mickey Mouse at the Disney parks in Anaheim and Orlando. After opening Disneyland, Disney carried around books on city planning, talking about traffic noise and neon signs, and studied planner Victor Gruen's *The Heart of Our Cities* (1964). Gruen was the father of the American shopping mall, a European émigré who attempted, with some success, to make modernist Main Streets in places, like Edina, Minnesota, and Southfield, Michigan, that had none. Midcentury Los Angeles was already home to a couple of these scenographic retail streets, including Crossroads of the World, a set of boutiques that opened in 1936 in a half-timbered village ornamented with a lighthouse and a ship. Today, Los Angeles has Santa Monica Place and the Grove, privately developed Main Streets that people drive to from neighborhoods without a pedestrian center.

In a 1966 film created to launch his second city, Walt Disney World, Disney proudly cited the praise of James Rouse, the developer of a number of urban "festival marketplaces" that inserted new commercial functions into historic buildings in the 1970s, attempting to put the pleasures of the mall back into the urban fabric. Rouse had told a room full of planners at the 1963 Urban Design Conference at Harvard, "The greatest piece of urban design in the United States today is Disneyland."[76] Rouse was not alone among architectural sophisticates in that opinion. Architect Charles Moore echoed his language almost exactly. "Disneyland must be regarded as the most important single piece of construction in the West, in the past several decades," wrote Moore in "You Have to Pay for the Public Life" (1965), one of the first postmodern critiques of urban America.[77] In that often misunderstood essay, Moore goes looking for public life in Southern California and finds its best representation at Disneyland. Students often think he's being ironic, but he's not: People at Disneyland are paying admission for the walkability and sociability, not to mention the freedom from traffic, that they can't get in their own public realm. They *could* get it if they were willing to pay the price another way: taxes, perhaps, or by shrinking their houses or yards. The houses they live in, Moore writes, are "separate and private, it has been pointed out: islands, alongside which are moored the automobiles that take the inhabitants off to other places."[78] It's the opposite of connected space, so they drive to Disneyland. Moore doesn't speak directly of children, or even of families, but he believes, like Walt Disney himself, that everyone is looking for a place to play in public. "Disneyland, it appears, is enormously important and successful just because it re-creates all the chances to respond to a public environment, which Los Angeles particularly no longer has. It allows play-acting, both to be watched and to be participated in, in a public sphere."[79] Disneyland has architectural scale and vehicular drama; it has an architectural backdrop and it is kept immaculately clean. Moore talks about disappointments in the real world, like fountains in Berkeley, California, that were immediately vandalized and turned off. This can't happen at Disneyland, and people are willing to pay for the security of knowing everything works. Moore is well aware that there is a downside to privatizing public life: There's no room for protest at Disneyland, for example, nor for poor people who can't pay the cost of admission. There's a danger in family-friendly planning that families might insist that the city become too much like Disneyland. That's often used as a pejorative for places that are too pretty, too neat, but the greater danger is that a healthy diversity and difference get swept away. It can also mean too cute: When planners start talking about making the whole city playable I cringe, since this often translates into streetside climbing equipment or lane markings in primary colors. I'd prefer safer streets and age-integrated parks—indeed, Walt Disney's more expansive and interconnected idea of fun: a legible environment, fueled by all possible forms of public transportation, designed to have something to catch everyone's eye.

Buoyed by the success of Disneyland, and perhaps by Rouse's words, Disney would go on to try to imagineer a real city: EPCOT, the Experimental Prototype Community of Tomorrow, code-named "Project X." It was to be built near Orlando, neighbor to a new, larger theme park, and home to twenty thousand people, with multimodal public transportation, a fifty-acre domed civic center with retail and entertainment streets copied from cities around the world, and easy commutes from suburban subdivisions organized much like Radburn. Cars on the outside, houses, kids, and lawns on the inside.[80] As Marling describes the plans: "Factories looked properly industrial, with their towers and stacks aglow in the darkness. But they were clean and eerily deserted, as if to suggest their unobtrusive silence. Houses were showpieces, grouped in amiable kaffeeklatsches around fortuitous lakes. Sealed away in its fifty-acre dome, the inner city had been sanitized for the protection of a generation of skittish suburbanites who never went downtown any more."[81] The dome was obviously inspired by Buckminster Fuller's sphere at Expo 67 in Montreal, itself a fragment of Fuller's earlier proposal to erect a great climate-controlled dome over Manhattan. The oval plan, with its wheel-shaped transportation corridors, recalled the turn-of-the-century garden cities of planner Ebenezer Howard, with a commercial center, a greenbelt, and pie wedges of residential development nested within each other in concentric circles. Car and truck traffic were restricted to ring roads, carried under the dome in subterranean levels. EPCOT wasn't so much disruptive of the status quo as a superorganized improvement upon it, gathering ideas from Detroit, Montreal, Chicago, Los Angeles, and Houston in one greenfield site in Florida. Maybe Disney himself could have pulled it off: He wanted corporations to buy in and build research and development facilities to be on permanent display in the town's industrial park. Imagine Silicon Valley office parks, served by a high-speed monorail, in central Florida, but not walled off by virtual security and you'll get the idea. But Disney died months after filming the 1966 presentation that showed EPCOT first to Florida legislators, then to the world. "It made great sense to Walt, but he didn't live long enough to get into the nitty gritty details of getting an idea to work," Marty Sklar, who joined Disney's marketing and publicity team in the 1950s, told *Esquire*. "There's a gigantic difference between the spark of a brilliant idea and the daily operation of an idea."[82] What was built, and opened in 1982, was a theme park of futurism that gestured at the grand ideas Disney hoped to make real. Like Disneyland before it, it combined nostalgia and new thinking along with a pedestrian-friendly and entertaining environment that cities struggled to provide.

•

"We have friends with large homes and they are constantly working on it, and we're like 'bye, we're going to the R[oyal] O[ntario] M[useum].' That's what we try to remember when it gets cramped and crazy in here."

—Joel and Frances, parents of Cormac (five)[83]

This quote, from a downtown condo–dwelling Toronto family in 2016, nicely sums up the private house versus public life debate that rages unabated into the twenty-first century. As we've seen, practically since the suburb was invented, visionary planners have been trying to unwind, hack, restructure, and regrow some combination of private family quarters, open space, and public transportation that privileges the smallest citizens. At the same time, designers, psychologists, and sociologists have charted the effect of the environment on children, arguing that rather than penned-in play space, they need access to the full complement of urban and outdoor experiences. Lacking this, children lose motivation, competence, and independence—all the qualities educators say children need to operate in postindustrial society. Backyard or museum? Reorganizing closets or living with less? Twenty-first-century family-friendly planning operates not on the new town model, or by reclaiming industrial land, but as infill: Just as apartment-dwelling families carve play space out of overbuilt parking structures so, finally, are urban designers, transportation engineers, school systems, and parks administrators carving connected space from cities as they are. Ideally, creating family-friendly buildings and neighborhoods within existing urban environments would allow the benefits of such planning to be distributed more equitably, without the racial, economic, and geographic stratification that bedeviled previous efforts. Whether this is possible remains to be seen.

Between 2006 and 2016 Toronto grew up, with 143,000 new units built within city limits, 80 percent of which were over five stories, and 3.8 percent of which were three-bedrooms. Meanwhile, the number of families with children living in high-rise buildings grew by ten thousand—despite the fact that few units were designed with these families in mind. Toronto's low-rise residential neighborhoods were planned with retail, community buildings, and schools close to home, but the city's future growth is more likely to be dense, in mid- to high-rise infill buildings, as single-family homes have become increasingly expensive for millennials, and retirees stay put. In response, in 2016, the City of Toronto initiated a research project to look at how the city of the future might be built for all ages and sizes of citizens—from the apartment to the neighborhood, from storage to the streets. They saw value in maintaining a diversity of life stages downtown, with different-size apartments to allow people to raise a family and age in place and community facilities and parks to increase social interaction and offset the loss of a yard. "Families loved not having to commute by car," says Andrea Oppedisano, a City of Toronto planner and one of the new guidelines' authors. "They preferred the walk to school instead of having to drop off their kids in a car."[84] The project's case studies bring together best practices from across the globe: New York City's Schoolyards to Playgrounds program, which put 290 schoolyards back into the public realm as accessible weekend open spaces; those *woonerfs*, or shared streets, with examples from Toronto, Brighton, and Seattle; mixed-use master-planned neighborhoods including Vancouver's Olympic Village (2010). The guidelines also go inside buildings, with sample apartment designs based on interviews with families about how they *really* use their apartments. "During the #CondoHack visits we saw many interesting solutions to storing the primary family vehicle," planner Julie Bogdanowicz remarked drily on Twitter, above an image of a stroller in a bathtub. "We were encouraged by the informal sharing economy that happens in vertical communities," adds Oppedisano, "Families prefer to have a playroom within the building where tricycles and toys can be shared among residents. This also frees up space within their home." Public space can then become an extension of the home: "A public realm that meets the needs of children also accommodates the population as a whole. For example, designing comfortable, safe streets that support public life will not only encourage families to linger and socialize, but they will become an asset to all users," write the authors of the guidelines.[85] Peñalosa's claim for children as the index of a successful city strikes again, but this time, there are diagrams.

Toronto is lucky to have a model on its doorstep: the St. Lawrence neighborhood, planned with resident Jane Jacobs's ideas in mind, which successfully integrated new mid- to low-rise housing, for both renters and condo owners, and commercial development with the existing urban fabric. When the forty-four-acre site was acquired in May 1974, it was industrial land; by 1979 it held thirty-five hundred residential units, along with schools, shops, a library, and a community center, as well as a dedicated bus line.[86] Alan Littlewood, who designed much of the public development, came up with three guiding principles to avoid what former mayor David Crombie describes as the "American model of the city," with downtowns purely for office buildings.[87] Rather than putting new residential towers in a park, taking people off the street grid and isolating apartments from retail corridors, the plan extended existing streets into the former railyards and parking lots and gave new streets historic names via a public contest. New buildings' front doors opened onto the sidewalk or a yard. And the housing itself was a mix of market and subsidized units, owned and rented,

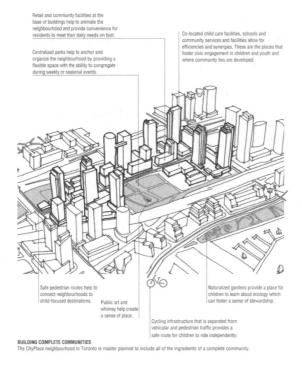

Retail and community facilities at the base of buildings help to animate the neighbourhood and provide convenience for residents to meet their daily needs on foot.

Co-located child care facilities, schools and community services and facilities allow for efficiencies and synergies. These are the places that foster civic engagement in children and youth and where community ties are developed.

Centralized parks help to anchor and organize the neighbourhood by providing a flexible space with the ability to congregate during weekly or seasonal events.

Safe pedestrian routes help to connect neighbourhoods to child-focused destinations.

Public art and whimsy help create a sense of place.

Cycling infrastructure that is separated from vehicular and pedestrian traffic provides a safe route for children to ride independently.

Naturalized gardens provide a place for children to learn about ecology which can foster a sense of stewardship.

BUILDING COMPLETE COMMUNITIES
The CityPlace neighbourhood in Toronto is master planned to include all of the ingredients of a complete community.

Building Complete Communities, "Growing Up: Planning for Children in New Vertical Communities" Draft Urban Design Guidelines, May 2017. [City of Toronto / Hariri Pontarini Architects]

to try to make the area mixed-income. The few so-called heritage buildings in the parcel were sold to new owners to restore. It was a built-from-scratch neighborhood with the elements of a place built over time, though later critics would question the application of quite so much red brick. Ken Greenberg, the city's urban design director after Littlewood, calls Jacobs the "mentor" for the neighborhood: "We would go to her to get advice, she would point out things in the fabric of Toronto, things people should incorporate in new development. It was about mix in all its senses, it was about walkability, small blocks, heritage; it kind of all came together."[88] The new guidelines propose something yet more surgical, which, if successful, could be imported to other North American cities that are trying to fit more families into their existing footprint.

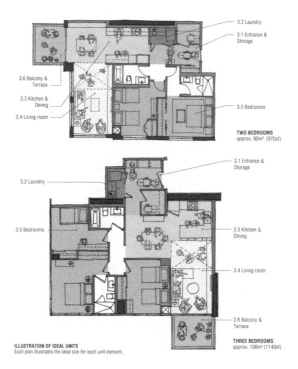

3.2 Laundry

3.1 Entrance &
Storage

3.6 Balcony &
Terrace

3.3 Kitchen &
Dining

3.4 Living room

3.5 Bedrooms

TWO BEDROOMS
approx. 90m² (970sf)

3.1 Entrance &
Storage

3.2 Laundry

3.5 Bedrooms

3.3 Kitchen &
Dining

3.4 Living room

3.6 Balcony &
Terrace

THREE BEDROOMS
approx. 106m² (1140sf)

ILLUSTRATION OF IDEAL UNITS
Each plan illustrates the ideal size for each unit element.

Ideal two- and three-bedroom units, "Growing Up: Planning for Children in New Vertical Communities" Draft Urban Design Guidelines, May 2017. [City of Toronto / Hariri Pontarini Architects]

Let's start at the front door of the apartments, either a 969-square-foot two-bedroom or a 1,140-square-foot three-bedroom. That door should be staggered or recessed so neighboring apartments can't look directly into your living room, wide enough for four people and a stroller, with two closets, one for coats and one for deep storage of scooters, boots, parkas, or small bikes. Bigger items might be stored in closets built into the unit's parking space below; in Vancouver, several families had told me they used their parking spots for storage or covered play, since they didn't own a car. There's also this note, which shows that storage walls remain relevant: "Maximize useable wall space to accommodate built-in storage walls or furniture."[89] (Also, amusingly, "Children generate a significant amount of laundry.") The kitchen, "the family hub," should, as the subjects of the

UCLA family-life study demonstrated, have an open plan and natural light, with cooking and countertops adjacent to a table large enough to fit the whole family and accommodate homework, located close to outlets sufficient for a whole family's-worth of charging. The guidelines suggest visual access to the living room and any outdoor play space that may be part of the unit. Bedrooms need to be large enough to be rearranged over time. Eleven square meters can accommodate a desk, a closet, and either twin beds, bunk beds, or a double bed, and nightstands. For visual and acoustic privacy, bedrooms should be separated from the living room, creating the sort of his, hers, and theirs zoning of the home that Christopher Alexander described as necessary for happy family life. Even in an apartment, even in a high-rise, every adult and every child needs their space.

The most radical concept may be the suggestion that the unit walls themselves be built to change, morphing, via demolition or movable storage partitions, from a three-bedroom apartment for a family with toddlers to a two-bedroom for the parents of college students to the one-bedroom empty nest.[90] It might be even more useful to be able to give back some of that space, and reduce your rent, when the square footage is no longer needed. I've seen the idea of building for intergenerational flexibility before, most notably in Studio Gang's Recombinant House, a speculative project developed for the Museum of Modern Art's 2012 *Foreclosed* exhibition.[91] Studio Gang took the 1920s bungalow of Cicero, Illinois—the classic small, detached family house proposed as the American dream—and broke it into parts, with private bedrooms and bathrooms as well as new, shared kitchens and commons that might better suit multigenerational families or cohabitating sets of adults. These pieces would be stacked into vertical neighborhoods, freeing the ground for more parks as well as work spaces, and allowing residents to lease only the type and number of pieces that they needed at the time. The whole building becomes a storage wall, in a sense, giving adults the ability to pop modules for living in and out as they might a cabinet for a stereo or a pegboard for tools.

Finally: outdoor access. These guidelines, like McAfee and Malczewski's, strongly advocate that families live on lower floors and ask architects to place a critical mass of large units in the base of the buildings, with direct access to ground-level and rooftop play spaces with the possibility of informal supervision, as well as small private terraces or yards. The new guidelines include an updated version of the diagram of the mother calling Joey in for dinner, with a planted courtyard, enclosed private balconies, and indoor amenity spaces (like community rooms) next to the courtyard. The first four or five floors immediately become more porous and sociable.[92] Once again missing-middle housing like rowhouses or midrise C- or L-shaped courtyard buildings are the preferred option from the point of view of both planners and potential buyers, splitting the difference between the single-family home and the tower. Taller buildings might have broad bases that wrap around a shared courtyard, with indoor and outdoor community spaces on the roof and widely spaced towers above, like Vancouver's point-and-podium designs. Buildings' outdoor spaces should prioritize play, if they are not within a five- to ten-minute walking distance of a park or playground, and offer midblock connections to child-oriented destinations, creating a secondary grid of pathways separated from trafficked streets. In St. Lawrence, David Crombie Park and the Esplanade combine to form what is essentially a linear, shared courtyard, running for blocks, though unfortunately separated from the buildings by a couple of lanes of car traffic.

When families move to denser housing, they give up private amenities like the yards, garages, and basements that act simultaneously as protective devices and expansion zones. The "islands" Charles Moore described as the essential Los Angeles residential landscape did have their purpose: storage, workshop, and play. Toronto's guidelines address the first within the footprint of the building, but it is the neighborhood that has to be restructured to provide opportunities for messy activity and recreation, and safe streets between home and amenities. Several cities, following the lead of Portland, Oregon, in 2012, have initiated programs to densify around the concept of "20-Minute Neighborhoods": areas where residents can walk or bike to all daily nonemployment needs within twenty minutes and take transit to work.[93] These actions aren't specifically framed as family friendly, but their goals and design suggestions are closely aligned with more explicitly child-oriented planning. When Growing Up Boulder did a study on local schoolchildren's ideal neighborhood in 2014–15, they found that many had only a two-minute neighborhood available for independent use, as most were not allowed out of sight of their homes until middle school.[94] To foster independent mobility, the Toronto guidelines propose wider sidewalks, with a landscape buffer of trees or other plantings between sidewalk and bike lane, and bike lanes sandwiched between that buffer and a line of parked cars. Parks need to offer a variety of different experiences, including bounded playgrounds with equipment and landscaped areas for adventure play; both should include "graduated levels of risk to allow children the opportunity to go up higher, or faster, as they become more comfortable and confident."[95] Linear parks can even be used as connections. Intersections and lane widths should be narrowed, to reduce cars' speeds, and when possible crosswalks should be raised and speed limits lowered. Child-focused destinations should be located on existing routes that meet these criteria, or ganged, in order to minimize the number of streets children must cross on their daily round. The guidelines even suggest child-size signage, including some with symbols, both to indicate the presence of children and to give them a sense that the city is made for them. As Colin Ward wrote, the goal is not a "Childhood City"—a purpose-built and soon-outgrown landscape of what adults think children love—the goal is a city in which children are one of many constituents whose health and welfare are taken into consideration.

Toronto isn't alone in its efforts at reform: Rotterdam, Amsterdam, Bogotá, Melbourne, Oslo, Portland, Seattle, among other cities, are researching and piloting initiatives involving redesigned streets, greenways, and parks, increasing family-size apartments in central cities, and collocating community facilities with open space and schools. Sometimes these initiatives are framed in terms of children's welfare, sometimes in terms of health, access to nature, or resilience. In 2010, the city of Rotterdam developed a program it called Building Blocks for a Child Friendly Rotterdam, a tool used to analyze neighborhoods for their existing amenities for children and identify places that could be improved. As their definition of "child-friendly city" made explicit, their goal was not more fenced, age-graded areas for children to play in, like playgrounds: "It means that children form an intrinsic part of the city and should be allowed space everywhere to be young, to blossom, and to become an asset to the city."[96] The building blocks are familiar: units large enough to easily accommodate children; direct connection to the street or, in a pinch, a communal playground; safer traffic routes; closer schools; more space for sociability.

Rotterdam's child-friendly guidelines are part of a larger government strategy to try to improve the economy of the Netherlands' poorest and most diverse city, but critics charge the city with focusing on only one kind of family: the middle-class one, for whom so many previous child-friendly environments have been created. "All this talk about families moving back into the city is very selective," Brian Doucet, a senior lecturer at Erasmus University College told *Next City*. "It's not talking about more space for larger families from non-Western backgrounds or working-class families living in social housing."[97] Marguerite van den Berg, a professor at the University of Amsterdam's Institute for Social Science Research, has also argued that "child-friendly" is a proxy for "middle-class friendly."[98] Rotterdam's Woonvisie 2030 plan set a goal of demolishing 10,000 public and 10,000 private properties and replacing them with 36,000 new, larger houses, as well as promoting the combination of smaller apartments into larger ones to meet new standards for minimum size, thus reducing the number of low-cost apartments available in the central city. New facilities being built in Rotterdam are aimed at selected activities for younger, middle-class children—playgrounds and walking and cycle routes—while older, inner-city youth are driven out of undesignated public spaces with aggressive technology like the "mosquito," a device which admits a high-pitched sound only young people can hear.[99] Van den Berg relates Rotterdam's efforts to reintegrate the middle-class nuclear family into the city to the previous generation of modernist planning, whose main thrust was to separate home and work: "The most telling example of this is the goal of the city to become an attractive *residential* city."[100] The ideal family that the houses described in the building blocks target is also a nuclear one with two parents and one to three children— not a multigenerational household or one run by several unrelated adults. (In this definition of family, Rotterdam is by no means an outlier, though Vancouver's guidelines do mention the single-parent household as deriving extra benefit from urban living.) A referendum in Rotterdam in 2016, organized by challengers to the city's 2030 plan, ended up with a null result due to low voter turnout, but the politicians and housing advocates behind it are continuing to ask Rotterdam to maintain its commitment to affordable housing and avoid displacement.[101]

As with the suburban middle-class ideal of the last century, it has typically been middle-class white families' interest in living centrally that has spurred planners to action. Poor and working-class families who remained in urban areas, by choice as well as by economic necessity, didn't force this dialogue. While each city has its own challenges, the questions being asked of Rotterdam's child-friendly strategy are definitely applicable elsewhere. There are already fears that new urban amenities that appeal to families, like playgrounds, are being unequally distributed in high-income neighborhoods, as major urban capital improvements are funded by public-private partnerships—and donors want new parks in their own backyard. Building any improved public facility can increase prices in a neighborhood unless measures are in place to protect renters from rent increases and building conversions. In Toronto, the new design guidelines don't directly address affordability, though they can be applied to rental and social housing as well as market-rate condominiums. The city has an existing rental protection policy to preserve or replace buildings with six or more units, as well as an inclusionary zoning policy applied to large sites whose developers ask for increased density. It is there that Toronto may have the leverage to organize the kind of economic diversity baked into False Creek South; it's more difficult building by building. In Vancouver, many families target the last generation of condominiums in their apartment searches: The two-bedrooms tend to be bigger, first of all, and tired 1990s lobby décor turns off those looking for an investment. Using the private development market to provide public services makes it incumbent upon cities to make up the difference with their own, freer funds, as when New York City's Parks Department launched the Community Parks Initiative in 2014: $130 million invested in upgrades to thirty-five parks identified as the city's neediest.[102]

Physical changes must happen all over the city, as a network of facilities and more generous apartment sizes will never be large enough to overcome the dominance of the automobile. Street designs that foster play and welcome pedestrians and cyclists can also address the question of equity—if not reserved for high-rent districts.[103] "Political will is a must for this type of work," says Hannah Wright, an urban planner at the global design, engineering and planning consultancy Arup. "You've got to have someone dedicated to joining up different disciplines, different departments, and different funding streams."[104] In a report published in December 2017, "Cities Alive: Designing for Urban Childhoods," Wright and her colleagues Josef Hargrave, Samuel Williams, and Felicitas zu Dohna use the term "children's infrastructure" to describe the coordinated planning required to put youth at the center of the urban agenda. "Perhaps uniquely," they write, "a child-friendly approach has the potential to unite a range of progressive agendas—including health and wellbeing, sustainability, resilience and safety—and to act as a catalyst for urban innovation."[105] To make the kind of large-scale and connected changes such planning requires, politicians and engineers need to tap into the agencies with the biggest budgets, like transportation and health, rather than the often overstressed parks and education departments. The Arup researchers looked at global examples of child-centric initiatives, extracting a checklist of interventions that echo initiatives seen in New York, Oslo, Rotterdam, and Vancouver, from child-mapped neighborhoods to temporary play streets, prioritizing pedestrian and bike routes to porous landscapes that absorb storm water and sequester carbon. The answer is not separate or childish spaces, as "then it becomes something that an adult provides rather than what children can do," says Williams.[106] "The problem we have when we talk about child-friendly cities or play is people sticking swings and slides everywhere, making everything colorful. Sticking the word *infrastructure* in there, a big serious word, combined with *children* gets them to stop and think about how things are connected as opposed to individual." Think of free time as spent not just on plastic playgrounds but in work in a community garden, which has the added bonus of being intergenerational. Think of parks as being resilient in the face of floods and necessary for public health, rather than as nice-to-have amenities. This network of open space, safe streets, natural settings, and useful equipment is the infrastructure. The result, in the authors' view, should be an increase in "everyday freedoms": the ability of children, wherever they are in the world, to travel independently and have time and space for independent play.[107]

I think of the Sallie Foster Adventure Playground in Omaha, Nebraska, where the junk playground is paired with a community garden, is around the corner from a bike shop, and is most popular when parents are shopping at a weekend farmers market: That's intergenerational, multiskilled urban planning, allowing everyone in a neighborhood to spend more time outdoors together without spending much money. It's also interactive and lets everyone get their hands dirty. In his book on "coddled kids," Peter Wyden includes a chapter on the "anti-coddlers": They are "the resistance fighters. Like all guerillas they are boring from within—traditionally the most strategic location to bore from."[108] Wyden's anti-coddlers are today's free-range parents, today's sponsors of junk playgrounds, today's peddlers of cargo bikes. He describes the mania of homeowner's associations for "lawn cosmetics," which severely limited children's options for places and modes of play. Families have moved to the suburbs for the open space and nature, and yet their lawns, at least in front, are meant to be kept as pristine as the day the landscapers laid down the sod. Wyden calls this phenomenon

"Grass, grass everywhere, but not a place to play." When a pair of anti-coddlers are asked what they do when neighbors side-eye their lawn, they respond, "We've just explained . . . that we're growing kids instead of grass right now."

CONCLUSION

They tore down my elementary school last week. The demolition of child-hood memories is enough to make anyone nostalgic, but in this case, there was something more. My school, Martin Luther King Jr. Elementary School in Cambridge, Massachusetts, was designed by Josep Lluís Sert: modernist master, former Harvard Graduate School of Design dean, and architect of the superb Peabody Terrace apartments just across the street. I didn't know Sert designed my school until last year, but the building had its effects. When I started kindergarten in 1977, the building was just six years old. I may have lived in a Victorian house, but I learned and played in a thoroughly contemporary environment, with red Tectum walls, folding retractable partitions and clerestory light.

—Alexandra Lange, "How Can You Learn About the World in Spaces Without Character?" (2014)

This story isn't fiction, though it is a little too perfect: Architecture critic finds that she was educated in a modernist landmark, minutes (poetic license) before its destruction. If this were a movie, I would run through

Cambridge's residential streets arriving just in time to see the digger's claw bite into the King School's yellow concrete. Or, better, my passionate defense of the school's late modern architecture would have allowed the powers that be to see the light and preserve the school for future generations of kids. As I now know, the King School sat at the intersection between the midcentury schools built on the Crow Island model and the open-plan schools promoted in the 1970s. I had not been back inside since my family left Cambridge in 1981, but I could still draw a rough plan from memory. The kindergarten classrooms were lined up along Putnam Avenue to the right of the front door, and each had its own outdoor courtyard, just like in Winnetka. But kindergarten and first grade, then second and third, were paired, and accordion doors allowed teachers to grow and shrink the daylit, linoleum-floored classrooms at will. I was enrolled in the open program, a mixed-age, hands-on, play-to-learn experiment in public education where math was taught with Cuisenaire rods (yet another type of educational block), and water and sand tables replaced the desks. The central hall, washed with light from above, formed an indoor thoroughfare between the street and the playground behind, a path that linked auditorium, gym, cafeteria, and classrooms on three levels. As you got older, your classroom was located farther and farther from the front door; having to go up the stairs to fourth grade felt like a graduation. The recessed, mouth-like entrance, echoing with noise before the doors opened in the morning, gave us a place to assemble, while the sprawling blacktop playground gave us a place to go wild. This was a building for children with a cast-in-place pedagogy and a concrete, modular frame that seemed adaptable for whatever educational innovation might come. It was also a city in miniature, á la Hertzberger, where the smallest citizens might feel comfortable as they began to explore the adult city on guided walks.[1]

Martin Luther King Jr. Elementary School, Cambridge, MA, 1971, Sert, Jackson & Associates (demolished 2014). Photograph by Lee Dykxhoorn. [Courtesy Lee Dykxhoorn]

New England Aquarium, Boston, MA, 1969, Cambridge Seven Associates, Inc.
[Courtesy Cambridge Seven Associates, Inc.]

It was a shock, when I wrote my dissertation on postwar corporate design, to realize that the Gilbreths, whom I knew as the efficiency-obsessed characters from *Cheaper by the Dozen*, had a decisive effect on the arrangement of modern factories and production lines, not just on their own children's lives. It has been a similar shock, as I researched this book, to discover many objects of my own 1970s childhood in the pages of the history books. Our Cambridge backyard, for example, was kitted out with a geodesic dome–shaped metal climber, which my brother and I and a gaggle of neighborhood kids used as mountain, fort, and uneven bars, just like Aldo van Eyck's igloos. Such domes, popularized by Buckminster Fuller, were all the rage after Montreal's Expo 67, which inspired the similar sphere at EPCOT.[2] My parents may even have ordered our dome kit from Creative Playthings. My blocks were unit blocks, and it was with them that I made my first architectural forays. Eventually I graduated to LEGO. In the 1970s LEGO introduced its first sets for girls, called Homemaker, but my own working mother never whispered their name.[3] My brother and I happily deployed minifig astronauts in an ever-expanding zero-gravity space landscape, creating our own planet on which to play *Star Wars*. Even my preferred dress, OshKosh B'Gosh overalls in bright shades of green, blue, and orange, were a product of the design culture of the time, strikingly similar to the outfit worn by the redheaded girl in the 1981 LEGO ad. Books like *In Christina's Toolbox* were written for mothers like mine to give to daughters like me. My childhood coincided with a brief unisex interregnum between eras that divided children's clothing into racks of pink and racks of blue.[4]

In other words, I was born during a decade-long revolution. Feminism, activism, environmentalism, movements typically associated with the young adults of 1968, percolated into the playroom, playground, and classroom. Parents feared for their children's future and wanted to offer them more freedom. I wasn't crazy that my children's options seemed different from my own, but my nostalgia was not for the neat and tidy midcentury lawn but for the often grubby Dana Park, just a few blocks from my house. I was nostalgic for the kids in the neighborhood, whose houses I never entered, whose last names I still don't know. Yes, I had objects that are now in museums, but what I mostly remember is all the things we made with them: sidewalk art shows; a slideshow film directed by my best friend's father, in which aliens invaded our neighborhood. Writer-director Mike Mills's *20th Century Women* (2016) includes a scene in which unrelated adult housemates watch President Jimmy Carter's 1979 Crisis of Confidence speech:

> In a nation that was proud of hard work, strong families,
> close-knit communities, and our faith in God, too
> many of us now tend to worship self-indulgence and
> consumption. Human identity is no longer defined by
> what one does, but by what one owns. But we've
> discovered that owning things and consuming things does
> not satisfy our longing for meaning. We've learned that
> piling up material goods cannot fill the emptiness of lives
> which have no confidence or purpose.[5]

In the film, as in reality, Carter's warning turns out not to be the beginning but the end. Reagan is elected, the 1981 report "A Nation at Risk" invokes panic about American children's "mediocre educational performance," the open classrooms get divided up and the desks march back in. The Federal Communications Commission deregulates children's television, allowing programs based on toy brands to flourish. Advances in science allow for earlier and earlier gender testing of babies, eliminating the need for gender-neutral clothing and clothes, even at birth. Pink becomes another overlay that one can add to a set of blocks. And yet, just as the child-development experts say, my early years proved formative. The reason I'm so attracted to the Hawkness table, or the 1960s playgrounds, is that I learned in environments that were their offspring. I sat out the conservatism of the 1980s in my open-plan middle school. Although I experienced the many problems of that model—the noise, the lack of heat, the disorganization—I learned what it is best at teaching: to think for yourself.

Descriptions of what happened in the 1980s remind me very much of what is happening today: retraction, commercialism, fear of freedom, and the invocation of "standards." And yet history shows us that the design of childhood is cyclical, and I think we are on the verge of another revolution. The makers of new toys, digital and physical, are building them out of blocks. Parents sick of stuff have created a sharing economy that has nothing to do with apps and everything to do with proximity. The Silicon Valley startups disrupting education have returned to desk-free classrooms and invoking John Dewey, though I still believe they need to invest in their environments. A frank discussion of risk has reentered playground design, and junk playgrounds are popping up in unexpected places. Some metropolises are welcoming families rather than pushing them out, and some families are choosing the communal green over the private island. I see signs everywhere that the 1970s, not to mention the 1910s, are not forgotten. They just went underground in the sea of stuff.

If I'm right, this book can be a guide to the dark as well as the light in previous progressive movements. I've always been uncomfortable telling other parents what to do: Kids are individuals, and abstracting from your child's individual potty-training, screen-time, learning-to-read experience seems to produce smugness, and then, with child number 2, comeuppance. This book is not a prescription but a description of things to look out for, with red flags for exclusion, green flags for progress. We need to think beyond our own offspring. The future design of childhood has to be public and accessible or it becomes just another product, traded among middle-class parents as a sign that they have given their children the best possible start on life, like the stocked suburban playrooms of the past. Schools built for project-based learning have better acoustics, and more built-in structure, than the circular satellites of the 1960s, and that's a good thing. If your child wants to learn coding and collaborative practice from Scratch blocks after she learns structure and cooperation from unit blocks, so be it. The best new technologies build on the past in specific, positive ways, acknowledge their debt, and ensure that spatial freedom is available to children of all races, abilities, and socioeconomic backgrounds. Innovators like to talk about networks, but what children need is a safety net: an environment designed to foster their development and growing independence and to provide a community for their family, step by step and brick by brick. Having a baby can feel like entering a new world, but it isn't one. For two centuries, protectors of childhood and promoters of products have told parents how to make their children better behaved, better citizens, more insightful, more social, more creative, more inquiring, more independent, and more active. Learn from them, and we make childhood a better place.

ACKNOWLEDGMENTS

There are many people without whom this book could not exist. First and foremost: my children, Paul and Romy, whose play and playthings set me off on an entirely new path through design history. Next, Rachel Silverman, known in my house as "the nice Nieman," who generously invited me to tag along with her at the Nieman Fellows publishing symposium in 2014, at which I met my future agent, Joseph Veltre, who sold my book to Nancy Miller, who passed it to Ben Hyman, who treated it as if he had acquired it himself. Katya Mezhibovskaya designed a cover as playful as the contents. I thank these adults for understanding a serious book about childish things.

A 2016 publication grant from the Graham Foundation for Advanced Studies in the Fine Arts generously supported research travel for this book. The Wertheim Room and the collections at the New York Public Library provided invaluable quiet and ample resources for my project. I thank Duncan McFadyen and Duke University Libraries for their last-minute help with images.

Many editors commissioned and published the essays that started my thinking about the design of childhood. Kelsey Keith at *Curbed*; Michael

Agger and Daniel Zalewski at the *New Yorker*; Marcus Fairs and Anna Winston at *Dezeen*; Elizabeth Glickfeld at *Dirty Furniture*; Iker Gil at *MAS Context*; Sam Grawe at Herman Miller; Adam Nathaniel Furman at *Saturated Space*; Sarah Rich at *re:form*; Julia Turner at *Slate*; Michael Silverberg at *Print*; Ann Friedman at *GOOD*; and Michael Bierut, Jessica Helfand, and the late William Drenttel at *Design Observer* all shepherded earlier versions of these stories.

An international community of archivists, curators, designers, teachers, and writers has been extraordinarily generous to me with time, references, and information. Some of them are even my neighbors. This book would be far less rich without the inspiring work and helpful suggestions of Darrin Alfred, Greg Allen, Lila Allen, Amy Auscherman, Norman Brosterman, Allison Dunnet, Colin Fanning, Russell Flinchum, Amy Fusselman, Tricia Gilson, Sara Grant, Dakin Hart, Sara Hendren, Karen Hewitt, Amanda Kolson Hurley, Jane Hutton, Mimi Ito, Liz Jackson, Julia Jacquette, Juliet Kinchin, Pat Kirkham, Mark Lamster, Sam Lubell, Maynard and Lu Lyndon, Dung Ngo, Jim Nickoll, Monica Obniski, Amy F. Ogata, Aidan O'Connor, Andrea Oppedisano, Chee Pearlman, Michelangelo Sabatino, Susan Solomon, Brent Toderian, Carol Troha, Alissa Walker, Sam Williams, Alexa Griffith Winton, and Hannah Wright. I miss Jane Thompson and wish she had lived to see this book, as Design Research sold so many of these wonderful toys and was an important part of my own designed childhood. It was a thrill to run across an essay of hers on the Bauhaus *Vorkurs* in the course of my research, and to feel I was still walking in her footsteps.

Friends who supported this project in other ways, including tours, spare rooms, conversation, and scouting photos include Beth Hebert and Laurie M. Petersen at the Crow Island School; Steve Forster, Erin and Brooke Hawkins, Louis Joyner, and Richard McCoy in Columbus; Naomi Pollock and Hiroshi Shimamura in Tokyo; Penny and Jim Peters in Cambridge; Angelyn Chandler and George Kroenert in Hudson; Ellen Cavanagh and Leslie Koch in New York. The Loeb Fellows Class of 2014 encouraged me to pursue this book idea, as did Jim Stockard and Sally Young.

I also have to thank my Twitter and Instagram followers for tagging and sending me relevant photos and links along the way. Benjamin Shaykin and Abigail Weinberg even went to the archives for me. You understood my project even when I didn't feel as if I did.

I remain indebted to my own great teachers from kindergarten on: Risa at the King Open program in Cambridge, Massachusetts; Norm Budnitz, Henry Walker, and Genie DeLamotte at Carolina Friends School in Durham, North Carolina; Ann Gibson, Wayne Koestenbaum, Alec Purves, Vincent Scully, Fred Strebeigh, and Laura Wexler at Yale; and Jean-Louis Cohen at the Institute of Fine Arts. My parents, Peter Lange and Martha Scotford, made sure my childhood was full of blocks and play.

My deepest appreciation is for my husband, Mark Dixon, and my babysitter, Margreta Skeete, who were there to play when I needed to work.

NOTES

Introduction

1. Jane Lancaster, *Making Time: Lillian Moller Gilbreth—A Life Beyond "Cheaper by the Dozen"* (Boston: Northeastern University Press, 2004), 221.
2. Some of this material was previously published, in slightly different form, in *Slate*. Alexandra Lange, "The Woman Who Invented the Kitchen," *Slate*, October 25, 2012, http://www.slate.com/articles/life/design/2012/10/lillian_gilbreth_s_kitchen_practical_how_it_reinvented_the_modern_kitchen.html (accessed February 1, 2017).
3. Frank B. Gilbreth Jr. and Ernestine Gilbreth Carey, *Belles on Their Toes* (New York: Thomas E. Crowell Co., 1950), 107.
4. Lancaster, *Making Time*, 266–67.
5. Frank B. Gilbreth Jr. and Ernestine Gilbreth Carey, *Cheaper by the Dozen* (New York: Thomas Y. Crowell Co., 1948), 4.
6. Lella Gandini, "Play and the Hundred Languages of Children: An Interview with Lella Gandini," *American Journal of Play* 4, no. 1 (Summer 2011).
7. Jonathan Zimmerman, *Small Wonder: The Little Red Schoolhouse in History and Memory* (New Haven, CT: Yale University Press, 2009).
8. Juliet Kinchin and Aidan O'Connor, eds., *Century of the Child: Growing by Design, 1900–2000* (New York: Museum of Modern Art, 2012), 16.
9. Jane Jacobs, "Can Big Plans Solve the Problem of Renewal?," in *Vital Little Plans: The Short Works of Jane Jacobs*, ed. Samuel Zipp and Nathan Storring (New York: Random House, 2016), 226.

Chapter One

1. Antoinette Portis, *Not a Box* (New York: HarperCollins, 2006).

2. *The Works of John Locke*, vol. 9, *Some Thoughts Concerning Education* (London: W. Otridge and Son, 1812 [© 1693]), 145.

3. Edith Ackermann, "Piaget's Constructivism, Papert's Constructionism: What's the Difference?" (2001), http://learning.media.mit.edu/content/publications/EA.Piaget%20_%20Papert.pdf (accessed September 27, 2017).

4. Ann Hulbert, *Raising America: Experts, Parents, and a Century of Advice About Children* (New York: Vintage Books, 2004 [© 2003]), 300.

5. Shelley Nickles, " 'Preserving Women': Refrigerator Design as Social Process in the 1930s," *Technology and Culture* 43, no. 4 (October 2002): 694.

6. Benjamin Spock, *The Common Sense Book of Baby and Child Care* (New York: Duell, Stone and Pearce, 1946), 248.

7. John Neuhart, Marilyn Neuhart, and Ray Eames, *Eames Design* (New York: Abrams, 1995), 157.

8. "Industrial Design: Another Toy to Tinker With," *Interiors* 111 (September 1951), 10.

9. Creative Playthings, "The Power of Play" (Princeton, NJ: Creative Playthings, 1967), 2, 27.

10. "Cardboard Box," National Toy Hall of Fame, http://www.toyhalloffame.org/toys /cardboard-box (accessed March 20, 2017).

11. Ellen Seiter, *Sold Separately: Parents and Children in Consumer Culture* (New Brunswick, NJ: Rutgers University Press, 1995); Gary Cross, *Kids' Stuff: Toys and the Changing World of American Childhood* (Cambridge, MA: Harvard University Press, 1999); Lisa Jacobson, *Raising Consumers: Children and the American Mass Market in the Early Twentieth Century* (New York: Columbia University Press, 2004).

12. Amy F. Ogata, "Good Toys," in *Century of the Child: Growing by Design, 1900–2000*, ed. Juliet Kinchin and Aidan O'Connor (New York: Museum of Modern Art, 2012), 171.

13. Karen Hewitt and Louise Roomet, eds., *Educational Toys in America: 1800 to the Present* (Burlington, VT: Robert Hull Fleming Museum, 1979), 1.

14. Teresa Michals, "Experiments before Breakfast: Toys, Education and Middle-Class Childhood," in *The Nineteenth-Century Child and Consumer Culture*, ed. Dennis Denisoff. (Hampshire, England: Ashgate, 2008), 32.

15. Maria Edgeworth and Richard Lovell Edgeworth, *Practical Education* (Boston: Samuel H. Parker, 1825 [© 1798]), 17, 22.

16. Evelyn Weber, "Play Materials in the Curriculum of Early Childhood," in *Educational Toys*, ed. Hewitt and Roomet, 33.

17. Karen Hewitt, "Blocks as a Tool for Learning: Historical and Contemporary Perspectives," *Young Children* (January 2001), 6–8.

18. Brenda and Robert Vale, *Architecture on the Carpet: The Curious Tale of Construction Toys and the Genesis of Modern Buildings* (London: Thames & Hudson, 2013), 8.

19. Seiter, *Sold Separately*, 68–70.

20. Ibid., 73.

21. Barbara Beatty, *Preschool Education in America: The Culture of Young Children from the Colonial Era to the Present* (New Haven, CT: Yale University Press, 1995), 10–12.

22. Norman Brosterman, *Inventing Kindergarten* (New York: Abrams, 1997), 20–21.

23. Ibid.

24. Beatty, *Preschool Education in America*, 38.

25. Brosterman, *Inventing Kindergarten*, 33.

26. "The Garden for the Children is the Kindergarten," illustration from *Friedrich Froebel's Education by Development*, trans. Josephine Jarvis (New York: D. Appleton and Co., 1899). Reproduced in Brosterman, *Inventing Kindergarten*, 31.

27. Maria Kraus-Boelte and John Kraus, *The Kindergarten Guide: An Illustrated Hand-Book*, vol. 1 (New York: E. Steiger, 1881 [© 1877]), 29.

28. Beatty, *Preschool Education in America*, 68. There is evidence that Anna Lloyd Jones, Frank Lloyd Wright's mother, saw the Froebel gifts at work as Burritt taught the eighteen orphans from a nearby charity home selected as pupils for the Kindergarten Cottage. Upon returning home to Boston, she bought a set of the gifts and enrolled in a training course on how to use them. Brosterman, *Inventing Kindergarten*, 10.

29. Ibid., 58.

30. Mrs. Horace Mann and Elizabeth P. Peabody, *Moral Culture of Infancy, and Kindergarten Guide*, 6th ed. (New York: J. W. Schermerhorn & Co., 1876) 13–14.

31. Brosterman, *Inventing Kindergarten*, 48.

32. Kraus-Boelte and Kraus, *Kindergarten Guide*, 28.

33. Brosterman, *Inventing Kindergarten*, 50–53.

34. Frank Lloyd Wright, *A Testament* (New York: Horizon Press, 1957), 19–20.

35. Juliet Kinchin and Aidan O'Connor, eds., *Century of the Child: Growing by Design, 1900–2000* (New York: Museum of Modern Art, 2012), 30–35.

36. *Buckminster Fuller, Thinking Out Loud*, produced and directed by Karen Goodman and Kirk Simon (Zeitgeist Films, 1996), quoted in Brosterman, *Inventing Kindergarten*, 84.

37. Beatty, *Preschool Education in America*, 69–70.

38. Anna Bryan, "The Letter Killeth" (address to the Kindergarten Department of the National Education Association [1890]), quoted in Beatty, *Preschool Education in America*, 82.

39. John Dewey, "Froebel's Educational Principles," *Elementary School Record* 1 (June 1900), 151.

40. Alice Temple, "Conference on Gifts and Occupations" (lecture, Seventh Annual Convention of the International Kindergarten Union [1900]), quoted in Weber, "Play Materials," 25.

41. Caroline Pratt, *I Learn from Children: An Adventure in Progressive Education* (New York: Grove Press, 2014 [© 1948]), 6.

42. "Woodwork for Girls," School Journal (November 23, 1895), 475, quoted in Jeroen Staring, "Caroline Pratt: Progressive Pedagogy *In Statu Nascendi*," *Living a Philosophy of*

Early Childhood Education: A Festschrift for Harriet Cuffaro, Bank Street College of Education Occasional Paper Series 32, https://www.bankstreet.edu/occasional-paper-series/32/caroline-pratt-progressive-pedagogy-in-statu-nascendi (accessed March 22, 2017).

43. Jeroen Staring, "Caroline Pratt: Progressive Pedagogy *In Statu Nascendi*," *Living a Philosophy of Early Childhood Education: A Festschrift for Harriet Cuffaro*, Bank Street College of Education Occasional Paper Series 32, https://www.bankstreet.edu/occasional-paper-series/32/caroline-pratt-progressive-pedagogy-in-statu-nascendi (accessed March 22, 2017).

44. Pratt, *I Learn from Children*, 10.

45. Caroline Pratt, "The Real Joy in Toys," (114–123) in Mary Harmon Weeks, ed., *Parents and Their Problems: Methods and Materials for Training*, Vol. IV (Washington, D.C.: The National Congress of Mothers and Parent-Teacher Associations), 119.

46. Caroline Pratt, "The Toys That Children Like," *Woman's Magazine*, December 1914, 34.

47. Patty Smith Hill, "Kindergarten" (1941), quoted in Karyn Wellhousen and Judith Kieff, *A Constructivist Approach to Block Play in Early Childhood* (Boston: Cengage Learning, 2001), 11.

48. Brosterman, *Inventing Kindergarten*, 102.

49. G. F., "How Do Unit Blocks Help Children Learn?" *The Economist*, July 11, 2013, http://www.economist.com/blogs/economist-explains/2013/07/economist-explains-6 (accessed May 15, 2017).

50. Jim Hughes and Chas Saunter, "History," Hilary Page Toys website, http://www.hilarypagetoys.com/Home/History and Jim Hughes, "1947—Kiddicraft," Brick Fetish, http://brickfetish.com/timeline/1947.html (accessed October 11, 2016).

51. Hewitt, "Blocks as a Tool for Learning," 7.

52. Hilary F. Page, *Playtime in the First Five Years*, rev. 2nd ed. (London: George Allen and Unwin Ltd., 1953), 10.

53. Hilary F. Page, "Plastics as a Medium for Toys," in *Daily Graphic Plastics Exhibition Catalogue*. Published in association with the British Plastics Federation, 1946. Text via Hilary Page Toys website, http://www.hilarypagetoys.com/Home/History/27/0 (accessed October 10, 2016).

54. "K280 Interlocking Building Cubes—1939," Hilary Page Toys website, http://www.hilarypagetoys.com/Home/Products/3/2 (accessed May 15, 2017).

55. Page, *Playtime*, 34.

56. Kiddicraft Self-Locking Building Brick print ad from *Boy's Own Paper*, June 1948. Brick Fetish, http://brickfetish.com/kiddicraft/ad_1948.html (accessed May 15, 2017).

57. Adrian Lithgow, "The Ghost That Is Haunting Lego Land," *Mail on Sunday*, July 26, 1987, reproduced on Hilary Page Toys website, http://www.hilarypagetoys.com/Home/History/26/0 (accessed October 11, 2016).

58. LEGO Group, *Developing a Product* (Billund, Denmark: The Lego Group, 1997), 2–3.

59. Colin Fanning, "The Plastic System: Architecture, Childhood, and LEGO 1949–2012" (MA qualifying paper, Bard Graduate Center, April 2013), 5ff.

60. "The LEGO Group History," LEGO website, https://www.lego.com/en-us/aboutus/lego-group/the_lego_history (accessed May 15, 2017).

61. Jim Hughes, "The Automatic Binding Brick," Brick Fetish website, http://brickfetish.com/timeline/1949.html (accessed October 11, 2016).

62. "LEGO System of Play," LEGO, https://www.lego.com/en-us/legohistory/system-of-play (accessed October 30, 2017); Jim Hughes, "*System I Leg*," Brick Fetish, http://brickfetish.com/timeline/1955.html (accessed October 11, 2016).

63. Fanning, "The Plastic System," 13.

64. Jim Hughes, "*System I Leg*," Brick Fetish, http://brickfetish.com/timeline/1955.html (accessed May 15, 2017).

65. Maaike Lauwaert, *The Place of Play: Toys and Digital Cultures* (Amsterdam: Amsterdam University Press, 2009), 58.

66. Ogata, "Good Toys," 171–73.

67. Elizabeth Licata, "Mokulock Wood Bricks: The Natural LEGOs," Apartment Therapy, March 27, 2013, http://www.apartmenttherapy.com/mokulock-wood-bricks-the-natural-legos-186976 (accessed May 15, 2017).

68. "Wooden LEGO Blocks by Mokurokku," *designboom*, February 10, 2013, http://www.designboom.com/design/lego (accessed May 15, 2017).

69. Amy F. Ogata, *Designing the Creative Child: Playthings and Places in Midcentury America* (Minneapolis: University of Minnesota Press, 2013), 46.

70. Roland Barthes, *Mythologies*, selected and trans. Annette Lavers (New York: Hill and Wang, 1984 [© 1957]), 53–55.

71. Jim Hughes, "The Lego System," Brick Fetish, http://brickfetish.com/timeline/1958.html (accessed May 15, 2017).

72. "10 Vigtige Kendetegn for Lego," (ca. 1962), reprinted in Jim Hughes, "*System I Leg*," Brick Fetish, http://brickfetish.com/photos/things/principles_1962.html (accessed May 15, 2017).

73. Lauwaert, *Place of Play*, 52.

74. Anthony Lane, "The Joy of Bricks," *New Yorker*, April 27, 1998. https://www.newyorker.com/magazine/1998/04/27/the-joy-of-bricks (accessed October 30, 2017).

75. Advertisements reproduced in Jim Hughes, "Samsonite," Brick Fetish, http://brickfetish.com/timeline/1961.html (accessed May 15, 2017).

76. Jim Hughes, "The Airport," Brick Fetish, http://brickfetish.com/timeline/1964.html (accessed May 15, 2017).

77. Fanning, "The Plastic System," 24–26.

78. Todd Wasserman, "Lego's 1981 Girl-Power Ad Comes with an Inspiring Backstory," Mashable, January 21, 2014, http://mashable.com/2014/01/21/lego-girl-power-ad-1981/#kYyooM7s3iqG (accessed May 15, 2017); Michel Martin, "Gender Controversy Stacks Up Against 'Lego Friends,'" NPR, January 18, 2012, http://www.npr.org/2012/01/18/145397007/gender-controversy-stacks-up-against-lego-friends (accessed May 15, 2017).

79. Colin Fanning, "LEGO Play on Display: *The Art of the Brick* and *The Collectivity Project*," *Response: The Digital Journal of Popular Culture Scholarship* (November 2016) https://responsejournal.net/issue/2016-11/feature/review-lego-play-display-art-brick-and-collectivity-project (accessed May 15, 2017).

80. Mitchel Resnick et al., "Scratch: Programming for All," *Communications of the ACM* 52, no. 11 (November 2009): 63.

81. Mitchel Resnick and Eric Rosenbaum, "Designing for Tinkerability," in *Design, Make, Play: Growing the Next Generation of STEM Innovators*, ed. Margaret Honey and David E. Kanter (New York: Routledge, 2013), 164–66.

82. Mitchel Resnick, "Computer as Paintbrush: Technology, Play, and the Creative Society," in *Play = Learning: How Play Motivates and Enhances Children's Cognitive and Social-Emotional Growth*, ed. Dorothy G. Singer, Roberta Michnick Golinkoff, and Kathy Hirsh-Pasek (New York: Oxford University Press, 2006), 3. http://web.media.mit.edu/~mres/papers/playlearn-handout.pdf (accessed March 27, 2017).

83. Marina Umaschi Bers, *Designing Digital Experiences for Positive Youth Development: From Playpen to Playground* (New York: Oxford University Press, 2012), 14.

84. Chris Berdik, "Can Coding Make the Classroom Better?" *Slate*, November 23, 2015; Laura Pappano, "Learning to Think like a Computer," *New York Times*, April 4, 2017.

85. Seymour Papert, "Project-Based Learning," Edutopia, November 1, 2001, https://www.edutopia.org/seymour-papert-project-based-learning (accessed May 15, 2017).

86. Bers, *Designing Digital Experiences*, 28–29.

87. Pappano, "Learning to Think."

88. Bers, *Designing Digital Experiences*, 29.

89. Ibid., 103.

90. Mimi Ito, "Why *Minecraft* Rewrites the Playbook for Learning," *Boing Boing*, June 6, 2015, http://boingboing.net/2015/06/06/why-minecraft-rewrites-the-pla.html (accessed March 27, 2017).

91. Colin Fanning and Rebecca Mir, "Teaching Tools: Progressive Pedagogy and the History of Construction Play," in *Understanding* Minecraft: *Essays on Play, Community and Possibilities* ed. Nate Garrelts (Jefferson, NC: McFarland & Co., 2014), 38.

92. "*Minecraft*: The Story of Mojang," 2 Player Productions, 2012: 33:15-35:02, quoted in Fanning, "Teaching Tools," 51.

93. Katja Borregaard, "Fraction Stories," *Minecraft* Education Edition, https://education.minecraft.net/lessons/fraction-stories (accessed March 27, 2017).

94. "Summer Camp: *Minecraft* Builders Unite!" Chicago Architecture Foundation, https://www.architecture.org/experience-caf/programs-events/detail/summer-camp-minecraft-builders-unite (accessed March 27, 2017).

95. Fanning and Mir, "Teaching Tools," 52.

96. Clive Thompson, "The *Minecraft* Generation," *New York Times Magazine*, April 17, 2016, https://www.nytimes.com/2016/04/17/magazine/the-minecraft-generation.html?_r=0 (accessed May 16, 2017).

97. Ibid.

98. Mimi Ito, interview with author, June 30, 2016.

99. Michael Joaquin Grey, interview with author, June 3, 2016.

100. "ZOOB with Michael Joaquin Grey 2 of 5," *YouTube*, January 9, 2010, https://www.youtube.com/watch?v=XfFMOOybqbY (accessed May 16, 2017).

101. Paola Antonelli, interview with author, October 7, 2016.

102. Michael Joaquin Grey, interview.

103. Andy Greenberg, "How a Geek Dad and His 3D Printer Aim to Liberate Legos," *Forbes*, April 5, 2012, https://www.forbes.com/sites/andygreenberg/2012/04/05/how-a-geek-dad-and-his-3d-printer-aim-to-liberate-legos/#310aa936108d (accessed October 18, 2017).

104. Andrew Liszewski, "Adapter Kit Lets Your Lego Bricks and Lincoln Logs Play Together," Gizmodo, March 19, 2012, https://gizmodo.com/5894539/adapter-kit-lets-your-lego-bricks-and-lincoln-logs-play-together (accessed October 18, 2017); Greenberg, "How a Geek Dad."

105. Pamela Popeson, "*This Is for Everyone*: Free Play," *Inside/Out*, Museum of Modern Art, March 27, 2015, https://www.moma.org/explore/inside_out/2015/03/27/this-is-for-every one-free-play (accessed May 15, 2017).

106. Ellen Lupton, ed., *Beautiful Users: Designing for People* (New York: Chronicle Books, 2014), 111.

Chapter Two

1. Ellen Lupton, ed., *Beautiful Users: Designing for People* (New York: Chronicle Books, 2014), 11.

2. Jeanne E. Arnold et al., *Life at Home in the Twenty-First Century: 32 Families Open Their Doors* (Los Angeles: Cotsen Institute of Archaeology Press, 2013).

3. Aidan O'Connor, "Design and the Universal Child," in *Century of the Child: Growing by Design, 1900–2000*, ed. Juliet Kinchin and Aidan O'Connor (New York: Museum of Modern Art, 2012), 233.

4. James Hennessey and Victor Papanek, *Nomadic Furniture* (New York: Pantheon, 1973), 121.

5. O'Connor, "Design and the Universal Child," 236.

6. Krabat Jockey website, http://www.krabat.no/en/products/krabat-jockey (accessed April 19, 2017).

7. Peter Opsvik, *Rethinking Sitting* (Oslo: Gaidaros Forlag AS, 2008), 158.

8. Sally Kevill-Davies, *Yesterday's Children: The Antiques and History of Childcare* (Suffolk, England: Antique Collectors' Club Ltd., 1991), 77–78.

9. Colin White, *The World of the Nursery* (New York: E. P. Dutton, 1984), 26.

10. Karin Calvert, *Children in the House: The Material Culture of Early Childhood, 1600–1900* (Boston: Northeastern University Press, 1992), 121.

11. White, *World of the Nursery*, 32.

12. Bryn Varley Hollenbeck, "Making Space for Children: The Material Culture of American Childhoods, 1900–1950" (PhD dissertation, University of Delaware, 2008), 102.

13. Calvert, *Children in the House*, 122.

14. *Hints for the Improvement of Early Education and Nursery Discipline* (Philadelphia: John H. Putnam, 1826), quoted in Calvert, *Children in the House*, 127–28.

15. Kevill-Davies, *Yesterday's Children*, 79.

16. Calvert, *Children in the House*, 127.

17. Kevill-Davies, *Yesterday's Children*, 81.

18. Calvert, *Children in the House*, 130.

19. Kevill-Davies, *Yesterday's Children*, 84–86.

20. Marta Gutman, "The Physical Spaces of Childhood," in *The Routledge History of Childhood in the Western World*, ed. Paula S. Fass (London: Routledge, 2013), 249.

21. Elizabeth Collins Cromley, "A History of American Beds and Bedrooms," *Perspectives in Vernacular Architecture* 4 (1991), 177.

22. Philippe Ariès, *Centuries of Childhood: A Social History of Family Life*, trans. Robert Baldick (New York: Vintage Books, 1962), 128.

23. Hugh Cunningham, *Children and Childhood in Western Society Since 1500* (New York: Longman, 1995), 61–64, 79.

24. Charles Richmond Henderson, *Proceedings of the Lake Placid Conference on Home Economics*, 1902, quoted in Gwendolyn Wright, *Building the Dream: A Social History of Housing in America* (Cambridge: MIT Press, 1983), 127.

25. Charles P. Neill, address to the New York School of Philanthropy, 1905, quoted in ibid., 126.

26. Calvert, *Children in the House*, 107.

27. Wright, *Building the Dream*, 128.

28. Ibid., 77.

29. Cromley, "A History of American Beds," 179.

30. Dolores Hayden, *The Grand Domestic Revolution: A History of Feminist Designs for American Homes, Neighborhoods, and Cities* (Cambridge: MIT Press, 1981), 67ff.

31. Wright, *Building the Dream*, 144.

32. Gutman, "Physical Spaces of Childhood," 250–51.

33. White, *World of the Nursery*, 12–13.

34. Wright, *Building the Dream*, 111–12.

35. White, *World of the Nursery*, 22.

36. Calvert, *Children in the House*, 146.

37. Helen Sprackling, "The Whole-Family House," *Parents* (March 1931), 27.

38. George Nelson and Henry Wright, *Tomorrow's House: A Complete Guide for the Home-Builder*, 2nd ed. (New York: Simon & Schuster, 1945), 2.

39. John Archer, *Architecture and Suburbia: From English Villa to American Dream House, 1690–2000* (Minneapolis: University of Minnesota Press, 2005), 263.

40. Carolyn M. Goldstein, *Do It Yourself: Home Improvement in 20th-Century America* (New York: National Building Museum/Princeton Architectural Press, 1998), 15.

41. Dennis Bryson, "Family and Home, Impact of the Great Depression On," in *Encyclopedia of the Great Depression*, ed. Robert S. McElvaine, vol. 1 (New York: Macmillan Reference USA, 2004), 310–15. *U.S. History in Context*, link.galegroup.com/apps/doc/CX3404500173 /UHIC?u=nysl_ro_rush&xid=c2eb346b. (accessed September 6 2017).

42. Dianne Harris, *Little White Houses: How the Postwar Home Constructed Race in America* (Minneapolis: University of Minnesota Press, 2013), 34.

43. Clifford Edward Clark Jr., *The American Family Home, 1800–1960* (Chapel Hill: University of North Carolina Press, 1986), xv.

44. Harris, *Little White Houses*, 21.

45. William H. Frey, "The Suburbs: Not Just for White People Anymore," *New Republic*, November 24, 2014, https://newrepublic.com/article/120372/white-suburbs-are-more -and-more-thing-past (accessed May 18, 2017).

46. Christopher Hawthorne, "How Arcadia Is Remaking Itself as a Magnet for Chinese Money," *Los Angeles Times*, December 3, 2014, http://www.latimes.com/entertainment/arts /la-et-cm-arcadia-immigration-architecture-20140511-story.html (accessed May 18, 2017).

47. Diana Selig, "*Parents* Magazine," in *Encyclopedia of Children and Childhood: In History and Society*, ed. Paula S. Fass, vol. 2. (New York: Macmillan Reference USA, 2004) 654–55.

48. Shirley G. Streshinsky, "The Berkeley Story: Commitment to Integration," *Parents* (May 1969); Bernard Ryan Jr. "A Last Look at the Little Red Schoolhouse," *Parents* (February 1969).

49. Amy M. Hostler, "Learning Through Play," *Parents* (January 1933); Virginia Wise Marx, "Play Equipment That Keeps Children Outdoors," *Parents* (April 1933).

50. H. Vandervoort Walsh, "The Whole-Family House," *Parents* (February 1929), 26.

51. Ruth Schwartz Cowan, *More Work for Mother: The Ironies of Household Technology from the Open Hearth to the Microwave* (New York: Basic Books, 1983), 177.

52. Ibid., 179.

53. Wright, *Building the Dream*, 210.

54. Walsh, "Whole-Family House," 50.

55. Douglas Haskell, "New Homes for Old," *Parents* (June 1933), 25, 44–45.

56. Rene and Harold Hawkins, "Better Homes for Children," *Parents* (January 1934) 26, 40.

57. Hollenbeck, "Making Space for Children," 70.

58. Ibid., 22.

59. Helen Sprackling, "*Parents* Magazine Presents a Health-First Nursery," *Parents* (October 1934), 33, 86–87.

60. Hollenbeck, "Making Space for Children," 43.

61. Sprackling, "*Parents* Magazine Presents," 87.

62. Cromley, "A History of American Beds," 183–84.

63. Ashley Brown, "Ilonka Karasz: Rediscovering a Modernist Pioneer," *Studies in the Decorative Arts* 8, no. 1 (Fall/Winter 2000–2001), 69–91.

64. Quoted in ibid., 80.

65. Ilonka Karasz, "Children Go Modern," *House and Garden* (October 1935), 64, quoted in Hollenbeck, "Making Space for Children," 74.

66. Joseph Aronson, quoted by Mary Roche, "Ideas for a Playroom," *New York Times*, October 5, 1947, quoted in Amy F. Ogata, *Designing the Creative Child: Playthings and Places in Midcentury America* (Minneapolis: University of Minnesota Press, 2013), 81.

67. Ronald Millar, "Science from Six to Sixteen," *Parents* (October 1933) 22–23, 52–53.

68. "A Model Playroom-Bedroom," *Parents* (September 1935), 33.

69. ROW Window Company ad, 1945, illustrated in Archer, *Architecture and Suburbia*, 274.

70. *New Yorker*, July 20, 1946, http://archives.newyorker.com/?i=1946-07-20#folio=CV1 (accessed May 17, 2017).

71. Goldstein, *Do It Yourself*, 35.

72. Ibid., 49.

73. *Time*, August 2, 1954, http://content.time.com/time/covers/0,16641,19540802,00.html (accessed May 17, 2017).

74. "The New Do-It Yourself Market," *Business Week*, June 14, 1952, quoted in Goldstein, *Do It Yourself*, 31.

75. Goldstein, *Do It Yourself*, 77.

76. Ibid., 66.

77. Ibid., 71.

78. Ibid., 79.

79. Dianne Homan, *In Christina's Toolbox* (Chapel Hill, NC: Lollipop Power, 1981).

80. Maxine Livingston, "Come Visit *Parents* Magazine Expandable Homes," *Parents* (October 1947), 41–48, 88–96.

81. Ibid., 92.

82. Christopher Alexander et al, *A Pattern Language: Towns, Buildings, Construction* (New York: Oxford University Press, 1977), 661.

83. "Median and Average Square Feet of Floor Area in New Single-Family Houses Completed by Location," U.S. Census, 2010, https://www.census.gov/const/C25Ann/sftotalmed avgsqft.pdf (accessed May 18, 2017).

84. Barbara T. Alexander, "The U.S. Homebuilding Industry: A Half Century of Building the American Dream," John T. Dunlop Lecture, Harvard University, October 12, 2000, http://www.jchs.harvard.edu/sites/jchs.harvard.edu/files/m00-1_alexander.pdf (accessed May 18, 2017).

85. Arnold et al., *Life at Home*, 81.

86. Elinor Ochs and Tamar Kremer-Sadlik, eds., *Fast Forward Family: Home, Work, and Relationships in Middle-Class America* (Berkeley: University of California Press, 2013), 40.

87. Arnold, *Life at Home*, 94.

88. Anthony P. Graesch, "At Home," in *Fast Forward Family: Home, Work, and Relationships in Middle-Class America*, ed. Elinor Ochs and Tamar Kremer-Sadlik, 41.

89. Maxine Livingston, "Best Homes for Families with Children," *Parents* (February 1955), 57, 59–64.

90. Maxine Livingston, "Every Family with Children Needs 2 Living Rooms," *Parents* (January 1955), 47–50.

91. Nelson and Wright, *Tomorrow's House*, 80.

92. Ibid., 1, 4.

93. Ibid., 79.

94. Mary and Russel Wright, *Guide to Easier Living* (New York: Simon & Schuster, 1951 [© 1950]).

95. Ibid., 71.

96. Ibid., 76–81.

97. "The Two-in-One-Room," *Parents* (April 1955), 63–67.

98. Arnold, *Life at Home*, 24.

99. Jeanne E. Arnold, "Mountains of Things," in *Fast Forward Family: Home, Work, and Relationships in Middle-Class America*, ed. Elinor Ochs and Tamar Kremer-Sadlik, 74.

100. Taffy Brodesser-Akner, "Marie Kondo and the Ruthless War on Stuff," *New York Times Magazine*, July 6, 2016, https://www.nytimes.com/2016/07/10/magazine/marie-kondo -and-the-ruthless-war-on-stuff.html?_r=0 (accessed May 17, 2017).

101. City of Toronto, "Growing Up: Planning for Children in New Vertical Communities," Draft Urban Design Guidelines (May 2017).

102. Wright, *Building the Dream*, 274.

103. Alex Truesdell, interview with author, April 28, 2017.

104. Mike Oliver, "The Individual and Social Models of Disability," paper presented at Joint Workshop of the Living Options Group and the Research Unit of the Royal College of Physicians, July 23, 1990, http://disability-studies.leeds.ac.uk/files/library/Oliver-in-soc -dis.pdf (accessed November 6, 2017.)

105. Hope Reese, "Alex Truesdell: Maker. Adaptive Designer. Advocate for Children with Special Needs," TechRepublic, December 14, 2015, http://www.techrepublic.com/article /alex-truesdell-maker-adaptive-designer-advocate-for-children-with-special-needs (accessed May 17, 2017).

106. Alex Truesdell, interview with author, April 28, 2017.

107. The U.S. Census reported that 56.7 million people, or 19 percent of the population, had a disability in 2010, https://www.census.gov/newsroom/releases/archives/miscellaneous /cb12-134.html (accessed May 1, 2017).

108. Quoted in Reese, "Alex Truesdell."

109. Jim Dwyer, "Using Cardboard to Bring Disabled Children Out of the Exile of Wrong Furniture," *New York Times*, July 29, 2014, https://www.nytimes.com/2014/07/30 /nyregion/using-cardboard-to-bring-disabled-children-out-of-the-exile-of-wrong-furni ture.html?_r=1 (accessed May 17, 2017).

110. George Cope and Phylis Morrison, *The Further Adventures of Cardboard Carpentry: Son of Cardboard Carpentry* (Cambridge, MA: Workshop for Learning Things, 1973).

111. Quoted in Reese, "Alex Truesdell."

112. Alex Truesdell, interview with author, April 28, 2017.

113. Rob Gilson, interview with author, January 17, 2017.

114. Alex Truesdell, interview with author, April 28, 2017.

Chapter Three

1. Laura Ingalls Wilder, *These Happy Golden Years* (New York: Harper & Row, 1971 [© 1943]).

2. *American Journal of Play*, "Play and the Hundred Languages of Children: An Interview with Lella Gandini," *American Journal of Play* 4, no. 1 (Summer 2011), 2.

3. Jonathan Zimmerman, *Small Wonder: The Little Red Schoolhouse in History and Memory* (New Haven, CT: Yale University Press, 2009), 17.

4. Bernard Ryan Jr., "A Last Look at the Little Red Schoolhouse," *Parents* (February 1968) 54–56.

5. Laura Ingalls Wilder, *Little Town on the Prairie* (New York: Harper & Row, 1971 [© 1941]), 291–93.

6. Pamela Smith Hill, ed., *Pioneer Girl: The Annotated Autobiography* (Pierre: South Dakota Historical Society Press, 2014), 292–93. This annotated version of the first memoir written by Laura Ingalls Wilder, on which the Little House books were based, includes a description of the school exhibition that closely follows the account in the published series, although she and daughter Rose Wilder Lane rearranged the chronology.

7. Sylvanus Cox and William W. Fanning, School Desk and Seat Patent Model (1873), National Museum of American History, http://americanhistory.si.edu/collections/search /object/nmah_742773 (accessed May 29, 2017).

8. Neil Gislason, *Building Innovation: History, Cases, and Perspectives on School Design* (Big Tancook Island, Nova Scotia: Backalong Books, 2011), 8.

9. John Glendenning, School Desk and Seat Patent Model (1880), National Museum of American History, http://americanhistory.si.edu/collections/search/object/nmah_679705 (accessed May 29, 2017).

10. Illustrated in "The History of Seating America," American Seating and the Grand Rapids Public Museum, http://www.americanseating.com/images/homepage/Seating_Ameri cawv.pdf (accessed May 29, 2017).

11. Cliff Kuang, "IDEO and Steelcase Unveil a School Desk for the Future of Teaching," Fast Company, June 16, 2010, https://www.fastcompany.com/1660576/ideo-and-steelcase -unveil-school-desk-future-teaching-updated (accessed May 29, 2017).

12. Katherine Towler, "History of Harkness: The Men behind the Plan," *Exeter Bulletin* (Fall 2006), http://www.exeter.edu/news/history-harkness (accessed March 30, 2017).

13. Edward Harkness to Lewis Perry, April 9, 1930, quoted in "The Harkness Gift," Phillips Exeter Academy website, https://www.exeter.edu/about-us/harkness-gift (accessed May 9, 2017).

14. This section was previously published, in slightly different form, in *Dirty Furniture*. Alexandra Lange, "Power Positions," *Dirty Furniture* 2 (Summer 2015).

15. *Creative Playthings Inc.: A Climate of Creativity for New World Builders* (Princeton, New Jersey: Creative Playthings, 1960), 5.

16. Amy F. Ogata, *Designing the Creative Child: Playthings and Places in Midcentury America* (Minneapolis: University of Minnesota Press, 2013), 140.

17. Ibid., 122.

18. William W. Caudill, *Toward Better School Design* (New York: F. W. Dodge Corporation, 1954), 168.

19. Gislason, *Building Innovation*, 13.

20. Harold Rugg and Ann Shumaker, *The Child-Centered School* (1928/1969), quoted in Gislason, *Building Innovation*, 15.

21. William W. Cutler III, "Cathedral of Culture: The Schoolhouse in American Educational Thought and Practice since 1820," *History of Education Quarterly* 29 (Spring 1989): 1.

22. Henry Barnard, *School Architecture* (1850), quoted in Amy S. Weisser, " 'Little Red School House, What Now?' Two Centuries of American Public School Architecture," *Journal of Planning History* 5, no. 3 (August 2006): 198.

23. Horace Mann, Twelfth Annual Report to the Board of Education, Together with the Twelfth Annual Report of the Secretary of the Board (Boston, 1849), quoted in Lawrence A. Cremin, *The Transformation of the School: Progressivism in American Education, 1876–1957* (New York: Alfred A. Knopf, 1961), 9.

24. Gislason, *Building Innovation*, 7.

25. Cutler, "Cathedral of Culture," 5.

26. Dale Allen Gyure, *The Chicago Schoolhouse: High School Architecture and Educational Reform, 1856–2006* (Chicago: University of Chicago Press, 2011), 58.

27. Ibid., 8–9.

28. Quoted in Cutler, "Cathedral of Culture," 35.

29. Amy S. Weisser, " 'Little Red School House, What Now?' Two Centuries of American Public School Architecture," *Journal of Planning History* 5, no. 3 (August 2006): 202.

30. Jennifer L. Gray, "Ready for Experiment: Dwight Perkins and Progressive Architectures in Chicago, 1893–1917" (PhD dissertation, Columbia University, 2011), 277.

31. Gislason, *Building Innovation*, 34–35.

32. "The Work of William B. Ittner, FAIA," *Architectural Record* 57 (Feb. 1925), 99, 101, Regional Planning Federation of the Philadelphia Tri-State District, *The Regional Plan of the Philadelphia Tri-State District* (Philadelphia, 1932), 66, both quoted in Cutler, "Cathedral of Culture," 25.

33. Gray, "Ready for Experiment," 273.

34. Ibid., 275–76.

35. Cutler, "Cathedral of Culture," 8–10.

36. John Dewey, *The School and Society & The Child and the Curriculum* (Chicago: University of Chicago Press, 1990 [© 1900, 1902]), 31–33.

37. Evelyn Weber, "Play Materials in the Curriculum of Early Childhood," in *Educational Toys in America: 1800 to the Present*, ed. Karen Hewitt and Louise Roomet (Burlington, VT: Robert Hull Fleming Museum, 1979), 30, 32.

38. Alice Dewey, "The University Elementary School," quoted in Anne Durst, *Women Educators in the Progressive Era: The Women Behind Dewey's Laboratory School* (New York: Palgrave Macmillan, 2010), 45–46.

39. John Dewey, "Three Years of the University Elementary School," postscript to *The School and Society*, quoted in Anne Durst, *Women Educators in the Progressive Era: The Women Behind Dewey's Laboratory School* (New York: Palgrave Macmillan, 2010), 48.

40. Althea Harmer, "Textile Work Connected with American Colonial History," *The Elementary School Teacher* 4, no. 9 (May 1904): 661, quoted in Anne Durst, *Women Educators in the Progressive Era: The Women behind Dewey's Laboratory School* (New York: Palgrave Macmillan, 2010), 85.

41. Witold Rybczynski, "Remembering the Rosenwald Schools," *Architect*, September 16, 2015, http://www.architectmagazine.com/design/culture/remembering-the-rosenwald -schools_o (accessed March 28, 2017).

42. Mabel O. Wilson, "Rosenwald School: Lessons in Progressive Education," in *Frank Lloyd Wright: Unpacking the Archive*, ed. Barry Bergdoll and Jennifer Gray (New York: Museum of Modern Art, 2017), 98.

43. Mary S. Hoffschwelle, "The Rosenwald Schools of the American South," in *Designing Modern Childhoods: History, Space, and the Material Culture of Children*, ed. Marta Gutman and Ning de Coninck-Smith (New Brunswick, NJ: Rutgers University Press, 2007) 213–32.

44. Rybczynski, "Remembering."

45. Hoffschwelle, "Rosenwald Schools," 221–23.

46. Frank Lloyd Wright to Darwin D. Martin, July 27, 1928, quoted in Wilson, "Rosenwald School," 101.

47. Wilson, "Rosenwald School," 103.

48. S. L. Smith, *Community School Plans*, Bulletin No. 3 (Julius Rosenwald Fund, 1924), 17.

49. "Schools," *Architectural Forum* 103 (October 1955), 129.

50. Frances Presler, "A Letter to the Architects," reprinted in "Crow Island School, Winnetka, Illinois," *Architectural Forum* 75 (August 1941): 80.

51. Jane H. Clarke, "Philosophy in Brick," *Inland Architect*, November/December 1989, 55.

52. Oral history of Lawrence Bradford Perkins. Interviewed by Betty J. Blum and compiled under the auspices of the Chicago Architects Oral History Project, Department of Architecture, the Art Institute of Chicago (November 1985), 59–60.

53. Grant Pick, "A School Fit for Children," *Chicago Reader*, February 28, 1991, http://www .chicagoreader.com/chicago/a-school-fit-for-children/Content?oid=877158 (accessed May 29, 2017).

54. Marion Stern, a retired Crow Island teacher, in Pick, "A School Fit for Children."

55. Carleton Washburne, quoted in Pick, "A School Fit for Children."

56. Pick, "A School Fit for Children."

57. Presler, "A Letter to the Architects," 80.

58. Ibid., 81.

59. Clarke, "Philosophy in Brick," 56.

60. Presler, "A Letter to the Architects," 80.

61. "*Modern Architecture for the Modern School*," Museum of Modern Art, press release, https://www.moma.org/calendar/exhibitions/2302?locale=en (accessed November 3, 2016).

62. Pick, "A School Fit for Children."

63. Pick, "A School Fit for Children"; Carleton W. Washburne and Sidney P. Marland Jr., *Winnetka: The History and Significance of an Educational Experiment* (Englewood Cliffs, NJ, Prentice Hall, 1963), quoted in Sheila Duran, " 'J' Is for Jungle Gym," Winnetka Historical Society, http://www.winnetkahistory.org/gazette/j-is-for-jungle-gym (accessed May 29, 2017).

64. Ogata, *Designing the Creative Child*, 113.

65. Pick, "A School Fit for Children."

66. William W. Caudill, *Toward Better School Design* (New York: F.W. Dodge Corporation, 1954), 10.

67. Ogata, *Designing the Creative Child*, 113.

68. Caudill, *Toward Better School Design*, 26.

69. Eleanor Nicholson, "The School Building as Third Teacher," in *Children's Spaces*, ed. Mark Dudek (Amsterdam: Architectural Press, 2005), 56.

70. Steven V. Roberts, "Is It too Late for a Man of Honesty, High Purpose and Intelligence to Be Elected President of the United States in 1968?" *Esquire*, October 1967, 89–93, 173–84; Eric Pace, "J. Irwin Miller, 95, Patron of Modern Architecture, Dies," *New York Times*, August 19, 2004, http://www.nytimes.com/2004/08/19/business/j-irwin-miller-95-patron-of-modern-architecture-dies.html?_r=0 (accessed December 12, 2016).

71. J. Irwin Miller, interviewed by Nancy Halik, December 28, 1978, Columbus Indiana Architectural Archives.

72. I am indebted to the research of J. E. Nickoll in the Columbus Indiana Architectural Archives for making the connection between the Cummins Foundation Architecture Program and the Booth-Setser and Clifty schools, as well as for pointing out that Bartholomew County had one-room schoolhouses into the 1950s.

73. "No 'Bargain Counter' Schools for Columbus, Architect Says," *Columbus Evening Republican*, May 22, 1956, Columbus Indiana Architectural Archives.

74. "Lillian C. Schmitt Elementary School, Columbus, Indiana," *Architectural Record*, November 1958, 223–25.

75. Ibid.

76. Harry McCawley, "Fireplace Breathes Warmth into Classroom," *The Republic*, December 26, 2013, 7.

77. Reed Karaim, "Is Columbus's Modernist Legacy at Risk?" *Architect*, July 26, 2016, http://www.architectmagazine.com/design/is-columbuss-modernist-legacy-at-risk_o (accessed May 29, 2017).

78. Randall Tucker, interview with author, July 13, 2016.

79. J. Irwin Miller's letter was read to the Columbus Board of School Trustees on December 16, 1957. Jeffrey L. Cruikshank and David B. Sicilia, *The Engine That Could: Seventy-Five Years of Values-Driven Change at Cummins Engine Company* (Cambridge, MA: Harvard Business Review, 1997), 181.

80. Eero Saarinen to John Carl Warnecke, March 21, 1958, Columbus Indiana Architectural Archives.

81. Eero Saarinen to John Carl Warnecke, February 3, 1959, Columbus Indiana Architectural Archives.

82. "Excellence in Indiana," *Architectural Forum* 117 (August 1962): 120–23.

83. Nikole Hannah-Jones, "The Resegregation of Jefferson County," *New York Times Magazine*, September 6, 2017, https://www.nytimes.com/2017/09/06/magazine/the-resegregation-of-jefferson-county.html?rref=collection%2Fsectioncollection%2Fmagazine&action=click&contentCollection=magazine&region=rank&module=package&version=highlights&contentPlacement=5&pgtype=sectionfront (accessed September 12, 2017).

84. Francine Stock, "Is There a Future for the Recent Past in New Orleans?" *MAS Context* 8 (Winter 2010): 73.

85. Helena Huntington Smith, "The Child Is the Monument," *Collier's*, September 3, 1949, quoted in Stock, "Is There a Future."

86. John C. Ferguson, "The Architecture of Education," in *Crescent City Schools: Public Education in New Orleans, 1841–1999*, ed. Donald E. DeVore and Joseph Logsdon (Lafayette, LA: University of Louisiana at Lafayette, 2012 [© 1991]), 338.

87. Donald E. DeVore and Joseph Logsdon, eds., *Crescent City Schools: Public Education in New Orleans, 1841–1991* [Lafayette, LA: University of Louisiana at Lafayette, 2012 [© 1991]), 232.

88. Ferguson, "Architecture of Education," 340.

89. "A Reason for Smiles in 'Back-of-Town,'" *Life*, March 29, 1954, 59–62.

90. Edward Waugh and Elizabeth Waugh, *The South Builds: New Architecture in the Old South* (Chapel Hill, NC: University of North Carolina Press, 1960), 46–47.

91. Hannah Miet, "Historic Phillis Wheatley Elementary School Torn Down in Treme," *New Orleans Times-Picayune*, June 17, 2011, http://www.nola.com/education/index.ssf/2011/06/historic_phillis_wheatley_elem.html; R. Stephanie Bruno, "2 New Orleans Public Schools Are Demolished in Post-Katrina Rebuilding Campaign," *New Orleans Times-Picayune*, September 4, 2011, http://www.nola.com/education/index.ssf/2011/09/2_new_orleans_public_schools_a.html (accessed March 28, 2017).

92. DeVore and Logsdon, eds., *Crescent City Schools*, 245.

93. Miet, "Historic Phillis Wheatley."

94. Cutler, "Cathedral of Culture," 37.

95. Ibid., 40.

96. Evan Mather, *A Plea for Modernism*, video, https://vimeo.com/23565526.

97. Spreadsheet prepared by J. E. Nickoll, Columbus Indiana Architectural Archives.

98. "John M. Johansen: Mummers (Stage Center) Theater Oklahoma City," *YouTube* video, https://www.youtube.com/watch?v=iz4GgZoTbJM (accessed May 29, 2017).

99. "Two More for Columbus," *Architectural Forum* 132 (March 1970): 22–27; Natalie Fairhead, "Smith—the In School," *The Republic*, December 18, 1970, 15.

100. Reprinted in Harry McCawley, "Building Debate: Architecture Talk Often Overheated," *Republic*, December 11, 2012.

101. Mildred F. Schmertz, "An Open Plan Elementary School," *Architectural Record*, September 1973, 121–28.

102. Larry Cuban, "The Open Classroom," *EducationNext* 4, no. 2 (Spring 2004), http://educationnext.org/theopenclassroom (accessed May 9, 2017).

103. Herman Hertzberger, *Space and Learning: Lessons in Architecture 3* (Amsterdam: 101 Publishers, 2008), 98.

104. "Interview with Herman Hertzberger," *Architecture and Education*, September 9, 2015, https://architectureandeducation.org/2016/02/03/interview-with-herman-hertzberger (accessed March 29, 2017).

105. Laura Lippman, "My Wild School Days at Hippie High," *Daily Mail*, July 10, 2016, http://www.dailymail.co.uk/home/you/article-3678676/My-wild-schooldays-Hippie-High-Writer-Laura-Lippman-remembers-experimental-1970s-education-fondness-horror.html (accessed March 29, 2017).

106. Graciela Sevilla, "Saying Goodbye to Wilde Lake High," *Washington Post*, May 26, 1994, https://www.washingtonpost.com/archive/local/1994/05/26/saying-goodbye-to-wilde-lake-high/8ccc0783-de32-40be-afe5-75d155e56c85/?utm_term=.98eee8a7e486 (accessed March 29, 2017).

107. Lippman, "My Wild School Days."

108. Schmertz, "An Open Plan Elementary School," 128.

109. Bridget Shield, Emma Greenland, and Julie Dockrell, "Noise in Open Plan Classrooms in Primary Schools: A Review," *Noise & Health* 12, no. 49 (2010), http://www.noiseandhealth.org/article.asp?issn=1463-1741;year=2010;volume=12;issue=49;spage=225;epage=234;aulast=Shield#ref19 (accessed March 29, 2017).

110. Charles Silberman, *The Open Classroom Reader* (New York: Random House, 1973), 297.

111. Cuban, "Open Classroom."

112. "Designing for a Better World Starts at School. Rosan Bosch at TEDxIndianapolis," *YouTube* video, https://www.youtube.com/watch?v=dRMJvmOoero (accessed May 29, 2017).

113. David Thornburg, "Campfires in Cyberspace: Primordial Metaphors for Learning in the 21st Century," handout, revised October 2007, http://tcpd.org/thornburg/Handouts/Campfires.pdf (accessed May 31, 2017).

114. Rosan Bosch, interview with author, February 6, 2017.

115. Alexia Elejalde-Ruiz, "Every Day Is Earth Day for Sarah Elizabeth Ippel," *Chicago Tribune*, April 22, 2013, http://articles.chicagotribune.com/2013-04-22/features/ct-tribu-remar kable-ippel-20130421_1_earth-day-chicken-coop-agc (accessed May 29, 2017).

116. Sarah Elizabeth Ippel, interview with author, May 17, 2017.

117. Elejalde-Ruiz, "Every Day Is Earth Day."

118. Matthew Messner, "Studio Gang Proposes Net-Zero School with Three-Acre Urban Farm (Complete with Its Own Goat)," *Architect's Newspaper*, August 22, 2016, https://archpaper .com/2016/08/academy-for-global-citizenship-studio-gang-2 (accessed May 29, 2017).

119. Sarah Elizabeth Ippel, e-mail to author, May 22, 2017.

120. Prakash Nair, "The Classroom Is Obsolete: It's Time for Something New," *Education Week*, July 29, 2011, http://www.fieldingnair.com/wp-content/uploads/2015/05/The_Class room_is_Obsolete-Ed-Week.pdf (accessed May 29, 2017).

121. Audrey Watters, "The Invented History of 'The Factory Model of Education,'" *Hack Education*, April 25, 2015, http://hackeducation.com/2015/04/25/factory-model (accessed January 2, 2017).

122. Stuart Brodsky, CannonDesign, interview with author, February 21, 2017; Jordan A. Carlson, Jessa K. Engelberg, Kelli L. Cain et. al., "Implementing Classroom Physical Activity Breaks: Associations with Student Physical Activity and Classroom Behavior," *Preventive Medicine* (August 2015), https://www.researchgate.net/publication/281166732 _Implementing_classroom_physical_activity_breaks_Associations_with_student _physical_activity_and_classroom_behavior; Donna de la Cruz, "Why Students Shouldn't Sit Still in Class," *New York Times*, March 21, 2017, https://www.nytimes .com/2017/03/21/well/family/why-kids-shouldnt-sit-still-in-class.html?_r=0 (accessed May 29, 2017).

123. Michael Kimmelman, "Reading, Writing and Renewal (the Urban Kind)," *New York Times*, March 18, 2014, https://www.nytimes.com/2014/03/18/arts/design/reading-writ ing-and-renewal-the-urban-kind.html?_r=0 (accessed May 9, 2017).

124. Maria Konnikova, "The Limits of Friendship," *New Yorker*, October 7, 2014, http://www .newyorker.com/science/maria-konnikova/social-media-affect-math-dunbar-number -friendships (accessed June 1, 2017).

125. Liz Bowie, "Bridging the Divide: Struggles of New East Baltimore School Show Challenges of Integration," *Baltimore Sun*, March 22, 2017, http://www.baltimoresun.com /news/maryland/investigations/bs-md-school-segregation-series-henderson-20170321 -story.html (accessed May 10, 2017).

126. Mariale Hardiman, interview with author, October 4, 2017.

127. Rob Rogers, interview with author, May 30, 2017.

128. Rebecca Mead, "Learn Different," *New Yorker*, March 7, 2016, http://www.newyorker.com /magazine/2016/03/07/altschools-disrupted-education (accessed May 29, 2017).

129. Alex Ragone, "Technology and Project-Based Learning," *Independent School* (Spring 2017), https://www.nais.org/magazine/independent-school/spring-2017/technology-and-pro ject-based-learning (accessed October 22, 2017).

130. Christopher Alexander et al., *A Pattern Language: Towns, Buildings, Construction* (New York: Oxford University Press, 1977), 421.

131. Adam Satariano, "Silicon Valley Tried to Reinvent Schools. Now It's Rebooting," Bloomberg, November 1, 2017, https://www.bloomberg.com/news/articles/2017-11-01 /silicon-valley-tried-to-reinvent-schools-now-it-s-rebooting (accessed November 1, 2017).

132. Devin Vodicka, interview with author, September 8, 2017.

133. Alex Ragone, interview with author, September 25, 2017.

Chapter Four

1. Alice McLerran, *The Legacy of Roxaboxen* (Spring, TX: Absey & Co., 1998).

2. Jon Mooallem, "Smallville," *California Sunday Magazine*, October 4, 2015, https://story .californiasunday.com/smallville-roxaboxen (accessed April 4, 2017).

3. Roy Kozlovsky, "Adventure Playgrounds and Postwar Reconstruction," in *Designing Modern Childhoods: History, Space, and the Material Culture of Children*, ed. Marta Gutman and Ning de Coninck-Smith (New Brunswick: Rutgers University Press, 2007), 171.

4. UN General Assembly Resolution 1386 (XIV), "Declaration of the Rights of the Child," Principle 7, November 20, 1959.

5. "Copenhagen's Traffic Playground for Kids—Renovated and Ready to Go," *Copenhagenize Design Co.*, January 5, 2015, http://www.copenhagenize.com/2015/01/copenhagens-traffic-playground-for-kids.html (accessed April 4, 2017).

6. Jen Kinney, "A Playground That Teaches Kids to Love Their Bike," *Next City*, October 4, 2016, https://nextcity.org/daily/entry/seattle-bike-playground-opens (accessed April 4, 2016).

7. Ruth Graham, "How the American Playground Was Born in Boston," *Boston Globe*, March 28, 2014, https://www.bostonglobe.com/ideas/2014/03/28/how-american-playground -was-born-boston/5i2XrMCjCkuu5521uxleEL/story.html (accessed December 1, 2016).

8. Joe Frost, "Evolution of American Playgrounds," *Scholarpedia* 7 (12): 30423, http://www .scholarpedia.org/article/Evolution_of_American_Playgrounds (accessed April 4, 2017).

9. Ibid.

10. Mrs. John Graham Brooks, "Cambridge Playgrounds," *The Playground*, no. 11 (February 1908), 4.

11. G. Stanley Hall, *The Story of a Sand-pile* (New York: E. L. Kellogg & Co., 1897), 3.

12. Frost, "Evolution of American Playgrounds."

13. John Dewey and Evelyn Dewey, *Schools of To-morrow* (New York: E. P. Dutton, 1915), 114. Thanks to Colin Fanning for providing this reference.

14. Hall, *Story of a Sand-pile*, 14.

15. Jay Mechling, "Sandwork," *Journal of Play* 9, no. 1 (Fall 2016): 19.

16. Roger Smith, "The Long History of Gaming in Military Training," *Simulation & Gaming* 41, no 1 (February 2010), www.dtic.mil/get-tr-doc/pdf?AD=ada550307 *(accessed May 19, 2017).*

17. Steve Breslin, "The History and Theory of Sandbox Gameplay," Gamasutra, July 16, 2009, http://www.gamasutra.com/view/feature/132470/the_history_and_theory_of_sand box_.php (accessed April 4, 2017).

18. Theodore Roosevelt to Cuno H. Rudolph, president of the Washington Playground Association, February 16, 1907, http://www.theodore-roosevelt.com/images/research /txtspeeches/239.txt (accessed May 19, 2017).

19. Dominick Cavallo, *Muscles and Morals: Organized Playgrounds and Urban Reform, 1880–1920* (Philadelphia: University of Pennsylvania Press, 1981), 26.

20. "Seward Park," New York City Department of Parks and Recreation, https://www .nycgovparks.org/parks/seward-park/history (accessed April 5, 2017).

21. Jennifer L. Gray, "Ready for Experiment: Dwight Perkins and Progressive Architectures in Chicago, 1893–1917" (PhD dissertation, Columbia University, 2011), 217.

22. Ibid., 222.

23. Viviana A. Zelizer, *Pricing the Priceless Child: The Changing Social Value of Children* (Princeton, NJ: Princeton University Press, 1985), 32.

24. Howard P. Chudacoff, *Children at Play: An American History* (New York: New York University Press, 2008), 108.

25. Jacob Riis, "The Genesis of the Gang," *Atlantic*, September 1899, https://www.theatlantic .com/magazine/archive/1899/09/the-genesis-of-the-gang/305737 (accessed May 10, 2017).

26. Robin F. Bachin, *Building the South Side: Urban Space and Civic Culture in Chicago, 1890–1919* (Chicago: University of Chicago Press, 2004), 115–16.

27. Gray, "Ready for Experiment," 227.

28. Cavallo, *Muscles and Morals*, 32

29. Henry S. Curtis, *The Play Movement and Its Significance* (Washington, D.C.: McGrath Publishing Co. & National Recreation and Park Association, 1917), 257, 337.

30. "Live Births, Deaths, Infant Deaths, and Maternal Deaths: 1900 to 1997," table no. 1420, U.S. Census Bureau, Statistical Abstract of the United States (1999), 874, https://www .census.gov/prod/99pubs/99statab/sec31.pdf (accessed September 27, 2017).

31. Gray, "Ready for Experiment," 229.

32. Edward B. DeGroot, "The Management of Playgrounds in Public Parks," *American City* 10 (1914): 127.

33. John H. Chase, "Points About Directors," *Playground* 3, no. 4 (July 1909), 13.

34. Cavallo, *Muscles and Morals*, 41.

35. Gray, "Ready for Experiment," 244.

36. Myron F. Floyd and Rasul A. Mowatt, "Leisure Among African Americans," in *Race, Ethnicity, and Leisure: Perspectives on Research, Theory, and Practice*, ed. Monica Stodolska, Kimberly J. Shinew, Myron F. Floyd, and Gordon J. Walker (Champaign, IL: Human Kinetics, 2013), 58.

37. Emmett J. Scott, "Leisure Time and the Colored Citizen," *Playground* 18 (January 1925), reprinted in David Kenneth Wiggins and Patrick B. Miller, eds. *The Unlevel Playing Field:*

A Documentary History of the African American Experience in Sport (Champaign, IL: University of Illinois Press, 2003), 88–90.

38. Curtis, *Play Movement*, 229.

39. Karin Calvert, *Children in the House: The Material Culture of Early Childhood, 1600–1900* (Boston: Northeastern University Press, 1992), 114.

40. Brenda Biondo, *Once Upon a Playground: A Celebration of Classic American Playgrounds, 1920–1975* (Lebanon, NH: ForeEdge, 2014), x–xv.

41. Ibid., x.

42. 1931 Karymor Playground Apparatus catalog, R.F. Lamar and Co., reproduced in Biondo, *Once Upon a Playground*, 10.

43. 1931 Giant Manufacturing Company catalog, reproduced in Biondo, *Once Upon a Playground*, 12.

44. Ibid., ix.

45. Hinton's patents, which include different methods of connecting the three-dimensional grid, include U.S. Patent 1,471,465, filed July 22, 1920; U.S. Patent 1,488,244, filed October 1, 1920; U.S. Patent 1,488,245, filed October 1, 1920; and U.S. Patent 1,488,246, filed October 24, 1921.

46. Grant Pick, "A School Fit for Children," *Chicago Reader*, February 28, 1991, http://www.chicagoreader.com/chicago/a-school-fit-for-children/Content?oid=877158 (accessed May 29, 2017); Carleton W. Washburne and Sidney P. Marland Jr., *Winnetka: The History and Significance of an Educational Experiment* (Englewood Cliffs, NJ, Prentice Hall, 1963), quoted in Sheila Duran, "'J' is for Jungle Gym," Winnetka Historical Society, http://www.winnetkahistory.org/gazette/j-is-for-jungle-gym (accessed May 19, 2017).

47. Biondo, *Once Upon a Playground*, 56.

48. Robert McCarter, *Aldo van Eyck* (New Haven, CT: Yale University Press, 2015), 7–8.

49. A previous version of this text on van Eyck's orphanage was published on *Curbed*, in slightly different form. Alexandra Lange, "Book Report: Aldo van Eyck, from Playground to Orphanage," *Curbed*, February 26, 2016, http://www.curbed.com/2016/2/26/11028076/aldo-van-eyck-playground-orphanage-dutch-design (accessed April 4, 2017).

50. McCarter, *Aldo van Eyck*, 85ff.

51. Quoted in ibid., 111.

52. Quoted in Liane Lefaivre and Ingeborg de Roode, eds., *Aldo van Eyck, the Playgrounds and the City* (Amsterdam: Stedelijk Museum/NAi Publishers, 2002), 70.

53. Lefaivre and de Roode, *Aldo Van Eyck*, 25.

54. Anna van Lingen and Denisa Kollarová, *Aldo van Eyck: Seventeen Playgrounds* (Eindhoven, Netherlands: Lecturis, 2016).

55. Liane Lefaivre, *Ground-Up City: Play as a Design Tool* (Amsterdam: 010 Publishers, 2007) 67–68.

56. Lefaivre and de Roode, *Aldo van Eyck*, 59.

57. McCarter, *Aldo van Eyck*, 51.

58. Lefaivre and de Roode, *Aldo van Eyck*, 81.

59. Paraphrased in McCarter, *Aldo van Eyck*, 51.

60. Ezra Jack Keats, *The Snowy Day* (New York: Viking Press, 1962).

61. A previous version of this section on Japanese adventure playgrounds appeared, in slightly different form, on the *New Yorker* website. Alexandra Lange, "What It Would Take to Set American Kids Free," *New Yorker*, November 18, 2016, http://www.newyorker.com /culture/cultural-comment/what-it-would-take-to-set-american-kids-free (accessed April 5, 2017).

62. Amy Fusselman, "Play Freely at Your Own Risk," *Atlantic*, January 15, 2015, https:// www.theatlantic.com/health/archive/2015/01/play-freely-at-your-own-risk/373625 (accessed April 5, 2017).

63. Richard Dattner, interview with author, June 6, 2016.

64. Melanie Thernstrom, "The Anti-Helicopter Parent's Plea: Let Kids Play!" *New York Times Magazine*, October 19, 2016, https://www.nytimes.com/2016/10/23/magazine/the-anti -helicopter-parents-plea-let-kids-play.html?_r=0 (accessed April 5, 2016).

65. Carl Theodor Sørensen, "Junk Playgrounds," *Danish Outlook* 4, no. 1 (1951), quoted in Kozlovsky, "Adventure Playgrounds," 174.

66. Marjory Gill Allen (Lady Allen of Hurtwood), "Why Not Use Our Bomb Sites Like This?" *Picture Post*, November 16, 1946, 26–29.

67. Quoted in Chris Steller, "When 'The Yard' Was Minnesota's Most Radical Park," *MinnPost*, July 25, 2014, https://www.minnpost.com/arts-culture/2014/07/when-yard-was -minnesota-s-most-radical-park (accessed April 7, 2017).

68. "Recreation: Junkyard Playgrounds," *Time*, June 25, 1965.

69. Aase Eriksen, *Playground Design: Outdoor Environments for Learning and Development* (New York: Van Nostrand Reinhold, 1986), 25.

70. Quoted in Lillian Ross, "Summer Glimpses," Talk of the Town, *New Yorker*, July 31, 1971, 25.

71. Hanna Rosin, "The Overprotected Kid," *Atlantic*, April 2014, https://www.theatlantic .com/magazine/archive/2014/04/hey-parents-leave-those-kids-alone/358631 (accessed April 6, 2017).

72. Quoted in Arvid Bengtsson, *Adventure Playgrounds* (London: Crosby Lockwood, 1972), 21.

73. Reilly Bergin Wilson, interview with author, April 7, 2017.

74. Casey Logan, "Playground for the Imagination Swaps Slides and Swings for Lumber and Tires," *Omaha World-Herald*, May 18, 2015, http://www.omaha.com/momaha/playground -for-the-imagination-swaps-slides-and-swings-for-lumber/article_1011bd8b-d611-54ba -b092-08b1cbc8d605.html (accessed May 19, 2017).

75. Quoted in Bengtsson, *Adventure Playgrounds*, 11.

76. Rosin, "The Overprotected Kid."

77. Charles Mount, "Boy Injured on Slide Gets $9.5 Million," *Chicago Tribune*, January 15, 1985.

78. Rosin, "The Overprotected Kid."

79. Sharon Otterman, "The Downward Slide of the Seesaw," *New York Times*, December 11, 2016, https://www.nytimes.com/2016/12/11/nyregion/the-downward-slide-of-the-seesaw.html (accessed April 6, 2017).

80. Douglas Martin, "That Upside-Down High Will Be Only a Memory; Monkey Bars Fall to Safety Pressures," *New York Times*, April 11, 1996, http://www.nytimes.com/1996/04/11/nyregion/that-upside-down-high-will-be-only-a-memory-monkey-bars-fall-to-safety-pressures.html (accessed April 6, 2017).

81. Teresa B. Hendy, interview with author, September 28, 2017.

82. Jeanette Fich Jespersen, interview with author, May 30, 2017; "The KOMPAN Saturn Carousel," *YouTube* video, September 26, 2014, https://www.youtube.com/watch?v=XbB_UHp9fn8 (accessed June 1, 2017).

83. Craig W. O'Brien, *Injuries and Investigated Deaths Associated with Playground Equipment, 2001–2008*, U.S. Consumer Product Safety Commission, October 2009, http://playgroundsafety.org/research/injuries (accessed April 6, 2017).

84. Quoted in Steller, "When 'The Yard.'"

85. Reilly Bergin Wilson, interview with author, April 7, 2017.

86. Helle Nebelong, speech at the Designs on Play conference, Playlink/Portsmouth City Council, 2002, quoted in Tim Gill, *No Fear: Growing Up in a Risk-Averse Society* (London: Calouste Gulbenkian Foundation, 2007), 35.

87. Ellen Beate Hansen Sandseter, "Characteristics of Risky Play," *Journal of Adventure Education and Outdoor Learning* 9, no. 1 (2009), 7; Ellen Beate Hansen Sandseter and Leif Edward Ottesen Kennair, "Children's Risky Play from an Evolutionary Perspective: The Anti-Phobic Effects of Thrilling Experiences," *Evolutionary Psychology* 9, no. 2 (April 2011), 265.

88. Tim Gill, *No Fear: Growing Up in a Risk-Averse Society* (London: Calouste Gulbenkian Foundation, 2007), 15.

89. Sandseter, "Children's Risky Play," 261.

90. Susan G. Solomon, *The Science of Play: How to Build Playgrounds That Enhance Development* (Lebanon, NH: University Press of New England, 2014), 34.

91. Sam Wang and Sandra Aamodt, "Play, Stress, and the Learning Brain," *Cerebrum* (September/October 2012), https://www.ncbi.nlm.nih.gov/pmc/articles/PMC3574776 (accessed April 6, 2017).

92. Gill, *No Fear*, 16.

93. Gill, *No Fear*, 36; Play Safety Forum, "Managing Risk in Play provision: A Position Statement," https://playsafetyforum.files.wordpress.com/2015/03/managing-risk-in-play-provision-position-statement.pdf (accessed April 6, 2017).

94. An earlier account of this trip to Morenuma was published on *Curbed*, in slightly different form. Alexandra Lange, "A journey to Isamu Noguchi's last work," *Curbed*, December 1, 2016, http://www.curbed.com/2016/12/1/13778884/noguchi-playground-moerenuma-japan (accessed April 7, 2017).

95. Ana Maria Torres, *Isamu Noguchi: A Study of Space* (New York: Monacelli Press, 2000), 25.

96. "Playground Equipment," *Architectural Forum* 73 (October 1940), 245.

97. *Fourteen Americans* Museum of Modern Art, September 10–December 8, 1946, https://www.moma.org/calendar/exhibitions/3196?locale=en (accessed May 19, 2017).

98. Shaina D. Larrivee, "Playscapes: Isamu Noguchi's Designs for Play," *Public Art Dialogue* 1, no. 1 (2011) 53–80.

99. Solomon, *American Playgrounds*, 24–25.

100. Letter, Isamu Noguchi to Brian O'Doherty, National Foundation on the Arts and Humanities, n.d. (1974), Archives of the Isamu Noguchi Foundation and Garden Museum.

101. Thomas B. Hess, "The Rejected Playground," *ARTNews*, April 1952.

102. Solomon, *American Playgrounds*, 25.

103. Hess, "The Rejected Playground."

104. Dakin Hart, interview with author, October 2, 2014.

105. Solomon, *American Playgrounds*, 45.

106. Letter, Newbold Morris to Helen Harris, United Neighborhood Houses of New York, February 20, 1962, quoted in Solomon, *American Playgrounds*, 49.

107. *Isamu Noguchi and Louis Kahn:* Play Mountain (Japan: Watari-Um, 1997), 100.

108. Larrivee, "Playscapes."

109. Joseph Lelyveld, "Model Play Area for Park Shown," *New York Times*, February 5, 1964; "Parks Are for Park Purposes," *New York Times*, February 8, 1964.

110. Larrivee, "Playscapes."

111. Hayden Herrera, *Listening to Stone: The Art and Life of Isamu Noguchi* (New York: Farrar, Straus and Giroux, 2015), 495.

112. Ibid.

113. Richard Dattner, *Design for Play* (New York: Van Nostrand Reinhold, 1969), 65.

114. Lewis Mumford, "Artful Blight," The Sky Line, *New Yorker*, May 5, 1951.

115. Robert A. M. Stern, David Fishman, and Thomas Mellins, *New York 1960: Architecture and Urbanism between the Second World War and the Bicentennial* (New York: Monacelli Press, 1997), 768.

116. Anthony Flint, *Wrestling with Moses: How Jane Jacobs Took on New York's Master Builder and Transformed the American City* (New York: Random House, 2009), 85.

117. "Park-Side Residents Gain Writ to Stay Parking Lot for Tavern," *New York Times*, May 3, 1956, 23.

118. Michael Gotkin, "The Politics of Play," in *Preserving Modern Landscape Architecture*, ed. Charles A. Birnbaum (New York: Spacemakers Press, 1999), 65.

119. Stern, Fishman, and Mellins, *New York 1960*, 776.

120. Richard Dattner, interview with author, June 6, 2016.

121. Dattner, *Design for Play*, 66.

122. Ibid., 70.

123. Charles L. Mee Jr., "Putting the Play in Playground," *New York Times Magazine*, November 6, 1966.

124. Julia Jacquette, *Playground of My Mind* (New York: DelMonico Books/Prestel/Wellin Museum of Art, 2017).

125. Julia Jacquette and James Trainor, "City as Playground," *Urban Omnibus*, September 21, 2016, http://urbanomnibus.net/2016/09/playground-of-my-mind (accessed Dec 7, 2016).

126. M. Paul Friedberg, interview with author, May 31, 2016.

127. Dattner, *Design for Play*, 109ff.

128. Ibid., 110–13.

129. Playworld, *Inclusive Play Design Guide* (Lewisburg, PA: Playworld Systems, 2015); Mimi Kirk, "Playgrounds Designed for Everyone," *CityLab*, February 27, 2017, https://www.citylab.com/navigator/2017/02/designing-playgrounds-for-all/517692 (accessed May 19, 2017).

130. Ian Proud, interview with author, May 16, 2017.

131. Jeanette Fich Jespersen, interview with author, May 30, 2017.

132. Richard Dattner, "Play Panels" sketch, December 3, 2012, shared with author, December 6, 2016.

133. "Bringing PlayCubes Back to Life," Playworld, May 16, 2016, https://playworld.com/press-room/playworld-and-architect-richard-dattner-bring-playcubes-back-life-boston (accessed May 19, 2017).

134. Simon Nicholson, "How Not to Cheat Children: The Theory of Loose Parts," *Landscape Architecture* 62, no. 1 (October 1971): 30–34.

135. Ibid., 30.

136. Ibid., 34.

137. Rebecca Mead, "State of Play," *New Yorker*, July 5, 2010, http://www.newyorker.com/magazine/2010/07/05/state-of-play (accessed Dec 7, 2016).

138. Reilly Bergin Wilson, interview with author, April 7, 2017.

139. Nicholson, "How Not to Cheat Children," 31.

140. A version of this text first appeared, in slightly different form, in the *New Yorker*. Alexandra Lange, "Play Ground," *New Yorker*, May 16, 2016, http://www.newyorker.com/magazine/2016/05/16/adriaan-geuzes-governors-island (accessed May 19, 2017).

141. Alexandra Lange, "A Playground That Parents Won't Come to Despise," *New Yorker*, July 6, 2012, http://www.newyorker.com/culture/culture-desk/a-playground-that-parents-wont-come-to-despise (accessed May 19, 2017).

Chapter Five

1. Maud Hart Lovelace, *Betsy and Tacy Go Over the Big Hill*, in *The Betsy-Tacy Treasury* (New York: Harper Perennial, 2011 [© 1942]), 283–84.

2. Ibid., 286.

3. Roger A. Hart, "Planning Cities with Children in Mind: A Background Paper for the State of the World's Children Report," April 30, 2011, http://cergnyc.org/files/2013/10/Hart-Planning-Cities-with-Children-in-Mind-SOWC-APRIL-2011.pdf (accessed May 26, 2017).

4. Dolores Hayden, *Redesigning the American Dream: The Future of Housing, Work, and Family Life* (New York: W .W. Norton, 2002 [© 1984]), 230.

5. Jia Tolentino, "The Little Syria of Deep Valley," *New Yorker*, February 16, 2017, https://www.newyorker.com/books/second-read/the-little-syria-of-deep-valley (accessed April 25, 2017).

6. Selena Hoy, "Why Japanese Kids Can Walk to School Alone," *Atlantic*, October 2, 2015, https://www.theatlantic.com/technology/archive/2015/10/why-japanese-kids-can-walk -to-school-alone/408475 (accessed April 25, 2017).

7. Lenore Skenazy, quoted in Lizzie Widdicombe, "Mother May I?" *New Yorker*, February 23 and March 2, 2015, http://www.newyorker.com/magazine/2015/02/23/mother-may (accessed May 26, 2017).

8. Dolores Hayden, *The Grand Domestic Revolution: A History of Feminist Designs for American Homes, Neighborhoods, and Cities* (Cambridge: MIT Press, 1981), 3.

9. Hart, "Planning Cities with Children in Mind," 8.

10. Denis Wood, "Free the Children! Down with Playgrounds!" *McGill Journal of Education* 12, no. 2 (1977): 229.

11. Tim Gill, "Space-Oriented Children's Policy: Creating Child-Friendly Communities to Improve Children's Well-Being," *Children & Society* 22 (March 2008), 136.

12. David Derbyshire, "How Children Lost the Right to Roam in Four Generations," *Daily Mail*, June 15, 2007, http://www.dailymail.co.uk/news/article-462091/How-children-lost -right-roam-generations.html (accessed May 26, 2017).

13. Widdicombe, "Mother May I?"

14. Gill, "Space-Oriented Children's Policy," 139.

15. Alexandra Lange, "The Moms Aren't Wrong: Why Planning for Children Would Make Cities Better for All," *GOOD*, February 1, 2011.

16. Enrique Peñalosa and Susan Ives, "The Politics of Happiness," *Yes* magazine, May 20, 2004, http://www.yesmagazine.org/issues/finding-courage/the-politics-of-happiness (accessed May 26, 2017).

17. Adrian Crook, interview with author, February 28, 2017; Centers for Disease Control and Prevention, "10 Leading Causes of Injury Deaths by Age Group Highlighting Unintentional Injury Deaths, United States—2015," https://www.cdc.gov/injury/images /lc-charts/leading_causes_of_injury_deaths_unintentional_injury_2015_1050w760h .gif (accessed May 26, 2017).

18. Ashifa Kassam, "Canada Father Prepares Lawsuit after Province Bars Kids from Riding Bus Alone," *Guardian*, October 1, 2017, https://www.theguardian.com/world/2017/oct/01 /canada-father-bus-children-adrian-crook (accessed October 4, 2017).

19. Adrian Crook, "Very Superstitious: How Fact-Free Parenting Policies Rob Our Kids of Independence," *5Kids1Condo*, September 5, 2017. https://5kids1condo.com/very-super stitious-how-fact-free-parenting-policies-rob-our-kids-of-independence (accessed October 4, 2017).

20. Ann McAfee and Andrew, *Housing Families at High Density*, City of Vancouver Planning Department, 1978, https://www.researchgate.net/publication/284698660_Housing _Families_at_High_Density (accessed April 25, 2017).

21. Ann McAfee, interview with author, March 8, 2017.

22. Donald Gutstein, *Vancouver Ltd.*, (Toronto: James Lorimer & Company, 1975), 98.

23. Amanda Kolson Hurley, "Will U.S. Cities Design Their Way Out of the Affordable Housing Crisis?" *Next City*, January 18, 2016, https://nextcity.org/features/view/cities -affordable-housing-design-solution-missing-middle (accessed April 25, 2017).

24. National Association of Realtors and Portland State University, *Community and Transportation Preferences Survey: U.S. Metro Areas, 2015*, July 23, 2015, https://www.nar.realtor /sites/default/files/reports/2015/nar-psu-2015-poll-report.pdf (accessed May 26, 2017).

25. McAfee and Malczewski, *Housing Families*, 21.

26. Ann McAfee, interview with author.

27. Larry Beasley, interview with author, February 22, 2017.

28. Maria Konnikova, "The Limits of Friendship," *New Yorker*, October 7, 2014, http://www .newyorker.com/science/maria-konnikova/social-media-affect-math-dunbar-number -friendships (accessed June 1, 2017).

29. Tom Cardoso and Matt Lundy, "Has Home Affordability Actually Improved in Vancouver?" *Globe and Mail*, April 24, 2017, https://beta.theglobeandmail.com/real-estate/ the-market/has-vancouver-home-affordability-actually-improved/article34796026/?ref =http://www.theglobeandmail.com (accessed November 3, 2017); Bob Dugan, "Why the Foreign Buyers Tax Isn't Making Vancouver More Affordable," *Maclean's*, August 17, 2017, http://www.macleans.ca/opinion/why-the-foreign-buyers-tax-isnt-making-vancouver -more-affordable (accessed November 3, 2017).

30. Jennifer Langston, "Are You Planning to Have Kids? (Part 2)," Sightline Institute, July 29, 2014, http://www.sightline.org/2014/07/29/are-you-planning-to-have-kids-part-2 (accessed May 26, 2017).

31. Brent Toderian, "Tall Tower Debates Could Use Less Dogma, Better Design," *Planetizen*, June 1, 2014, https://www.planetizen.com/node/69073 (accessed May 27, 2017).

32. Alvin Martin, interview with author, March 28, 2017.

33. Dan Fumano, "A Balancing Act in One of the City's Greatest Neighbourhoods," *Vancouver Sun*, May 26, 2017, http://vancouversun.com/opinion/columnists/dan-fumano-a-balan cing-act-in-one-of-citys-greatest-neighbourhoods (accessed May 27, 2017); "False Creek South Neighbourhood Association and *RePlan Principles," http://www.falsecreeksouth .org/replanprinciples (accessed October 24, 2017); City of Vancouver, *False Creek South Planning: Terms of Reference*, May 16, 2017, http://council.vancouver.ca/20170530/docu ments/rr1.pdf (accessed June 1, 2017).

34. Cory Verbauwhede, "How to Grow a City: South False Creek's Forgotten Visionaries," *West Coast Line* (July 2005): 198, http://newcity.ca/Pages/south-false-creek-history.pdf (accessed April 27, 2017).

35. John Punter, *The Vancouver Achievement: Urban Planning and Design* (Vancouver: University of British Columbia Press, 2014), 37.

36. Christopher Alexander et al., *A Pattern Language: Towns, Buildings, Construction* (New York: Oxford University Press, 1977), 342.

37. Ibid., 342.

38. Colin Ward, *The Child in the City* [London: Bedford Square Press, 1990 [© 1969]), 179.

39. Clare Foran, "How to Design a City for Women," *CityLab*, September 13, 2013, https://www.citylab.com/transportation/2013/09/how-design-city-women/6739 (accessed June 1, 2017).

40. Sarane Spence Boocock, "The Life Space of Children," in *Building for Women*, ed. Suzanne Keller (Lexington, MA: Lexington Books, 1981), 99–100.

41. Iona Archibald Opie and Peter Opie, *Children's Games in Street and Playground* (Oxford, England: Oxford University Press, 1969).

42. Alexander et al., *Pattern Language*, 421.

43. Witold Rybczynski, "Do You See a Pattern?" *Slate*, December 2, 2009.

44. Bernard van Leer Foundation, Urban95 project website, https://bernardvanleer.org/solutions/urban95 (accessed May 26, 2017).

45. Caroline Pratt, *I Learn from Children: An Adventure in Progressive Education* (New York: Grove Press, 2014 [© 1948]), 56.

46. Ibid., 113.

47. Ibid., 122.

48. Kevin Lynch, *The Image of the City* (Cambridge, MA: MIT Press, 1960).

49. Robin C. Moore, *Childhood's Domain: Play and Place in Childhood Development* (London: Croom Helm, 1986), 2.

50. Ibid., 14.

51. Ibid., 109–10.

52. Ibid., 21.

53. Naomi Larsson, "The App That Gives Oslo's Children a Direct Say over Their Own Road Safety," *Guardian*, September 2, 2016, https://www.theguardian.com/public-leaders-network/2016/sep/02/app-oslo-children-traffic-road-safety (accessed November 3, 2017).

54. Toole Design Group, *How I Get to School! A Complete Streets Story*, http://www.tooledesign.com/sites/default/files/TDG_How%20I%20Get%20to%20School.pdf (accessed April 27, 2017).

55. Kenneth T. Jackson, *Crabgrass Frontier: The Suburbanization of the United States* (New York: Oxford University Press, 1987), 58.

56. Ralph Waldo Emerson, "Journal," 1865, quoted in Jackson, *Crabgrass Frontier*, 59; Lewis Mumford, *The City in History: Its Origins, Its Transformations, and Its Prospects* (Boston: Houghton Mifflin Harcourt, 1981 [© 1961]), 495–96.

57. United States Department of the Interior, National Park Service, *National Historic Landmark Nomination: Radburn*, https://www.nps.gov/nhl/find/statelists/nj/Radburn.pdf (accessed May 26, 2017).

58. Clarence Perry, "The Neighborhood Unit" (1929), reproduced in "The Neighborhood Unit: How Does Perry's Concept Apply to Modern Day Planning?" EVStudio website, October 8, 2014 http://evstudio.com/the-neighborhood-unit-how-does-perrys-concept -apply-to-modern-day-planning (accessed May 26, 2017.)

59. Gwendolyn Wright, *Building the Dream: A Social History of Housing in America* (Cambridge, MA: MIT Press, 1981), 205, 207.

60. Eugenie L. Birch, "Radburn and the American Planning Movement," *Journal of the American Planning Association* 46, no. 4 (October 1980) 424–31.

61. United States Department of the Interior, National Park Service, *National Historic Landmark Nomination: Baldwin Hills Village*, https://www.nps.gov/nhl/find/statelists/ca /Baldwin.pdf (accessed May 26, 2017).

62. Jackson, *Crabgrass Frontier*, 238–39.

63. Peter Wyden, *Suburbia's Coddled Kids* (Garden City, NY: Doubleday & Co., 1962), 1.

64. Jackson, *Crabgrass Frontier*, 301.

65. Wyden, *Suburbia's Coddled Kids*, 14.

66. United States Department of the Interior, National Park Service, *National Historic Register Nomination: Lafayette Park*, https://www.nps.gov/nhl/news/LC/fall2014/LafayettePark.pdf (accessed May 26, 2017).

67. "Redevelopment F.O.B. Detroit," *Architectural Forum* 102 (March 1955): 119.

68. "Housing Reversing a Trend?" *Detroit Free Press*, September 17, 1959, 21.

69. "A Tower Plus Row Houses in Detroit," *Architectural Forum* 112 (May 1960): 112.

70. Ibid., 106.

71. Don Beck, "Here's a One-Room School in the Heart of Detroit," *Detroit Free Press*, September 17, 1959, https://www.newspapers.com/image/98337157 (accessed May 26, 2017).

72. Karal Ann Marling, ed., *Designing Disney's Theme Parks: The Architecture of Reassurance* (Montreal: Canadian Centre for Architecture, 1997) 78–79.

73. Brigid Beaubien, "Come to the Fair! Laying the Groundwork for the Early Childhood Profession," *Young Children* (September 2013).

74. Marling, *Designing Disney*, 36.

75. Ibid., 87.

76. James Rouse, "The Regional Shopping Center: Its Role in the Community It Serves," Seventh Urban Design Conference, Harvard University, April 26, 1963.

77. Charles W. Moore, "You Have to Pay for the Public Life" in *You Have to Pay for the Public Life: Selected Essays of Charles W. Moore*, ed. Kevin Keim (Cambridge, MA: MIT Press, 2004), 124.

78. Ibid., 113.

79. Ibid., 126.

80. "Walt Disney's Original EPCOT film" (1966), YouTube video, https://www.youtube.com/ watch?v=sLCHg9mUBag (accessed November 3, 2017).

81. Marling, *Designing Disney*, 152.

82. Matt Patches, "Inside Disney's Ambitious, Failed Plan to Build the City of Tomorrow," *Esquire*, May 20, 2015, http://www.esquire.com/entertainment/news/a35104/walt-disney-epcot-history-city-of-tomorrow (accessed May 12, 2017).

83. "Condohacks: Mount Pleasant & Davisville," City of Toronto, Planning Studies & Initiatives, https://www1.toronto.ca/City%20Of%20Toronto/City%20Planning/SIPA/Files/pdf/V/Condohack2_Mount_Pleasant_Davisville_AODA.pdf (accessed May 25, 2017).

84. Andrea Oppedisano, e-mail to author, May 29, 2017.

85. City of Toronto, "Growing Up: Planning for Children in New Vertical Communities," Draft Urban Design Guidelines (May 2017), 9.

86. Christopher Hume, "Big Ideas: Learning the Lessons of St. Lawrence Neighbourhood," *Toronto Star*, May 3, 2014, https://www.thestar.com/news/gta/2014/05/03/big_ideas_learning_the_lessons_of_st_lawrence_neighbourhood.html (accessed May 25, 2017).

87. Dave LeBlanc, "35 Years On, St. Lawrence Is a Template for Urban Housing," *Globe and Mail*, February 6, 2013, https://www.theglobeandmail.com/life/home-and-garden/architecture/35-years-on-st-lawrence-is-a-template-for-urban-housing/article8296990 (accessed May 25, 2017).

88. Shawn Micallef, "Jane Up North," *Curbed*, May 4, 2016, https://www.curbed.com/2016/5/4/11521812/jane-jacobs-toronto-spadina-expressway (accessed May 25, 2017).

89. City of Toronto, "Growing Up," 42–44.

90. Ibid., 48.

91. Studio Gang, "The Garden in the Machine: Cicero, Ill.," in *Foreclosed: Rehousing the American Dream*, Museum of Modern Art, https://www.moma.org/interactives/exhibitions/2012/foreclosed/cicero (accessed May 27, 2017).

92. City of Toronto," Growing Up," 30.

93. City of Portland, "5b. 20-Minute Neighborhoods," *Portland Plan* (2012), http://www.portlandonline.com/portlandplan/index.cfm?a=288098&c=52256 (accessed June 1, 2017).

94. Mara Mintzer, Joanna Mendoza, Louise Chawla, and Aria Dellepiane, "Growing Up Boulder: Young People's Ideas for 15-Minute Neighborhoods," report (September 2016), http://www.growingupboulder.org/uploads/1/3/3/5/13350974/15_min_neighborhood_report.pdf (accessed May 27, 2017).

95. City of Toronto, "Growing Up," 19.

96. City of Rotterdam, "Rotterdam, City with a Future," Youth, Education, and Society Department (October 2010), http://www.robedrijf.nl/JOS/kindvriendelijk/Rotterdam%20City%20with%20a%20future.pdf (accessed November 3, 2017).

97. Quoted in Ashley Renders, "Critics Keep Pressure on Rotterdam's Affordable Housing Plan," *Next City*, April 5, 2017, https://nextcity.org/daily/entry/rotterdam-affordable-housing-teardown-plan-protest (accessed May 27, 2017).

98. Marguerite van den Berg, *Gender in the Post-Fordist Urban: The Gender Revolution in Planning and Public Policy* (Berlin: Springer, 2017), 63.

99. Arjen Schreuder, "The Mosquito's Bite: Dutch Debate Use of 'Teen Repellent,'" *Der Spiegel*, April 24, 2009, http://www.spiegel.de/international/europe/the-mosquito-s-bite -dutch-debate-use-of-teen-repellent-a-621025.html (accessed May 27, 2017).

100. Van den Berg, *Gender in the Post-Fordist Urban*, 65.

101. Renders, "Critics Keep Pressure."

102. New York City Office of the Mayor, "De Blasio Administration Launches Community Parks Initiative to Build More Inclusive and Equitable Park System," press release, October 7, 2014, http://www1.nyc.gov/office-of-the-mayor/news/468-14/de-blasio-adminis tration-launches-community-parks-initiative-build-more-inclusive-equitable#/0 (accessed May 27, 2017).

103. Helen Forman, "Residential Street Design and Play," Playing Out (January 2017), http:// playingout.net/wp-content/uploads/2017/02/Helen-Forman-Street-design-and-play.pdf (accessed May 12, 2017).

104. Samuel Williams and Hannah Wright, interview with author, May 16, 2017.

105. Josef Hargrave, Samuel Williams, Hannah Wright, and Felicitas zu Dohna, "Cities Alive: Designing for Urban Childhoods," Arup, December 2017, 7.

106. Williams and Wright, interview with author.

107. Hargrave et al., "Cities Alive," 15–17.

108. Wyden, *Suburbia's Coddled Kids*, 107–8.

Conclusion

1. Additional discussion of the King School's history and architecture was published, in slightly different form, in *MAS Context*. Alexandra Lange, "Never-Loved Buildings Rarely Stand a Chance," *MAS Context* 25–26 (Spring/Summer 2015), http://www.mascontext .com/tag/alexandra-lange (accessed June 2, 2017).

2. Charles E. Rhine, "PS Projects: Amazing Sun Dome," *Popular Science* (May 1968), 108–12.

3. David Pickett, "The LEGO Gender Gap: A Historical Perspective," *Thinking Brickly*, January 2, 2012, http://thinkingbrickly.blogspot.com/2012/01/lego-gender-gap.html (accessed June 2, 2017).

4. Jo B. Paoletti, *Pink and Blue: Telling the Boys from the Girls in America* (Bloomington, IN: Indiana University Press, 2012) 108–9.

5. President Jimmy Carter, "Energy and the National Goals—A Crisis of Confidence," delivered July 15, 1979, http://www.americanrhetoric.com/speeches/jimmycartercrisi sofconfidence.htm (accessed June 2, 2017).

BIBLIOGRAPHY

Adams, Annmarie. "The Eichler Home: Intention and Experience in Postwar Suburbia." *Perspectives in Vernacular Architecture* 5 (1995).

Alexander, Barbara T. "The U.S. Homebuilding Industry: A Half Century of Building the American Dream." John T. Dunlop Lecture, Harvard University, October 12, 2000.

Alexander, Christopher, Sara Ishikawa, and Murray Silverstein. *A Pattern Language: Towns, Buildings, Construction.* New York: Oxford University Press, 1977.

Allen, Marjory Gill. (Lady Allen of Hurtwood). "Why Not Use Our Bomb Sites Like This?" *Picture Post*, November 16, 1946.

———. *Planning for Play.* London, Thames & Hudson, 1969 (© 1968).

American Journal of Play. "Play and the Hundred Languages of Children: An Interview with Lella Gandini." *American Journal of Play* 4, no. 1 (Summer 2011): 1–19.

Archer, John. *Architecture and Suburbia: From English Villa to American Dream House, 1690–2000.* Minneapolis: University of Minnesota Press, 2005.

Ariès, Philippe. *Centuries of Childhood: A Social History of Family Life.* Translated by Robert Baldick. New York: Vintage Books, 1962.

Arnold, Jeanne E., Anthony P. Graesch, Enzo Ragazzini, and Elinor Ochs. *Life at Home in the Twenty-First Century: 32 Families Open Their Doors.* Los Angeles: Cotsen Institute of Archaeology Press, 2013.

Bachin, Robin F. *Building the South Side: Urban Space and Civic Culture in Chicago, 1890–1919.* Chicago: University of Chicago Press, 2004.

Barthes, Roland. "Toys." In *Mythologies*. Selected and translated by Annette Lavers. New York: Hill and Wang, 1984 (© 1957).

Beatty, Barbara. *Preschool Education in America: The Culture of Young Children from the Colonial Era to the Present*. New Haven, CT: Yale University Press, 1995.

Beaubien, Brigid. "Come to the Fair! Laying the Groundwork for the Early Childhood Profession." *Young Children* (September 2013): 96–99.

Beck, Don. "Here's a One-Room School in the Heart of Detroit." *Detroit Free Press*, September 17, 1959.

Bengtsson, Arvid. *Adventure Playgrounds*. London: Crosby Lockwood, 1972.

Bergdoll, Barry, and John H. Beyer. "Marcel Breuer: Bauhaus Tradition, Brutalist Invention." *Metropolitan Museum of Art Bulletin* (Summer 2015).

Bers, Marina Umaschi. *Designing Digital Experiences for Positive Youth Development: From Playpen to Playground*. New York: Oxford University Press, 2012.

"The Big Play in Paper." *Life*, November 3, 1967.

Biondo, Brenda. *Once Upon a Playground: A Celebration of Classic American Playgrounds, 1920–1975*. Lebanon, NH: ForeEdge, 2014.

Birch, Eugenie L. "Radburn and the American Planning Movement." *Journal of the American Planning Association* 46, no. 4 (October 1980): 424–31.

Bliss, Anna Campbell. Children's Furniture. *Design Quarterly* 57 (1963).

Boocock, Sarane Spence. "The Life Space of Children." In *Building for Women*, edited by Suzanne Keller, 93–116. Lexington, MA: Lexington Books, 1981.

Breslin, Steve. "The History and Theory of Sandbox Gameplay." Gamasutra, July 16, 2009.

Brodesser-Akner, Taffy. "Marie Kondo and the Ruthless War on Stuff." *New York Times Magazine*, July 6, 2016.

Brosterman, Norman. *Inventing Kindergarten*. New York: Abrams, 1997.

Brown, Ashley. "Ilonka Karasz: Rediscovering a Modernist Pioneer." *Studies in the Decorative Arts* 8, no. 1 (Fall/Winter 2000–2001): 69–91.

Bruce, Gordon. *Eliot Noyes*. New York: Phaidon, 2007.

Burkhalter, Gabriela, ed. *The Playground Project*. Zurich: JRP/Ringier, 2016.

Calvert, Karin. *Children in the House: The Material Culture of Early Childhood, 1600–1900*. Boston: Northeastern University Press, 1992.

Caudill, William W. *Toward Better School Design*. New York: F. W. Dodge Corporation, 1954.

Cavallo, Dominick. *Muscles and Morals: Organized Playgrounds and Urban Reform, 1880–1920*. Philadelphia: University of Pennsylvania Press, 1981.

Chase, John H. "Points about Directors." *Playground* 3, no. 4 (July 1909): 13–15.

Cherner, Norman. *How to Build Children's Toys and Furniture*. New York: McGraw-Hill, 1954.

Chudacoff, Howard P. *Children at Play: An American History*. New York: New York University Press, 2008.

City of Rotterdam. "Rotterdam, City with a Future." Youth, Education, and Society Department (October 2010).

City of Toronto. "Growing Up: Planning for Children in New Vertical Communities." Draft Urban Design Guidelines (May 2017).

Clark, Clifford Edward Jr. *The American Family Home, 1800–1960*. Chapel Hill: University of North Carolina Press, 1986.

Clarke, Jane H. "Philosophy in Brick." *Inland Architect* (November/December 1989): 54–59.

Columbus, Indiana: A Look at Architecture. Columbus, IN: Columbus Area Visitors Center, 1974.

Cook, Daniel Thomas. *The Commodification of Childhood: The Children's Clothing Industry and the Rise of the Child Consumer*. Durham, NC: Duke University Press, 2004.

Cooper, Clare C. "Adventure Playgrounds." *Landscape Architecture* 61, no. 1 (October 1970): 18–29, 88–91.

Cope, George, and Phylis Morrison. *The Further Adventures of Cardboard Carpentry: Son of Cardboard Carpentry*. Cambridge, MA: Workshop for Learning Things, 1973.

Cowan, Ruth Schwartz. *More Work for Mother: The Ironies of Household Technology from the Open Hearth to the Microwave*. New York: Basic Books, 1983.

Cremin, Lawrence A. *The Transformation of the School: Progressivism in American Education, 1876–1957*. New York: Alfred A. Knopf, 1961.

Cromley, Elizabeth Collins. "A History of American Beds and Bedrooms." *Perspectives in Vernacular Architecture* 4 (1991): 177–86.

Cross, Gary. *Kids' Stuff: Toys and the Changing World of American Childhood*. Cambridge, MA: Harvard University Press, 1999.

"Crow Island School." *Architectural Forum* 75 (August 1941): 79–92.

Cuban, Larry. "The Open Classroom." *EducationNext* 4, no. 2 (Spring 2004): 69–71.

Cunningham, Hugh. *Children and Childhood in Western Society since 1500*. New York: Longman, 1995.

Curtis, Henry S. *The Play Movement and Its Significance*. Washington, D.C.: McGrath Publishing Co. & National Recreation and Park Association, 1917.

Cutler, William W. III. "Cathedral of Culture: The Schoolhouse in American Educational Thought and Practice since 1820." *History of Education Quarterly* 29 (Spring 1989): 1–40.

Dattner, Richard. *Design for Play*. New York: Van Nostrand Reinhold, 1969.

DeVore, Donald E., and Joseph Logsdon. *Crescent City Schools: Public Education in New Orleans, 1841–1991*. Lafayette, LA: University of Louisiana at Lafayette, 2012 (© 1991).

Dewey, John. *The School and Society and the Child and the Curriculum*. Chicago: University of Chicago Press, 1990 (© 1900, 1902).

Dewey, John, and Evelyn Dewey. *Schools of To-morrow*. New York: E. P. Dutton, 1915.

Dudek, Mark, ed. *Children's Spaces*. Amsterdam: Architectural Press, 2005.

Durst, Anne. *Women Educators in the Progressive Era: The Women behind Dewey's Laboratory School*. New York: Palgrave Macmillan, 2010.

Edgeworth, Maria, and Richard Lovell Edgeworth. *Practical Education*. Boston: Samuel H. Parker, 1825 (© 1798).

Educational Facilities Laboratories, Inc. *Educational Change and Architectural Consequences*. New York: EFL, 1968.

Eriksen, Aase. *Playground Design: Outdoor Environments for Learning and Development*. New York: Van Nostrand Reinhold, 1985.

Fanning, Colin. "LEGO Play on Display: *The Art of the Brick* and *The Collectivity Project*," *Response: The Digital Journal of Popular Culture Scholarship* (November 2016).

———. "The Plastic System: Architecture, Childhood, and LEGO 1949–2012." Masters qualifying paper, Bard Graduate Center, 2013.

Fanning, Colin, and Rebecca Mir. "Teaching Tools: Progressive Pedagogy and the History of Construction Play." In *Understanding* Minecraft: *Essays on Play, Community and Possibilities*, edited by Nate Garrelts. Jefferson, NC: McFarland & Co., 2014.

Fass, Paula S., ed. *Encyclopedia of Children and Childhood: In History and Society*. Vol. 1. New York: Macmillan Reference USA, 2004.

———. *The Routledge History of Childhood in the Western World*. New York: Routledge, 2013.

Ferguson, John C. "The Architecture of Education: The Public School Buildings of New Orleans." In *Crescent City Schools: Public Education in New Orleans, 1841–1991*, edited by Donald E. DeVore and Joseph Logsdon. Lafayette, LA: University of Louisiana at Lafayette, 2012 (© 1991).

Flint, Anthony. *Wrestling with Moses: How Jane Jacobs Took on New York's Master Builder and Transformed the American City*. New York: Random House, 2009.

Floyd, Myron F., and Rasul A. Mowatt. "Leisure among African Americans." In *Race, Ethnicity, and Leisure: Perspectives on Research, Theory, and Practice*, edited by Monica Stodolska, Kimberly J. Shinew, Myron F. Floyd, and Gordon J. Walker, 53–74. Champaign, IL: Human Kinetics, 2013.

Foran, Clare. "How to Design a City for Women." *CityLab*, September 13, 2013.

Frazier, Ian. "Form and Fungus." *New Yorker*, May 20, 2013.

Friedberg, M. Paul, and Ellen Perry Berkeley. *Play and Interplay: A Manifesto for New Design in Urban Recreational Environment*. New York: Macmillan, 1970.

Frost, Joe. "Evolution of American Playgrounds." *Scholarpedia*, 7 (12): 30423.

Fusselman, Amy. "Play Freely at Your Own Risk." *Atlantic*, January 15, 2015.

———. *Savage Park: A Meditation on Play, Space, and Risk for Americans Who Are Nervous, Distracted, and Afraid to Die*. New York: Houghton Mifflin Harcourt, 2015.

Gilbreth, Frank B. Jr., and Ernestine Gilbreth Carey. *Belles on Their Toes*. New York: Thomas Y. Crowell Co., 1950.

———. *Cheaper by the Dozen*. New York: Thomas Y. Crowell Co., 1948.

Gill, Tim. *No Fear: Growing Up in a Risk-Averse Society*. London: Calouste Gulbenkian Foundation, 2007.

———. "Space-Oriented Children's Policy: Creating Child-Friendly Communities to Improve Children's Well-Being." *Children & Society* 22 (March 2008): 136–42.

Gislason, Neil. *Building Innovation: History, Cases, and Perspectives on School Design*. Big Tancook Island, Nova Scotia: Backalong Books, 2011.

Goldstein, Carolyn M. *Do It Yourself: Home Improvement in 20th-Century America*. New York: National Building Museum/Princeton Architectural Press, 1998.

Gotkin, Michael. "The Politics of Play." In *Preserving Modern Landscape Architecture*, edited by Charles A. Birnbaum, 60–75. New York: Spacemakers Press, 1999.

Graham, Ruth. "How the American Playground Was Born in Boston." *Boston Globe*, March 28, 2014.

Gray, Jennifer L. "Bodies at Play, the Body Politic: The Playground Movement in Chicago." Lecture. Museum of Modern Art, September 23, 2010.

———. "Ready for Experiment: Dwight Perkins and Progressive Architectures in Chicago, 1893–1917." PhD diss., Columbia University, 2011.

Greenberg, Andy. "How a Geek Dad and His 3D Printer Aim to Liberate Legos." *Forbes*, April 5, 2012.

Gyure, Dale Allen. *The Chicago Schoolhouse: High School Architecture and Educational Reform, 1856–2006*. Chicago: University of Chicago Press, 2011.

Hall, G. Stanley. *The Story of a Sand-pile*. New York: E. L. Kellogg & Co., 1897.

Hargrave, Josef, Samuel Williams, Hannah Wright and Felicitas zu Dohna. "Cities Alive: Designing for Urban Childhoods," Arup, December 2017.

Harris, Dianne. *Little White Houses: How the Postwar Home Constructed Race in America*. Minneapolis: University of Minnesota Press, 2013.

Hart, Roger A. "Planning Cities with Children in Mind: A Background Paper for the State of the World's Children Report." April 30, 2011, http://cergnyc.org/files/2013/10/Hart-Planning -Cities-with-Children-in-Mind-SOWC-APRIL-2011.pdf (accessed May 26, 2017).

Hawes, Joseph M. *Children between the Wars: American Childhood, 1920–1940*. New York: Twayne Publishers, 1997.

Hayden, Dolores. *The Grand Domestic Revolution: A History of Feminist Designs for American Homes, Neighborhoods, and Cities*. Cambridge: MIT Press, 1981.

———. *Redesigning the American Dream: The Future of Housing, Work and Family Life*. New York: W. W. Norton, 2002 (© 1984).

Hennessey, James, and Victor Papanek. *Nomadic Furniture*. New York: Pantheon, 1973.

Herrera, Hayden. *Listening to Stone: The Art and Life of Isamu Noguchi*. New York: Farrar, Straus and Giroux, 2015.

Hertzberger, Herman. *Space and Learning: Lessons in Architecture 3*. Amsterdam: 101 Publishers, 2008.

Hess, Thomas B. "The Rejected Playground." *ARTNews*, April 1952.

Hewitt, Karen. "Blocks as a Tool for Learning: Historical and Contemporary Perspectives." *Young Children* (January 2001): 6–13.

Hewitt, Karen, and Louise Roomet, eds. *Educational Toys in America: 1800 to the Present*. Burlington, VT: Robert Hull Fleming Museum, 1979.

Hille, R. Thomas. *Modern Schools: A Century of Design for Education*. New York: Wiley & Sons, 2011.

Hirsch, Elisabeth S., ed. *The Block Book*. 3rd Ed. Washington, D.C.: National Association for the Education of Young Children, 1996 (© 1984).

Hoffschwelle, Mary S. "The Rosenwald Schools of the American South." In *Designing Modern Childhoods: History, Space, and the Material Culture of Children*, edited by Marta Gutman and Ning de Coninck-Smith, 213–32. New Brunswick, NJ: Rutgers University Press, 2007.

Hollenbeck, Bryn Varley. "Making Space for Children: The Material Culture of American Childhoods, 1900–1950." PhD diss., University of Delaware, 2008.

Hoy, Selena. "Why Japanese Kids Can Walk to School Alone." *Atlantic*, October 2, 2015.

Hughes, Jim. *Brick Fetish*. 3rd ed. Hughes Press, 2009.

Hulbert, Ann. *Raising America: Experts, Parents, and a Century of Advice about Children*. New York: Vintage Books, 2004.

Hurley, Amanda Kolson. "Welcome to Disturbia." *Curbed*, May 25, 2016.

———. "Will U.S. Cities Design Their Way Out of the Affordable Housing Crisis?" *Next City*, January 18, 2016.

Huxtable, Ada Louise. "Fully Planned Town Opens in Virginia." *New York Times*, December 5, 1965.

Isamu Noguchi: Playscapes. Mexico City: RM/Museo Tamayo Arte Contemporáneo, 2016.

Isenstadt, Sandy. "Visions of Plenty: Refrigerators in America Around 1950." *Journal of Design History* 11, no. 4 (1998): 311–21.

Ito, Mimi. "Why *Minecraft* Rewrites the Playbook for Learning." *Boing Boing*, June 6, 2015.

Ito, Mizuko. *Engineering Play: A Cultural History of Children's Software*. Cambridge, MA: MIT Press, 2009.

Jackson, Kenneth T. *Crabgrass Frontier: The Suburbanization of the United States*. New York: Oxford University Press, 1987.

Jacobs, Jay. "Projects for Playgrounds." *Art in America* 55, no. 6 (November/December 1967): 39–53.

Jacobson, Lisa. *Raising Consumers: Children and the American Mass Market in the Early Twentieth Century*. New York: Columbia University Press, 2004.

Jacquette, Julia. *Playground of My Mind*. New York: DelMonico Books/Prestel/Wellin Museum of Art, 2017.

Keats, Ezra Jack. *The Snowy Day*. New York, Viking Press, 1962.

Kevill-Davies, Sally. *Yesterday's Children: The Antiques and History of Childcare*. Suffolk, England: Antique Collectors' Club Ltd., 1991.

Key, Ellen. *The Century of the Child*. New York and London: G. P. Putnam's Sons, 1909.

Kinchin, Juliet, and Aidan O'Connor, eds. *Century of the Child: Growing by Design, 1900–2000*. New York: Museum of Modern Art, 2012.

Kirkham, Pat. *Charles and Ray Eames: Designers of the Twentieth Century*. Cambridge, MA: MIT Press, 1998.

Kozlovsky, Roy. "Adventure Playgrounds and Postwar Reconstruction." In *Designing Modern Childhoods: History, Space, and the Material Culture of Children*, edited by Marta Gutman and Ning de Coninck-Smith, 171–92. New Brunswick, NJ: Rutgers University Press, 2007.

Kraus-Boelte, Maria, and John Kraus. *The Kindergarten Guide: An Illustrated Hand-Book*. Vol. 1, *The Gifts*. New York: E. Steiger, 1881 (© 1877).

Lancaster, Jane. *Making Time: Lillian Moller Gilbreth—A Life Beyond "Cheaper By the Dozen."* Boston: Northeastern University Press, 2004.

Lane, Anthony. "The Joy of Bricks." *New Yorker*, April 27, 1998.

Lane, Barbara Miller. *Houses for a New World: Builders and Buyers in American Suburbs, 1945–1965*. Princeton, NJ: Princeton University Press, 2015.

Langston, Jennifer. "Are You Planning to Have Kids? (Part 2)." Sightline Institute, July 29, 2014.

Larrivee, Shaina D. "Playscapes: Isamu Noguchi's Designs for Play." *Public Art Dialogue* 1, no. 1 (2011).

Larsson, Naomi. "The App That Gives Oslo's Children a Direct Say over Their Own Road Safety." *Guardian*, September 2, 2016.

Lauwaert, Maaike. *The Place of Play: Toys and Digital Cultures*. Amsterdam: Amsterdam University Press, 2009.

Lefaivre, Liane. *Ground-Up City: Play as a Design Tool*. Amsterdam: 010 Publishers, 2007.

Lefaivre, Liane, and Ingeborg de Roode, eds. *Aldo van Eyck: The Playgrounds and the City*. Amsterdam: Stedelijk Museum/NAi Publishers, 2002.

LEGO Group. *Developing a Product*. Billund, Denmark: The Lego Group, 1997.

Lippman, Laura. "My Wild School Days at Hippie High." *Daily Mail*, July 10, 2016.

Locke, John. *The Works of John Locke*. Vol. 9, *Some Thoughts Concerning Education*. London: W. Otridge and Son, 1812 (© 1693).

Lovelace, Maud Hart. *Betsy and Tacy Go Over the Big Hill*. In *The Betsy-Tacy Treasury*. New York: Harper Perennial, 2011 (© 1942).

Lupton, Ellen, ed. *Beautiful Users: Designing for People*. New York: Chronicle Books, 2014.

Lupton, Ellen, and J. Abbott Miller, eds. *The ABCs of the Bauhaus: The Bauhaus and Design Theory*. New York: Princeton Architectural Press, 1991.

Lynch, Kevin. *The Image of the City*. Cambridge, MA: MIT Press, 1960.

Mann, Mrs. Horace, and Elizabeth P. Peabody. *Moral Culture of Infancy, and Kindergarten Guide*. 6th ed. New York: J. W. Schermerhorn & Co., 1876.

Marling, Karal Ann, ed. *Designing Disney's Theme Parks: The Architecture of Reassurance*. Montreal: Canadian Centre for Architecture, 1997.

Mather, Evan. *A Plea for Modernism*. Posted May 10, 2011. https://vimeo.com/23565526.

McAfee, Ann, and Andrew Malczewski. *Housing Families at High Density*. City of Vancouver, Canada, 1978.

McCarter, Robert. *Aldo van Eyck*. New Haven, CT: Yale University Press, 2015.

McGrath, Molly, and Norman McGrath. *Children's Spaces: 50 Architects and Designers Create Environments for the Young*. New York: William Morrow and Co., 1978.

McLerran, Alice. *The Legacy of Roxaboxen*. Spring, TX: Absey & Co., 1998.

———. *Roxaboxen*. New York: HarperCollins, 1991.

McPartland, John. *No Down Payment*. New York: Pocket Books, 1957.

Mead, Margaret. *A Creative Life for Your Children*. Washington, D.C.: Children's Bureau, 1962.

Mead, Rebecca. "Learn Different." *New Yorker*, March 7, 2016.

———. "State of Play." *New Yorker*, July 5, 2010.

———. "When I Grow Up." *New Yorker*, January 19, 2015.

Mechling, Jay. "Sandwork." *Journal of Play* 9, no. 1 (Fall 2016).

Mee, Charles L. Jr. "Putting the Play in Playground." *New York Times Magazine*, November 6, 1966.

Micallef, Shawn. "Jane Up North." *Curbed*, May 4, 2016.

Michals, Teresa. "Experiments before Breakfast: Toys, Education and Middle-Class Childhood." In *The Nineteenth-Century Child and Consumer Culture*, edited by Dennis Denisoff, 29–42. Hampshire, England: Ashgate, 2008.

Mintz, Steven. *Huck's Raft: A History of American Childhood*. Cambridge, MA: Belknap Press, 2006.

Mooallem, Jon. "Smallville." *California Sunday Magazine*, October 4, 2015.

Moore, Charles W. "You Have to Pay for the Public Life" (1965) in *You Have to Pay for the Public Life: Selected Essays of Charles W. Moore*, edited by Kevin Keim, 111–41. Cambridge, MA: MIT Press, 2004.

Moore, Robin C. *Childhood's Domain: Play and Place in Childhood Development*. London: Croom Helm, 1986.

Mumford, Lewis. *The City in History: Its Origins, Its Transformations, and Its Prospects*. Boston: Houghton Mifflin Harcourt, 1981 (© 1961).

———. "Plight of the Prosperous." The Sky Line, *New Yorker*, March 4, 1950.

Nasaw, David. *Children of the City: At Work and at Play*. New York: Doubleday, 1985.

Nelson, George, and Henry Wright. *Tomorrow's House: A Complete Guide for the Home-Builder*. 2nd ed. New York: Simon & Schuster, 1945.

Neuhart, John, Marilyn Neuhart, and Ray Eames. *Eames Design*. New York: Abrams, 1995.

Neutra, Richard J. "New Elementary Schools for America." *Architectural Forum* 62 (January 1935): 24–35.

Nicholson, Simon. "How Not to Cheat Children: The Theory of Loose Parts." *Landscape Architecture* 62, no. 1 (October 1971): 30–34.

Norman, Nils. *An Architecture of Play: A Survey of London's Adventure Playgrounds*. London: Four Corners Books, 2003.

Norton, Mary. *The Borrowers*. New York: Harcourt Young Classics, 1998 (© 1952).

Ochs, Elinor, and Tamar Kremer-Sadlik, eds. *Fast Forward Family: Home, Work, and Relationships in Middle-Class America*. Berkeley: University of California Press, 2013.

Ogata, Amy F. "Building for Learning in Postwar American Elementary Schools." *Journal of the Society of Architectural Historians* 67, no. 4 (December 2008): 562–91.

———. "Creative Playthings: Educational Toys and Postwar American Culture." *Winterthur Portfolio* 39, no. 2/3 (Summer/Autumn 2004): 129–56.

———. *Designing the Creative Child: Playthings and Places in Midcentury America*. Minneapolis: University of Minnesota Press, 2013.

———. "Good Toys." In *Century of the Child: Growing by Design, 1900–2000*, edited by Juliet Kinchin and Aidan O'Connor, 171–73. New York: Museum of Modern Art, 2012.

Ogata, Amy F., and Susan Weber, eds. *Swedish Wooden Toys*. New Haven, CT: Bard Graduate Center/Yale University Press, 2014.

Opie, Iona Archibald, and Peter Opie. *Children's Games in Street and Playground.* Oxford: Oxford University Press, 1969.

Opsvik, Peter. *Rethinking Sitting.* Oslo: Gaidaros Forlag AS, 2008.

OWP/P Architects + VS Furniture + Bruce Mau Design. *The Third Teacher: 79 Ways You Can Use Design to Transform Teaching and Learning.* New York: Abrams, 2010.

Page, Hilary F. "Plastics as a Medium for Toys." In *Daily Graphic Plastics Exhibition Catalogue.* Published in association with the British Plastics Federation. Dorland Hall, November 7–27, 1946.

———. *Playtime in the First Five Years.* Rev. 2nd ed. London: George Allen and Unwin Ltd., 1953.

Palmer, Bruce. *Making Children's Furniture and Play Structures.* New York: Workman Publishing, 1974.

Paoletti, Jo B. *Pink and Blue: Telling the Boys from the Girls in America.* Bloomington, IN: Indiana University Press, 2012.

Papert, Seymour. *Mindstorms: Children, Computers, and Powerful Ideas.* New York: Basic Books, 1980.

———. "Project-Based Learning." Edutopia, November 1, 2001.

Pappano, Laura. "Learning to Think Like a Computer." *New York Times*, April 4, 2017.

Piaget, Jean, and Bärbel Inhelder, *The Child's Conception of Space.* New York: W. W. Norton & Co., 1967 (© 1948).

Pick, Grant. "A School Fit for Children." *Chicago Reader*, February 28, 1991.

Portis, Antoinette. *Not a Box.* New York: HarperCollins, 2006.

Punter, John. *The Vancouver Achievement: Urban Planning and Design.* Vancouver: University of British Columbia Press, 2014.

Pratt, Caroline. *I Learn from Children: An Adventure in Progressive Education.* New York: Grove Press, 2014 (© 1948).

Pursell, Carroll. *From Playgrounds to PlayStation: The Interaction of Technology and Play.* Baltimore: Johns Hopkins University Press, 2015.

Reese, Hope. "Alex Truesdell: Maker. Adaptive Designer. Advocate for Children with Special Needs." TechRepublic, December 14, 2015.

Reif, Rita. "Instead of Ending on Scrap Heap, This Furniture Began There." *New York Times*, December 30, 1972.

Resnick, Mitchel. "Computer as Paintbrush: Technology, Play, and the Creative Society." In *Play = Learning: How Play Motivates and Enhances Children's Cognitive and Social-Emotional Growth*, edited by Dorothy G. Singer, Roberta Michnik Golinkoff, and Kathy Hirsh-Pasek, 192–206. New York: Oxford University Press, 2006.

Resnick, Mitchel, and Eric Rosenbaum. "Designing for Tinkerability." In *Design, Make, Play: Growing the Next Generation of STEM Innovators*, edited by Margaret Honey and David E. Kanter, 163–82. New York: Routledge, 2013.

Resnick, Mitchel, et al. "Scratch: Programming for All." *Communications of the ACM* 52, no. 11 (November 2009): 60–67.

Riis, Jacob. "The Genesis of the Gang." *Atlantic*, September 1899.

Rosin, Hanna. "The Overprotected Kid." *Atlantic*, April 2014.

Ross, Lillian. "Summer Glimpses." Talk of the Town. *New Yorker*, July 31, 1971.

Roth, Alfred. *The New School*. New York: Praeger, 1958.

Rouse, James. "The Regional Shopping Center: Its Role in the Community It Serves." Seventh Urban Design Conference. Harvard University, April 26, 1963.

Ryan, Bernard Jr. "A Last Look at the Little Red Schoolhouse." *Parents* (February 1968).

Rybczynski, Witold. *Now I Sit Me Down*. New York: Farrar, Straus and Giroux, 2016.

———. "Remembering the Rosenwald Schools." *Architect*, September 16, 2015.

Sanders, James. "Adventure Playground: John V. Lindsay and the Transformation of Modern New York." *Design Observer*, May 4, 2010.

Sandseter, Ellen Beate Hansen. "Characteristics of Risky Play." *Journal of Adventure Education and Outdoor Learning* 9, no. 1 (2009): 3–21.

Sandseter, Ellen Beate Hansen, and Leif Edward Ottesen Kennair. "Children's Risky Play from an Evolutionary Perspective: The Anti-Phobic Effects of Thrilling Experiences." *Evolutionary Psychology* 9, no. 2 (April 2011): 257–84.

Schmertz, Mildred F. "An Open Plan Elementary School." *Architectural Record* (September 1973).

Seiter, Ellen. *Sold Separately: Parents and Children in Consumer Culture*. New Brunswick, NJ: Rutgers University Press, 1995.

Sherman, Thomas, and Greg Logan, eds. *Tezuka Architects: The Yellow Book*. Berlin: JOVIS, 2016.

Smith, Elizabeth A. T. *Case Study Houses: The Complete Program, 1945–1966*. Los Angeles: Taschen, 2009.

Smith Hill, Pamela, ed. *Pioneer Girl: The Annotated Autobiography*. Pierre: South Dakota Historical Society Press, 2014.

Solomon, Susan G. *American Playgrounds: Revitalizing Community Space*. Hanover, NH: University Press of New England, 2005.

———. *The Science of Play: How to Build Playgrounds That Enhance Development*. Lebanon NH: University Press of New England, 2014.

Spock, Benjamin. *The Common Sense Book of Baby and Child Care*. New York: Duell, Stone and Pearce, 1946.

Staring, Jeroen. "Caroline Pratt: Progressive Pedagogy *In Statu Nascendi*." *Living a Philosophy of Early Childhood Education: A Festschrift for Harriet Cuffaro*, Bank Street College of Education Occasional Paper Series 32.

Steller, Chris. "When 'The Yard' Was Minnesota's Most Radical Park." *MinnPost*, July 25, 2014.

Stern, Robert A. M., David Fishman, and Thomas Mellins. *New York 1960: Architecture and Urbanism between the Second World War and the Bicentennial*. New York: Monacelli Press, 1997.

Stock, Francine. "Is There a Future for the Recent Past in New Orleans?" *MAS Context* 8 (Winter 2010): 70–87.

Sunset Ideas for Children's Rooms and Play Yards. Menlo Park, CA: Lane Publishing Co. 1980.

Thernstrom, Melanie. "The Anti-Helicopter Parent's Plea: Let Kids Play!" *New York Times Magazine*, October 19, 2016.

Thompson, Clive. "The *Minecraft* Generation." *New York Times Magazine*, April 4, 2016.

Toderian, Brent. "Tall Tower Debates Could Use Less Dogma, Better Design." *Planetizen*, June 1, 2014.

Tolentino, Jia. "The Little Syria of Deep Valley." *New Yorker*, February 16, 2017.

Torres, Ana Maria. *Isamu Noguchi: A Study of Space*. New York: Monacelli Press, 2000.

"A Tower Plus Row Houses in Detroit." *Architectural Forum* 112 (May 1960): 104–113, 222.

Towler, Katherine. "History of Harkness: The Men behind the Plan." *Exeter Bulletin* (Fall 2006).

Trainor, James. "Reimagining Recreation." *Cabinet* 45 (Spring 2012), http://www.cabinetmagazine .org/issues/45/trainor.php (accessed November 5, 2017).

Tromm, J. H. *Cardboard Construction*. Springfield, MA: Milton Bradley Co., 1907.

United Nations General Assembly. Resolution 1386 (XIV). "Declaration of the Rights of the Child." Principle 7. UN doc A/4354 (1959).

Vale, Brenda, and Robert Vale. *Architecture on the Carpet: The Curious Tale of Construction Toys and the Genesis of Modern Buildings.* London: Thames & Hudson, 2013.

Van den Berg, Marguerite. *Gender in the Post-Fordist Urban: The Gender Revolution in Planning and Public Policy.* Berlin: Springer, 2017.

Van Lingen, Anna, and Denisa Kollarová. *Aldo van Eyck: Seventeen Playgrounds.* Eindhoven, Netherlands: Lecturis, 2016.

Verbauwhede, Cory. "How to Grow a City: South False Creek's Forgotten Visionaries." *West Coast Line* (July 2005): 195–203.

Von Vegesack, Alexander, ed. *Kid Size: The Material World of Childhood.* Milan: Skira; Vitra Design Museum, 1997.

Walker, Rob. "Dedigitization." *Design Observer,* June 8, 2011.

———. "Digital Culture, Meet Analog Fever." *New York Times Sunday Review,* November 28, 2015.

Wang, Sam, and Sandra Aamodt. "Play, Stress, and the Learning Brain." *Cerebrum* (September/October 2012).

Ward, Colin. *The Child in the City.* London: Bedford Square Press, 1990 (© 1978).

Watters, Audrey. "The Invented History of 'The Factory Model of Education,'" *Hack Education* (blog), April 25, 2015.

———. "What Does (and Doesn't) Progressive Education Plus Technology Look Like? Thoughts on AltSchool." *Hack Education,* August 7, 2014.

Waugh, Edward, and Elizabeth Waugh. *The South Builds: New Architecture in the Old South.* Chapel Hill, NC: University of North Carolina Press, 1960.

Weber, Evelyn. "Play Materials in the Curriculum of Early Childhood." In *Educational Toys in America: 1800 to the Present,* edited by Karen Hewitt and Louise Roomet, 25–37. (Burlington, VT: Robert Hull Fleming Museum, 1979).

Weisser, Amy S. "'Little Red School House, What Now?' Two Centuries of American Public School Architecture." *Journal of Planning History* 5, no. 3 (August 2006): 196–217.

Wellhousen, Karyn, and Judith Kieff. *A Constructivist Approach to Block Play in Early Childhood.* Boston: Cengage Learning, 2001.

White, Colin. *The World of the Nursery.* New York: E. P. Dutton, 1984.

Widdicombe, Lizzie. "Mother May I?" *New Yorker,* February 23 and March 2, 2015.

Wiggins, David Kenneth, and Patrick B. Miller, eds. *The Unlevel Playing Field: A Documentary History of the African American Experience in Sport*. Champaign, IL: University of Illinois Press, 2003.

Wilder, Laura Ingalls. *Little Town on the Prairie*. New York: Harper & Row, 1971 (© 1941).

———. *On the Banks of Plum Creek*. New York: Harper & Row, 1971 (© 1937).

———. *These Happy Golden Years*. New York: Harper & Row, 1971 (© 1943).

Wilson, Mabel O. "Rosenwald School: Lessons in Progressive Education." In *Frank Lloyd Wright: Unpacking the Archive*, edited by Barry Bergdoll and Jennifer Gray, 96–104. New York: Museum of Modern Art, 2017.

Wilson, Penny. *The Playwork Primer*. College Park, MD: Alliance for Childhood, 2009.

Wood, Denis. "Free the Children! Down with Playgrounds!" *McGill Journal of Education* 12, no. 2 (1977): 227–42.

Wright, Frank Lloyd. *A Testament*. New York: Horizon Press, 1957.

Wright, Gwendolyn. *Building the Dream: A Social History of Housing in America*. Cambridge: MIT Press, 1983.

Wright, Mary, and Russel Wright. *Guide to Easier Living*. 2nd ed. New York: Simon & Schuster, 1951 (© 1950).

Wyden, Peter. *Suburbia's Coddled Kids*. Garden City, NY: Doubleday & Co., 1962.

Zelizer, Viviana A. *Pricing the Priceless Child: The Changing Social Value of Children*. Princeton, NJ: Princeton University Press, 1985.

Zimmerman, Jonathan. *Small Wonder: The Little Red Schoolhouse in History and Memory*. New Haven, CT: Yale University Press, 2014.

Zinguer, Tamar. *Architecture in Play: Imitations of Modernism in Architectural Toys*. Charlottesville, VA: University of Virginia Press, 2015.

Zipp, Samuel, and Nathan Storring, eds. *Vital Little Plans: The Short Works of Jane Jacobs*. New York: Random House, 2016.

INDEX

Note: Italic page numbers refer to illustrations.

A NOTE
ON THE
AUTHOR

ALEXANDRA LANGE is an architecture and design critic whose essays, reviews, and features have appeared in design journals, *New York*, the *New Yorker*, the *New York Times*, *Curbed*, *Design Observer*, *Dezeen*, and many other publications. She received a PhD in twentieth-century architecture history from the Institute of Fine Arts at New York University in 2005. She is the author of *Writing about Architecture: Mastering the Language of Buildings and Cities* and the e-book *The Dot-Com City: Silicon Valley Urbanism*, and co-author of *Design Research: The Store That Brought Modern Living to American Homes*. She lives in Brooklyn, New York, with her family.